# POLAND

Garland Reference Library
of the Humanities
Volume 743

# POLAND

## An Annotated Bibliography of Books in English

### AUGUST GERALD KANKA

Garland Publishing, Inc. • New York & London
1988

© 1988 by August Gerald Kanka
All rights reserved

**Library of Congress Cataloging-in-Publication Data**

Kanka, August Gerald, 1928–
   Poland : an annotated bibliography of books in English.
   (Garland reference library of the humanities ; v. 743)
    Includes index.
    1. Poland—Bibliography.  I. Title.  II. Series: Garland reference library of the humanities ; vol. 743.
Z2526.K28  1988  [DK4040]  016.9438  88-4064
ISBN 0-8240-8492-6 (alk. paper)

Printed on acid-free, 250-year-life paper
Manufactured in the United States of America

TO MY MOTHER AND FATHER

THANK YOU!

CONTENTS

| | |
|---|---|
| Preface | xi |
| Introduction | xiii |
| List of Abbreviations | xxiii |

| | | |
|---|---|---|
| I. | GENERAL WORKS | 3 |
| II. | SPECIAL WORKS | 21 |
| | Aeronautics | 21 |
| | Agriculture | 21 |
| | Antiquities | 21 |
| | Architecture | 23 |
| | Armed Forces | 26 |
| | Arms and Armor | 31 |
| | Art | 32 |
| | Bibliography | 36 |
| | Biography--General | 40 |
| | Biography--Specific | 42 |
| | Birds | 93 |
| | Botany | 94 |
| | Boundaries | 94 |
| | Cities and Towns | 107 |
| | Commerce | 114 |
| | Cookery | 114 |
| | Culture | 116 |
| | Czestochowa | 116 |
| | Dance | 116 |
| | Decorations of Honor | 117 |
| | Description and Travel | 117 |
| | Economic Conditions | 128 |
| | Education | 135 |
| | Fiction | 135 |
| | Folklore | 138 |
| | Foreign Relations | 139 |
| | Genealogy | 153 |
| | Geographical Conditions | 153 |
| | Geography | 154 |
| | German Occupation, 1939-1945 | 155 |
| | Heraldry | 159 |
| | History | 159 |
| | History, 962-1386. Piasts. | 168 |

*vii*

| | |
|---|---|
| History, 1386-1573. Jagiellonians. | 170 |
| History, 1573-1795. Including Partitions. | 171 |
| History, 1795-1918. Partitioned Poland. | 175 |
| History, 1918-1939. First Polish Republic. | 180 |
| History, 1939-1945. Worl War II. | 184 |
| History, 1945- | 188 |
| History--Fiction | 195 |
| Industries | 199 |
| Intellectual Life | 200 |
| Jews in Poland | 205 |
| Jews in Poland--Fiction | 222 |
| Juvenile Literature | 224 |
| Karaims | 230 |
| Kaszuby | 230 |
| Katyn Forest Massacre, 1940 | 231 |
| Language | 233 |
| Law | 233 |
| Learning and Scholarship | 234 |
| Libraries and Librarianship | 235 |
| Literature--History and Criticism | 236 |
| Literature--Translations Into English | 239 |
| Military Techniques | 241 |
| Minorities | 241 |
| Moving Pictures | 243 |
| Music | 244 |
| Oświecim | 245 |
| Personal Narratives | 249 |
| Poles in Argentina--Fiction | 261 |
| Poles in Austrailia | 261 |
| Poles in Canada | 262 |
| Poles in Great Britain | 264 |
| Poles in New Zealand | 265 |
| Poles in the United States | 266 |
| Poles in the United States--Fiction | 288 |
| Poles in Uruguay--Fiction | 298 |
| Poles Outside Poland | 298 |
| Polish Jews in America--Fiction | 299 |
| Polish National Catholic Church | 300 |
| Polish Question | 302 |
| Polish Roman Catholic Chuch--U.S. | 306 |
| Politics and Government | 307 |
| Population | 318 |
| Public Opinion | 319 |
| Religious Conditions | 319 |
| Russian Occupation, 1939-1945 | 324 |
| Social Conditions | 325 |
| Social Life and Customs | 332 |
| Socialism | 333 |

Contents

|  |  |
|---|---|
| Solidarność | 335 |
| Sports | 338 |
| Statistics | 339 |
| Tales | 339 |
| Theatre | 343 |
| Transportation | 344 |
| Warszawa--History--Uprising of 1943 | 345 |
| Warszawa--History--Uprising of 1944 | 346 |
| Wycinanki | 348 |
| Author Index | 351 |
| Title Index | 367 |

PREFACE

The election of a Pope from Poland, the emergence of the Solidarity movement, the declaration of martial law in Poland and the award of the 1983 Nobel Peace Prize to Lech Walesa, a leader in the Solidarity movement, are all events which have generated a good deal of publicity in the United States and the rest of the English-speaking world. This publicity, centered as it was on affairs in Poland or on prominent Poles, demonstrated how important Poland and the Polish people are to the western world. Furthermore, a significant number of new books about Poland or the Poles have been published within the last few years. Even that great American story-teller, James Michener, popularized the country with the appearance of his best-selling novel entitled simply, POLAND.

It should be pointed out, however, that this recent outpouring of works about Poland and the Poles is not something of recent origin. Indeed, literally hundreds of books in English have been published during the past two hundred years. This interest in Poland in the English-speaking world seems to have begun shortly after the infamous partitions of that country which took place during the last quarter of the eighteenth century. The eclipse of the Polish state ironically did more to arouse interest in Poland among western observers than did the partitions themselves. Ever since the last partition which occurred in 1795, there have been periodic outbursts of publications about Poland or the Poles. Often these outbursts have coincided with revolutionary events within the country or achievements made by famous Poles, either at home or abroad. This latest outburst of publications appears to be just another in that series.

From time to time, lists of these titles have been compiled and published. Some are more comprehensive than others. None yet exists which attempts to include all the titles which have appeared on all aspects of Polish life and culture. The bibliography which follows attempts to be the most exhaustive and the most comprehensive list of works in the English language. Of greatest value to the reader are the annotations for it is only annotations which will lead to an intelligent choice by the user. In effect, the annotations are mini-reviews. Often the compiler attempted to alert the user of the bibliography to some particularly valuable feature of the book annotated.

This list has been in preparation for many years. An attempt has been made to search out every title which has been published in English during the last one hundred and fifty years. Every book has been either read in its entirety, studied or thoroughly scanned. Each work has been examined individually in order to provide a meaningful annotation. It should be noted that an attempt has been made to provide information about the locations for each and every title which is not in the Library of Congress.

Many libraries, too numerous to mention, have been visited and used in compiling this bibliography. Major collections such as the Library of Congress and the New York Public Library have played prominent roles. Of special help has been Marvin F. Bielawski of the Princeton University Libraries and Michael Kraus of the European Division of the Library of Congress. Last, but not least, I wish to acknowledge the contribution of Dr. George Barany of the University of Denver without whose initial inspiration this book would not have taken shape.

INTRODUCTION

Almost a century has passed since the beginning of the great migration to the United States of persons from the overcrowded and relatively backward agricultural communities of eastern Europe. Many of these immigrants were Slavs who most often settled in the burgeoning industrial centers. The various individual ethnic groups tended to congregate in one particular part of a city. Living in this "splendid isolation," these Slavic immigrants often remained divorced from the mainstream of American life and institutions. Eventually, the presence in America of so many Slavs and their offspring was bound to have an effect on the academic world. The mere presence of such sizeable ethnic groups aroused the curiosity of some scholars. Impressive sociological studies such as the work about the Polish peasant by Thomas and Znaniecki appeared.[1] Scholars sought to know as much as possible not only about the Slavic immigrants themselves but also about the areas from whence they had come. The First World War destroyed the Austro-Hungarian, the German, the Russian, and the Ottoman Empires. As a result of this destruction, entirely new nation-states appeared on the quickly redrawn map of Europe. Politically annihilated in 1795, Poland re-emerged as a sovereign state in 1918. In attempting to analyze the causes and results of World War I, scholars often found it necessary to study and to learn about these new nations. They were no longer mere geographical expressions, they were real nation-states with problems which were to have repercussions even for the United States. These areas could no longer be ignored or studied as parts of now defunct empires. Titles about them as individual states began to appear in ever-increasing numbers.

Many of the pioneers of Slavic studies in the United States were themselves of Slavic ancestry. The first comprehensive bibliography about the Slavs published in English and entitled, *Slavic Europe*,[2] was compiled by Robert Joseph Kerner, whose mother, Rose Veselak, was herself of Czech descent. It seems likely that Professor Kerner's interest in Slavic studies was related somehow to his Czech ancestry. Many scholars, who were not of Slavic origin, were also interested in Slavic studies. Among these persons, such a distinguished scholar as George Rapall Noyes comes to mind. His English translation of the Polish classic epic, *Pan Tadeusz* by Adam Mickiewicz,[3] is unparalleled. But few of these scholars have given their full and undivided attention to making the general public aware of the rich cultural heritage of the eastern Europeans. Nor have they been successful in publicizing the availability of a vast number of books about the eastern European nations and their peoples in the English language. Their works appealed mainly to their fellow scholars.

While numerous works of a scholarly nature were being written and published about the eastern European nations—their cultures and their peoples—a great many books also were being published of a popular nature. Novels about these countries and peoples and those who had made their homes in the United States appeared. Probably the most well-known of these novels was written by Upton Sinclair about a Lithuanian immigrant family in Chicago and their misadventures around the turn of the century.[4] Many prominent persons of eastern European origin wrote their own life stories.[5] Others, such as Marie Curie (née Sklodowska), became the subjects of popular biographies.[6] Travel after World War I often included trips to eastern Europe resulting in excellent accounts of impressions obtained by these visitors and published for popular consumption.[7] Turbulance characterized the inter-war period and often impressive personal narratives of harrowing experiences were written either in English or in the author's native tongue and translated into English.[8] Many of these non-scholarly books are of great interest and often shed the light necessary for an understanding of these peoples. The sheer volume of publications continually increased particularly immediately before, during and after the outbreak of World War II. Unless these various works are listed, classified, annotated and brought to the attention of the general reading public, their value to a knowledge and understanding of eastern Europe and its peoples is virtually lost.

My own search for information about my ancestry was a difficult task. No central source then existed to direct me to works which might enlighten me about my Kashubian background. Yet, while I was growing up, three very competent scholars were writing a book in the English language about the customs and traditions of my ancestral people.[9] I came across this work many years later, having had to content myself meanwhile, with what I later learned to be an erroneous interpretation of my origins, i.e. Kashubians were "half-Polish and half-German." Many students, aspiring scholars and the just plain curious, experience similar difficulties partially because they are unable to find a useful tool to guide them in their research. Even when they seek aid from professional librarians, they are frustrated for few, if any, librarians

*Introduction* xv

have any idea of just how rich and plentiful are the sources of information in the English language about the eastern Europeans. Few, if any, comprehensive, annotated bibliographies about eastern Europeans in the English language exist to help them.

Turning to academia once again, some impressive bibliographies have been compiled and published about eastern Europe. Works such as Horecky's[10] are exhaustive but, in addition to listing and describing titles of interest mainly to scholars, they often include works in languages other than English. During a time and in a nation such as the United States where a fluent reading knowledge of any modern foreign language is an exception rather than a rule, these non-English works, therefore, become the luxuries of the educated few.

On the other hand, attempts at compiling less esoteric bibliographies have been made, e.g. two recent works published about Poland and the Poles. Norman Davies recently published a bibliography[11] which was well received. The work is sparsely annotated and, although purported to be a list of works in English, indeed does contain many titles in other languages. In addition, the Davies' book focuses largely on history.

Another work by Joseph W. Zurawski[12] is a notable attempt at comprehensiveness but apparently was prepared hastily. A careful editing might have eliminated many entries in this bibliography impossible to obtain anymore. Furthermore, this compilation contains much non-book material including periodical articles, local histories, etc. Having stated my case why I compiled this bibliography, I would like to describe the work itself.

## Constraints of Time and Place

As the collection of titles progressed, certain chronological limitations became apparent. No attempt has been made to include incunabula, for example, simply because such items are difficult to locate. The very beginnings of the publications of works in English seems to coincide with the era of the partitions of Poland (1772-1795). Apparently the political plight of the Polish nation generated interest among English-speaking readers. After the political eclipse of the Polish state, interest continued and works about Poland were published. A new phrase was coined, viz. the Polish Question.

Persistent political unrest among the Poles generated a steady stream of publications in English about this beleaguered people. Often, books about the Poles alone were replaced by books which discussed the Polish people as a minority group of one or another of the occupying powers. This trend gradually gave way to another due to the appearance in western

Europe and in the western hemisphere, principally the United States, of large numbers of Polish emigrants and the popularization of the contemporary ideology of nationalism.

Concern over the Polish Question accounted for an increase in the number of books published about Poland and the Poles dealing primarily with political or historical topics. Many of these books appeared to have been written to persuade the reader to sympathize with the Polish viewpoint concerning independence. As the number of Polish emigrés seeking refuge in western Europe and the United States increased, so did the variety and number of publications increase. Personal narratives, translations of Polish literary classics, and fictional accounts about Poland and the Poles appeared in ever-increasing numbers. The outbreak of World War I put a stop to the emigration of Polish people but not to the number and variety of works published about them. Polish agitation for the re-establishment of the Polish state increased and many books about the Polish Question continued to be published during the war years many of which were apparently written in order to further the independence movement. In 1918 a new Polish state was established and the efforts of the patriots were rewarded.

While the war put an end to large-scale emigration of the Poles to the United States, the hundreds of thousands of Poles already settled in this country became the subject of numerous publications in English. Some scholars became interested in them and made them the subjects of their research. Writers of fiction such as the Anzia Yerzierska found the Polish immigrants' condition a fertile source of material. In her case, however, the purely political or historical definition of the term, "Pole," was lost. The subjects of her novels, although born in a territory which was later to become politically Polish, were treated as Russians simply because they had been born in and had emigrated from the Russian Empire. Thus, unless one adds the dimension of nationality to works such as hers, the fact that the stories were about Poles may be lost.

This question of cultural identity becomes even more confused when trying to classify the large number of Jews who had emigrated to this country from "Polish" cities such as Wilno, Bialystok, Warszawa, Kraków, Lódz, etc. Then too, one must not forget the immigrants who did not always identify themselves as Poles. Many of them rapidly disappeared into the so-called "melting-pot"; others preferred to be identified with a province or a region of Poland instead of the entire country; while, still others, never lost sight of the fact that their passports were either Austrian, Russian or German and accepted citizenship as being identical with nationality.

The reason for this digression into the status of the Polish immigrants in this country was to illustrate the diffi-

*Introduction* xvii

culty of identifying someone as Polish once that person has moved out of Poland. A stated aim of this work was to include titles not only about Poland and the Polish people in their native land but also to include works about the Polish diaspora. Extreme care, then, was necessary in collecting works because of the possibility of overlooking items about the Poles who might have been categorized as Austrian, German or Russian citizens. This problem gradually diminished, however, so that by the 1930s clear lines of cultural identity among the Poles in this country seem to have been drawn.

But, how does one define a Pole? By 1939, many persons with Polish surnames had attained prominence in the United States. Many had become the subjects of biographies. For the purpose of this bibliography, if a person clearly came from a so-called "Polish-American" family, he or she is considered a Pole, that is, a "Pole in the United States." Obviously, some arbitrary decisions had to be made and it is hoped that the majority of the users of this bibliography will agree with them. It is also hoped that no serious omissions have been made.

During the first half of the twentieth century, there was a flurry of publishing activity in the Polish-American community. At first, most of the works were published in the Polish language. Gradually, however, works in English began to appear. The publications of an ever-increasing number of titles about Polish-Americans and their activities emanating from private sources and religious and cultural organizations continues. Keeping track of the sheer volume of these publications has become something of a problem.

Meanwhile, back in Europe, some interesting developments regarding publications about Poland and the Poles were taking place. Well over three million Jews had lived in Poland before the German invasion. Most of them had resided in cities. The most prominent Jewish settlement was known as the "Warsaw Ghetto." Hitler's policy of extermination of the Jews is legendary. In Poland and the West, a great quantity of high quality works about the plight of the Jews, or the Holocaust, have been published. In fact, probably no other portion of Polish history has been so well documented and written about. Many exhaustive accounts, some fictional, continue to appear in print.

As a new Poland emerged, once again visitors were first permitted and later encouraged to go there. Many fine accounts of these visits have appeared in print. Also, the Polish government through its publishing houses, began to print many books about the country. The bulk of the early publications were descriptions of the country and its people. English translations of Polish literary classics also appeared. Many contemporary Polish writers had their works quickly translated into English. Some, like Czeslaw Milosz, eventually left the country and began to write in English. This bibliography excludes such works of literature, be they classical or contemporary. All other works about Poland and the Polish diaspora recently published in Poland have been included. As this book goes to press, the volume of works published about Poland and the Poles continues to grow and soon a supplement will have to be written. For the time being, however, this list will have to suffice.

Topical Limitations

In addition to the rather obvious stated chronological limitation, there were other and, perhaps more important, choices which had to be made: Which kinds of works should be included and which should be excluded? The bibliography speaks for itself concerning what was included. I should like to anticipate possible criticism of what was excluded, however, by listing the exclusions and then explaining why they were left out.

1. *Incunabula*. Few titles exist in this catagory. No great effort was made to include materials of this sort mainly because of the fact that such items would be of very limited interest. Furthermore, their age would necessitate being stored in rare book collections with very limited access.

2. *Translations of classical works of Polish Literature.* A bibliographic tool, now somewhat dated, covering this category already exists.[13] Also, this is a special category and often the literary works do not necessarily shed any light upon the subject of Poland or the Polish people.

3. *Translations of works by contemporary Polish writers.* Often, Polish writers have had their works published simultaneously in the Polish and English languages. Since most of them fall in the category of *belles lettres*, they were left out.

4. *Monographs by prominent Polish writers not dealing with the country or the Polish people.* Works dealing with subjects which do not discuss the land, its people, culture or its institutions are excluded. Thus, a famous Polish philosopher might publish a book dealing with philosophy. Since the subject-matter lies outside the scope of this bibliography, his or her work is excluded.

5. *Government publications.* Care should be taken here to distinguish between actual documents and items published under the aegis of a governmental agency. Utmost care has been exercised to include only those publications of a governmental agency which have been written by individuals. Other

# Introduction

governmental documents such as treaties, statistical tables, etc. have not been included. They are too numerous and are of concern principally to the research scholar.

6. *Institutional publications*. Innumerable works have been published by religious and fraternal organizations. These works serve mainly to explain their institutional activities rather than to enlighten a reader about Poland or the Poles. Parish Jubilee books, however, may be a rich source of data about individual Polish settlements in the United States. Most of these items have not been catalogued and are scattered in libraries all over the country. A special bibliography could be prepared just for them.

7. *Collections*. Any book which covered other countries or peoples in addition to Poland and the Poles were excluded.

8. *Language books*. Only books which were written about the Polish language have been included. Teaching manuals, dictionaries, phrase books, etc. have been excluded.

9. *Ephemeral materials*. Pamphlets and brochures have been left out.

10. *Works without text*. Books containing only illustrations have been excluded. The best example of this kind of work is a recently published book about Polish poster art.

11. *Articles from scholarly journals or periodicals*. There are literally hundreds of scholarly articles written about Poland and the Polish people. Unless these items were published in monographic form, either before or after they appeared in serial form, they were excluded. Sufficient indices exist to tap these resources.

12. *Dissertations and theses*. Unless the dissertation or thesis was published for sale to the general public through a publisher, they were not included in this bibliography.

## Subject Headings

The compiler of a bibliography must quickly resolve the problem of subject headings. Rather than create an entirely new set of headings, it seemed logical to rely upon the subject headings used by the Library of Congress. It is important to note that primary subject headings were used only. In the biographical section, the birth dates and death dates, if applicable, were the ones established by the Library of Congress.

## Entry Format

The format presented here incorporates standard bibliographical features with the addition of two rather important features, i.e. the location and call number of the book if it is not in the Library of Congress. First, each item is presented according to established rules determining authorship. The so-called "main entry" is almost always established by the Library of Congress. In the event of personal authorship, the author's surname, using Polish orthography if Polish, is given followed by the first name, again using Polish orthography if Polish. All other names are indicated by the use of an initial or initials. In the case of joint authorship, the name of the author which appears first on the title page becomes the main entry. All other authors are acknowledged after the title, and appear in the author index. Non-personal authorship follows Library of Congress decisions. The title is stated exactly as it appears on the title page of the book. In the case of translations, the non-English title appears in the annotation in the original language in which the book was written, usually Polish. Translators' names appear after the title. Imprint information includes place of publication, publisher and date of publication. The number of volumes or pages is also given. The final item listed is the location of the book. If it is part of the collection of the Library of Congress, then the LC card number is noted. If in another library, the abbreviation for that library as furnished by the National Union Catalog is given followed by the call number of the book. All other features of the book are covered in the annotations.

## Annotations

The most valuable feature of this bibliography is the annotation. Far too many bibliographies merely list authors and titles. If the annotations are given, they are ordinarily too brief or too vague. The author's aim in writing the book is stated. If the book is a multi-volume work, or contains articles by many different authors, the titles of the articles are given together with the names of the persons who wrote the articles. The aim of the annotation is to describe the work as breifly, but as comprehensively, as possible alerting the user to special features of the book which might otherwise have been overlooked.

In some cases, descriptive notes appeared to be insufficient. For instance, to indicate merely that a book contains maps may not be necessarily useful. On the other hand, if the type of map is noted, that could be helpful. The same explanation applies to notes about illustrative materials. If portraits are contained in the book, these are noted. Also, some distinction is made between colored and black-and-white illustrations.

*Introduction* xxi

## The Index

A complete author and title index has been prepared. The user will find it helpful to consult the index because of the arrangement of the bibliography.

It is hoped that the user of this bibliography will be amply rewarded in the search for book materials about Poland and the Poles. The bibliography, at best, will aid the person who knows little or nothing about the subject at hand. Some of the books listed in the bibliography contain bibliographies themselves which will further assist the searcher. At worst, it will be a select list which will not satisfy all users. Many might object to the arbitrariness in which items were included or excluded. But, it is certain that most, if not all users of this bibliography, will be astounded by the sheer volume and great richness of the works about Poland and the Poles available in the English language.

## Notes

1. William I. Thomas and Florian Znaniecki, *The Polish Peasant in Europe and America*, 2 vols. (New York: Alfred A. Knopf, Inc., 1928).

2. Robert J Kerner, *Slavic Europe*, (Cambridge, Mass.: Harvard University Press, 1918).

3. Adam Mickiewicz, *Pan Tadeusz*, trans. by George R. Noyes, (New York: E.P. Dutton & Co., Inc., 1917).

4. Upton B. Sinclair, Jr., *The Jungle*, (New York: Doubleday & Co., 1906).

5. Józef Pilsudski, *The Memoirs of a Polish Revolutionary and Soldier*, (London: Faber and Faber, Ltd., 1931).

6. Eve Curie, *Madame Curie, a Biography*, (Garden City, N.Y.: Garden City Publishing Co., 1937).

7. Paul Super, *The Polish Tradition*, (London: George Allen & Unwin, Ltd., 1939).

8. Zofia Kossak-Szczucka, *The Blaze: Reminiscences of Volhynia, 1917-1919*, (London: George Allen & Unwin, Ltd., 1927).

9. Friedrich Lorentz, Adam Fischer and Tadeusz Lehr-Splawinski, *The Cassubian Civilization*, (London: Faber and Faber, Ltd., 1935).

10. Paul L. Horecky, ed., *East Central Europe: A Guide to Basic Publications*, (Berkeley: University of California Press, 1970).

11. Norman Davies, *Select Bibliography of Works in English on Polish History*, (Cambridge, Eng.: Oriental Research Partners, 1975).

12. Joseph W. Zurawski, comp., *Polish American History and Culture: A Classified Bibliography*, (Chicago: Polish Museum of America, 1975).

13. Marion M Coleman, *Polish Literature in English Translation: A Bibliography*, (Cheshire, Conn.: Cherry Hill Books, 1963).

## LIST OF ABBREVIATIONS

| | |
|---|---|
| CtY | Yale University |
| MCC | Macomb Community College, Warren, Michigan |
| MiD | Detroit Public Library |
| MiU | The University of Michigan, Ann Arbor |
| NN | New York Public Library |
| NjP | Princeton University |
| NIC | Cornell University |
| OL | Orchard Lake Schools (Michigan) |
| ScU | University of South Carolina |
| UW | University of Windsor (Ontario) |

POLAND

An Annotated Bibliography of Books in English

# I
# GENERAL WORKS

1. Alcuin, pseud. POLAND, text by Alcuin; drawings by M. Zuławski. Middlesex, Eng.: Atlantis, 1943. 53p. 43-12441.

   "A comprehensive account of the multitude of things bundled together under the common label, Poland, to enable the reader to form an idea of one of the major problems of the war." Particularly valuable are sections devoted to a brief discussion of the Polish armed forces. No documentation. Maps. Illustrations.

2. Barnett, Clifford R. POLAND, ITS PEOPLE, ITS SOCIETY, ITS CULTURE, in collaboration with Robert J. Feldman and others. New Haven, Conn.: HRAF Press, 1958. 470p. 58-11469.

   Concerned with all aspects of Polish society and culture: history, geography, ethnic groups, religion, politics, law, foreign relations, economics, finance, agriculture, industry, foreign trade, public health and welfare. Part of the Human Relations Area Files. Tables. Maps. Bibliography, pp. 443-460.

3. Brant, Irving. NEW LIFE IN POLAND. London: D. Dobson, Ltd., 1946. 64p. 47-22045.

   The British edition of the book entitled, THE NEW POLAND, omitting out-of-date material.

4. Brant, Irving. THE NEW POLAND. New York: Universe Publishers, 1946. 116p. 46-3920.

   Although aimed at defining the new Polish economic system, this book is the story of Poland at the time "in which the thread of the new economy is interwoven with the life of the people."

5. Budrewicz, Olgierd. INTRODUCTION TO POLAND. Miami: American Institute of Polish Culture, 1985. 216p. 84-073027.

   Highly personal, emotional but extremely informative introduction to Poland, Polish towns and villages, historical places and history of the Polish nation. Illustrations. Maps.

6. Cameron, Charles O. THE NEW POLAND. Chicago: National Polish Department of America, 1919. 100p. 19-19925.

   Contains a "series of articles reprinted from the DETROIT JOURNAL dealing with the reappearance of a Polish state after World War I."

7. Czarnomski, Francis B., ed. THE POLISH HANDBOOK, 1925: A GUIDE TO THE COUNTRY AND RESOURCES OF THE REPUBLIC OF POLAND. London: Eyre and Spottiswoode, Ltd., 1925. 704p. 26-26534.

   Extremely valuable retrospective comprehensive guide. Data obtained from Polish specialists in Poland who wrote the articles. Contains the English text of the Constitution of March 21, 1921. Subjects covered are: constitution and government of Poland; history; physical characteristics; education and religion; production: agriculture, forestry, mining, industries; trade and commerce; transport and communications; labor and social welfare; finance; national defense; cultural life; and general information. Coats of arms. Maps.

8. de Colonna, Bertram. POLAND FROM THE INSIDE. London: Heath, Cranton, Limited, 1939. 167p. 48-42050.

   Popular survey of Poland including history, economic conditions, social life and customs and basically an attempt by an Englishman to appeal to readers to understand the country. Appendix includes such items as exports and imports, figures on educational institutions and a list of "important dates in Polish history." Portraits. Three folded maps, one showing the "historical frontiers" of Poland.

9. Dobrzyński, Wacław T. POLAND, LIGHTS AND SHADOWS IN THE LIFE OF AN ANCIENT NATION. Dublin: Talbot Press Limited, 1941. 112p. A42-1234.

A selection of papers, addresses, and speeches given by the author at the request of numerous Irish bodies, scientific and other, on the subject of Polish history and other aspects of Polish culture as well as articles on the same subjects published in the Irish Press.

10. Drogosław, pseud. POLAND AND THE POLISH NATION, trans. by Marie Busch. London: Polish Information Committee, 1917. 106p. 17-24671.

    Survey of Poland written in response to the concern of the British public for the political re-establishment of an independent Poland.

11. Dyboski, Roman. POLAND. New York: Charles Scribner's Sons, 1933. 443p. 33-31276.

    A comprehensive survey of the life and culture of Poland. Divided into history, geography, minority problems, economic life, education and research, literature, and "Poland's position in the world of to-day and to-morrow." Bibliography, pp. 425-430.

12. Dyboski, Roman. POLAND IN WORLD CIVILIZATION, ed. by Ludwik Krzyżanowski. New York: J.M. Barrett Corporation, 1950. 285p. MiU: DK-411-.D96-1950a

    Offers readers of English a summary presentation of what Poland has stood for in the annals of civilized humanity and what justifies her claim to a permanent place among the free nations of the world. Stress has been laid on the ideas governing the intellectual and moral development of the nation instead of on the outward spectacle of its efforts and attainments in the sphere of international action, whether political or economic. Maps on lining papers. Bibliographical notes, pp. 259-263.

13. Dyboski, Roman. POLAND, OLD AND NEW, THREE LECTURES. London: Oxford University Press, 1926. 68p. 27-7793.

    Lectures delivered at Geneva in 1925 in an attempt to use historical argument to justify Poland's claim to a seat in the Council of the League of Nations. One map depicting the historical frontiers of Poland.

14. Elgoth-Ligocki, Edward. LEGENDS AND HISTORY OF POLAND.
    New York: Thomas Nelson and Sons, 1943. 120p.
    44-4712.

    A brief, undocumented survey of the history of Poland.
    Also contains four Polish legends: The white eagle;
    Prince Cracus and the dragon; Princess Wanda; Princess
    Kinga's ring; and The legend of Pan Twardowski. Brief
    biography of General Władysław Sikorski. Illustrations
    and many portraits of Polish historical figures. Maps.

15. Elgoth-Ligocki, Edward. POLAND. London: MacDonald and
    Co., Ltd., 1944. 167p. 44-3890.

    Half of the book is history; the other half discusses
    the contemporary scene, the Church, literature, social
    state and political future. One map.

16. FIFTEEN YEARS OF PEOPLE'S POLAND. Warszawa: Polonia
    Publishing House, 1959. 237p. NN: D-12-1617.

    Brief review of the most important spheres of cultural
    activity in post-war Poland: political system,
    industry, agriculture, Poland's western territories,
    education, science, cultural achievements. Tables.
    Maps. Illustrations.

17. Giergielewicz, Mieczysław, ed. POLISH CIVILIZATION:
    ESSAYS AND STUDIES. New York: New York University
    Press, 1979. 318p. 78-52747.

    Contents: Polish peasant rituals and seasonal cus-
    toms, by Cezaria Beaudouin de Jędrzejewicz; Towns in
    medieval Poland by Jan Ptaśnik; Nicolaus Copernicus by
    Alexandre Kayre; Polish Reformation in the sixteenth
    century by Aleksander Bruckner; From radicalism to
    humanitarianism by Stanisław Kot; Helping the Danish
    ally by Jan Pasek; Protection of Jewish religious rights
    by royal edicts in pre-partition Poland by Isaac Lewin;
    Seventeenth-century Padua in the intellectual life of
    Poland by Henryk Barycz; Twilight of the leaders:
    Julian Ursyn Niemcewicz by Wacław Berent; Mickiewicz at
    the College de France by Wacław Lednicki; Catholicism
    and Christian democracy in Poland by Adam Żółtowski;
    Polish illegal publications under Russian rule by Józef
    Piłsudski; Working class in Poland by Feliks Gross; and,
    Recollections of the camp at Sachsenhausen, 1939-1940
    by Stanisław Pigoń.

*General Works* 7

18. Giertych, Jędrzej. CHRISTIAN POLAND'S MILLENARY.
London: Veritas Foundation Publication Centre, 1966.
63p. 66-74363.

   Brief historical sketch of Christianity in Poland.

19. Giertych, Jędrzej. IN DEFENSE OF MY COUNTRY. London:
Veritas Foundation Press, 1981. 732p. 82-187976.

   Justification of the re-establishment of a Polish
state based upon frontiers affixed along ethnic lines.
Discussion of the historical rights to the territories
accompanied by numerous facsimiles of documents from
German, Russian and Polish sources. Illustrations.
Maps. Publications of the Roman Dmowski Society, No. 19.

20. Great Britain. Foreign Office. AUSTRIAN POLAND.
London: H.M. Stationery Office, 1920. 78p. NjP:
1638.406.

   Handbook prepared by the British Foreign Office for
use by its delegates to the Paris Peace Conference.
Contents: geography, physical and political; political
history; social and political conditions; economic
conditions.

21. Great Britain. Foreign Office. PRUSSIAN POLAND.
London: H.M. Stationery Office, 1920. 58p. NjP:
1638.4063.

   Handbook prepared by the British Foreign Office for
use by its delegates to the Paris Peace Conference.
Contents: geography, physical and political; political
history; social and political conditions; economic
conditions. Of particular importance is a rather extensive discussion of KULTURKAMPF.

22. Great Britain. Foreign Office. RUSSIAN POLAND,
LITHUANIA AND WHITE RUSSIA. London: H.M. Stationery
Office, 1920. 144p. MiD: D914X-G77.

   Handbook prepared by the British Foreign Office for
use by its delegates to the Paris Peace Conference.
Contents: geography, physical and political; political
history, social and political conditions; economic
conditions.

23. Gronowicz, Antoni. THE PIASTS OF POLAND, trans. by
    Joseph Vetter. New York: Charles Scribner's Sons,
    1945. 199p. 45-9938.

    The story of the growth of Poland as a nation and her
    relationships throughout the ages with her neighbors,
    Germany and Russia, as seen through the eyes of a farmer,
    Stefan Piast. Appeals to juvenile reader. Illustrations.
    Maps.

24. Halecki, Oskar, ed. POLAND UNDER THE COMMUNISTS. New
    York: F.A. Praeger, 1957. 601p. 57-9331.

    Volume 50 in Praeger series on Russian history and
    world Communism. Various articles on politics, culture,
    the economy of Poland. Biographical sketches of leading
    figures of the Communist regime. Brief chronology,
    April, 1943 to March, 1956. Maps. Bibliography, pp.
    572-586.

25. Holzer, Jerzy Z. FIFTY YEARS OF POLISH INDEPENDENCE.
    Warszawa: Interpress Publishers, 1968. 89p. UW:
    DK440.H7.

    Divided into three sections: Poland's place in Europe,
    the nation and internal policy. Polish viewpoint.
    Chronological table covers principal events from
    November 6, 1918 through August 2, 1945.

26. Iwanicka, Halina. A THOUSAND YEARS OF POLISH HERITAGE.
    Chicago: Commerce Clearing House, 1966. 87p.
    66-23479.

    Historical sketch divided into six periods: Piast
    dynasty, Jagiellonian era, elective kings, struggle for
    independence, interwar independence period, and Poland
    today. Final chapter attempts to cover all phases of
    life in Poland c. 1966. Maps.

27. Iwańska, Alicja, ed. CONTEMPORARY POLAND: SOCIETY,
    POLITICS, ECONOMY. New Haven: Human Relations Area
    Files, 1955. 56-32388.

    Contents: Geography, by Benjamin Nimer; History, by
    Zbigniew Kruszewski; Population, by Leon Novar; Language,
    by Alicja Iwańska; Social Institutions and Society by
    Alicja Iwańska; Political Institutions, Constitution and

Judiciary, by Samuel P. Lyon; Political Structure of Poland, 1918 to the Communist Seizure of Power, by Zbigniew Kruszewski; Installation of the Communist Regime in Poland, by Zbigniew Kruszewski; Marxism-Leninism in Poland, by Samuel P. Lyon; The Polish Communist Party, by Samuel P. Lyon; The Police, by Samuel P. Lyon; Government of Poland, by Zbigniew Kruszewski; Army and Paramilitary Organizations, by Zbigniew Kruszewski; Economic Institutions, by Michał Zawadzki. Prepared by the University of Chicago. Maps. Bibliography, pp. 571-578.

28. Jarecka, Louise L. MADE IN POLAND: LIVING TRADITIONS OF THE LAND, illus. by M.G. Nowicki. New York: Alfred A. Knopf, 1949. 289p. 49-8468.

Excellent survey of Polish history and Polish culture, including folk culture, designed for the teen-age reader. Especially good ethnographic materials. Illustrations. Maps.

29. Keefe, Eugene K. AREA HANDBOOK FOR POLAND, by E.K. Keefe and others. Washington, D.C.: U.S. Government Printing Office, 1973. 335p. 72-600380.

One of a series of handbooks prepared by Foreign Area Studies of the American University. Designed for military and other personnel who need a convenient compilation of basic facts about the social, economic, political and military institutions and practices of Poland. Maps. Bibliography, pp. 305-319.

30. Lineberry, William P. POLAND. New York: H.W. Wilson Company, 1984. 169p. 84-11977.

First section describes the historical background, the rise of Solidarity, and the economic conditions that did much to provoke a crisis. The second section concentrates on Poland's international importance and poses the question of how the West should respond to events that threaten the stability of its political adversary. The third section describes Poland in the aftermath of martial law, presenting a picture of a population aware of its own power, but uncertain how to use it. Bibliography, pp. 161-169.

31. Mała Encyklopedia Powszechna. POLAND: LAND, HISTORY, CULTURE, AN OUTLINE, trans. by T.A. Malanowski and C. Kozłowska. Warszawa: Państwowe Wydawnitctwo Naukowe, 1959. 156p. 60-1981.

    Reprint of articles pertinent to Poland in the MAŁA ENCYKLOPEDIA POWSZECHNA published for foreigners. Illustrations. Maps.

32. Morfill, William R. POLAND. New York: Ayer Co., Publishers, 1972. 389p. 75-39494.

    Reprint (Select Bibliographic Reprint Series) of the author's book entitled, THE STORY OF POLAND, published in 1893.

33. Morfill, William R. THE STORY OF POLAND. New York: G.P. Putnam's Sons, 1893. 389p. 4-17621.

    Readable history of the country bringing into prominence the most stirring episodes and salient characteristics, and putting in the background and details which must prove less interesting. In addition to being a brief history of Poland for the general reader, it devotes a chapter to a discussion of Polish literature, another to the social condition of Poland, and a third to political and literary landmarks. Many portraits reproduced from old prints in the British Museum. List of Polish kings. Genealogical tables.

34. Newman, Bernard. RUSSIA'S NEIGHBOR: THE NEW POLAND. London: Victor Gollancz, Ltd., 1946. 256p. 47-72.

    A seasoned traveler to Poland comments on Poland from 1945 to date of publication with reference to Polish history in an attempt to advise the English-speaking world of the Polish situation as he saw it. Maps.

35. Newman, Bernard. THE STORY OF POLAND. New York: Hutchinson and Co., Ltd., 1943. 288p. 43-14495.

    A comprehensive discussion of the history and social life and customs of Poland. In addition, the author discusses the problems of Poland devoting much space to the invasion of Poland in 1939 including maps of the progress of the German occupation. Illustrations. Portraits. Maps.

36. Paneth, Philip.   IS POLAND LOST?   London:   Nicholson and Watson, 1939.   253p.   40-5627.

    The object of this book is to give a survey of Polish history, both recent and past, and to show how and to what extent it has been informed by the spirit of religion.

37. THE PATTERN OF LIFE IN POLAND.  Paris:   Mid-European Research and Planning Centre, 1952-.   16v.   52-35431.

    A factual and objective survey of the organization and principles applied in the chief domain of life in present-day Poland under the Communist system.  Twenty-one volumes planned.

38. Pawłowski, Jerome I.  POLAND AND HER PEOPLE.  Detroit: Barc Brothers Printing Co., 1929.  211p.  29-22408.

    First section covers evolution of the Polish classes; cultural Poland; idealism of Poland; Poland in the World War; and What American Poles did for Poland.  Second section is a travelogue which attempts to acquaint English-speaking peoples with the extraordinary richness of Poland, her people and institutions, with the political and cultural life of Poland, and the effect of Polish heredity and environment on its genesis.

39. Piltz, Erasmus, ed.  POLAND, HER PEOPLE, HISTORY, INDUSTRIES, FINANCE, SCIENCE, LITERATURE, ART AND SOCIAL DEVELOPMENT, ed. by E. Piltz et al.  London: H. Jenkins Limited, 1909.  416p.  18-23343.

    Authorized English version of the PÉTITE ENCYCLOPÉDIE POLONAISE.  Maps.

40. Poland.  Komisariat Generalny.  Nowojorska Wystawa Światowa, 1939-1940.  OFFICIAL CATALOG OF THE POLISH PAVILION AT THE WORLD'S FAIR, NEW YORK, 1939. Warszawa:   Drukarnia Polska, Ltd., 1939.   503p. 40-51535.

    A kaleidoscope of Polonica as it was viewed by the best minds of the country for presentation to the world at the New York World's Fair.  Contains numerous black-and-white and colored illustrations of works of art, architecture, maps, charts, etc.; many not easily found elsewhere. Numerous texts on Polish subjects, e.g. history, engineering, etc. Covers all aspects of Polish life EXCEPT religion.

41. POLAND, A COUNTRY STUDY, ed. by Harold D. Nelson. Washington, D.C.: U.S. Government Printing Office, 1983. 483p. 83-22431.

    One of a series prepared by the Foreign Area Studies, the American University, under the Country Studies/Area Handbook Program. Describes Poland's economic, national security, political and social systems and institutions and examines the inter-relationship of those systems and institutions and the ways they are shared by cultural factors. Written by a multi-disciplinary team of social scientists. Includes major ground, air force and national air defense and naval weapons, 1982, as well as other useful military data. Bibliography, pp. 429-466. Illustrations. Maps.

42. POLAND, A HANDBOOK. Warszawa: Interpress Publishers, 1977. 613p. NjP: DK4040.P62813.

    Contents: National emblem, colours, anthem - Stefan K. Kuczyński. A thousand years of Poland - Andrzej Ajnenkiel. The country - Jerzy Kondracki. Polish society - Jerzy J. Wiatr. Poles abroad - Euzebiusz Basiński. The state - Adam Łopatka. Organization of political and social life - Jerzy Janitz. The national economy - Janusz Kaliński. Social policy - Marek Piątkowski. Education - Andrzej Świecki. Science and learning - Zdzisław Każimierczak. The arts - Mirosław Żuławski et al. Development and dissemination of culture - Włodzimierz Sandecki and Stanisław Lorentz. Poland and the world - Ryszard Baturo et al. Sport - Stefan Sieniarski. Tourism - Leonard Ostrębski and Jerzy Kondracki. Poland in the years 1971-1980 - Zygmunt Szeliga.

43. POLAND, GENERAL SKETCH OF HISTORY, 1569-1815. London: H.M. Stationery Office, 1920. 30p. NjP: 1638.4065.

    One of a series of pamphlets prepared for the British delegation to the peace conference of 1918. A brief historical sketch by trained writers.

General Works 13

44. POLAND OF TODAY. Warszawa: Polonia Foreign Languages
Publishing House, 1954. 144p. 55-33650.

Purpose of the book is to acquaint the reader abroad
with the great changes which have taken place in Poland
during the decade, 1945-1955. Illustrations. Maps.

45. POLAND'S CASE FOR INDEPENDENCE. New York: Dodd, Mead
and Company, 1916. 352p. NjP: 1638.72787.

Series of essays designed to illustrate the continuance of Polish national life and to interpret the manifestation of that life to foreigners and especially to
the people of Great Britain.

46. POLISH ENCYCLOPEDIA, published by the Committee for the
Polish Encyclopaedic Publications at Fribourg and
Geneva. Geneva: Atar Ltd., 1922-1926. MiD:
R914.38-P755.

Contents: Volume I - The Polish language by Stanisław
Dobrzycki. History of literature, from Middle Ages
through pseudo-classicism by Stanisław Dobrzycki.
Romanticism and contemporary literature by M. Szyjkowski.
History of Poland by L. Konopczynski. Volume II -
Territory and population of Poland. Geography and
ethnography by William J. Rose. General demography by
Stefan L. Zaleski. Territorial development of the
Polish nation by Włodzimierz Wakar. The Jews in Poland
by Adam Skierko. The population of present-day Poland
by Martin Nadobnik. Volume III - Economic Life in
Poland. Natural wealth by Tadeusz Estreicher et al.
Prussian Poland: Introduction by Jan Żółtowski. Agriculture by Stefan L. Zaleski. Industry by Józef
Frejlich. Commerce by Stefan L. Zaleski and Jan
Żółtowski. Means of communication by Adam Rzewuski.
Credit by Marcel Scheffs. Polish cooperative societies
by Józef Adamek and Marcel Scheffs. Labour question by
Józef Adamek. Public finance by Jan Żółtowski. Galicia
and Silesia of Cieszyn: Introduction by Franciszek
Bujak. Agriculture by Jan Rozwadowski. Industry by Jan
Rozwadowski and Franciszek Bujak. Means of communication
by Józef Frejlich. Commerce by Arthur Benes and Jan
Rozwadowski. Credit by Jan Rozwadowski. Cooperative
societies by Józef Adamek and Józef Bek. The labour
question by Alexander Szczepański. Public finances by
Stanisław Głabinski. Silesia of Cieszyn by Stanisław

Filasiewicz. Kingdom of Poland: Agriculture by Wacław Ponikowski and Stefan L. Zaleski. Industry by Józef Frejlich. Commerce by Stefan L. Zaleski. Means of communication by Józef Frejlich. Credit by Henryk Kaden and Jan Żółtowski. Cooperative societies by Józef Adamek. Labour question by Leo Klimecki. Public finances by Stefan L. Zaleski. Lithuania and Ruthenia by Bronisław Cinet-Piłsudski, rev. and completed by Konstantyn Skirmunt and Jan Żółtowski. Courland by Andrew Plater-Syberg. Bibliography, Vol. III, pp. xxxi-xxxv. Maps.

47. POLISH LANGUAGE AND HERITAGE: A STUDY GUIDE FOR STUDENTS AND TEACHERS. Orchard Lake, Mich.: Center for Polish Studies and Culture, 1969. 162p. OL: DK411.P6.

    Reference for those interested in reflective and effective study of the Polish contributions to social living. Bibliography, pp. i-x.

48. POLISH PEOPLE'S REPUBLIC, trans. by Halina Markiewicz, Warszawa: PWN-Polish Scientific Publishers, 1976. 200p. 77-378739.

    Contents: Natural conditions; history; population; economy and living conditions; social structure; state system; Party system; the armed forces; educational system; science; culture; Poland in the present-day world; and a brief section on Poles abroad entitled, Polonia.

49. Polish Research Centre. London. EASTERN POLAND. Ditchling, Hassocks, Sussex: Ditchling Press, Ltd., 1941. 53p. 42-25455.

    Comprehensive sketch of regions of Wilno, Nowogródek, Polesia, Wółhynia, Lwów, Tarnopol and Stanisławów. Maps.

50. PORTRAIT OF POLAND, comp. by Jan Krok-Paszkowski. Illustrations by Bruno Barbey. New York: Thames & Hudson, 1982. 172p. 82-50740.

    Exquisite collection of colored photographs taken throughout urban and rural Poland primarily during the 1980s. Includes selections from writings by famous

*General Works* 15

personages, Polish and non-Polish, a propos to the subject. Maps.

51. REMEMBRANCES OF A POLISH EXILE, by August A. Jakubowski. Albany: Packard and van Bentyhuysen, 1835. 69p. 1-1476.

 Contents: Essay on Polish poetry, pp. 11-30; Historical Sketch of Education in Poland, pp. 31-42; The Polish Lovers, pp. 43-51; The Causes of Emigration of the Poles, pp. 52-60. Appendix contains short notice of Ukraine and Podolia, pp. 61-69.

52. Retinger, Joseph H., ed. ALL ABOUT POLAND: FACTS, FIGURES, DOCUMENTS. London: Minerva Publishing Co., Ltd., 1941. 292p. 42-8385.

 Furnishes the Anglo-Saxon reader with the main historical, cultural and political data and statistics relating to Poland and Polish affairs as they were before 1939. Includes an English translation of extracts of the 1935 Constitution and the English words and music to the Polish national anthem. Data on Roman Catholic Church includes names of bishops, etc. Bibliography, pp. 289-292. One map, folded in pocket.

53. Rose, William J. POLAND, OLD AND NEW. London: G. Bell and Sons, Ltd., 1948. 354p. 49-13370.

 A thorough sketch of Polish history as well as the national economy, folk culture, religion and education, literature and art and sciences. References to further readings in English given at the end of each chapter. Appendix II contains names of cabinet ministers with their portfolios as of June, 1945. List of members of the Provisional Government of National Unity. Portraits. Maps.

54. Schmitt, Bernadotte E., ed. POLAND. Berkeley: University of California Press, 1945. 500p. A45-933.

 Contents: Poland and Europe: geographic position, by Oskar Halecki. Anthropology of Poland: prehistory and race, by John L. Angel. Formation of the Polish state, by Frank F. Nowak. Poland as a European power, by Oskar Halecki. Partitioned Poland, 1795-1914, by Julia Swift Orvis. Rebirth of Poland, 1914-1923, by Bernadotte E. Schmitt. Constitutional development of Poland, by

Joseph C. Gedyński. Polish political parties, by
Malbone W. Graham. Polish politics, 1918-1939, by
Malbone W. Graham. Minorities, by Joseph S. Rouček.
Poland's monetary and financial policy, 1919-1939, by
Zygmunt Karpinski. Agricultural reconstruction in
Poland, by Jerzy Radwan. Social progress in Poland,
1918-1939, by Jan K. Kasprzak. Religious life, by Oskar
Halecki. Education, by Wojciech Swiętosławski. Science
and scientific institutions, by Wojciech Swietosławski.
Polish literature, by Manfred Kridl. Fine arts, by
Irena Piotrowska. Music, by Felix R. Lobienski. Polish
national spirit, by Edmund Zawacki. Polish-American
cultural relationships, by Stephen P. Mizwa. Polish-
American political and economic relations, by Eldon R.
Burke. Foreign relations, by S. Harrison Thomson.
Poland and the war, by Stanisław Strzetelski. Epilogue,
by Robert J. Kerner. Illustrations. Portraits. Maps.

55. Singleton, Aileen M.W. POLAND INDOMITABLE. London:
George E.J. Coldwell, Ltd., 1936. 72p. 39-32224.

An outline of Polish history and culture with special
chapters on Sobieski, Stanislaus Leszczynski, Kośćiuszko.
Author appears to defend Poland's existence at the time,
1936, when German designs toward the east became
apparent.

56. Singleton, Aileen M.W. THE RIDDLE OF POLAND. London:
Washbourne and Bogan, Ltd., 1933. 61p. 35-11278.

Written to inform the general English reading public
in 1932-1933 about Poland, especially its Catholic
aspects with special attention given to similarities in
the histories of Poland and Ireland.

57. Skrzyński, Alexander J. POLAND AND PEACE. London:
George Allen and Unwin, Ltd., 1923. 154p. 24-14727.

This book aims to be a complete picture of contemporary Poland, based entirely on facts. Author was
Minister of Foreign Affairs. Portrait of author on
frontispiece.

58. Statkowski, Józef. POLAND, OLD AND NEW. Warszawa: M.
Arct, 1938. 134p. 39-4451.

A general historical sketch of Polish history for the
general reader. Author attempts to place the country in

*General Works*

the perspective of the time the book was published.
Contains list of famous Poles. Chronology of important
dates in Polish history. Illustrations. Portraits.
Maps.

59. Statkowski, Józef. POLAND, THE COUNTRY OF YOUR FATHERS.
Warszawa: Światowy Związek Polaków z Zagranicy, 1935.
53p. 39-23118.

    Provides the American of Polish extraction with a
    brief description of Polish history and life. Illustrations. Maps.

60. Steven, Stewart. THE POLES. New York: Macmillan
Publishing Co., 1982. 427p. 82-9924.

    A vivid account, through anecdotes and vignettes, of
    life in Poland in 1980-1981. Based on hundreds of
    interviews with Polish labor organizers, government
    officials, churchmen, Communists, artists, and workers.
    Set of notes, pp. 409-414, explains sources of information. Bibliography, pp. 415-417.

61. STUDIES IN POLISH CIVILIZATION. New York: Columbia
University Press, 1971. 549p. 76-25103.

    Selected papers presented at the first congress of the
    Polish Institute of Arts and Sciences in America,
    November 25-27, 1966. Includes bibliographical references. Illustrations. Plans.

62. Super, Paul. THE POLISH TRADITION: AN INTERPRETATION
OF A NATION. London: George Allen and Unwin, Ltd.,
1939. 215p. 40-6246.

    Author desired to crystallize into very definite form
    the observations of seventeen years of residence among
    the Poles and extensive study of their land, life, and
    literature. Illustrations. Maps.

63. Swicz, V. POLAND STILL UNKNOWN. Kilmarnock, Scotland:
Standard Printing Works, 1942. 2d ed. 148p.
43-14938.

    Purpose of the book is to present a brief record of
    history and a plain statement of present problems and to
    contribute to a better understanding of Poland among the
    English-speaking people. Maps.

64. Swidziński, Natalia. POLAND, FACTS AND FIGURES, trans.
by Stanisław Tarnowski. Warszawa: Interpress
Publishers, 1973. 67p. 73-15173.

    Fact book about contemporary Poland. Statistical data
    given on charts. Many black-and-white and colored illustrations.

65. Szturm de Sztrem, Edward. STATISTICAL ATLAS OF POLAND.
London: Polish Ministry of Information, 1945. 120p.
45-6926.

    Provides a concise and comprehensive survey of Poland
    between the two great wars. Maps, tables, graphs, often
    multi-colored, provided retrospective data. Author was
    Professor of Statistics at the Free University of Warsaw
    and Director of Polish Chief Statistical Bureau. Maps.

66. TWENTY YEARS OF THE POLISH PEOPLE'S REPUBLIC, by
Stanisław W. Balicki et al. Trans. by Eugene Lepa
et al. Warszawa: Państwowe Wydawnictwo Ekonomiczne,
1964. 313p. 65-2869.

    The purpose of this book is to present the achievements of People's Poland over the past twenty years in
    all fields, to throw light on the role of this historically brief but extremely important period in the
    thousand-year old history of the popular names in the
    fight for national and social liberation, and to define
    the place of socialist Poland in the present-day world
    and the prospects for her future development. Chronicle
    of main events, 1944-1964. Illustrations. Portraits.
    Maps.

67. Wieniewski, Ignacy. HERITAGE: THE FOUNDATIONS OF
POLISH CULTURE, trans. by Marta Zaborska. Toronto:
Polish-Canadian Women's Federation in Canada, 1981.
96p. MiU: DK4110.W653.

    Account of the basic foundations of Polish culture and
    those elements which constituted its essence and determined its type. Considers the native element, the
    Christian element, and the Latin element. Illustrations. Portraits. Maps.

68. Woroniecki, Edouard, comp. POLAND: HER PEOPLE, HISTORY,
INDUSTRIES, FINANCE, SCIENCE, LITERATURE, ART, AND

SOCIAL DEVELOPMENT. London: Herbert Jenkins, Ltd., 1909. 416p. 18-23343.

Object was to furnish the public with concise information concerning Poland at a moment when the future of Europe was being decided. Offers a picture of the country as it was on the eve of World War I. Maps.

69. Zieleniewicz, Andrzej. POLAND, trans., rev., and ed. by Robert Strybel and others in cooperation with Edward J. Piszek. Orchard Lake, Mich.: Center for Polish Studies and Culture, 1971. 277p. 72-187180.

A guide to the geography, people, history, culture, economy, and capital city of Poland. Poor scholarship. Mainly illustrations in color. No bibliography. No documentation. Maps.

II
SPECIAL WORKS

Aeronautics

70. Cynk, Jerzy B. HISTORY OF THE POLISH AIR FORCE, 1918-1968. Reading, Eng.: Osprey Publishing Ltd., 1972. 307p. OL: TL515.P57C9.

History of the air force from the time of its conception to 1968. Profusely illustrated in black-and-white.

71. Cynk, Jerzy B. POLISH AIRCRAFT, 1893-1939. London: Putnam and Company, 1971. 760p. 79-879715.

Covers the history of Polish aircraft design and industry. Attempts to include all Polish heavier-than-air designs which evolved prior to September, 1939. Includes work of Poles in neighboring countries and in France. Contains photographs and drawings. Bibliography: pp. 736-738.

Agriculture

72. Korbonski, Andrzej. POLITICS OF SOCIALIST AGRICULTURE IN POLAND: 1945-1960. New York: Columbia University Press, 1965. 330p. 64-22153.

Analysis of Communist agrarian policies in Poland. Includes agrarian scene during the interwar period. Bibliography: pp. 317-322.

Antiquities

73. Czarnecki, Jan. THE GOTHS IN ANCIENT POLAND: A STUDY ON THE HISTORICAL GEOGRAPHY OF THE ODER-VISTULA REGION DURING FIRST TWO CENTURIES OF OUR ERA. Coral Gables,

Fla.: University of Miami Press, 1975. 184p.
74-20750.

An historical-geographical investigation of the territory occupied and the moves made by the Goths in the Odrawista region during the first two centuries of our era. Many charts and maps. Adequately documented. Bibliography: pp. 161-174.

74. Gayre, George R. TEUTON AND SLAV ON THE POLISH FRONTIER: A DIAGNOSIS OF THE RACIAL BASIS OF THE GERMANO-POLISH BORDERLANDS, WITH SUGGESTIONS FOR THE SETTLEMENT OF GERMAN AND SLAV CLAIMS. London: Eyre and Spottiswoode, Ltd., 1944. 11-76p. A44-4815.

Anthropological study of people living in the areas where the Polish frontier meets the German frontier. Discusses the geographical background of the Germano-Polish borderland, the races involved, the influences of ethnographic and linguistic factors, the distribution of the Slav-speaking population. Numerous ethnological and ethnographical maps. Of particular note are several black-and-white illustrations of racial types. Maps.

75. Hensel, Witold. ARCHAEOLOGICAL RESEARCH IN POLAND, by Witold Hensel and Aleksander Gieysztor. Warszawa: Polonia Publishing House, 1958. MiU: DK409.H52.

General information on archaeological research carried on in Poland after World War II. Deals with results obtained during the course of excavations. Contains list of important post-war archaeological institutes in Poland. Illustrations. Map. Bibliography: pp. 71-75.

76. Hensel, Witold. THE BEGINNING OF THE POLISH STATE. Warszawa: Polonia Publishing House, 1960. 178p. MiU: DK421.H53.

Considers the probable period at which Slavonic peoples settled on Polish territory, the beginnings of political organization on Polish territory, the formation of the Polish state, main factors in the development of early Polish culture. Illustrations. Maps.

77. Jażdżewski, Konrad. POLAND, trans. by Maria Abramowicz and Robin Place. New York: F.A. Praeger, 1965. 240p. 64-17679.

## Special Works

Discusses the archaeology and cultural history of Poland from the Paleolithic, Mesolithic, Neolithic, Bronze and early Iron Ages and later Iron Ages using the latest in archaeological findings. Includes 77 plates in black-and-white with notes. Drawings. Maps. Tables. Bibliography: pp. 178-190.

78. Kmietowicz, Frank A. ANCIENT SLAVS. Stevens Point, Wisc.: Worzalla Publishing Co., 1976. 250p.

    Concentrates on pre-history of Poles. No index, no bibliography. Illustrations. Maps.

79. THE NEOLITHIC IN POLAND, ed. by Tadeusz Wiślanski, trans. by Krystyna Kozłowska. Wrocław: Zakład Narodowy im. Ossolinskich, 1970. 520p. 72-262187.

    Reflects the present state of knowledge of the Neolithic in Poland. A collection of papers depicting the stage that has been reached in investigations of most of Neolithic cultures. Drawings of artifacts on folded sheets. Maps. Bibliography: pp. 450-493.

80. Rajewski, Zdzisław. BISKUPIN POLISH EXCAVATIONS, trans. by Leopold Widymski. Warszawa: Polonia Publishing House, 1959. 77p. MiD: 913.36 R137b.

    Sketch with numerous illustrations of the archaeological findings in and around Biskupin. Divided into three sections: oldest settlement, settlement in the first centuries and the early middle ages, and information for visitors. Illustrations. Maps.

81. Roemer, Ferdinand. THE BONE CAVES OF OJCÓW IN POLAND, trans. by John Edward Lee. London: Longmans, Green and Co., 1884. 41p. 1-4140.

    Description of caves and contents of them in Ojców in Silesia, an area which at the time the archaeological remains were discovered, was part of the German Empire. Numerous illustrations of artifacts.

### Architecture

82. BUILDING AND ARCHITECTURE IN POLAND, 1945-1966, by Juliusz Dumnicki et al. Warszawa: Interpress Publishers, 1968. 116p. 72-5276.

Several articles about contemporary architecture in Poland. Includes all types. Numerous black-and-white illustrations. Some elevations. Maps.

83. Chrościcki, Juliusz A. ATLAS OF WARSAW'S ARCHITECTURE, by Juliusz A. Chrościcki and Andrzej Rottermund. Warszawa: Arkady Publishers, 1977. 248p. 78-324485.

    Intended to serve tourists who visit Poland's capital, as well as its inhabitants and all who are interested in Warszawa's history and art. History of architecture and a catalog of particular structures. Complete list of Warszawa's architectural monuments. Illustrations in black-and-white and color. Maps.

84. Dmochowski, Zbigniew. THE ARCHITECTURE OF POLAND, AN HISTORICAL SURVEY, with a foreword by Lionel B. Budden. London: Polish Research Centre, Limited, 1956. 429p. 57-45822.

    Covers the development of architecture in Poland from tenth century to early years of the nineteenth century. Follows chronological order but buildings are analyzed in groups representative of a given architectural style. Profusely illustrated. Bibliography: pp. 411-416.

85. Faczyński, Jerzy. STUDIES IN POLISH ARCHITECTURE, trans. by Peter Jordan. London: Hodder and Stoughton, Limited, 1945. 120p. 45-9353.

    Black-and-white illustrations with marginal notes chosen from those made by Polish art historians. Introduction is a clear, concise description of Polish architecture.

86. Knox, Brian. THE ARCHITECTURE OF POLAND. London: Barrie and Jenkins, 1971. 161p. 73-597292.

    Illustrative description of the principal architectural monuments of Poland. Comprehensive and scholarly. Many floor plans. Maps.

87. Lisowski, Bohdan. MODERN ARCHITECTURE IN POLAND. Warszawa: Interpress Publishers, 1963. 41p. 69-135181.

    Brief overview of the historical development of modern architecture in Poland by an architect. Includes some

## Special Works

elevations. List of prizes and honorable mentions received by Polish architects in international competition in the years 1959-1967. Illustrations.

88. Łozinski, Jerzy Z. GUIDE TO ARCHITECTURE IN POLAND, by J.Z. Łozinski and Adam Miłobedzki, trans. by Agnieszka Glinka. Warszawa: Polonia Publishing House, 1967. 286p. 68-630.

    Exhaustive guide to architecture of Poland intended primarily for tourists. Numerous black-and-white photographs of both interiors and exteriors of buildings. Arranged in alphabetical order by location. Maps and plans are in color.

89. Piechotka, Maria. WOODEN SYNAGOGUES, by Maria Piechotka and Każimierz Piechotka, trans. by Rulka Langer. Warszawa: Arkady Publishers, 1959. 218p. 60-31583.

    History of the wooden synagogues which were destroyed by the Germans during the occupation, 1939-1945. Mostly illustrations. Some elevations. Description of objects: pp. 196-210.

90. Soltynski, Roman. GLIMPSES OF POLISH ARCHITECTURE, trans. by Peter Jordan. London: Maxlove Publishing Co., Ltd., 1943. 56p. 43-15644.

    Comprehensive overview of architecture in Poland just prior to the Nazi invasion in 1939. Includes representative specimens of buildings extant in 1939. Emphasis on functional structures such as hospitals, banks, etc. Profusely illustrated. Map of the towns and villages mentioned in the book.

91. Zachwatowicz, Jan. POLISH ARCHITECTURE UP TO THE MID-NINETEENTH CENTURY. Warszawa: Budownictwo i Architektura, 1956. 29p. MiD: R720.949.W26p.

    Text followed by 499 illustrations each individually titled. Includes map of Poland which is an index of localities of objects included in the book.

92. Zachwatowicz, Jan. PROTECTION OF HISTORICAL MONUMENTS IN POLAND, trans. by Krystyna Cękalska. Warszawa: Polonia Publishing House, 1965. 147p. 67-56283.

Story of the destruction and gradual restoration of various historical monuments after World War II. Includes numerous black-and-white illustrations of monuments often before reconstruction and after restoration.

### Armed Forces

93. Anders, Władysław. AN ARMY IN EXILE; THE STORY OF THE SECOND POLISH CORPS. London: Macmillan and Co., Ltd., 1949. 319p. 49-5681.

    Story of the Polish army-in-exile with the Allies in France, in the Battle of Britain of 1940, at Tobruk in 1941, at Monte Cassino, Ancona, Bologna and simultaneously in Normandy, Belgium and Holland. Portraits. Maps.

94. Arct, Bohdan. POLES AGAINST THE V WEAPONS. Warszawa: Interpress Publishers, 1972. 126p.

    Story of how Poles contributed to the battle against the V weapons developed by Germany during World War II both on the continent and as participants in Great Britain. Maps. Illustrations.

95. Arct, Bohdan. POLISH WINGS IN THE WEST; AFTER THE SEPTEMBER DISASTER, THE BATTLE OF BRITAIN, AIR OFFENSIVES AND FINAL VICTORY, trans. by Beryl Arct. Warszawa: Interpress Publishers, 1971. 146p. 73-26311.

    Popular account of Polish airmen from the beginning to the end of World War II. Contains a summary of fight results, a list of victories gained by the leading fighter pilots from September 1, 1939 to May 6, 1945. Numerous black-and-white illustrations.

96. Biegański, Witold. POLES IN THE BATTLE OF NARVIK, trans. by Jan Alekandrowicz. Warszawa: Interpress Publishers, 1969. 106p. 74-7765.

    Account of the Polish participation in the Battle of Narvik, May 28-31, 1940. Black-and-white illustrations. Maps.

*Special Works* 27

97. Biegański, Witold. POLES IN THE BATTLE OF WESTERN EUROPE, trans. by Beryl Arct. Warszawa: Interpress Publishers, 1971. 158p. 75-306118.

    Translation of POLACY W WALKACH O ZACHODNIA EUROPIE. Important for illustrations of Polish forces in action in western European battles. Foreword states that this is one volume in a proposed series which will show the Polish contribution to freeing of Europe during World War II.

98. DESTINY CAN WAIT: THE POLISH AIR FORCE IN THE SECOND WORLD WAR, trans. by A. Truscoe. London: William Heinemann, Ltd., 1949. 402p. 50-2584.

    Story of the Polish Air Force based upon combat reports, squadron diaries and other official records and on personal narratives of members of the Air Force. Covers period from the summer of 1940 through 1945. Illustrations. Maps.

99. Fiedler, Arkady. SQUADRON 303: THE STORY OF THE POLISH FIGHTER SQUADRON WITH THE RAF. New York: Roy Publishers, 1943. 182p. 43-4047.

    Written anecdotally. No documentation. Reports of activities of those Poles who served really with the Royal Air force. Illustrations. Portraits.

100. Garliński, Józef. POLAND, S.O.E. AND THE ALLIES; trans. by Paul Stevenson. London: George Allen and Unwin, Ltd., 1969. 248p. NjP: 14101.169.378.03.

    S.O.E. stands for the "Special Operations Executive" of the British government. Covers activities of this unit in Poland from February 15, 1941 to October 2, 1944. Illustrations. Portraits of important officers in the unit. Maps.

101. Jamar, K. WITH THE TANKS OF THE 1ST POLISH ARMOURED DIVISION, trans. by M.C. Słomczanka. Hengelo, Netherlands: H.L. Smit and Zn., 1946. 332p. OL: D765.J313.

    Story of a unit of the Polish armed forces which fought with the Allied armies during World War II. Illustrations. Portraits. Maps.

102. Karolevitz, Robert F. FLIGHT OF EAGLES: THE STORY OF THE AMERICAN KOŚĆIUSZKO SQUADRON IN THE POLISH-RUSSIAN WAR, 1919-1920, by F.F. Karolevitz and Ross S. Fenn. Sioux Falls, S.D.: Brevet Press, Inc., 1974. 280p. 74-80769.

    Particularly valuable for photographs, mostly black-and-white. Story of a small coterie of American flying officers who offered their services to the Polish cause pieced together from diaries, letters and personal reminiscences of the men who wore the distinctive uniforms of the embryonic Polish Air Force. Portraits. Maps.

103. Koc, Leon Wacław, ed. THE POLISH ARMY AND THE POLISH NAVY. Warszawa: Central Military Booksellers Magazine, 1939. 111p. A44-787.

    Principally illustrations with six pages of text in English and German. Portraits.

104. Komorowski, Taduesz. THE SECRET ARMY. New York: Macmillan Company, 1950. 407p. 51-5124.

    Story of the Polish Underground Movement as it developed from 1939 to the end of 1944 by the author who was one of its organizers and later, from 1943 onwards, Commander of the Home Army. Part two is a history of the Warsaw Uprising of 1944 as told by the author who was a participant. Contains map of Warszawa and portrait of the author.

105. Lorentz, Leopold. CAEN TO WILHELMSHAVEN. Edinburgh: Erroll Publishing Co., Ltd., 1945. 104p. OL: D765.L6.

    Story of the Polish First Armoured Division by an American soldier of Polish descent. Short account of battles won by the division while operating as an integral part of British Liberation Army. Illustrations. Portraits.

106. Maclaren, Anna. POLAND AT ARMS. London: John Murray, 1942. 116p. A42-3614.

    Stories told to the author by Polish sailors, airmen and soldiers of the part they played in the battles of Poland, France, Norway and Britain. Illustrations. Maps.

*Special Works* 29

107. Malcher, George C. POLAND'S POLITICIZED ARMY: COMMU-
NISTS IN UNIFORM. New York: Praeger Publishers,
1984. 287p. 84-6894.

 Purpose of this book is "to explain how the Polish
 Army had the will and means to destroy the organizational structure of Solidarity, the story of an army
 within an army, an instrument of a committed nucleus of
 politicians in uniform led by General Jaruzelski."

108. Meissner, Janusz. POLISH WINGS OVER EUROPE, trans. by
Peter Jordan. Harrow, Eng.: Atlantis Publishing
Co., Ltd., 1945. 91p. A45-1631.

 Brief history of the Polish Air Force up to 1940.
 Segments written by various authors.

109. Murray, Kenneth M. WINGS OVER POLAND: THE STORY OF
THE 7TH KOŚCIUSZKO SQUADRON OF THE POLISH AIR
SERVICE, 1919, 1920, 1921. New York: D. Appleton
and Company, 1932. 362p. 32-24006.

 Includes roster of the squadron, May 1921. Group of
 highly experienced American military pilots of World
 War I who fought for Poland in the Russo-Polish War of
 1920-1921. Story based on logs kept by the pilots.
 Also based upon stories told by the pilots themselves.

110. Pawlowicz, Bohdan. O.R.P. GARLAND IN CONVOY TO RUSSIA,
trans. by J.M. Aldredge and M. Peczkowski. Metcham,
Surrey, Eng.: Surrey Press, Ltd., 1943. 79p.
43-17557.

 The record of a Polish destroyer on her journey from
 Great Britain to Murmansk and Archangel in the Spring
 of 1942. Contains numerous black-and-white photographs.

111. POLISH TROOPS IN NORWAY: A PHOTOGRAPHIC RECORD OF THE
CAMPAIGN AT NARVIK. London: M.I. Kolin Publishers,
Ltd., 1943. 155p. 44-4640.

 Photographic story of the Polish Highland Brigade.

112. Pruszyński, Ksawery. POLAND FIGHTS BACK: FROM WESTER-
PLATTE TO MONTE CASINO, trans. by Peter Jordan. New
York: Roy Publishers, 1944. 191p. 44-8374.

113. Rudnicki, Klemens S. THE LAST OF THE WAR HORSES.
London: Bachman and Turner, 1974. 255p. 75-302869.

   Story of General Rudnicki and his Polish army regiments' "path of destiny" from August 6, 1939 to 1944. Contains portraits of General Władysław Sikorski, General Władysław Anders and General Tadeusz Bor-Komorowski. Undocumented. Path took the regiment through the U.S.S.R. and eventually through the Middle East to Italy, France and England.

114. Sopocko, Eryk K. "ORZEL'S PATROL"; THE STORY OF THE POLISH SUBMARINE. London: Methuen and Co., Ltd., 1942. 146p. A42-4075.

   Attempt to present to the British public the ordinary everyday life of the crew of a Polish submarine in the Atlantic Ocean in the summer of 1941.

115. Swięcicki, Marek. WITH THE RED DEVILS AT ARNHEM, trans. by H.C. Stevens. London: Maxlove Publishing Co., Ltd., 1945. 91p. 45-7266.

   Contains a graphic description of the very gallant part played in the Battle of Arnhem by the 1st Polish Parachute Brigade Group in 1944. Many black-and-white illustrations. Portraits. Maps.

116. Terlecki, Olgierd. POLES IN THE ITALIAN CAMPAIGN, 1943-1945, trans. by Beryl Arct. Warszawa: Interpress Publishers, 1972. 136p. NjP: 14101.923.898.

   An account of Polish participation in the Italian campaign during World War II. Numerous black-and-white illustrations. Maps. One chapter devoted to the Battle of Monte Cassino.

117. THE UNSEEN AND THE SILENT; ADVENTURES FROM THE UNDERGROUND MOVEMENT NARRATED BY PARATROOPS OF THE POLISH HOME ARMY, trans. by George Iranek-Osmecki. New York: Sheed and Ward, 1954. 350p. 54-3848.

   Forty studies describing the activities of the Polish paratroops during World War II. Includes training of the troops in England, jumps over England, and work they did in Poland. Illustrations.

*Special Works* 31

118. Zaloga, Steven J. THE POLISH ARMY, 1939-45. London: Osprey Publishing, 1982. 40p.

    Descriptive history of the Polish Army. Of special value are colored plates of uniforms of the Army. Portraits.

119. Zaloga, Steven J. THE POLISH CAMPAIGN 1939, by S.J. Zaloga and Victor Madej. New York: Hippocrene Books, Inc., 1985. 195p. NjP: D765.Z34.

    A provocative look at the battles of the 1939 campaign from the perspective of the Polish Army. Contains a combat chronology of Polish units in the 1939 war. Illustrations. Maps. Bibliography: pp. 193-195.

120. Zbyszewski, Karol. THE FIGHT FOR NARVIK. London: Lindsay Drummond, Ltd., 1941. 2d ed. 30p. A41-18583.

    Impressions of the Polish campaign in Norway in 1940 where the author and the illustrator, Józef Natanson, fought.

121. Żyw, Aleksander. POLES IN UNIFORM; SKETCHES OF THE POLISH ARMY, NAVY AND AIR FORCE. New York: Thomas Nelson and Sons, Ltd., 1943. 128p. 43-13170.

    An artist's notebook filled with everyday impressions of life in the Polish Army, Navy and Air Force, in Great Britain during 1940 and beyond. Author was soldier and the book is mainly his sketches. Text by Edwin Meier.

### Arms and Armor

122. Barbarski, Krzysztof. POLISH ARMOUR, 1939-1945. London: Osprey Publishing, 1982. 40p.

    Description of key units and weapons systems with illustrations of authentic details of armour and supporting vehicles, camouflage, markings, uniforms, insignia and weapons. Bibliography: p. 39.

123. Nadolski, Andrzej. POLISH ARMS, SIDE-ARMS, trans. by
Maria Abramowiczowa. Wrocław: Ossolineum, 1974.
235p. 75-325333.

Detailed history of Polish Arms and side-arms from
the beginnings of the Polish state to 1945 with numerous illustrations, some colored.

Art

124. Bochnak, Adam. DECORATIVE ARTS IN POLAND, by A. Bochnak
and Każimierz Buczkowski, trans. by Paul Crossley and
Marek Łatyński. Warszawa: Arkady, 1972. 331p.
72-17172.

Book divided into six periods: Romanesque, Gothic,
Renaissance, Baroque and Rococo, Classic and
Biedermeier, and second half of the 19th century and
20th century. 325 plates, some in color, preceded by
explanatory text.

125. CRACOW: CITY OF MUSEUMS: THE MOST BEAUTIFUL WORKS OF
ART FROM SEVEN MUSEUMS, ed. by Jerzy Banach; trans.
by Neil Jones. Warszawa: Arkady, 1976. 183p.
78-309473.

Covers collections of the Wawel, the National Museum
in Cracow, the Museum of the Jagiellonian University,
the Jagiellonian Library, the Archaeological Museum,
the Ethnographic Museum and the Historical Museum of
the City of Cracow. Fifty-four pages of text followed
by illustrations, some colored, of some of the items in
the various collections. Text for each section written
by the directors and scientific staff of the museums
and of the Jagiellonian Library.

126. Detroit. Institute of Arts. POLISH PAINTINGS.
Detroit: Detroit Institute of Arts, 1945. 56p.

Black-and-white illustrations of paintings on loan
and exhibited at the Institute from June 1 to July 1,
1945. Text valuable for biographical sketches of
artists and critical evaluation of their works.

127. Dobrowolski, Tadeusz. POLISH PAINTING FROM THE ENLIGHTENMENT TO RECENT TIMES, trans. by Tadeusz Rybowski.

*Special Works* 33

Wrocław: Ossolineum, 1981. 36p. NjP: (SA) ND691.D62.

Mostly plates, many colored, of major works in the last two hundred years of Polish painting.

128. Gotlib, Henryk. POLISH PAINTING. London: Minerva Publishing Co., 1942. 147p. 43-1925.

    History of Polish painting by a Polish artist followed by black-and-white illustrations. Contains biographical sketches of major Polish painters with birth and death dates in text.

129. Holewinski, Jan. A SKETCH OF THE HISTORY OF POLISH ART. London: George Allen and Unwin, Ltd., 1916. 42p. 17-27767.

    A synopsis of the general conditions of art in Poland around 1916; epoch of Romanticism, coming of Gothic style, Renaissance epoch in Polish art.

130. Jackowski, Alesksander. FOLK ART IN POLAND, by A. Jackowski and Jadwiga Jarnuszkiewicz. Warszawa: Arkady, 1968. 476p. 69-136033.

    Principally illustrations, some colored, of architecture, paintings, sculpture and various other kinds of folk art, including costumes of Poland. Introduction defines and describes folk art. Catalogue, pp. 457-473, contains a brief description of each of the 521 plates. Includes a map of ethnical regions of Poland. Bibliography: pp. 475-477.

131. Jakimowicz, Irena. CONTEMPORARY POLISH GRAPHIC ART, trans. by Edward Rothert. Warszawa: Arkady Publishers, 1975. 206p. 76-383649.

    Black-and-white and colored reproductions of 172 works of graphic art by Polish artists working from 1946 to 1972. Contains biographical notes which are brief sketches of the professional activities of the artists represented in the book.

132. Kozakiewicz, Stefan. BERNARDO BELLOTTO, trans. by Mary Whiteall. Greenwich, Conn.: New York Graphic Society, 1972. 2v. 78-143465.

Contents: Vol. I deals with the principal aspects of Bellotto's work in the context of his life. Volume II is a catalogue of the authentic works of Bellotto, with 435 entries covering his paintings, drawings and etchings, and a further list, comprising some 580 entries of works which have been attributed to him.

133. Kozakiewiczowa, Helena. THE RENAISSANCE IN POLAND, by Helena Kozakiewiczowa and Stefan Kozakiewicz, trans. by Doreen H. Potworowska. Warszawa: Arkady Publishers, 1976. 329p. 78-295548.

Covers works of art executed in Poland but also a few examples of artistic imports from other countries, closely connected with Polish culture and commissioned by Polish patrons. Map, list of illustrations, selected literature, index of places and antiquities and index of artists. Some elevations. Most illustrations are black-and-white but some are colored. Chronology 1500-1640.

134. Krauze, Andrzej, ed. THE SACRAL ART IN POLAND: ARCHITECTURE. Warszawa: Ars Christiana, 1956. 366p. 59-48688.

Acquaints the reader with a domain of ancient Polish spiritual culture which grew out of the religious and artistic creative thought. The history of sacral art in Poland is followed by 308 sepia photographs of the exteriors and interiors of churches in Poland. Notes to the illustrations, pp. 345-367, describes each of the photographs. Also contains several colored reproductions of paintings of churches.

135. London. Royal Academy of Arts. 1000 YEARS OF ART IN POLAND. Uxbridge, Middlesex, Eng.: Westminster Press Limited, 1970. 2d ed. 158p. MiD: R709.438-L846o.

Catalog of an exhibition at the Royal Academy of Arts, London, held from January 3rd to March 1, 1970. Items from eight national collections. Covers fine arts and decorative arts. Includes colored or black-and-white illustrations of some of the exhibit items. Of value are brief biographical sketches of many but not all of the artists exhibited.

## Special Works

136. Lorentz, Stanisław. THE RENAISSANCE IN POLAND. Warszawa: Prasa, 1955. 95p. 57-3503.

    Cheifly black-and-white illustrations of architecture, sculpture, woodcuts, and other extant objects d'art, produced in Poland during the Renaissance. Text beneath illustrations explains each one.

137. New York City. Museum of Modern Art. 15 POLISH PAINTERS, by Peter Selz. New York: Museum of Modern Art, 1961. 64p. 61-16522.

    Exhibition booklet of post-war Polish painting on exhibit at the Museum of Modern Art in New York in 1961. Contains biographies of the exhibited artists and a catalogue of the exhibition. Black-and-white illustrations. One colored.

138. Piotrowska, Irena. THE ART OF POLAND. New York: Philosophical Library, 1947. 238p. 47-3695.

    Attempts to present to the English-speaking reader the facts one must know in order to understand Polish art. Covers architecture, sculpture, painting, the graphic arts, the decorative arts, fold art, and art protection. Some of the more esoteric items covered include the art of the Polish postage stamp, Polish Christmas time festivals in art, the athletic sports in Polish art, Polish horse and battle painters, the Annunciation in Polish art, Polish lace and white embroidery and the essentials of Polish peasant art.

139. PLAKAT POLSKI. THE POLISH POSTER, with an introduction by Jerzy Wasniewski. Warszawa: Wydawnictwo Artystyczno-Graficzne, 1972. unpaged. OL: NC1807.P6.W3.

    Mainly black-and-white or colored illustrations of posters. Contains biographical notes of illustrators. Posters cover the period 1945-1964 and are divided by subject area: political and public service; theater and concert; film; exhibition and commercial; sports and circus.

140. SYMBOLISM IN POLAND: COLLECTED ESSAYS. Detroit: Detroit Institute of Arts, 1984. 63p. OL: ND955.P6S89.1984.

Published in conjunction with the exhibition "Symbolism in Polish Painting 1890-1914," July 30 - September 23, 1984. Essays provide information on various aspects of both art and the literature of the Młoda Polska period. Illustrations.

141. UNESCO. POLAND: PAINTING OF THE FIFTEENTH CENTURY. New York: New York Graphic Society, 1964. 21p.

    Preface by Rene Hughes. Introduction by Michał Walicki. The introduction describes the art of Poland during the fifteenth century followed by 32 colored plates of representative pieces.

142. Wojciechowski, Aleksander. CONTEMPORARY POLISH PAINTING: TRENDS, GOALS, WORKS, trans. by E.J. Czerwinski. Warszawa: Interpress Publishers, 1977. MiD: 749.38-W829c.

    Black-and-white and colored illustrations. A history of Polish painting from 1944 to 1976. Published simultaneously in Polish, French and German.

143. Zanoziński, Jerzy. CONTEMPORARY POLISH PAINTING. Warszawa: Arkady Publishers, 1975. 140p. MiD: 759.38-Z17c.

    Attempts to present in a condensed form characterizations of individual artists and, in many cases, detailed information on those of their paintings contained therein. Sixty-three colored reproductions with biographical sketches of each artist.

Bibliography

144. Baxter, James H. WHAT TO READ ABOUT POLAND, rev. and enlarged by George H. Bushnell. Edinburgh: Oliver and Boyd, 1942. 19p. 48-41801.

    List of books and articles about Poland for the use of those who may wish to pursue a course of reading on Polish life and history. Divided into general, geography, travel and descriptions; history, literature, translations; grammars and dictionaries.

*Special Works* 37

145. Davies, Norman. SELECT BIBLIOGRAPHY OF WORKS IN
ENGLISH ON POLISH HISTORY. Cambridge, Eng.:
Oriental Research Partners, 1975. 187p.

Author was a lecturer in Polish at the University of
London and this list appears to have been prepared for
the lectures. Divided into bibliography; handbooks and
reference books; historiography; biography and memoirs;
general history; archaeology and prehistory; society;
economy; constitutional and legal history; political
history; religious history; cultural and intellectual
history; military history; nationalities and minorities; regional and local history; emigration; foreign
relations; governmental publications. Scattered annotations. Many items in other than the English language.

146. Drzewieniecki, Walter M. POLONICA BUFFALONENSIS.
Buffalo, N.Y.: Buffalo and Erie County Historical
Society, 1976. 148p. 76-47407.

Annotated bibliography of source and printed materials
dealing with the Polish-American community in the
Buffalo, New York area.

147. Fryde, Matthew M. SELECTED WORKS IN POLISH AGRARIAN
HISTORY AND AGRICULTURE, A BIBLIOGRAPHICAL SURVEY.
New York: Mid-European Studies Center, 1952. 87p.
52-43903.

Bibliographical survey of Polish agrarian history.
Multilingual listing. Divided into: guide and source
materials; general works; and special works.

148. Hoskins, Janina W. EARLY AND RARE POLONICA OF THE
15TH-17TH CENTURIES IN AMERICAN LIBRARIES; A BIBLIOGRAPHICAL SURVEY. Boston: G.K. Hall and Co., 1973.
193p. 73-1270.

Rare Polonica, in all languages, dating from 1475
through 1700 in American libraries. Includes 1,231
entries, mostly non-annotated. Map on lining papers.
Bibliography, pp. 181-187.

149. Hoskins, Janina W. POLISH BOOKS IN ENGLISH, 1945-1971.
Washington, D.C.: Library of Congress, 1974. 163p.
74-6163.

Record of translated Polish works in the fields of
the humanities and social sciences. Contains listing
of over 1,000 English-language books and pamphlets
which were published in Poland or translated into
English outside Poland in the years 1945-1971.
Includes belles-lettres.

150. Ledbetter, Eleanor, comp. THE POLISH IMMIGRANT AND HIS
READING. Chicago: American Library Association,
1924. 40p. 25-26028.

Suggested list of titles for a beginning collection
in the Polish language, pp. 24-40. First part lists
works of value to the immigrant.

151. Ledbetter, Eleanor, comp. POLISH LITERATURE IN ENGLISH
TRANSLATION; A BIBLIOGRAPHY WITH A LIST OF BOOKS
ABOUT POLAND AND THE POLES. New York: H.W. Wilson
Company, 1932. 45p. 32-10973.

Initial attempt to bring "together all important bibliographic items of Polish literature, history and art
ever published in English." Divided into: language,
folklore, literary history and criticism, Polish literature in English translation, works about Poland and the
Poles. Annotated. Includes periodical articles.
Selective and small. Dated.

152. Lewański, Richard C., comp. POLAND. Oxford: Clio
Press, Ltd., 1984. 267p. NjP: (DR)Z2526.L48.

Annotated bibliography of 901 items, many of which are
periodical articles. Part of World Bibliographical
Series. Pays particular attention to "Poland's long
and crucially important history." Many works pertain
to eastern Europe, in general. Includes works in the
Polish language.

153. Nowak, Chester M. CZECHOSLOVAK-POLISH RELATIONS.
1918-1939: A SELECTED AND ANNOTATED BIBLIOGRAPHY.
Stanford: Hoover Institution Press, 1976. 219p.
75-39562.

Originated as part of a doctoral dissertation at
Boston University. Includes books in several languages.
Divided into categories. 869 items.

154. Obal, Thaddeus J. A BIBLIOGRAPHY FOR GENEALOGICAL RESEARCH INVOLVING POLISH ANCESTRY. Hillsdale, New Jersey, n.p., 1978.

   Designed primarily to be of help in genealogical research involving ancestry in old and new Poland.

155. POLISH DISSIDENT PUBLICATIONS: AN ANNOTATED BIBLIOGRAPHY. New York: F.A. Praeger, 1982. 382p. 82-7677.

   Bibliography divided into journals, books and monographs and documents. Amply annotated covering post-1976 period.

156. Polish Roman Catholic Union of America. Archives and Museum. POLONICA IN ENGLISH, ANNOTATED CATALOGUE OF THE ARCHIVES AND MUSEUM OF THE POLISH ROMAN CATHOLIC UNION, by Alphonse S. Wolanin. Chicago: Polish Roman Catholic Union, 1945. 186p. A46-888.

   Tool to archives at time of publication, c. 1945. Divided into history; monographs; biographies; description, travel, customs; language; literature; art; fiction and poetry on Poland; non-fiction by Polish authors; and miscellaneous.

157. Polish University College. London. Library. BIBLIOGRAPHY OF BOOKS IN POLISH OR RELATING TO POLAND PUBLISHED OUTSIDE POLAND SINCE SEPTEMBER 1, 1939, compiled by Janina Zabielska. London: Polish University College Library, 1953- v. 54-1761.

   Comprehensive, non-annotated listing. Includes non-Polish subjects, e.g. Malinowski, Bronisław--Magic, science and religion and other essays.

158. Polskie Towarzystwo Naukowena Obczyźnie. BIBLIOGRAPHY OF WORKS BY POLISH SCHOLARS AND SCIENTISTS PUBLISHED OUTSIDE OF POLAND IN LANGUAGES OTHER THAN POLISH, compiled by Maria Danilewicz and Jadwiga Nowak. London: Polish Society of Arts and Sciences Abroad, 1964- v. 66-51431.

   Attempt at compiling an inventory of the works of individual Polish scholars residing outside Poland between the years 1939 and 1962. Includes published articles as well as monographs.

159. Turek, Wiktor. POLONICA CANADIANA; A BIBLIOGRAPHICAL
LIST OF THE CANADIAN POLISH IMPRINTS, 1848-1957.
Toronto: Polish Alliance Press, Limited, 1958. 138p.
65-46092.

Annotated compilation of items in English, French and
Polish published about Poland and the Poles in Canada
between 1848 and 1957.

160. U.S. Library of Congress. POLAND IN THE COLLECTIONS OF
THE LIBRARY OF CONGRESS; AN OVERVIEW by Każimierz
Grzybowski. Washington, D.C.: U.S. Government
Printing Office, 1968. 26p. 69-60009.

Short, general overview of Polonica in the Library
with an emphasis on primary materials of all sorts and
no secondary sources.

161. Zolobka, Vincent, comp. POLONICA CANADIANA, 1958-1970,
comp. by Vincent Zolobka and Wiktor Turek. Toronto:
Polish Alliance Press, Ltd., 1978. 414p. UW:
Z1377.P6Z6.1978.

Second volume in series.

162. Żurawski, Joseph W., comp. POLISH AMERICAN HISTORY AND
CULTURE: A CLASSIFIED BIBLIOGRAPHY. Chicago:
Polish Museum of America Press, 1975. 218p.
75-24789.

An attempt at compiling a comprehensive bibliography
of items, largely monographic, on Polish-America. Lacks
careful selection. Includes many periodical articles.
Scattered throughout are annotations of little use because of the lack of judgement. Most items are in
Polish Museum of America in Chicago.

Biography--General

163. Klarkowski, Claude E. THE QUEEN'S GEMS: SHORT LIVES
OF THE PATRON SAINTS OF POLAND. Pulaski, Wisc.:
Franciscan Publishers, 1958. 63p.

Acquaints English-speaking Catholics of the United
States with the true heroes of Poland--her saints.
Pamphlet-style sketches of the lives of SS. Cyril and
Methodius, St. Adalbert, the five Holy Martyrs of
Poland, SS. Andrew and Benedict, St. Stanislaus, St.
Florian, St. Hyacinth, St. John Cantius, St. Casimir,

Special Works                                                           41

St. Stanislaus Kostka, St. Josaphat, St. Andrew Bobola,
and St. Clement Dvorak. Illustrations. Portraits.

164. McLean, W.M. NOTABLE PERSONAGES OF POLISH ANCESTRY.
Detroit: Unique Press, 1938. 186p. 38-13303.

Short and concise biographies of famous men and women
of Polish nationality, classified according to the
accomplishments for which posterity will always honor
them.

165. Madison, Arnold. POLISH GREATS. New York: David
McKay Company, Inc., 1980. 114p. 79-3462.

Brief biographies of Jadwiga, Copernicus, Tadeusz
Kośćiuszko, Casimir Pułaski, Adam Mickiewicz, Frederic
Chopin, Helena Modjeska, Joseph Conrad, Ignace
Paderewski, Władysław Reymont, Marie Curie, Arthur
Rubinstein, and Pope John Paul II.

166. Marshall, Christabel. A LITTLE BOOK OF POLISH SAINTS.
London: Burns: Oates, Ltd., 1918. 87p. OL:
BX4659.P6S2.

Brief sketches of the lives of "SS. Adalbert,
Stanislaus, Hyacinth, Casimir, John Cantius, Josaphat,
Stanislaus Kostka, and the Blessed Ladislaus of Gielnow,
James of Strepa, Vincent Kadłubek, Salome, Ceslaus,
Bronisława, Andrew Bobola, the Five Polish Brothers,
Michael of Gedioc, John of Dukla and Kunegunda."

167. Mizwa, Stephen Paul, ed. GREAT MEN AND WOMEN OF POLAND.
New York: Macmillan Company, 1941. 397p. 41-26856.

Thirty biographies of famous Poles throughout history
judiciously selected and ranked by scholars. Sketches
written by famous historians and biographical sketch of
each writer included in table of contents. There is a
portrait of each person. No documentation; no bibliography. Entries vary in length.

168. Pilarski, Laura. THEY CAME FROM POLAND: THE STORIES
OF FAMOUS POLISH-AMERICANS. New York: Dodd, Mead
and Company, 1969. 178p. 69-17599.

Brief biographies of famous Poles or descendents of
Polish immigrants emphasizing their unique contributions

to their adopted homeland. Intended for the young reader. Illustrations. Portraits. Maps. Bibliography: pp. 163-167.

169. WHO'S WHO IN POLAND. Warszawa: Interpress Publishers, 1982. 1107p. MiU: CT1230.W62.1982.

 First WHO'S WHO compiled in People's Poland, which contains biographies of individuals from the worlds of science, politics, the arts, etc., whose position or achievement makes them note-worthy. Biographies furnished their own data. 4,000 entries. Index contains list of associations, institutions, etc. with addresses.

170. Wiśniewski, Joseph. WHO'S WHO IN POLAND. Toronto: Professional Translators and Publishers, 1981. 239p. OL: REF-DK443.4W5.

 Brief biographical sketches of living persons of prominence in Poland at the time the publication was prepared. In addition, the book contains numerous lists of personages, political, religious, e.g. list of all Roman Catholic dioceses with names of the bishops, etc.

Biography--Specific

JÓZEF BECK, 1894-1944

* Beck, Józef. FINAL REPORT. Cited below as item 624.

171. Harley, John H. THE AUTHENTIC BIOGRAPHY OF COLONEL BECK, based on the Polish by Conrad Wrzos, with an introduction by Count Edward Raczyński. London: Hutchinson and Company, 1939. 198p. 39-29585.

 A clear and authentic biographical sketch of the life of Józef Beck. Based mainly upon materials collected by Conrad Wrzos. Includes 14 speeches made by Beck between 1933 and 1939. Dwells principally on his career as foreign minister. Illustrations. Portraits.

CELINA BORZECKA, 1833-1913

172. Kalkstein, Teresa. WITNESS TO THE RESURRECTION: THE SERVANT OF GOD, MOTHER CELINA BORZECKA, FOUNDRESS OF THE CONGREGATION OF THE RESURRECTION OF OUR LORD JESUS CHRIST. Castleton-on-Hudson, New York: Sisters of the Resurrection, 1967. 212p. 67-29594.

Special Works                                                         43

A biographical sketch by a member of the Congregation
of the Sisters of the Resurrection of Our Lord Jesus
Christ of the Congregation's foundress, Celina Borzecka.
Contains numerous black-and-white illustrations; some
portraits.

FRYDERYK FRANCISZEK CHOPIN, 1810-1849

173. Bidou, Henry. CHOPIN, trans. by Catherine A. Phillips.
New York: Alfred A. Knopf, 1927. 267p. 27-19025.

   Originally published in French in Paris in 1927.
   Standard popular biography. Chronological list of
   Chopin's works, 1825-1847, pp. 259-264. Illustrations.
   Portraits.

174. Boucourechliev, Andre. CHOPIN, A PICTORIAL BIOGRAPHY,
trans. by Edward Hyams. London: Thames and Hudson,
1963. 144 p. 63-8850.

   A pictorial biographical account of the life of
   Chopin. Illustrations include scenes of the places
   associated with Chopin's life as well as pictures of
   some of his musical scores and pictures of Chopin himself. A chronology of Chopin's life is contained, pp.
   130-133; descriptive notes on pictures, pp. 134-142.
   Bibliography, p. 142.

175. Byron, May Clarissa. A DAY WITH FREDERIC CHOPIN.
London: Hodder and Stoughton, 1927. 47p. 29-1434.

   Author proposes what a day would be like if spent
   with Fryderyk Chopin. Illustrations. Portraits.

176. Cortot, Alfred. IN SEARCH OF CHOPIN, trans. by Cyril
and Rena Clarke. New York: Abelard Press, 1952.
268p. 52-12542.

   Not a biography but rather a treatment of Chopin as a
   composer and performer. Contains discography, pp. 231-
   268. Illustrations. Portraits. Bibliography, pp.
   220-230.

177. Gavoty, Bernard. FREDERIC CHOPIN, trans. by Martin
Sokolinsky. New York: Scribner's, 1977. 452p.
77-3966.

Includes bibliographical references. Chronological table of the life and works of Chopin.

178. Gide, Andre. NOTES ON CHOPIN, trans. by Bernard Frechtman. New York: Philosophical Library, 1949. 126p. 49-10766.

    The thoughts of an outstanding literary figure on Chopin. Contains fragments of music.

179. Glinski, Matteo. CHOPIN THE UNKNOWN. Windsor, Ontario: Assumption University of Windsor Press, 1963. 84p. 63-15502.

    Outgrowth of lectures on Chopin given at The University of Michigan and other American colleges and universities. Stresses Chopin's constant attachment to the Christian faith. Illustrations. Portraits.

180. Gronowicz, Antoni. CHOPIN, trans. by Jessie McEwen. New York: T. Nelson and Sons, 1943. 202p. 43-15248.

    A biographical sketch written for the juvenile. Contains numerous drawings illustrating the composer and his surroundings and also George Sand. Bibliography, pp. 195-196.

181. Hadden, James C. CHOPIN. New York: E.P. Dutton and Co., Inc., 1934. 243p. 35-11189.

    Biography simply and directly told to give a clear picture of the man and to discuss the composer without trenching on the ground of the formalist. Contains a calendar, a catalogue of works and personalia, brief sketches of lives of persons important in Chopin's life. Illustrations. Portraits. Bibliography, pp. 229-231.

182. Hedley, Arthur. CHOPIN. London: J.M. Dent and Sons, Ltd., 1947. 214p. 48-12992.

    A biography based upon original Polish sources. Appendices include a calendar; a catalogue of works; Personalia, very brief biographical sketches of persons important in Chopin's life. Facsimiles. Portraits. Bibliography, pp. 202-204.

Special Works                                                45

183.  Huneker, James G.  CHOPIN:  THE MAN AND HIS MUSIC.  New
      York:  Charles Scribner's Sons, 1900.  415p.  0-2094.

      Classic biography of Chopin in English.  Divided into
      two parts:  the man and his music.  Portraits.  Bibliog-
      raphy, pp. 391-396.

184.  Karasowski, Moritz.  FREDERIC CHOPIN, HIS LIFE AND
      LETTERS, trans. by Emily Hill.  London:  William
      Reeves Booksellers, Limited, 1938.  OL:  ML410.C54K3.

      First edition published in 1879 in two volumes.
      Second revised edition published in 1906.  Author was a
      close friend of Chopin family and was intimate with
      them for several years.  He was given access to the
      letters written by Chopin to his family in Poland
      throughout his life abroad.

185.  Kelley, Edgar Stillman.  CHOPIN, THE COMPOSER.  New
      York:  G. Schirmer, 1913.  190p.  13-25409.

      A discussion of the structural art and that which
      admits of little or no dispute in the musical structure
      of Chopin.  Portrait.

186.  Kobylańska, Krystyna.  CHOPIN IN HIS OWN LAND:  DOCU-
      MENTS AND SOUVENIRS collected and edited by Claire
      Grece-Dąbrowska and Mary Filippi.  Kraków:  Polskie
      Wydawnictwo Muzyczne, 1955.  296p.  58-18405.

      This unusually rich collection of momentoes shows us
      the first half of Chopin's life from many sides and in
      varied lights.  It enables us to become acquainted with
      the surroundings, with the milieu, even with the tri-
      fles of daily life which make up the manners and cus-
      toms, fashions, social and artistic relations as a
      whole.  Illustrations.  Maps.  Portraits.  Bibliography,
      pp. 295-296.

187.  Liszt, Franz.  LIFE OF CHOPIN, trans. by John Broad-
      house.  London:  William Reeves, Publisher, 1899.
      240p.  6-2347.

      First complete English translation of biography of
      Chopin by Liszt.  Medallion portrait of Chopin appears
      as a frontispiece.

188. Liszt, Franz. FREDERIC CHOPIN, trans. by Edward N. Waters. New York: The Free Press of Glencoe, 1963. 184p. 63-10651.

Liszt's product is an appreciation, a memoir, a revelation of much of Liszt's reaction to Chopin's music in the mid-nineteenth century.

189. Marek, George R. CHOPIN, by G.R. Marek and Maria Gordon-Smith. New York: Harper and Row, 1978. 282p. 76-57880.

Tells the story of a man, who was worldly yet an enigma, one who hugged success yet remained dissatisfied and one whose work has given pleasure to the musically naive. Illustrations. Portraits. Bibliography, pp. 277-282.

190. Mizwa, Stephen P. FREDERIC CHOPIN, 1810-1849. New York: Macmillan, 1949. 108p. 49-11025.

Centennial publication intended as a tribute to a great artist pointing out his place in the literature of music as understood by critic, artist and composer at the half-turn of the twentieth century. An anthology of articles about Chopin. Numerous portraits, illustrations and facsimiles. Also, list of works by Chopin compiled by Bronosław E. Sydow, pp. 97-108.

191. Murdoch, William D. CHOPIN: HIS LIFE. New York: Macmillan Company, 1935. 410p. 35-6561.

Biographical account based on additional material made available after the publication of the classical Niecks' work. Emphasizes the man not his work as a composer, pianist and teacher. Contains a chronological listing of Chopin's published works. Portraits of Chopin and his parents, George Sand.

192. Niecks, Frederick. FREDERICK CHOPIN, AS A MAN AND MUSICIAN. New York: Novello, Ewer and Co., 1890. 2d ed. 2v. 4-7719.

Standard biography in English. Author's researches had for their object the whole of Chopin's life and his historical, political, artistical, social and personal surroundings, but they were chiefly directed to the least known and most interesting period of his career--

*Special Works* 47

his life in France and his visits to Germany and Great Britain. Contains a list of the published works of Chopin including dates of publication and original German and French publishers. Portraits.

193. Orga, Ates. CHOPIN: HIS LIFE AND TIMES. London: Midas Books, 1976. 144p. 76-378024.

    Well-written up-to-date biography excellently illustrated by a music scholar. Portraits. Bibliography, p. 7.

\* Rayson, Ethel. POLISH MUSIC AND CHOPIN, ITS LAUREATE. Cited below as item 1122.

194. Schallenberg, Evert W. FREDERIC CHOPIN, trans. by M. Smedts. Stockholm: Continental Book Co., 1949. 57p. 49-49601.

    Brief historical sketch of the life of Chopin. Illustrations. Portraits. Bibliography, p. 57.

195. Seroff, Victor. FREDERIC CHOPIN. New York: Macmillan and Company, 1964. 118p. 64-20733.

    Concise, readable biography intended for the juvenile reader. Includes selected discography, pp. 113-115. Illustrations. Portraits.

196. Strachey, Marjorie C. THE NIGHTINGALE, A LIFE OF CHOPIN. London: Longmans, Green and Co., 1925. 305p. 25-9887.

    Chopin's life in story form. Reconstructed from his letters and elaborated as to detail, the musician's friendships and loves, his triumphs and griefs, and the distressing illness of his later years are here made very real. Portraits.

197. Tarnowski, Stanisław. CHOPIN AS REVEALED BY EXTRACTS FROM HIS DIARY, trans. by Natalie Janotka. London: W. Reeves, 1906. 69p. 6-39985.

    Sketch was intended for one of a course of public lectures which took place in Kraków in 1871. A reevaluation of Chopin's musical reaction to the defeat of the Polish Insurrection in 1831 based upon

authenticated notes written by Chopin while in
Stuttgart during the final days. Portraits.

198. Uminska, Zofia. CHOPIN, THE CHILD AND THE LAD, by Z.
Uminska and H.E. Kennedy. London: Metheun and Co.,
Ltd., 1925. 91p. 26-14089.

A biography of the early years of Chopin based upon
information obtained personally from Władysław Zelenski,
the Polish composer, friend of Chopin's favorite pupil,
Princess Marcelina Czartoryska. Contains musical
scores. Illustrations. Portraits.

199. Walker, Alan, ed. FREDERIC CHOPIN: PROFILES OF THE
MAN AND THE MUSICIAN, by Paul Badura-Skoda and
edited by Alan Walker. New York: Taplinger
Publishing Co., 1967. 334p. 67-16594.

Eleven essays on Chopin by contemporary musicians,
composers, musicologists. Editor states book addressed
primarily to musicians. Contains specimens of scores.
Biographical summary by Arthur Hedley arranged in
chronological order. General catalogue of Chopin's
works. Discography listings. Illustrations.
Portraits. Bibliography, pp. 323-324.

200. Wheeler, Opal. FREDERIC CHOPIN, SON OF POLAND, LATER
YEARS. New York: E.P. Dutton, 1949. 155p.
48-10153.

A fictional life of Chopin for children, with excerpts
from his music arranged for the piano. Illustrations.

201. Wierzynski, Kaźimierz. THE LIFE AND DEATH OF CHOPIN,
trans. by Norbert Guterman and a foreword by Arthur
Rubinstein. New York: Simon and Schuster, 1949.
444p. 49-11707.

A biography which claims to amplify what M. Rubinstein
considers the most important--the formative years.
Author attempts to demonstrate how important were the
years spent in Poland as "the spirit of Poland remained
the living source of his inspiration, the touchstone of
his being, to the end of his life." Illustrations.
Portraits. Bibliography, pp. 425-429.

## Special Works

202. Willeby, Charles. FREDERIC FRANCOIS CHOPIN. London: Sampson Low, Marston and Company, Limited, 1892. 316p. 6-4809.

   In the main, a discussion of Chopin the composer. Contains specimens of Chopin's music. Portrait.

### JOHN BAPTIST CIEPLAK, 1857-1926

203. Lédit, Joseph. ARCHBISHOP JOHN BAPTIST CIEPLAK. Montreal: Palm Publishers, 1963. 138p. 65-73738.

   Sympathetic account of the life of John Baptist Cieplak, last archbishop of Mogilev, the old Russian imperialist diocese, who subsequently was arrested, imprisoned, tortured and exiled.

### NICOLAUS COPERNICUS, 1473-1543

204. Adamczewski, Jan. NICOLAUS COPERNICUS AND HIS EPOCH, in cooperation with Edward J. Piszek. Philadelphia: Copernicus Society of America, 1974. 160p. 74-174362.

   Translation of MIKOŁAJ KOPERNIK I JEGO EPOKA. Thoroughly researched biography of Mikołaj Kopernik and a history of his theories. Many illustrations, in black-and-white, and in color. Illustrations contain many segments of documents, pictures of surroundings, etc. No index, no bibliography, no documentation.

205. Armitage, Angus. SUN, STAND THOU STILL: THE LIFE AND WORKS OF COPERNICUS THE ASTRONOMER. New York: Henry Schuman, 1947. 210p. 47-11441.

   Personal story and some of the historical motives at the back of the great sixteenth century revolution in man's outlook on the universe explaining the origin of the situation in which Copernicus played his decisive part. Illustrations. Portrait. "Books for further reading," pp. 203-205.

206. Armitage, Angus. COPERNICUS, THE FOUNDER OF MODERN ASTRONOMY. London: G. Allen and Unwin, Ltd., 1938. 183p. 39-9166.

   Short account of the astronomer, Copernicus, and of the historic book in which he laid the foundations of the heliocentric theory of the planetary motions. Concise biography. Diagrams. Bibliography, pp. 179-180.

207. Biskup, Marian. COPERNICUS, SCHOLAR AND CITIZEN, by M. Biskup and Jerzy Dobrzycki. Warszawa: Interpress Publishers, 1972. 119p. MiD: B-C792B5.

    Brief outline of the life and work of Copernicus with some general information about the society of that time and the Polish state. Black-and-white illustrations at end of work including portrait. Facsimile of Copernicus' signature on frontispiece. Maps.

208. Cynarski, Stanisław. RECEPTION OF THE COPERNICAN THEORY IN POLAND IN THE SEVENTEENTH AND EIGHTEENTH CENTURIES. Warszawa: Polish Science Publishers, 1973. 63p. 73-176448.

    Well-documented brief survey of the Copernican theory in Poland. Well illustrated. Not an in-depth study or analysis. Portraits.

209. Hoyle, Fred. NICOLAUS COPERNICUS, AN ESSAY ON HIS LIFE AND WORK. New York: Harper and Row, Publishers, 1973. 94p. 73-4092.

    Mainly works but includes a "biographical sketch" in chapter 3. Illustrations. Portraits. Maps. Bibliography, p. 89.

210. Kesten, Hermann. COPERNICUS AND HIS WORLD, trans. by E.B. Ashton and Norbert Guterman. New York: Roy Publishers, 1945. 408p. 45-35022.

    Popular biography. Illustrations. Portraits.

211. Mizwa, Stephen P. NICHOLAS COPERNICUS, 1543-1943. New York: Kośćiuszko Foundation, 1943. 88p. 43-5107.

    In addition to being a life story, it is also about the cult of Copernicus including his origin, monuments to him, map of Poland during his time. Many illustrations including "how Polish students dressed in the student days of Copernicus, 1491-1495." Bibliographical suggestions and comments, pp. 60-64, both Polish and English works. Program suggestions for 1943 Copernican Quadricentennial, containing lyrics and

*Special Works* 51

music to the Hejnał, Gaude Mater Poloniae and Jeszcze Polska nie zginęła in Polish and English.

212. Rudnicki, Józef. NICHOLAS COPERNICUS, 1473-1543, trans. by B.W.A. Massey. London: The Copernicus Quatercentenary Celebration Committee, 1943. 53p. 43-16916.

 Written to commemorate the four-hundredth anniversary of the death of Copernicus and of the publication of his great work, DE REVOLUTIONIBUS ORBIUM COELESTIUM. Includes biographical sketch, his work, the Copernican system in Great Britain. Numerous black-and-white illustrations. Portraits.

213. Rusinek, Michał. LAND OF NICHOLAS COPERNICUS, trans. by A.T. Jordan. New York: Twayne Publishers, Inc., 1973. 235p. OL: QB36.C8R97.

 Photographs by Magdalena Rusinek-Kwilecka. A sketch of the life of Copernicus "against the background of his times and the world in which he lived." Numerous black-and-white photographs as well as some colored. Also, some sketches. Portraits. References, p. 235.

MARIE SKŁODOWSKA CURIE, 1867-1934

214. Abrahall, Clare C. THE YOUNG MARIE CURIE. New York: Roy Publishers, 1961. 128p. 61-11042.

 A biographical sketch of Maria Skłodowska designed for the juvenile reader. Drawings by Denise Brown.

215. Bigland, Eileen. MADAME CURIE. New York: Criterion Books, 1957. 191p. 57-5540.

 Biography aimed at the juvenile audience. Illustrations.

216. Curie, Eve. MADAME CURIE, A BIOGRAPHY, trans. by Vincent Sheean. Garden City, N.Y.: Doubleday, Doran and Company, Inc., 1943. 393p. 38-1015.

 Biographical account written by Marie's youngest daughter, from long research among records published and unpublished and from personal remembrances. Appendix contains a list of Mme. Curie's prizes, medals and decorations, honorary titles. No bibliography. No documentation. Portrait on dust jacket only.

217. Doorly, Eleanor. THE RADIUM WOMAN, A YOUTH EDITION OF THE LIFE OF MADAME CURIE. London: W. Heinemann, Limited, 1940. 184p. 41-11657.

   A biography of Marie Curie for the young adult reader. Illustrations. Portraits.

218. Giroud, Françoise. MARIE CURIE: A LIFE, trans. by Lydia Davis. New York: Holmes and Meier, 1986. 291p. 85-27241.

   Author's interpretation of Marie Curie's life, how her life has appeared to her. Illustrations. Portraits. Bibliography, pp. 288-289.

JAN CWIKLIŃSKI, 1901-

219. Cwikliński, Jan. THE CAPTAIN LEAVES HIS SHIP: THE STORY OF THE CAPTAIN OF THE S.S. BATORY AS TOLD TO HAWTHORNE DANIEL. Garden City, N.Y.: Doubleday and Company, 1955. 313p. 55-5262.

   Captain Cwikliński "jumped" ship in England on June 19, 1953. This is the story of the captain's life at sea and of the political forces that changed his life. No illustrations. Story told to Hawthorne Daniel who wrote the book in English.

ADAM JERZY CZARTORYSKI, 1770-1861

220. Czartoryski, Adam Jerzy, książę. MEMOIRS OF PRINCE ADAM CZARTORYSKI AND HIS CORRESPONDENCE WITH ALEXANDER I. With documents relative to the Prince's negotiations with Pitt, Fox, and Brougham, and an account of his conversations with Lord Palmerston and other English statesmen in London in 1832, ed. by Adam Gielgud. London: Remington and Co., 1888. 2d ed. 2v. 5-23388.

   Memoirs, the greater part of which were written from his dictation in occasional hours of leisure in Paris, end at the Battle of Austerlitz, 1805. They give vivid pictures of the life of the Polish aristocracy during the latter part of the eighteenth century. The

*Special Works* 53

remainder of the work consists of the Prince's correspondence which completes the story of his life. Individual portraits of the Prince and his mother.

\* Kukiel, Marjan. CZARTORYSKI AND EUROPEAN UNITY. Cited below as item 804.

MARIA DĄBROWSKA, 1889-

221. Folejewski, Zbigniew. MARIA DĄBROWSKA. New York: Twayne Publishers, Inc., 1967. 123p. 67-12267.

Great contemporary writer. Intellectual background and literary heritage, her appearance on the literary scene, her artistic development, main work as a novelist, her place in contemporary trends, reception of author as an artist. Bibliography, pp. 115-117.

ROMAN DMOWSKI, 1864-1939

222. Fountain, Alvin M. ROMAN DMOWSKI: PARTY, TACTICS, IDEOLOGY, 1895-1907. New York: Columbia University Press, 1980. 240p. 79-53834.

A biography principally focusing on the years 1895 through 1907, the pivotal years in the development of Dmowski's political ideology and his development of the Stronnictwo Demokratyczyno-Narodowe or National Democratic Party. Contains a biographical and party register as well as a descriptive sketch of each of the following parties: The National Democratic Party, the Polish Socialist Party, Social Democracy of the Kingdom of Poland and Lithuania. Bibliography, pp. 217-231.

MOTHER MARYA TERESA DUDZIK, 1860-1918

223. Malak, Henryk M. THE APOSTLE OF MERCY FROM CHICAGO, trans. by Sister Mary Hugoline. London: Veritas, 1962. 139p. 64-54792.

Biography of Mother Mary Teresa, foundress of the Franciscan Sisters of Blessed Kunegunda. Illustrations. Portraits. Bibliography, pp. 133-137.

ROMAN DYBOSKI, 1883-1945

\* Dyboski, Roman. SEVEN YEARS IN RUSSIA AND SIBERIA. Cited below as item 1149.

## KORNEL FILIPOWICZ, 1913-

224. Maciąg, Włodzimierz. FILIPOWICZ, trans. by Krystyna Cękalska. Warszawa: Author's Agency, 1972. 56p.

   Biographical sketch and evaluation of Filipowicz's principal works. Of particular value are bibliography of principal works, pp. 51-54 and of translations in various languages, pp. 53-54. Illustrations. Portrait of Filipowicz on front cover.

## KAŹIMIERZ FUNK, 1884-1967

225. Harrow, Benjamin. CASIMIR FUNK: PIONEER IN VITAMINS AND HORMONES. New York: Dodd, Mead and Co., 1955. 209p. 55-6935.

   Biography of a famous Polish-born scientist. As of the publication of the book, Funk was still living. Contains a list of "Scientific Papers of C. Funk and Collaborators" listed in alphabetical order. Illustrations. Portraits.

## HENRYK GOLSZMIT, 1878-1942

226. Falkowska, Maria. A CHRONOLOGY OF THE LIFE, ACTIVITIES, AND WORKS OF JANUSZ KORCZAK, trans. by Edwin Kulawiec. New York: Kościuszko Foundation, 1980. 50p.

   A chronology of the major achievements in the life of Henryk Goldszmit, Janusz Korczak, pseud. Portraits.

227. Goldszmit, Henryk. THE WARSAW GHETTO MEMOIRS OF JANUSZ KORCZAK, pseud., trans. by Edwin P. Kulawiec. Washington, D.C.: University Press of America, 1978. 127p. 78-63065.

   Memoirs. Autobiographical. Written in an episodic form.

\*  Hyams, Joseph. A FIELD OF BUTTERCUPS. Cited below as item 964.

228. Morkowicz-Olczakowa, Hanna. MISTER DOCTOR: THE LIFE OF JANUSZ KORCZAK, trans. by Romuald J. Kruk and Harold Gresswell. London: Peter Davies, 1965. 227p. 66-99127.

Biography whereby the author aimed "to bring to the reader's notice only the facts concerning the life and death of Janusz Korczak." She drew freely from Korczak's memoirs and his numerous works, as well as upon personal knowledge of him, conversations and remarks and letters of people closely acquainted with him.

WITOLD MARIAN GOMBROWICZ, 1904-1969

229. Thompson, Ewa M. WITOLD GOMBROWICZ. Boston: Twayne Publishers, 1979. 171p. 78-15571.

   Primarily a concise analysis of Gombrowicz's literary works. Also a biography. Contains a chronology of his life and work. Portraits. Bibliography, pp. 163-168.

WŁADYSŁAW GOMUŁKA, 1905-

230. Bethell, Nicholas. GOMUŁKA, HIS POLAND AND HIS COMMUNISM. London: Longmans, Ltd., 1969. 296p. 75-436368.

   Biography of a man who by his example if not by his actual achievement changed the course of recent European history. The only European Communist leader, apart from Marshal Tito, to have successfully challenged the autocracy of Stalin. Maps.

231. Weit, Erwin. EYEWITNESS: THE AUTOBIOGRAPHY OF GOMUŁKA'S INTERPRETER, trans. by Mary Schofield. London: Andre Deutsch, 1973. 224p. 73-160319.

   Although titled an autobiography, the book is concerned principally with the author's life when he was an interpreter while Gomułka was in prison.

ADAM GUROWSKI, HRABIA, 1805-1866

232. Fischer, LeRoy H. LINCOLN'S CADFLY, ADAM GUROWSKI. Norman: University of Oklahoma Press, 1964. 301p. 64-20756.

   Recounting of the Civil War actions and opinions of Count Adam Gurowski based on the Count's Civil War diaries and letters. Purpose of the author was "to understand the Count as he revealed himself during the war years and to make a pattern of the multitude of opinions on men and issues found in the jungle of his writing." Illustrations. Portraits. Bibliography, pp. 272-288.

SAINT HYACINTHUS, 1185-1257

233. Windeatt, Mary F. NORTHERN LIGHTS: THE STORY OF SAINT HYACINTH OF POLAND AND HIS COMPANIONS. New York: Sheed and Ward, 1945. 171p. 46-916.

First English biography of Saint Hyacinth of Poland. Only sources were from Dominican communities in U.S.A. and Canada. Illustrations.

JAROSŁAW IWASZKIEWICZ, 1894-

234. Matuszewski, Ryszard. IWASZKIEWICZ, trans. by Marsha Brochewicz. Warszawa: Author's Agency, 1972. 51p.

Biographical sketch and evaluation of principal works of Iwaszkiewicz. Of particular value are bibliographies at end of book, pp. 41-44, translations, pp. 45-46, translations into foreign languages, pp. 47-51.

JADWIGA, CONSORT OF VLADISLAUS II JAGIEŁŁO,
KING OF POLAND, 1371-1399

235. Gardner, Monica M. QUEEN JADWIGA OF POLAND. St. Louis: B. Herder Book Co., 1934. 191p. 35-16733.

Biographical sketch intended to depict the heroine as a "saint and a woman." Frontispiece shows portrait of Queen Jadwiga.

236. Kellogg, Charlotte. THE GIRL WHO RULED A KINGDOM, illus. by Aniela Pruszynska. New York: D. Appleton-Century Company, Inc., 1938. 154p. 38-21859.

Fictionalized biography written for the young adult reader. Illustrations.

237. Kellogg, Charlotte. JADWIGA, POLAND'S GREAT QUEEN, with a preface by Ignaz Jan Paderewski and an introduction by Frank H. Simonds. New York: Macmillan, 1931. 304p. 31-31956.

*Special Works*

A biography published without documentation. In the foreword, the author acknowledges indebtedness to many prominent scholars in the field of Polish studies for her information. One black-and-white portrait, a reproduction of a painting by Jan Matejko.

238. Kellogg, Charlotte. JADWIGA, QUEEN OF POLAND, with a preface by Ignace Jan Paderewski and an introduction by Frank A. Simonds. Washington, D.C.: Anderson House, 1936. 244p. 36-16011.

 Provides an authentic portrait of a noble and romantic figure and a fascinating picture of the pageantry of medieval ceremony seized upon one of the great and illuminating events in the history of the Polish people. Portraits.

\* Mills, Lois. SO YOUNG A QUEEN. Cited below as item 1043.

LEON JASTREMSKI, 1843-1907

239. Pinkowski, Edward. PILLS, PENS AND POLITICS: THE STORY OF GENERAL LEON JASTREMSKI, 1843-1907. Wilmington, Del.: Capt. Stanislaus Młotkowski Brigade Society, 1974. 172p. 74-29094.

 Biographical account of "Polish-Franco-American, Leon Jastremski." A preliminary look at subject in a way to understand his part in the drama of American culture. Adequate documentation. Illustrations. Portraits.

JOHN PAUL II, POPE, 1920-

240. Blazynski, George. POPE JOHN PAUL II: A MAN FROM KRAKÓW. London: Weidenfeld and Nicholson, 1979. 176p.

 Author of this biography is a broadcast interviewer for the BBC and used sources all over Europe. Places the figure of John Paul in perspective using his Polish background. Illustrations.

241. Craig, Mary. MAN FROM A FAR COUNTRY: AN INFORMAL PORTRAIT OF POPE JOHN PAUL II. New York: William Morrow and Co., 1979. 191p. 79-318565.

A very readable account of the life of Karol Wojtyła up to his election to the papacy interwoven with national, political and social events in Poland and Europe. Author is a British journalist and did some research in Poland. Bibliography, p. 191.

242. Hebblethwaite, Peter. JOHN PAUL II, A PICTORIAL BIOGRAPHY, by P. Hebblethwaite and Ludwig Kaufmann. New York: McGraw-Hill Book Co., 1979. 128p. 79-9169.

    Covers life of Karol Wojtyła from birth through visit to his native Poland as Pope. Many illustrations in color.

243. Karolak, Tadeusz. JOHN PAUL II, THE POPE FROM POLAND, trans. by David Evans. Warszawa: Interpress Publishers, 1979. 157p. 80-19307.

    Richly illustrated biography of John Paul II from his birth to his selection as Pope. Many of the illustrations are in color. Portraits.

244. Malinski, Mieczysław. POPE JOHN PAUL II, THE LIFE OF KAROL WOJTYŁA. New York: Seabury Press, 1979. 283p. 79-4906.

    As only a lifelong friend could, the author writes from the point of view of a fellow priest and a fellow Pole who knew Wojtyła from boyhood. Emphasizes his life before becoming Pope. Illustrations. Portraits.

245. Murphy, Francis X. JOHN PAUL II: A SON FROM POLAND, by F.X. Murphy and Norman Shaifer. South Hackensack, N.J.: Shepherd Press, 1978. 80p. 78-66213.

    Contents: Biographical sketch, conclave and the voting process for Pope, election of Pope John Paul II, John Paul's investiture, speeches of John Paul, a future vision. Also contains a brief history of the Polish people by Michael Krolewski. Illustrations. Portraits.

246. Murphy, Francis X. THE PILGRIM POPE: A MAN FOR ALL PEOPLE. South Hackensack, N.J.: Shepherd Press, 1979. 106p. 79-67391.

    A sketch of the papal visits to Mexico, Poland, Ireland and the United States with numerous photographs, some in color. Portraits.

Special Works                                                59

247.  Nemec, Ludwik.  POPE JOHN PAUL II:  A FESTIVE PROFILE.
      New York:  Catholic Book Publishing Co., 1979.  242p.
      OL:  BX1378.5.N45.

      Not just another biography, this book is also a his-
      tory of many factors which influenced and helped to
      form the character of John Paul II.  It includes
      little-known facts about Poland and his background.
      Illustrations.  Portraits.  Maps.  Bibliography, pp.
      232-235.

248.  Oram, James.  THE PEOPLE'S POPE:  THE STORY OF KAROL
      WOJTYŁA OF POLAND.  San Francisco:  Chronicle Books,
      1979.  OL:  BX1378.5.07.

      Author, an Australian journalist, presents an in-depth
      look at the life of John Paul II.  Illustrations.
      Portraits.  Bibliography, p. 224.

249.  St. John-Stevas, Norman.  POPE JOHN PAUL II:  HIS
      TRAVELS AND MISSION.  London:  Faber and Faber, 1982.
      160p.  82-01435.

      The author presents his impressions of the ten tra-
      vels and missions of Pope John Paul II up to 1982.  Last
      chapter is a clear portrait of the Pope.  Illustrations.
      Portraits.

250.  Szostak, John M.  IN THE FOOTSTEPS OF POPE JOHN PAUL II:
      AN INTIMATE PORTRAIT BY HIS AMERICAN FRIEND.
      Englewood Cliffs, N.J.:  Prentice-Hall, Inc., 1980.
      230p.  80-20258.

      Author knew the Pope when Wojtyła was Cardinal-
      Archbishop of Kraków.  He was a White House corre-
      spondent of Polish descent.  This book is not a biog-
      raphy; it is instead a portrait of a man as viewed by
      the author.  Illustrations.  Portraits.

251.  Williams, George H.  THE MIND OF JOHN PAUL II.  New
      York:  Seabury Press, 1981.  415p.  80-19947.

      An in-depth exploration of the intellectual and spir-
      itual character of John Paul II with a rigorous inves-
      tigation of the influences of his past in Poland.
      Maps.

252. Wolfe, Rinna. THE SINGING POPE: THE STORY OF POPE
JOHN PAUL II. New York: Seabury Press, 1980. 120p.
80-17531.

Story of Pope John Paul II told for young people.
Illustrations. Portraits.

JOZEF KARGE, 1823-1892

\*   Grzelonski, Bogdan. POLES IN THE UNITED STATES OF
AMERICA, 1776-1865. Cited below as item 1248.

253. Kajencki, Francis C. STAR ON MANY A BATTLEFIELD,
BREVOORT GENERAL JOSEP KARGE IN THE AMERICAN CIVIL
WAR. Cranbury, N.J.: Associated University Presses,
Inc., 1980. 280p. 77-89781.

A military biography of a native Pole who came to
America and joined the Union Army during the Civil War.
Tells of his missions and actions based on complete
documentation. Illustrations. Maps. Bibliography,
pp. 259-266.

SAINT KAŻIMIERZ, 1458-1484

254. Uminski, Sigmund H. THE ROYAL PRINCE: THE STORY OF
SAINT CASIMIR. New York: Polish Publication Society
of America, 1971. 146p. 76-147844.

Biography as well as a bit of history of Poland in
the fifteenth century. Illustrations. Portraits.
Bibliography, pp. 136-141.

JAN KOCHANOWSKI, 1530-1584

255. Welsh, David J. JAN KOCHANOWSKI. New York: Twayne
Publishers, Inc., 1974. 160p. 74-6391.

Chronology on p. 11. A biographical, but more impor-
tantly, a discussion of Kochanowski's works. Contains
specimens of his works in both Polish and English.

DOMINIK HIPPOLYT KOLASINSKI, 1838-1898

256. Orton, Lawrence D. POLISH DETROIT AND THE KOLASINSKI
AFFAIR. Detroit: Wayne State University Press,
1981. 229p. 80-25290.

*Special Works*

More than just a biography of Fr. Dominik H. Kolasinski, the author also has "tried to provide a broad portrait of the beginnings, expansion and consolidation of Detroit's Polish community in the late nineteenth century. Particular attention is paid to the perception and attitude of native Detroiters toward the immigrant ways." Illustrations. Portraits. Maps. Bibliography, pp. 221-224.

257. Skendzel, Edward A. THE KOLASINSKI STORY. Grand Rapids, Mich.: Littleshield Press, 1979. 126p. 79-64404.

A study of the controversial figure in the history of the Poles in the United States. The work appears to be adequately documented. The sources used include numerous newspaper accounts. Translations into English of pertinent letters is of special interest. The work is more an account of Fr. Kolasinski's career than a full biography. Illustrations. Portraits.

SAINT MAXIMILIAN KOLBE, 1894-1942

258. Dewar, Diana. SAINT OF AUSCHWITZ: THE STORY OF MAXIMILIAN KOLBE. San Francisco: Harper & Row, 1982. 146p. 81-48926.

"A popular account of the life journey and abiding influence of Maximilian Kolbe" by an English free-lance journalist and author. Illustrations. Portraits. Bibliography, pp. 138-139.

259. Hanley, Boniface. MAXIMILIAN KOLBE: NO GREATER LOVE. Notre Dame, IN: Ave Maria Press, 1982. 80p. 82-72656.

Simple, sympathetic account of the life and martyrdom of Maximilian Kolbe by a member of the Franciscan order in the United States, the same order to which Kolbe belonged. Illustrations. Portraits.

260. Lorit, Sergius. THE LAST DAYS OF MAXIMILIAN KOLBE. New York: New City Press, 1968. 152p. 67-30841.

Simple biography. No documentation.

261. MORE THAN A KNIGHT: THE TRUE STORY OF ST. MAXIMILIAN KOLBE, by the Daughters of St. Paul. Boston: Daughters of St. Paul, 1982. 100p. 82-18340.

   A simple version of the life of St. Maximilian Kolbe for the young reader. Illustrations.

262. Treece, Patricia. A MAN FOR OTHERS: MAXIMILIAN KOLBE, SAINT OF AUSCHWITZ, IN THE WORDS OF THOSE WHO KNEW HIM. San Francisco: Harper & Row, 1982. 198p. 82-48404.

   Told chiefly in the words of his family, friends, acquaintances and death-camp survivors, including the man he died for, this book is the story of an innovative, down-to-earth, and immensely likeable man, Maximilian Kolbe. Illustrations. Portraits. Bibliography, pp. 185-192.

263. Winowska, Maria. THE DEATH CAMP PROVED HIM REAL: THE LIFE OF FATHER MAXIMILIAN KOLBE, FRANCISCAN. Kenosha, Wisc.: Author, 1971. 190p. 71-178762.

   Life of St. Maximilian Kolbe. First published as OUR LADY'S FOOL. This new American edition, revised and enlarged. No documentation. Illustrations. Portraits.

264. Winowska, Maria. OUR LADY'S FOOL, FATHER MAXIMILIAN KOLBE, trans. by Jacqueline Bowers and Bernard M. Geiger. Westminster, Md.: Newman Press, 1952. 173p. 52-7503.

   An undocumented biography of St. Maximilian Kolbe written shortly after his death. Illustrations. Portraits.

STANISŁAW KONARSKI, 1700-1773

265. Rose, William J. STANISLAUS KONARSKI, REFORMER OF EDUCATION IN EIGHTEENTH CENTURY POLAND. London: Jonathan Cape, 1929. 288p. 29-28696.

   More than just a biography, this book is a scholarly study of Konarski's work. Origininally presented as a thesis offered to the Faculty of Philosophy of the University of Kraków by the author in partial

## Special Works

fulfillment for the degree of Doctor of Philosophy. Bibliography, pp. 279-283.

### CASIMIR JAMES KONSTANTY, 1917-

266. Yeutter, Franklin W. JIM KONSTANTY. New York: A.S. Barnes and Company, 1951. 181p. 51-11575.

> The subject was the son of Polish immigrants whose Christian name was Casimir (Kaźimierz), and thus can be classed as a Polish-American sports figure. Illustrations. Portraits.

### HENRYK KORWIN-KAŁUSSOWSKI, 1806-1894

* Grzelonski, Bogdan. POLES IN THE UNITED STATES OF AMERICA, 1776-1865. Cited below as item 1248.

### JÓZEF KORZENIOWSKI, 1857-1924

267. Morf, Gustav. THE POLISH HERITAGE OF JOSEPH CONRAD, 1857-1924. London: Sampson Low, Marston and Co., Ltd., 1929. 248p. NjP: 3687.3.823.

> A study of Joseph Conrad's ancestral roots. Also covers how Polish background influenced his writing. Contains portrait of Conrad's ancestors. Bibliography, pp. 241-243.

268. Morf, Gustav. THE POLISH SHADES AND GHOSTS OF JOSEPH CONRAD. New York: Astra Books, 1976. 334p. 75-18281.

> Reprint of British edition listed immediately above. Illustrations. Portraits. Bibliography, pp. 327-330.

### TADEUSZ KOŚĆIUSZKO, 1746-1817

269. Abodaher, David J. WARRIOR ON TWO CONTINENTS: THADDEUS KOŚĆIUSZKO. New York: Julian Messner, 1968. 192p. 68-14943.

> Biography of Kośćiuszko written for the young reader. Describes background and education. Contrived dialogue. Bibliography, p. 185.

270. Bushnell, George H. KOSĆIUSZKO, A SHORT BIOGRAPHY OF
THE POLISH PATRIOT. St. Andrews, Scotland: W.C.
Henderson and Son, Ltd., 1943. 54p.

   Main details of Kosćiuszko's life have been recorded.
   Portraits.

271. Evans, Anthony W.W. MEMOIR OF THADDEUS KOSĆIUSZKO,
POLAND'S HERO AND PATRIOT, AN OFFICER IN THE AMERICAN
ARMY OF THE REVOLUTION AND MEMBER OF THE SOCIETY OF
THE CINCINNATI. New York: G.A. Thitchener, Printer,
1883. 58p. 15-2486.

   Not memoirs but reminiscences of stories and historical points in Kosćiuszko's life recounted by author
   whose grandfather was a warm, personal friend of
   Kosćiuszko. Portraits. Maps.

272. Gardner, Monica M. KOSĆIUSZKO, A BIOGRAPHY. New York:
Charles Scribner's Sons, 1920. 211p. 21-1692.

   Author was earliest to obtain access to original
   Polish sources. Handles essential features of
   Kosćiuszko's character.

273. Gardner, Monica M. KOSĆIUSZKO, A BIOGRAPHY, ed. by
Mary Corbridge. London: George Allen and Unwin,
Ltd., 1942. Rev. ed. 148p. 42-20865.

   Revised edition of American published in 1920.
   Portraits. "Chief works consulted," p. 143.

274. Gronowicz, Antoni. GALLANT GENERAL: GENERAL
KOSĆIUSZKO, trans. by Samuel Sorgenstein. New York:
Charles Scribner's Sons, 1947. 136p. 47-12010.

   Readable biography for the juvenile, grades 7-9.
   Selected bibliography in English and Polish, pp. 134-
   136.

\*   Grzelonski, Bogdan. POLES IN THE UNITED STATES OF
AMERICA, 1776-1865. Cited below as item 1248.

275. Haiman, Miecislaus. KOSĆIUSZKO IN THE AMERICAN REVOLU-
TION. New York: Polish Institute of Arts and
Sciences in America, 1943. 198p. 43-16897.

   Reprint of the 1943 edition listed immediately above.

## Special Works

276. Omitted.

277. Haiman, Miecislaus. KOSĆIUSZKO, LEADER AND EXILE. New York: Polish Institute of Arts and Sciences in America, 1946. 183p. 47-17160.

    The second and the last part of a biography of Kosćiuszko, the first part of which has been published under the title, KOSĆIUSZKO IN THE AMERICAN REVOLUTION intended to mark and to honor the bicentennial of Kosćiuszko's birth in 1746. Illustrations. Portraits. Bibliography, pp. 157-167.

\* Haiman, Miecislaus. POLAND AND THE REVOLUTIONARY WAR. Cited below as item 1249.

278. Hoskins, Janina W. TADEUSZ KOSĆIUSZKO, 1746-1817: A SELECTED LIST OF READING MATERIALS IN ENGLISH. Washington, D.C.: Library of Congress, European Division, 1980. 24p.

    List of works contained in the Library of Congress and a brief biographical sketch of the life of Kosćiuszko. Illustrations. Portraits. Maps.

279. Johns, Joseph P. KOSĆIUSZKO, A BIOGRAPHICAL STUDY WITH A HISTORICAL BACKGROUND OF THE TIMES. Detroit, Mich.: Endurance Press, 1965. 99p. 64-15908.

    Designed for the juvenile reader. Covers life story as well as remarks about Poland at the time. Includes questions for discussion and review. Illustrations. Maps.

280. Kopczewski, Jan S. KOSĆIUSZKO AND PUŁANSKI. Warszawa: Interpress Publishers, 1976. 328p. NjP: DK4348.K67 xK613.

    A richly and profusely illustrated work of lives of both Kosćiuszko and Pułanski emphasizing their respective roles in the American Revolutionary War. Interesting section dealing with monuments, coins, stamps, money, etc. dedicated to them.

281. Kosćiuszko. Tadeusz A. THE KOSĆIUSZKO LETTERS, ed. by Metchie J.E. Budka. Chicago: Polish Museum of America, 1977. 202p. 77-78733.

Autographed letters of Kościuszko in the American Revolution as well as those by and about him connected with that event found in the collections of the Polish Museum of America. Contains facsimiles. Illustrations. Portraits.

JERZY KOSINSKI, 1933-

282. Lavers, Norman. JERZY KOSINSKI. Boston: Twayne Publishers, 1982. 176p. 81-7045.

 Contains biographical information, a chronology, but fundamentally this book is a series of essays on the works of Kosinski. Portrait. Bibliography, pp. 169-70.

IGNACY KRASICKI, HRABIA, ABP. OF GNIEZNO, 1735-1801

283. Welsh, David J. IGNACY KRASICKI. New York: Twayne Publishers, 1969. 150p. 68-57247.

 Concerned primarily with the literary efforts and results of Krasicki's work. Contains chronology. Bibliography, pp. 143-148.

FRANCISZKA KRASINSKA, 1744-1795

284. Kelly, Eric P. A GIRL WHO WOULD BE QUEEN, THE STORY AND DIARY OF THE YOUNG COUNTESS KRASINSKA, by E.P. Kelly and Hofmanowa. Chicago: A.C. McClurg and Co., 1939. 201p. 39-27806.

 Parts one and three are the work of Kelly; part two is the full text of the journal of the Countess Krasinska which was written in Polish by Klementyna z Tanskich Hofmanowa, a well-known figure of Polish literature. The journal, though fictional, is based on actual historical fact. Illustrations.

285. Krasinska, Francoise. Countess. THE JOURNAL OF COUNTESS FRANCOISE KRASINSKA, GREAT GRANDMOTHER OF VICTOR EMMANUEL, by Kasimer Dziekonska. Chicago: A.C. McClurg and Co., 1896. 182p.

 Journal covers period from Monday, January 1, 1759 to Tuesday, January 15, 1761. Illustrations. Portraits.

## ZYGMUNT KRASIŃSKI, 1812-1859

286. Gardner, Monica M. THE ANONYMOUS POET OF POLAND: ZYGMUNT KRASIŃSKI. Cambridge: Cambridge University Press, 1919. 320p. 20-4041.

    "Attempts to give the English reader some idea of Zygmunt Krasiński as the poet, the patriot, the mystic.... Limited to those details that seemed to be calculated to further the object for which this book was written, that is, to draw English attention to a poetry and a line of thought that are not only of a national but also of a world-wide appeal." Portrait of Krasiński on frontispiece. Bibliographical note gives only Polish language sources, pp. 315-316.

287. Lednicki, Wacław. ZYGMUNT KRASIŃSKI, ROMANTIC UNIVERSALIST, AN INTERNATIONAL TRIBUTE. New York: Polish Institute of Arts and Sciences in America, 1964. 228p. 65-51405.

    "... to give the Anglo-Saxon reader information about the life and work of the poet and to provide new facts and interpretations of his work." Consists of a series of articles by various authors. Portraits.

## WŁODZIMIERZ KRZYZANOWSKI, 1824-1887

\*   Grzelonski, Bogdan. POLES IN THE UNITED STATES OF AMERICA, 1776-1865. Cited below as item 1248.

288. Krzyzanowski, Włodzimierz. THE MEMOIRS OF WLADIMIR KRZYZANOWSKI, ed. by James S. Pula. San Francisco: R. and E. Research Associates, 1978. 91p. 77-081016.

    Translation of the MEMOIRS OF MY SOJOURN IN AMERICA DURING THE WAR, 1861-1864 in their entirety as they appeared in the Polish language version published by the Roman Catholic Union in 1963. Portraits. Sources, pp. 75-80.

289. Pula, James S. FOR LIBERTY AND JUSTICE: THE LIFE AND TIMES OF WŁODZIMIERZ KRZYZANOWSKI. Chicago: Polish American Congress Charitable Foundation, 1978. 288p. 77-080746.

    Biography of a Pole who emigrated to the United States and then became a Brigadier General and fought

in the Civil War. Illustrations. Portraits. Maps.
Bibliography, pp. 272-281.

WANDA LANDOWSKA, 1879-1959

290. Landowska, Wanda. LANDOWSKA ON MUSIC, collected, edited, and trans. by Denise Restout. New York: Stein and Day, 1964. 434p. 64-22698.

Collection of Wanda Landowska's writings on music. Includes large selections from Wanda Landowska's previously unpublished notebooks. Also includes Landowska's writings in French and complete text of her book MUSIQUE ANCIENNE. Facsimiles. Discography, pp. 411-422. List of musical works. Illustrations. Portraits.

WACŁAW LEDNICKI, 1891-1967

291. Lednicki, Wacław. REMINISCENCES: THE ADVENTURES OF A MODERN GIL BLAS DURING THE LAST WAR. The Hague: Mouton, 1972. 278p. 68-23199.

Reminiscences of the author on his Polish-European experiences of 1939-1940. Of note are remarks made about the United States after the author first arrived in this country.

MARJA TERESA LEDÓCHOWSKA, COUNTESS, 1863-1922

292. Bielak, Stanisława Kostka, siostra. THE SERVANT OF GOD, MARY THERESA COUNTESS LEDÓCHOWSKA; FOUNDRESS OF THE SODALITY OF SAINT PETER CLAVER. St. Paul, Minn.: Society of St. Peter Claver, 1944. 226p. 44-12886.

Biography of foundress of Society of St. Peter Claver with illustrations and portraits.

JOACHIM LELEWEL, 1786-1861

293. Skurnowicz, Joan S. ROMANTIC NATIONALISM AND LIBERALISM: JOACHIM LELEWEL AND THE POLISH NATIONAL IDEA. New York: Columbia University Press, 1981. 202p. 80-68446.

Revised version of author's doctoral dissertation completed at the University of Wisconsin. It is an analysis of an historian as well as the story of Lelewel's life. Bibliography, pp. 172-185.

## STANISŁAW LEM, 1921-

294. Ziegfeld, Richard E. STANISŁAW LEM. New York: Frederick Ungar Pub. Co., 1986. 188p. 83-13009.

   One of the first full-length books on Lem in the English language. It is an overview of his career, biographical background, and indication of what the key books are about, and a survey of the major themes and literary techniques. Bibliography, pp. 162-175.

## BOLESŁAW LEŚMIAN, 1877-1937

295. Stone, Rochelle H. BOLESŁAW LEŚMIAN, THE POET AND HIS POETRY. Berkeley: University of California Press, 1976. 364p. 73-84382.

   A study designed "to acquaint the English-speaking reader with Leśmian's life and the magic of his work. Study traces the convergence of Leśmian's theory and his poetry within the contemporary Polish and Russian literary scene out of which he emerged as a man and as a poet." Contains poetry in Polish and in translation. Bibliography, pp. 338-353.

## LIBERACE, 1919-1987

296. Liberace, Władysław Valentino. LIBERACE: AN AUTOBIOGRAPHY. New York: G.P. Putnam's Sons, 1973. 316p. 73-82031.

   Entertainer-pianist, Liberace, tells the story of his life and successful career in radio, television, and on the concert platform. Illustrations.

## BOLESŁAW LIMANOWSKI, 1835-1935

297. Cottam, Kazimiera J. BOLESŁAW LIMANOWSKI, 1835-1935; A STUDY IN SOCIALISM AND NATIONALISM. New York: Columbia University Press, 1978. 365p. 77-82395.

   Originally a doctoral dissertation at the University of Toronto. A study in an aspect of the nationality problem in Tsarist Russia in the second half of the

nineteenth and the beginning of the twentieth century.
Bibliography, pp. 331-349.

THADDEUS MICHAEL MACHROWICZ, 1899-1970

298. Święcicki, Marek. THE GENTLEMAN FROM MICHIGAN, by M.
Święcicki and Róża Nowotarska; trans. by Edward
Cynarski. London: Polish Cultural Foundation, 1974.
303p. MiD: B.M18559.

Originally published in Polish in 1970. Biography
based upon conversation with the biographee. Illustrations. Portraits.

MARYA, QUEEN CONSORT OF JOHN III SOBIESKI,
KING OF POLAND, 1641-1716

299. Waliszewski, Każimierz. MARYŚIENKA: MARIE DE LA
GRANGE D'ARQUIEN, QUEEN OF POLAND AND WIFE OF
SOBIESKI, 1641-1716, trans. by Lady Mary Loyd. New
York: Dodd, Mead and Company, 1899. 297p. 99-859.

Biographical sketch. Portraits. List of authorities
consulted, pp. viii-xvi.

MARJA LUDWIKA, QUEEN CONSORT OF JOHN II CASIMIR,
KING OF POLAND, 1611-1667

300. Batcheller, Tryphosa. THE SOUL OF A QUEEN. New York:
Brentano's, 1943. 280p. 44-1538.

Fictionalized biography of romantic and heroic Louise
Marie de Gonzague, Duchess of Nevers and Queen of
Poland, wife of Jan Każimierz II. Many illustrations
including portraits. Maps.

ADAM MICKIEWICZ, 1798-1855

301. Agatstein, Mieczysław. ADAM MICKIEWICZ. Warszawa:
Polonia Publishing House, 1955. 78p. 58-42213.

Not merely a biography of Mickiewicz, it speaks also
of his importance to the Polish people and of his influence upon Slavonic literature. Contains a two-page
English bibliography which is a listing of principal
English translations up to 1955. Portraits. Illustrations.

## Special Works

302. Buffalo. University. MICKIEWICZ AND THE WEST: A SYMPOSIUM by Zbigniew Folejewski and others, ed. by B.R. Bugelski. Buffalo, N.Y.: University of Buffalo, 1956. 75p. 56-58752.

    Five lectures by scholars delivered in 1955 at the annual convention of Polish Cultural Clubs.

303. Coleman, Arthur P. ADAM MICKIEWICZ IN ENGLISH, by A.P. Coleman and Marion M. Coleman. Schnectady, N.Y.: Electric City Press, Inc., 1940. 550. MiU: 891.858.M620.C69.

    History of English translations of Mickiewicz's works and a bibliography of translations as of 1940. Illustrations. Portraits.

304. Coleman, Marion M. YOUNG MICKIEWICZ. Cambridge Springs, Penn.: Alliance College, 1956. 380p. 55-9778.

    Covers Mickiewicz's life to the year, 1834. Intended as a story rather than a straight biography. No documentation. Illustrations. Portraits.

305. Gardner, Monica M. ADAM MICKIEWICZ, THE NATIONAL POET OF POLAND. New York: E.P. Dutton and Co., 1911. 317p. 11-29636.

    A sketch of the work and character of Mickiewicz. Contains excerpts in English of some of his writings. Portraits. "List of books," pp. 301-302.

306. Kapuścieńska. Marie, ed. ADAM MICKIEWICZ: HIS LIFE AND WORK IN DOCUMENTS, PORTRAITS AND ILLUSTRATIONS, ed. by M. Kapuścieńska and Wanda Markowska. Warszawa: Polonia Publishing House, 1956. 158p. 57-45143.

    Merely a collection of documents, portraits, and illustrations preceded by a brief biographicl sketch by Jan Z. Jakubowski marking the centennial of Mickiewicz's death.

307. Kridl, Manfred. ADAM MICKIEWICZ, POET OF POLAND. New York: Columbia University Press, 1951. 292p. 51-12310.

Aim of the book is to contribute to the commemoration of the 150th anniversary of Adam Mickiewicz's birth in 1798. The purpose was to present to the American public the universal significance of the work of the great Polish poet and leader, his contribution to world culture and the appreciation of this contribution by foreign writers. Essays divided into two parts: the man and the poet; and Mickiewicz in foreign years--Russia, Germany, Bohemia, France, Switzerland, Italy, and the United States and India. Illustrations. Portraits.

308. Lednicki, Wacław. ADAM MICKIEWICZ IN WORLD LITERATURE; A SYMPOSIUM. Berkeley, Cal.: University of California Press, 1956. 626p. 56-11898.

Purpose of the book is "to trace Mickiewicz's relationships with various literatures of the Old World and the New, and to delineate his role and destiny in them." Contains several articles about Mickiewicz in various countries and a biographical sketch by Wiktor Weintraub. Illustrations. Portraits.

309. Pruszynski, Ksawery. ADAM MICKIEWICZ: THE LIFE STORY OF THE GREATEST POLISH POET, with a foreword by Jack Lindsay. London: Polish Cultural Institute, 1955. 72p. A57-5521.

A clear and engrossing account of Mickiewicz's life and work. Portraits.

310. Welsh, David J. ADAM MICKIEWICZ. New York: Twayne Publishers, 1966. 168p. 66-21740.

This study is concerned with the nature of Mickiewicz's creative imagination as expressed in his poetry, and only with his biography when his philosophical and religious ideas offset his work. Contains excerpts of his poetry in English translation only. Chronology. Bibliography, pp. 159-165.

CZESŁAW MIŁOSZ, 1911-

311. Volynska-Bogert, Rimma, comp. CZESŁAW MIŁOSZ, AN INTERNATIONAL BIBLIOGRAPHY, 1930-1980, comp. by R. Volynska-Bogert and Wojciech Zalewski. Ann Arbor: The University of Michigan, Department of Slavic Languages and Literature. 1983. 162p. OL: Z8576.27 V641983.

## Special Works

Research tool aimed at aiding the study of Czesław Miłosz' entire literary output. Some annotations.

## HELENA MODJESKA, 1844-1909

312. Coleman, Arthur P. WANDERERS TWAIN: MODJESKA AND SIENKIEWICZ: A VIEW FROM CALIFORNIA, by A.P. Coleman and Marion M. Coleman. Cheshire, Conn.: Cherry Hill Books, 1964. 111p. 63-20948.

    Purpose of book is to illustrate the role the California scene played in the lives of Modjeska and Sienkiewicz. Modjeska was identified with Anaheim, California for 33 years; Sienkiewicz lived there a few months. An authentic, definitive and sympathetic story of the little group of Polish emigrés who came to America. Emphasis is on Modjeska. Portraits.

313. Coleman, Marion M. FAIR ROSALIND: THE AMERICAN CAREER OF HELENA MODJESKA. Cheshire, Conn.: Cherry Hill Books, 1969. 1019p. 69-10370.

    An exhaustive and comprehensive account of the American episode in the life of Helena Modjeska arranged in careful chronological order. Also contains a chronological list of plays presented by Modjeska, an alphabetical list of plays presented by her and a chronological list of appearances by her between 1877 and 1907. Illustrations. Portraits.

314. Cook, Mabel C. THE STORY OF HELENA MODJESKA, MADAME CHLAPOWSKA. London: W.H. Allen and Co., 1883. 296p. 12-19451.

    Simple biography emphasizing her acting career.

315. Gronowicz, Antoni. MODJESKA, HER LIFE AND LOVES. New York: Thomas Yoseloff, Inc., 1956. 254p. 56-8956.

    This book is based on twenty years of research, interviews, and travel throughout Europe and America gathering material on the life of the great Shakespearean actress, Helena Modjeska. The dialogue introduced in these pages is conceived from the Polish notes of Modjeska, together with conversations held by the author with those who lived with the actress and worked with her. New and unknown facts coming to the attention of the author have enabled him to present what he sincerely hoped is a complete picture of Modjeska's life and her contribution to the art of the theatre.

316. Gronowicz, Antoni. AN ORANGE FULL OF DREAMS. New York: Dodd, Mead and Co., 1971. 276p. 77-173884.

   A fictionalized version of the life of the great stage star of the nineteenth century, the Polish-born Helena Modjeska, here called Greta Galingala. Foreword by Greta Garbo. This book was written for Greta Garbo at her request to portray a dream she kept having and to realize her happiest fantasy of being a stage actress.

317. Modjeska, Helena. MEMORIES AND IMPRESSIONS OF HELENA MODJESKA: AN AUTOBIOGRAPHY. New York: Macmillan Company, 1969. 571p. 75-81212.

   Reprint of the 1910 edition published by Benjamin Blom, this book is a series of reminiscences of the life of Modjeska as expressed by herself. Illustrations. Portraits.

318. Payne, Theodore. LIFE ON THE MODJESKA RANCH IN THE GAY NINETIES. Los Angeles: Kruckeberg Press, 1962. 101p. 60-170.

   A brief history, a condensed account of her life, with special emphasis on her theatrical career. The remainder of the book is descriptive of the life and happenings on the Modjeska Ranch during the period from July, 1983 to January, 1896. Includes a portrait of Madame Modjeska. Illustrations.

319. Sienkiewicz, Henryk. AMERICAN DEBUT: SOURCE MATERIALS ON THE FIRST APPEARANCE OF THE POLISH ACTRESS, HELENA MODJESKA, ON THE AMERICAN STAGE, trans. by Marion M. Coleman. Cheshire, Conn.: Cherry Hill Books, 1965. 36p. 65-2614.

   A description of the California debut of the famous actress as described in the title. Illustrations. Portraits.

*Special Works* 75

STANLEY FRANK MUSIAL, 1920-

320. Meany, Thomas. STANLEY FRANK MUSIAL: THE MAN. New York: A.S. Barnes and Company, 1951. 25p. MiD: Burton: B.M9735.M462.

Musial was the son of Polish immigrants. This work is not so much a biography as a description of Musial's baseball career. Illustrations. Portraits.

321. Musial, Stanley F. STAN MUSIAL: "THE MAN'S OWN STORY," as told to Bob Broeg. Garden City, N.Y.: Doubleday and Company, 1964. 328p. 64-11753.

Popular biography by the sports editor of the St. Louis Post-Dispatch. Illustrations. Portraits.

322. Schoor, Gene. THE STAN MUSIAL STORY, by G. Schoor and Henry Gilfond. New York: Julian Messner, Inc., 1955. 192p. 55-6929.

Biography written for the teenage reader by an author who specializes in writing about sports figures. Illustrations. Portraits.

EDMUND SIXTUS MUSKIE, 1914-

323. Lippman, Theo, Jr. MUSKIE, by T. Lippman, Jr. and Donald C. Muskie. New York: W.W. Norton and Company, Inc., 1971. 237p. 78-141941.

Biographical account based upon "information learned in interviews with Senator Muskie, his friends, enemies, colleagues, family members, and staff members ... conducted in 1969 and 1970." Also based upon press accounts. Original family name was Marciszewski. Illustrations. Portraits.

324. Muskie, Edmund S. JOURNEYS. Garden City, N.Y.: Doubleday and Company, 1972. 204p. 71-109432.

An autobiographical sketch in which Muskie "describes his experiences and ideals, his observations and opinions." Author states that "this book reflects the influence of my mother and father and my life with Jane and our children."

325. Nevin, David.  MUSKIE OF MAINE.  New York:  Random House, 1972.  238p.  72-159361.

   Not only a standard biography, but also an attempt to determine Muskie's political popularity in 1968 when he was the Democratic nominee for Vice-President of the U.S. Author is a journalist.

ADAM STANISŁAW NARUSZEWICZ, 1733-1795

326. Rutkowska, Neomisia, sister.  BISHOP ADAM NARUSZEWICZ AND HIS HISTORY OF THE POLISH NATION:  A CRITICAL STUDY.  Washington, D.C.:  Catholic University of America, 1941.  138p.  A41-4909.

   Ph.D. thesis at the Catholic University of America. An historiographical study.  Entire chapter devoted to life and works of Naruszewicz.  Also a chapter on Polish historiography up to Naruszewicz.  Bibliography, pp. 130-135.

JULIAN URSYN NIEMCEWICZ, 1758-1841

*   Grzelonski, Bogdan.  POLES IN THE UNITED STATES OF AMERICA, 1776-1865.  Cited below as item 1248.

*   Haiman, Miecislaus.  POLAND AND THE REVOLUTIONARY WAR. Cited below as item 1249.

CYPRIAN NORWID, 1821-1883

327. Gömöri, George.  CYPRIAN WORWID.  New York:  Twayne Publishers, 1974.  162p.  73-17341.

   First full-length study on Norwid for the English-speaking reader.  Tries to provide a sketch of Norwid's life.  Gives some idea of Norwid's thought and historiosophy while indicating his connections with Christian tradition and nineteenth-century European thought. Chronology, pp. 11-12.  Portraits.  Bibliography, pp. 155-158.

IGNACY JAN PADEREWSKI, 1860-1941

328. Gronowicz, Antoni.  PADEREWSKI:  PIANIST AND PATRIOT. New York:  Thomas Nelson and Sons, 1943.  216p. 43-51131.

*Special Works* 77

A biography of Paderewski written for the young adult. The author was an acquaintance of Paderewski. Contains a list of "The compositions of Ignacy Jan Paderewski." Contains no documentation. Portraits.

329. Hoskins, Janina W. IGNACY JAN PADEREWSKI, 1860-1941: A BIOGRAPHICAL SKETCH AND A SELECTIVE LIST OF READING MATERIALS. Washington, D.C.: Library of Congress, 1984. 32p. 83-600314.

    Biography, bibliography, and a list of works in chronological order. Facsimile of page of music, inside back cover. Illustrations. Portraits.

330. Kellogg, Charlotte H. PADEREWSKI. New York: Viking Press, 1956. 224p. 56-14300.

    Critics agree that this biography is for older boys and girls and adults. Lacks bibliography, illustrations, documentation.

331. Landau, Rom. IGNACE PADEREWSKI, MUSICIAN AND STATESMAN. New York: Thomas Y. Crowell, 1934. 34-27054.

    A popular biography of Paderewski which covers his life as a musician, a statesman and, as the author states it, "a great man." Author indicates he based his book upon the "personal revelations of Paderewski himself and of his friends and collaborators." Numerous black-and-white photographs. Bibliography is annotated. Illustrations. Portraits. Maps. Bibliography, pp. 289-305.

332. Lengyel, Emil. IGNACE PADEREWSKI: MUSICIAN AND STATESMAN. New York: Franklin Watts, Inc., 1970. 113p. 70-11543.

    A brief biographical sketch of Paderewski. Chronology of his life. Illustrations. Portraits. Selected bibliography.

333. Paderewski, Ignacy Jan. THE PADEREWSKI MEMOIRS, by I.J. Paderewski and Mary Lawton. New York: Charles Scribner's Sons, 1938. 404p. 38-27960.

    Authentic biography. Numerous black-and-white illustrations, including many portraits of Paderewski. Covers period only to 1914.

334. Phillips, Charles J.M. PADEREWSKI, THE STORY OF A
 MODERN IMMORTAL. New York: Macmillan Companu, 1933.
 563p. 34-384.

 An introduction by Edward Mandell House. Portraits
 of Paderewski and Madame Paderewski. Postscript is, in
 effect, a brief bibliographical sketch of works about
 Paderewski. Appendix A: Paderewski's musical compositions. Appendix B: A list of Paderewski's recordings.
 A detailed and scholarly arrangement of facts. Author
 knew subject personally.

335. Strakacz, Aniela. PADEREWSKI AS I KNEW HIM: FROM THE
 DIARY OF ANIELA STRAKACZ, trans. by Halina Chybowska.
 New Brunswick, N.J.: Rutgers University Press, 1949.
 338p. 49-11799.

 Portions of the author's diary as "it relates only my
 personal experiences and observations I made as the wife
 of Paderewski's private secretary during the last
 twenty-three years of his life, 1918-1941." Author
 states that her diary omits "many facts and events
 extremely important and essential for recreating the
 full personality of Paderewski." Contains numerous
 photographs. Portraits.

336. Zamoyski, Adam. PADEREWSKI, A BIOGRAPHY OF THE PIANIST
 AND STATESMAN. New York: Atheneum Press, 1982.
 289p. 81-69136.

 A biography and an attempt by the author "to review,
 with the help of new research, the ... story of his
 life." Contains a list of works in chronological
 order, Paderewski's repertoire, and recordings. Illustrations. Portraits. Maps. Sources, pp. 267-275.

JAN PARANDOWSKI, 1895-

337. Harjan, George. JAN PARANDOWSKI. New York: Twayne
 Publishers, 1971. 160p. 68-57250.

 Important work since, as author states in his preface, not a single biography of the author exists.
 Bibliography, pp. 153-155.

*Special Works*

JAN CHRYZOSTOM Z GOSŁAWIEC, 1636-1701

338. Pasek, Jan Chryzostom. THE MEMOIRS OF JAN CHRYZOSTOM PASEK, trans. by Maria A.J. Święcicka. New York: Kościuszko Foundation, 1973. 529p. 77-79788.

Translation of a classic memoir by a nobleman covering the period 1656, when the author was but twenty years of age and ending in 1688, some thirty-two years later at the Diet of Grodno. "The Memoirs are ... an excellent reflection of the living speech of an ordinary Polish nobleman in the second half of the seventeenth century, a fine example of chatty style and, an excellent source of Polish customs of the time." Illustrations. Bibliography, pp. 56-65.

339. Pasek, Jan Chryzostom. MEMOIRS OF THE POLISH BAROQUE: THE WRITINGS OF JAN CHRYZOSTOM PASEK, A SQUIRE OF THE COMMONWEALTH OF POLAND AND LITHUANIA, ed. by Catharine S. Leach, with an introduction and notes by Wiktor Weintraub. Berkeley, Calif.: University of California Press, 1976. 327p. 74-77371.

Translation of PAMIĘTNIKI. Illustrations.

BOLESŁAW PIASECKI, 1915-

340. Blit, Łucjan. THE EASTERN PRETENDER: BOLESŁAW PIASECKI, HIS LIFE AND TIMES. London: Hutchinson and Co., Ltd., 1965. 223p. 68-2205.

The biography of "an extraordinary man," the leader of the Roman Catholic Communist Pax movement. Incomplete as Piasecki was still alive at the time book was written. Portraits.

KAROL FRYDERYK JULIUSZ PIĄTKOWSKI, 1796-1849

341. Watson, George Leo de St. M. A POLISH EXILE WITH NAPOLEON. Boston: Little, Brown and Company, 1912. 304p. A14-1848.

"... embodying the letters of Capt. Piontkowski to General Sir Robert Wilson and many documents from the Lowe Papers, the Colonial Office Records, the Wilson Manuscripts, the Capel Lofft Correspondence, and the French and Geneva archives hitherto unpublished." A biography of Piątkowski followed by letters which he wrote in the summer of 1817 to Sir Robert T. Wilson dealing with Napoleon and others. Illustrations. Portraits.

JOZEF PIŁSUDSKI, 1867-1935

342. Dziewanowski, Marian K. JOSEPH PIŁSUDSKI: A EUROPEAN FEDERALIST, 1918-1922. Stanford, California: Hoover Institution Press, 1969. 379p. 68-54094.

   This book represents an attempt to rescue Piłsudski from his admirers as well as from his enemies. It is also a modest attempt to recast a little-known aspect of eastern European history. Purely historical in character. Maps. Bibliography, pp. 355-372.

343. Humphrey, Grace. PIŁSUDSKI--BUILDER OF POLAND. New York: Scott and Moore, 1936. 301p. 36-12285.

   Numerous candid shots of Piłsudski of particular value. A popular account written and published shortly after his death. Illustrations. Portraits. Maps.

344. Jędrzejewicz, Wacław. PIŁSUDSKI: A LIFE FOR POLAND. New York: Hippocrene Books, 1982. 385p. 81-86441.

   A generally favorable and sympathetic account of Piłsudski's life. Lacks interpretation of why events happened. First major biographical work in English since publication of Reddaway's work published in 1939. Illustrations. Portraits. Bibliography, pp. 375-376.

345. Kaspryzycki, Tadeusz. JÓZEF PIŁSUDSKI AND HIS IDEAS ON INTERNATIONAL PEACE. New York: Piłsudski Centennial Memorial Committee, 1968. 42p. MiU: DK440.5.P6K19.

   Author was general of the Polish Army and in 1939 Minister of War. Covers author's impressions of Piłsudski's ideas. Portraits.

346. Landau, Rom. PIŁSUDSKI AND POLAND, trans. by Geoffrey Dunlop. New York: Dial Press, 1929. 305p. 29-25940.

   A history of Poland insofar as that country's history was determined by the life and work of Józef

*Special Works* 81

Piłsudski. It is also a biography of Piłsudski. Undocumented. Seven portraits of Piłsudski during different periods in his life.

347. Patterson, Eric J. PIŁSUDSKI, MARSHAL OF POLAND. London: P. Allen, 1934. 27p.

 Brief biographical sketch of Piłsudski. Portraits.

348. Piłsudska, Aleksandra. PIŁSUDSKI, A BIOGRAPHY BY HIS WIFE. New York: Dodd, Mead and Company, 1941. 352p. 41-3952.

 This biography of the Polish leader, Piłsudski, emphasizes his roots in historic Polish nationalism. In part, it is also Mme. Piłsudska's autobiography since it draws freely on her experiences while growing up in Russian-controlled-and-ruled Poland before 1900. Portraits.

349. Piłsudski, Józef. THE MEMOIRS OF A POLISH REVOLUTIONARY AND SOLDIER, trans. and ed. by D.R. Gillie. London: Faber and Faber Limited, 1931. 377p. 31-15807.

 Collection of Piłsudski's writings about his personal experiences prior to 1923 except ROK 1920, a book about his campaign against the Red Army. Translator and editor, responsible for details. Three military maps and one folded map of Poland, past and present. Illustrations.

350. Piłsudski, Józef. JOSEPH PIŁSUDSKI, THE MEMORIES OF A POLISH REVOLUTIONARY AND SOLDIER, trans. by D.R. Gillie. New York: AMS Press, Inc., 1971. 277p. 70-101275.

 Reprint of the 1931 edition with slightly different title as immediately above.

\* Piłsudski, Józef. THE YEAR 1920 AND ITS CLIMAX ... Cited below as item 829.

351. Reddaway, William F. MARSHALL PIŁSUDSKI. London: G. Routledge and Son, Ltd., 1939. 334p. 39-21584.

 Biography dispassionately using what is already public, particularly his own words, resulting in a true outline of one who in talents, ideals and force ranks high among modern men and who receives widespread worship from a great and fertile nation. Illustrations. Portraits. Maps. Bibliography included in Preface.

ANNA TYSZKIEWICZ POTOCKA, HRABINA, 1776-1867

352. Potocka, Anna (Tyszkiewicz), hrabina. MEMOIRS OF THE COUNTESS POTOCKA, ed. by Casimir Stryienski with an authorized translation by Lionel Strachey. New York: Doubleday and McClure Co., 1900. 253p. 0-5535.

Autobiography based upon memoirs for the period 1794-1820. Contains numerous portraits of important Polish and non-Polish personages of the period. Also numerous illustrations based upon lithographs and engravings of places and events of significance in the Countess's life. Maps.

ALFRED POTOCKI, HRABIA, 1886-

353. Potocki, Alfred, hrabia. MASTER OF LANCUT; THE MEMOIRS OF COUNT ALFRED POTOCKI. London: W.H. Allen & Co., 1959. 336p. 59-2303.

Memoirs and reminiscences of a member of a distinguished Polish family. The book covers the life of the author and the various aspects of his family's life. Includes many black-and-white photographs as well as black-and-white reproductions of various portraits.

KAŹIMIERZ PUŁASKI, 1748-1779

354. Abodaher, David J. FREEDOM FIGHTER: CASIMIR PUŁASKI. New York: Julian Messner, 1969. 190p. 69-13048.

Published simultaneously in the United States and Canada. Biography intended for the young adult reader. Bibliography, p. 183.

355. Adams, Dorothy. CAVALRY HERO: CASIMIR PUŁASKI, illus. by Irena Lorentowicz. New York: P.J. Kennedy and Sons, 1957. 190p. 57-6542.

"Tells the story of the colorful and freedom-loving eighteenth-century Polish count, Casimir Pułaski, who, exiled after fighting against the Russians for the

## Special Works

freedom of Poland, eventually joined the American forces and exercised a major influence on the course of military events in the American Revolutionary War." Aimed at the young adult reader. Illustrations.

\* Grzelonski, Bogdan. POLES IN THE UNITED STATES OF AMERICA, 1776-1865. Cited below as 1248.

\* Haiman, Miecislaus. POLAND AND THE REVOLUTIONARY WAR. Cited below as item 1249.

356. Hoskins, Janina W. CASIMIR PUŁASKI, 1747-1779: A SELECTIVE LIST OF READING MATERIALS IN ENGLISH. Washington, D.C.: Library of Congress. European Division, 1979. 24p.

List of works in English contained in the Library of Congress about Pułaski. Includes also a brief biographical sketch of the life of Pułaski. List is not annotated.

357. Konopczyński, Władysław. CASIMIR PUŁASKI, trans. by Irena Makarewicz. Chicago: Polish Roman Catholic Union of America, 1947. 62p. 47-7044.

An account of the life of Pułaski, the bulk of the study dealing with his role in the American Revolutionary War. Contains a black-and-white reproduction of painting entitled Pułaski at Savannah by John Lewis Brown.

358. Manning, Clarence A. SOLDIER OF LIBERTY: CASIMIR PUŁASKI. New York: Philosophical Library, 1945. 304p. 46-2998.

A biographical account written for popular reading public. No documentation or bibliographical references. Portrait of Pułaski on frontispiece.

RADZIWIŁŁ FAMILY

359. Nowakowski, Tadeusz. THE RADZIWIŁŁS: THE SOCIAL HISTORY OF A GREAT EUROPEAN FAMILY, trans. by E.B. Garside. New York: Delacorte Press, 1974. 325p. 74-692.

The history of the Radziwiłł family complete with illustrations of some of the illustrious members, a genealogical table of the Radziwiłł family, some dates in Polish history and a list of names. No documentation.

## MICHAEL RADZIWIŁŁ, PRINCE, 1907–

360. Radziwiłł, Michael, prince. ONE OF THE RADZIWIŁŁS. London: John Murray, 1971. 221p. 71-851783.

    A brief description of the Radziwiłł family is followed by an autobiography of the author from his birth in 1907 to his departure from Poland in 1946. Illustrations. Portraits. Maps.

## JÓZEF HIERONIM RETINGER, 1888–1860

361. Retinger, Joseph H. JOSEPH RETINGER: MEMOIRS OF AN EMINENCE GRISE, ed. by John Pomian. London: Chatto and Windus, 1972. 265p. 72-183688.

    An autobiography heavily weighed in favor of the subject's activities as a diplomat. Illustrations. Portraits.

## WŁADYSŁAW STANISŁAW REYMONT, 1867–1925

362. Krzyżanowski, Jerzy R. WŁADYSŁAW STANISŁAW REYMONT. New York: Twayne Publishers, Inc., 1972. 169p. 72-187632.

    Survey of Reymont's life, particularly his literary achievements. A discussion of Reymont's major works. Contains a list of critical works in English. Bibliography, pp. 163-165.

## HALINA RODZINSKA, 1904–

363. Rodzinska, Halina. OUR TWO LIVES. New York: Charles Scribner's Sons, 1976. 403p. 75-37519.

    Recollections of twenty-five years of marriage. Story covers period from her meeting with Mr. Rodzinski in 1932 through the years of his rising to fame in America. Contains a list of "Arthur Rodzinski on records," pp. 389-391. Illustrations. Portraits.

*Special Works*

RODZINSKI, ARTHUR, 1894-1958

\* Rodzinska, Halina. OUR TWO LIVES. Cited above as item 363.

WILLIAM J. ROSE, 1885-1968

364. Rose, William J. THE POLISH MEMOIRS OF WILLIAM ROSE, ed. by Daniel Stone. Toronto: University of Toronto Press, 1975. 248p. 74-79986.

Contains a biographical sketch of Mr. Rose, eight chapters on Mr. Rose's sojourn in Poland directly after World War I and, time spent at the University of London School of Slavonic Studies. Portraits.

TADEUSZ RÓŻEWICZ, 1921-

365. Vogler, Henryk. RÓŻEWICZ, trans. by Marsha Brochewicz. Warszawa: Author's Agency, 1972. 49p.

Biographical sketch of Różewicz and an evaluation of his principal works. Particularly valuable are the bibliographies, pp. 42-49. Illustrations.

MOTHER MARY FRANCES SIEDLISKA, 1842-1902

366. Burton, Katherine K. WHERE THERE IS LOVE: THE LIFE OF MOTHER MARY FRANCES SIEDLISKA OF JESUS THE GOOD SHEPHERD. New York: P.J. Kenedy and Sons, 1951. 200p. 51-14256.

Biographical sketch of the foundress of the Sisters of the Holy Family of Nazareth. Contains portraits of the foundress and her successor, Mother Mary Lauretta. It also serves as an historical sketch of the congregation. Illustrations.

367. Ricciardi, Antonio. HIS WILL ALONE: THE LIFE OF MOTHER MARY OF JESUS THE GOOD SHEPHERD, trans. by Regis N. Barwig. Oshkosh, Wisc.: Castle-Pierce Press, 1971. 453p. OL: BX4705.S624R5.

Complete biography of the foundress of the Sisters of the Holy Family of Nazareth. Contains a biographical synopsis. Illustrations. Portraits. Bibliography, pp. xxvi-xxviii.

## HENRYK SIENKIEWICZ, 1846-1916

368. Gardner, Monica M. THE PATRIOT NOVELIST OF POLAND: HENRYK SIENKIEWICZ. New York: E.P. Dutton, 1926. 281p. 27-13972.

    Book aims "at giving the reader some idea of the finest of Sienkiewicz's novels and short stories, with such references to the conditions under which he wrote them and the intentions which underlie them as are necessary to throw light on the character of their work." Individual chapters devoted to the more prominent works. Portrait of Sienkiewicz in frontispiece.

369. Giergielewicz, Mieczysław. HENRYK SIENKIEWICZ. New York: Twayne Publishers, Inc., 1968. 192p. 68-24311.

    More a work of criticism than a biography in order to put Sienkiewicz and his work in historical perspective. Chronology 1846-1955, pp. 17-19. Bibliography, pp. 177-185.

370. Lednicki, Wacław. HENRYK SIENKIEWICZ: A RETROSPECTIVE SYNTHESIS. s'Gravenhage: Mouton, 1960. 81p. 76-206120.

    A short biography with bibliographical notes. Chronological list of Sienkiewicz's main works in order of the date of publication. Comments on the writer as man and as writer. Illustrations. Portraits.

## WŁADYSŁAW EUGENIUSZ SIKORSKI, 1881-1943

371. Irving, David J.C. ACCIDENT: THE DEATH OF GENERAL SIKORSKI. London: William Kimber, 1967. 231p. 67-111277.

    The story by an English observer about the events surrounding the fatal airplane crash which claimed the life of General Władysław Sikorski. Numerous illustrations. Well-documented to suggest that the crash was more than just an accident. Maps. Notes and Sources, pp. 195-231.

*Special Works*

## PIÓTR SKARGA, 1536-1612

372. Bolek, Francis. THE LIFE OF FATHER SKARGA. Buffalo, N.Y.: The Riverside Press of Buffalo, Inc., 1943. 67p. 43-16722.

    A reverent, brief account of the life of Piótr Skarga, S.J. designed "to see Father Skarga's name in the United States." Many illustrations. Portraits. Bibliography, pp. 65-68.

## JULIUSZ SŁOWACKI, 1804-1849

373. Treugutt, Stefan. JULIUSZ SŁOWACKI: ROMANTIC POET. Warszawa: Polonia Publishing House, 1959. 132p. OL: 891.525T726.

    A descriptive biography with many black-and-white illustrations, facsimiles of Słowacki's work, and a list of some of his works translated into English. Portraits.

## JAN III SOBIESKI, KING OF POLAND, 1629-1696

374. Laskowski, Otton. SOBIESKI, KING OF POLAND, trans. by F.C. Anstruther. Glasgow: Polish Library, 1944. 237p. MiU: DK431.L343.

    Originally published in Polish. An up-to-date biography. Illustrations. Portraits. Maps. Bibliography, pp. 233-236.

375. Palmer, Alicia T. AUTHENTIC MEMOIRS OF THE LIFE OF JOHN SOBIESKI, KING OF POLAND. London: Longmans and Co., 1815. 303p. 5-6819.

    Subtitle reads, "illustrative of the inherent errors in the former constitution of that kingdom, which, though arrested for a time by the genius of a hero and a patriot, gradually paved the way to its downfall." Not really the actual memoirs but instead a narrative of the life of Jan Sobieski. One engraved portrait.

## JOHN SOBIESKI, 1842-

376. Sobieski, John. THE LIFE-STORY AND PERSONAL REMINISCENCES OF COL. JOHN SOBIESKI. Shelbyville, Ill.: J.L. Douthit and Son, Publishers, 1900. 384p. 0-3379.

Author was a lineal descendent of King John III, of Poland. Autobiography. Illustrations. Portraits.

ROMUALD SPASOWSKI, 1920-

377. Spasowski, Romuald. THE LIBERATION OF ONE. New York: Harcourt, Brace, Jovanovich, 1986. 687p. 85-24899.

An autobiography of the former Ambassador of Poland to the United States who defected in 1981, shortly after the imposition of martial law in Poland. In this autobiography, the author also presents "a history of the birth and growth of Communism in Poland." Illustrations. Portraits. Maps.

SAINT STANISŁAW, BISHOP OF KRAKÓW, 1030-1079

378. SAINT STANISŁAW: BISHOP OF KRAKÓW, IN COMMEMORATION OF THE 900TH ANNIVERSARY OF HIS MARTYRDOM IN 1079, ed. by Doyce B. Nunis, Jr. Santa Barbara, Calif.: Saint Stanisław Publications Committee, 1979. 83p. 79-65592.

A festschrift. Several articles written about Saint Stanisław. Illustrations. Portraits.

SAINT STANISŁAW KOSTKA, 1550-1568

379. Kane, William T. FOR GREATER THINGS: THE STORY OF SAINT STANISLAUS KOSTKA. St. Louis: B. Herder Book Co., 1915. 99p. 15-22696.

Although biographical, it can also serve as an inspirational work. Portraits.

380. Kerns, Joseph E. PORTRAIT OF A CHAMPION: A LIFE OF ST. STANLEY KOSTKA. Westminster, Md.: Newman Press, 1957. 278p. 57-8613.

Author refers to his work as a "portrait" of the life of St. Stanisław Kostka. Biography based on reliable sources. Bibliography, pp. 269-272.

381. Sigismund, brother. THE LAD WHO HIKED TO HEAVEN, A STORY OF ST. STANISLAUS KOSTKA, S.J. Notre Dame, Ind.: Dujarie Press, 1945. 91p. 46-12027.

*Special Works*

An undocumented biographical sketch for young readers.

STEFAN STARZYŃSKI, 1893-1943

382. Konwinski, Norbert. "THE MAYOR." Posen, Michigan: Diversified Enterprises, 1978. 153p. 78-52637.

Life story of the mayor of Warszawa at the time of the invasion of Poland in 1939. Also a history of the city. The narrative ends with the imprisonment of the mayor on October 27, 1939. Numerous illustrations, many of the destruction of the city in 1939. Portraits. Maps.

LEOPOLD STOKOWSKI, 1882-1977

383. Robinson, Paul. STOKOWSKI. New York: Vanguard Press, 1977. 154p.

A full-length study of Stokowski's life and work. Illustrations. Portraits. Discography, pp. 123-152.

KAROL SZYMANOWSKI, 1882-1937

384. Bronowicz-Chylińska, Teresa. SZYMANOWSKI, trans. by A.T. Jordan. New York: Twayne Publishers, 1973. 224p. 78-33360.

An album containing "a documentary collection of pictures and memorabilia." An attempt "to arrange the material as to evoke a vision of the people and things around Szymanowski." Contains list of compositions, pp. 211-214 and a list of recorded works, pp. 215-221. Illustrations. Portraits. Sources, pp. 207-209.

385. Maciejewski, B.M. KAROL SZYMANOWSKI: HIS LIFE AND MUSIC. London: Poets and Painters' Press, 1967. 147p. 67-86858 LMN.

First book about Szymanowski in English. Brief account of Szymanowski's life and work. Includes catalogue of Szymanowski's works and a discography. Also, a calendar of his life and work. Illustrations. Portraits. Bibliography, pp. 133-134.

MICHAŁ TARNOWSKI, 1895-

386. Tarnowski, Michał. POLISH PORTRAIT: AN AUTOBIOGRAPHY. New York: The Third Press-Joseph Okpaku Publishing Co., Inc., 1972. 224p. 72-80187.

   A personal narrative in an autobiographical form about the author and his family.

KACPER TOCHMAN, 1796-1880

\* Grzelonski, Bogdan. POLES IN THE UNITED STATES OF AMERICA, 1776-1865. Cited below as item 1248.

MARIA ANGELA TRUSZKOWSKA, 1825-1899

387. Cegielka, Francis A. THE PIERCED HEART: THE LIFE OF MOTHER MARY ANGELA TRUSZKOWSKA, FOUNDRESS OF THE CONGREGATION OF THE SISTERS OF ST. FELIX, FELICIAN SISTERS. Milwaukee, Wisc.: Bruce Publishing Co., 1955. 76p. 55-3134.

   General statistics of the congregation in 1955, p. 69. Bibliography, pp. 70-71. Portraits. Biographee was the foundress of the Congregation of Sisters of St. Felix, Felician Sisters.

JAN TYSSOWSKI, 1811-1857

388. Rutkowska, Neomisia, sister. JOHN TYSSOWSKI. Chicago: Polish Roman Catholic Union, 1943. 80p. 43-17846.

   Brief biographical sketch of the life of John Tyssowski. Illustrations. Portraits.

LECH WAŁESA, 1943-

\* Dobbes, Michael. POLAND: SOLIDARITY: WAŁESA. Cited below as item 1523.

MARIA ŁACZYNSKA WALEWSKA, 1789-1817

389. Ornano, Philippe Antoine, comte d'. LIFE AND LOVES OF MARIE WALEWSKA. London: Hutchinson and Co., Ltd., 1934. 287p. 35-16294.

   Biography of Marie Walewska. Contains portraits of Marie and a picture of her son by Napoleon and the three grandchildren. Illustrations.

*Special Works* 91

GANNA WALSKA, 1893-

390. Walska, Ganna. ALWAYS ROOM AT THE TOP. New York: Richard R. Smith, 1943. 504p. 43-13487.

"An autobiography which is something more than the story of a Polish soprano who married two American millionaires. It also offers detailed, documentary evidence of experiences living in New York, London and Paris." BOOK REVIEW DIGEST, 1943.

STANISŁAW IGNACY WITKIEWICZ, 1885-1939

391. Gerould, Daniel C. WITKACY: STANISŁAW IGNACY WITKIEWICZ AS AN IMAGINATIVE WRITER. Seattle: University of Washington Press, 1981. 362p. 79-3872.

More than just a biography, the author also presents Witkiewicz's formation as an artist and a chronological discussion of his major plays and novels. The first full-length critical study of Witkiewicz's works.

JÓZEF WITTLIN, 1896-

392. Yurieff, Zoya. JOSEPH WITTLIN. New York: Twayne Publishers, Inc., 1973. 175p. 70-186716.

Brief biographical sketch. Chronology of Wittlin's life. Extensive critique of his SALT OF THE EARTH. Appendix contains many of Wittlin's poems in English translation. Selected bibliography, pp. 164-169.

STANISŁAW WYŚPIAŃSKI, 1869-1907

393. Zimmer, Szczepan K. STANISŁAW WYŚPIAŃSKI, A BIOGRAPHICAL SKETCH, trans. by Halina Zimmer. Essen, West Gy.: Dr. Leopold Sanicki, 1959. 92p. 59-35734.

A brief biography written marking the fiftieth anniversary of Wyśpiański's death in 1957. Contains black-and-white reproductions of many of his paintings. Portraits.

STEFAN CARDINAL WYSZYŃSKI, 1901-1981

394. Micewski, Andrzej. CARDINAL WYSZYŃSKI: A BIOGRAPHY, trans. by William R. Brand and Catarzyna M. Brand.

New York: Harcourt, Brace, Jovanovich, 1984. 474p. 84-4683.

A sympathetic biography and a "major contribution by a native Polish journalist." The work was originally written in Polish and published in Poland under the title, KARDYNAŁ WYSZYŃSKI, PRYMAS I MĄŻ STANIE. Illustrations. Portraits.

395. Wyszyński, Stefan, Cardinal. THE DEEDS OF FAITH, selected and translated by Alexander T. Jordan. New York: Harper and Row, 1966. 187p. 66-20794.

Although Cardinal Wyszyński's sermons and addresses collected here are primarily of a spiritual nature, they nevertheless provide "an authentic portrait of the life and time of the cardinal." Illustrations. Portraits.

CARL M. YASTRZEMSKI, 1939-

396. Yastrzemski, Carl. YAZ, with Al Hirshberg. New York: Viking Press, 1968. 183p. 68-18115.

Covers boyhood as a potato farmer, family life, years at Notre Dame, courtship and marriage and his outstanding baseball career. Illustrations. Portraits.

ANNA YEZIERSKA, 1885-1970

397. Yezierska, Anzia. RED RIBBON ON A WHITE HORSE. New York: Scribner's Sons, 1950. 220p. 50-9574.

Autobiography of Andzia Jezierska, "an immigrant girl from Poland, reared in poverty in New York."

MARIE ELIZABETH ZAKRZEWSKA, 1829-1902

398. Zakrzewska, Maria. A WOMAN'S QUEST, ed. by Agnes C. Victor. New York: Arno Press, 1972. 72-2630.

"Earlier chapters are autobiographical and most of them were written in the form of a letter to Miss Mary L. Booth of New York." Remainder is biographical. Portraits. A reprint of the 1924 book published in New York by Appleton and Company.

## KORCZAK ŻIÓŁKOWSKI, 1908-1982

399. Swastek, Joseph. KORCZAK ŻIÓŁKOWSKI: MOUNTAIN CARVER. Detroit: The Conventual Press, 1950. 28p.

Brief biographical sketch of the Pole who carved the heads of the four U.S. Presidents on Mt. Rushmore. Illustrations.

## WOJCIECH ŻUKROWSKI, 1916-

400. Bartelski, Lesław M. ŻUKROWSKI, trans. by Marsha Brochewicz. Warszawa: Author's Agency, 1972. 56p.

Biographical sketch and evaluation of principal works. Of particular value are bibliographies: pp. 53-54, major works of W. Żukrowski; pp. 55-57, translations into various languages of his works. Illustrations. Portraits.

## Birds

401. Tomiałajc, Ludwik. BIRDS OF POLAND: A LIST OF SPECIES AND THEIR DISTRIBUTION. Warszawa: Foreign Scientific Publications Department of the National Center for Scientific, Technical and Economic Information, 1976. 253p. 76-602804.

An attempt to determine the composition of the avifauna within the present borders of Poland. It is also a history of avifauna in Poland from 1800 to 1970. Lists species in systematic order. Maps. Bibliography, pp. 202-241.

402. Wdowinski, Zdzisław. AMIDST FORESTS AND LAKES, trans. by Maria Paczyński. Warszawa: Wydawnictwo "Sport i Turystyka," 1955. 166p. 56-22610.

Author's adventures in the Masurian Lake District and unforgettable impressions thereof. Several months a member of the ornithological expedition organized for the purpose of ringing birds. Mainly photographs of nature.

## Botany

403. Szafer, Władysław, ed. THE VEGETATION OF POLAND, trans. by Witold H. Paryski; illustrations prepared by M. Lańcucka-Srodoniowa. New York: Oxford University Press, 1966. 738p. 63-17171.

    Contents: Historical outline of the development of plant geography in Poland by Władysław Szafer. Factors affecting the geographical distribution of plants in Poland by Anna Medwecka-Kornaś. Influences of man and his economic activities on the vegetation of Poland by Jan Kornaś. Floristic statistics and the elements of the Polish flora, by Stanisława Pawłowska. Review of terrestrial and freshwater plant communities by Bogumił Pawłowski et al. The vegetation of the Polish Baltic by Anna Medwecka-Korna and Jan Kornaś. Outlines of the historical development of the vegetation of Poland in the late-glacial and post-glacial periods by Andrzej Srodoń. Role of cultivated plants in the historical development of material culture in Poland by Aniela Kozłowska. Foundations of a globotanical division of Poland, by Władysław Szafer. Illustrations. Maps. Portraits.

## Boundaries

404. Arski, Stefan. THE NEW POLISH-GERMAN BORDER: SAFEGUARD OF PEACE. Washington, D.C.: Polish Embassy, 1947. 63p. 47-5772.

    Purpose of book is "to present to the American reader the problem of the Polish-German frontier." A defense at time of writing of the revised western boundaries by a Polish journalist and economist. Many black-and-white illustrations. Maps.

405. Askenazy, Szymon. DANTZIG AND POLAND, trans. by William J. Rose. London: George Allen and Unwin, Ltd., 1921. 132p. 21-18960.

    Reminiscences of Gdańsk's (Danzig's) past "intended to foreshadow the future of the city in a restored union with the restored Polish Republic."

## Special Works

406. Bagiński, Henryk. POLAND AND THE BALTIC: THE PROBLEM OF POLAND'S ACCESS TO THE SEA, trans. by Peter Jordan. London: Oliver and Boyd, 1942. 211p. 42-50883.

    Particularly noteworthy is mapwork including harbors of "Gdynia, Danzig, Stettin, Konigsberg, Memel, Libau, Windau and Riga." Also valuable tables. Bibliographies at the end of each of three parts.

407. Bagiński, Henryk. POLAND'S FREEDOM OF THE SEA, foreword by Marian Kukiel, trans. by Peter Jordan. Kirkcaldy, Scotland: Allen Lithographic Co., Ltd., 1942. 137p. 43-967.

    Contains many valuable photographs of Polish naval vessels. Several maps. Author is Polish officer. Written "to consolidate in the mind of the nation the knowledge that Poland must stand firm on the Baltic coast, hold it without thought or surrender and build its future on the sea." Bibliography, pp. 107-129.

408. Bilainkin, George. WITHIN TWO YEARS, BEING THE NARRATIVE OF A JOURNEY TO THE POLISH CORRIDOR, THE TINDER BOX OF EUROPE. London: Sampson, Low, Marston and Co., Ltd., 1934. 187p. 35-9713.

    Author covered Polish Corridor and Gdańsk (Danzig) in a journey made in 1933. These are his impressions. Attempts to show how area is a potentially dangerous area at the time. Illustrations are photographs of areas he saw plus two portraits. Narrative based upon interviews. Maps.

409. Bużiński, Józef. THE ROLE OF OPOLE SILESIA IN THE POLISH PEOPLE'S REPUBLIC, trans. by Anna Monkiewicz, et al. Opole: Instytut Sląski w Opole, 1962. 45p. 66-6703.

    An evaluation of the role of the region to Poland. Brief historical sketch assuming area "Polish" territory from an historical viewpoint. Surveys development of region from 1945-1961. Illustrations.

410. Donald, Robert. THE POLISH CORRIDOR AND THE CONSEQUENCES. London: Thornton Butterworth, Ltd., 1929. 301p. 29-20604.

An English account of the "Polish Corridor Question:" how it emerged and what problems exist. Author breaks the question into an historical background, then he discusses Upper Silesia separately, minority problems, the consequences and the future. Nine maps. Several black-and-white illustrations.

411. Drożdzyński, Aleksander. OBERLANDER: A STUDY IN GERMAN EAST POLICIES, by A. Drożdzyński and Jan Zaborowski. Poznań: Wydawnictwo Zachodnie, 1960. 324p. 61-24552.

    A Polish rebuttal to claims made by Dr. Oberlander in the Federal Republic of West Germany for the regained western territories. Most of documents amassed to support Oberlander's OSTPOLITIK. Illustrations. Sources, pp. 9-11.

412. Drzewieniecki, Walter M. THE GERMAN-POLISH FRONTIER. Chicago: Polish Western Association of America, 1959. 166p. 59-14336.

    Investigates in detail the course of events across the Polish-German frontier which led to the separation of the Germans from Polish populations. It concludes with observations upon the wider significance of this process. Contains many illustrations of the "new Polish Western Territories." Maps. Selected bibliography, pp. 155-160.

413. Feldman, Józef. POLISH-GERMAN ANTAGONISM IN HISTORY. Toruń: Baltic Institute, 1935. 80p. 37-14910.

    Brief discussion of the history of the age-old struggle between Germany and Poland from a Polish viewpoint. Maps. Bibliography, p. 4.

414. Fuchs, Werner, ed. POLAND'S POLICY OF EXPANSION AS REVEALED BY POLISH TESTIMONIES. Berlin: Deutscher-Ostmarken Verein, 1932. 44p. 73-238348.

    American-British edition of extracts from DER NEUE POLENSPIEGEL by Robert Sherwood Allan. Anti-Polish documents selected to illustrate unreasonableness of Polish demands.

Special Works 97

415. Giertych, Jędrzej. POLAND AND GERMANY: A REPLY TO
CONGRESSMAN B. CARROLL REECE OF TENNESSEE. London:
Author, 1958. 158p. 59-161.

A defense, in the form of a lengthy reply, to certain
remarks made concerning the territories taken from
Germany by Poland or regained by Poland in 1945. Reply
considers historical claims by Poland to these territories.

\* Grabski, Stanislaw. THE POLISH-SOVIET FRONTIER.
Cited below as item 636.

416. Hamel, Joost van. DANZIG AND THE POLISH PROBLEM. New
York: Carnegie Endowment for International Peace,
1933. 33p. 33-7999.

Author was High Commissioner of the League of Nations
in Gdańsk (Danzig) from 1925. Discussion of Gdańsk
(Danzig) and German-Polish relations as author
appraised them as a result of his tenure in Gdańsk
(Danzig).

417. Hamilton, F.E. POLAND'S WESTERN AND NORTHERN TERRI-
TORIES. London: Oxford University Press, 1975.
48p. 75-313256.

Written by a geographer as part of a series identified arbitrarily as "Problem Regions of Europe" describing and analyzing the problem area in Polish
geography: the so-called western territories. Illustrations. Maps.

418. Hansen, Ernst R.B. POLAND'S WESTWARD TREND; with a
foreword by August Muller. London: George Allen
and Unwin, Ltd., 1928. 92p. 29-7226.

The opposite position to the DRANG NACH OSTEN by an
English writer. An apologia for the DRANG or a sharp
criticism of Polish westward movement specifically
after World War I and how it affected a region for over
a century part of the German Empire.

419. Hutchison, Graham S. SILESIA REVISITED, 1929. London:
Simpkin Marshall, Ltd., 1929. 111p. 41-39671.

An examination of the problems arising from the
plebiscite and the partition and the relation between

the British coal problem and Silesia. Illustrations. Portraits. Maps.

420. Jordan Zbigniew A. ODER-NEISSE LINE: A STUDY OF THE POLITICAL, ECONOMIC AND EUROPEAN SIGNIFICANCE OF POLAND'S WESTERN FRONTIER. London: Polish Freedom Movement "Independence and Democracy," 1952. 141p. 54-18539.

Aim of the book is to expound the constructive and European aspect of the problem of the Oder-Neisse frontier which hitherto had been given the character of a purely local Polish-German conflict or one of the elements of the Soviet political strategy in its cold war against the West. Prepared outside Poland by emigré Poles. Maps. Bibliographical footnotes.

421. Kaeckenbeeck, Georges S.F.C. THE INTERNATIONAL EXPERIMENT OF UPPER SILESIA: A STUDY IN THE WORKING OF THE UPPER SILESIAN SETTLEMENT, 1922-1937. London: Oxford University Press, 1942. 859p. A43-561.

The author was, from 1922 to 1937, president of the Arbitral Tribunal of Upper Silesia. He has comprehensively and exhaustively recorded the history of this settlement. Documents relative to this question included. Maps.

422. Kaltenbach, Frederick W. SELF-DETERMINATION, 1919: A STUDY IN FRONTIER-MAKING BETWEEN GERMANY AND POLAND. London: Jarrolds Publishers, 1938. 150p. SD40-73.

Author examines the nationality problems of the prewar era, particularly those in the Polish Corridor and Upper Silesia. A large part of the study deals with the interpretation of the principle of self-determination by the Peace Conference, and with the part played by this principle in the delimitation of the frontier between Germany and Poland. Maps. Bibliography, pp. 143-146.

423. Kimmich, Christoph M. THE FREE CITY: DANZIG AND GERMAN FOREIGN POLICY, 1919-1934. New Haven, Conn.: Yale University Press, 1968. 196p. 68-27758.

Purpose of this book is to describe and interpret the stages of territorial revisionism in the Weimar Republic as it affected recovery of the eastern territories--West Prussia, Upper Silesia and Gdańsk (Danzig). Throughout, German spelling of place-names used. Maps on lining papers. Bibliography, pp. 167-187.

424. Kirkien, Leszek. RUSSIA, POLAND AND THE CURZON LINE. Duns, Scotland: Caldra House, Ltd., 1944. 62p. 44-47457.

Present book was written to enable the reader to judge for himself how far the resolutions of the Conferences at Teheran and Yalta accord with the ethnical, cultural and economic realities in the disputed areas of eastern Poland. Maps.

425. Klafkowski, Alfons. THE POLISH-GERMAN FRONTIER AFTER WORLD WAR II, trans. by Edward Rothert. Poznań: Wydawnictwo Poznańskie, 1972. 125p. MiU: DK418.5.G3K623.

Covers legal foundation of the final settlement of the Polish-German frontier; Polish-German frontier as a foundation of the European territorial system; recovered territories within the organism of the Polish state; guarantees of the security of the Polish-German frontier in the system of alliances concluded by Poland; and, the Potsdam agreement as a substitute for a peace treaty with Germany.

426. Korniłowicz, Maria ed. WESTERN AND NORTHERN POLAND: HISTORICAL OUTLINE, NATIONALITY PROBLEMS, LEGAL ASPECT, NEW SOCIETY, ECONOMIC SURVEY. Poznań: Zachodnia Agencja Prasowa, 1962. 534p. 65-76334.

This book contains basic information relating to the western and northern territories of Poland, their past and present, the analysis of the social and economic processes which shape the present day life of these territories and outlines simultaneously the prospects of further development of these territories as an organic component part of Poland. Illustrations. Maps. Bibliographical references included in "Notes," pp. 351-387.

427. Kruszewski, Z.A. THE ODER-NEISSE BOUNDARY AND POLAND'S MODERNIZATION. New York: F. Praeger Publishers, 1972. 285p. 74-159411.

Study analyzes the underlying causes of Poland's rapid modernization. It is concerned especially with the bases for the process of modernization which can be traced largely to problems associated with the 1945 changes in both the eastern and western borders of Poland. Maps. Bibliography, pp. 231-245.

428. Kudlicki, Stanisław. UPPER SILESIA. London: Polish Research Centre, 1944. 35p. 45-21319.

    Brief sketch of the place of Silesia in Poland's history--from the Polish point of view. Contains a map of Upper Silesia and Environs and table showing "Results of the 1910 Census and 1921 Plebiscite" in the Upper Silesian districts.

429. Lachs, Manfred. THE POLISH-GERMAN FRONTIER: LAW, LIFE AND LOGIC OF HISTORY. Warszawa: Polish Scientific Publishers, 1964. 80p. 65-71365.

    Brief resumé and defense of the new western frontiers. Bibliography, pp. 75-80.

430. Machray, Robert. EAST PRUSSIA: MENACE TO POLAND AND PEACE. Chicago: American Polish Council, 1943. 110p. 44-3892.

    Author proposes that East Prussia become part of recreated Poland after the Second World War and marshals evidence to support this position, historically and strategically. Page 93 contains map showing "German administrative Division of East Prussia after 1939" where three border regions around Memel, Suwałki and Ciechanów were incorporated into East Prussia.

431. Martel, Rene. THE EASTERN FRONTIERS OF GERMANY. London: Williams and Norgate, Ltd., 1930. 199p. 31-8690.

    Purpose of this book is to enlighten public opinion in all countries. Documentation contained in notes, pp. 185-190. Divided into historical retrospect and after Versailles. Discusses all major viewpoints, i.e. German, Polish, French. Maps. Bibliography, pp. 191-196.

432. Matuszewski, Ignacy. WHAT POLAND WANTS. New York: National Committee of Americans of Polish Descent, 1942. 35p. 43-14346.

*Special Works*  101

Brief summary of the undeniable rights of Poland. This refers to its territirial aspirations.

433. Morrow, Ian F.D. THE PEACE SETTLEMENT IN THE GERMAN-POLISH BORDERLANDS. London: Oxford University Press, 1936. 558p. 35-1244.

    A study of conditions today in the pre-war Prussian provinces of East and West Prussia, being a truly exhaustive scholarly account of the German-Polish problem covering the territories in question put in historical perspective. Contains thorough documentation. Maps. Bibliography, pp. 519-526.

434. Ocioszyński, Tadeusz. POLAND ON THE BALTIC, trans. by Krystyna Cękalska and Eugeniusz Lepa. Warszawa: Polonia Publishing House, 1960. 167p. 67-57332.

    Includes an historical outline of "Poland's ties with the Baltic, Poland's return to the coast after World War I, Poland's second return to the coast after World War II, Polish maritime achievements during 1945-1959, the development of Poland's seacoast and a summary." Illustrations. Maps.

435. Osborne, Arthur. LANDOWNERSHIP AND POPULATION IN POMERANIA. Toruń: Baltic Institute, 1934. 47p. MiU: D965.A2B208.

    Discussion of area given to Poland after World War I subsequently referred to as the Polish Corridor and a defense of Polish position from "official Polish statistics and on studies of eminent scholars on the question." Maps. Bibliography, p. 6.

436. Osborne, Sidney. THE UPPER SILESIAN QUESTION AND GERMANY'S COAL PROBLEM. London: George Allen and Unwin, Ltd., 1920. 285p. 21-5306.

    Author presents a pro-German defense of the loss of Upper Silesia with its coal resources to the new Polish state: "... the facts that bear upon the question of the natural, political and economic unity of Upper Silesia ... and the problem of Germany's coal production." Bibliography, pp. 160-162.

437. Poliakoff, Vladimir. A BULWARK OF DEMOCRACY, by Augur, pseud. New York: D. Appleton and Comapny, 1931. 207p. 32-3274.

 Deals with Poznań province. An apologia for this area having been incorporated as part of interwar Poland. Maps.

438. Poliakoff, Vladimir. EAGLES BLACK AND WHITE, THE FIGHT FOR THE SEA, by Augur, pseud. New York: D. Appleton and Company, 1929. 205p. 29-20661.

 "This book is written to present the case not of Poland alone, but of Germany and Poland together, as equal nations among equals." Contains an appendix entitled, KARL MARX ON THE POLISH QUESTION. Portrait of author. Maps.

439. Poliakoff, Vladimir. THE "POLISH CORRIDOR." London: Author, 1934. 32p. 35-7581.

 Summary of investigation of the German-Polish dispute with regard to the so-called Polish Corridor. Maps.

440. Polish Research Centre. London. THE BRIDGEHEAD OF EAST PRUSSIA. Edinburgh: Polish Books Depot, 1944. 44p. A44-2009.

 An historical sketch of East Prussia. Colored maps by Dr. Ludwik Grodzicki. Bibliographical footnotes.

441. Polish Research Centre. London. GERMAN WITHDRAWAL IN THE EAST: A STUDY IN VITAL GERMAN AND POLISH STA- TISTICS. London: Polish Research Centre, n.d. 50p. 42-14558.

 A study of the historical attempts by the Germans to possess persons and territory which have remained stub- bornly Polish for over a thousand years. Contains tables and charts. Includes bibliographies.

442. POLISH WESTERN TERRITORIES, trans. by Wanda Libicka. Poznań: Instytut Zachodni, 1959. 267p. A59-8094.

 A series of essays by Polish authors on the Western territories gained from Germany after World War II.

## Special Works

Subjects covered are geography, history, legal status, demographic changes and prospects for the region. Maps. Bibliographical notes.

443. Popiołek, Kaźimierz, ed. THE LAST ATTEMPT TO GERMANIZE OPOLE SILESIA, ed. by K. Popiołek and Wacław Sobański. Poznań: Western Press Agency, 1959. 82p. MiU: DD491.S53.P833.

    Contains original texts of German documents and materials bent on a complete suppression of the Polish element in Opole Silesia in the opening period of the Second World War. Maps.

444. Pounds, Norman J.G. POLAND BETWEEN EAST AND WEST. Princeton: Van Nostrand Company, Inc., 1964. 132p. 64-4686.

    Author attempts to prove that the weakness which has led on two occasions to the extinction of the Polish state springs from social and political not geographical considerations. Emphasizes enormous changes in Poland's boundaries during a thousand years and continuity of the spirit of Polish nationalism. Maps. Bibliography, pp. 126-127.

445. Rechowicz, Henryk. WESTERN AND NORTHERN POLAND. Warszawa: Interpress Publishers, 1972. 139p. 73-158302.

    Illustrate these territories' role in present-day Poland and to show the changes that have been wrought in them under Poland's rule. Covers economy, agriculture, education and science, and culture and recreational aspects in these areas. Maps. "Selected reading," pp. 137-139.

446. Shotwell, James T. POLAND AND RUSSIA, 1919-1945, by J.T. Shotwell and Max M. Laserson. New York: Carnegie Endowment for International Peace, 1945. 114p. A45-4954.

    Deals with postwar settlement and political problems of Europe. Main concern is the settlement of Poland's frontier with Russia which had not been stabilized since 1918. A narrative of events rather than an interpretation. Maps. Bibliography, pp. 112-114.

447. Skrzypek, Stanisław. THE PROBLEM OF EASTERN GALICIA. London: Polish Association for the South-Eastern Provinces, 1948. 93p. 50-800.

    Defense of Polish claims to eastern Galicia written in 1944 when restoration of Poland and her eastern boundaries were in question. Describes conditions in eastern Galicia at the outbreak of World War II, i.e. 1939. Maps. Bibliography, pp. 61-64.

448. Smogorzewski, Każimierz M. POLAND, GERMANY AND THE CORRIDOR. London: Williams and Norgate, Ltd., 1930. 163p. 31-7363.

    Brief defense of Polish claims to the Corridor written to offset German propaganda which saw this area as rightfully German in order to link East Prussia to post-World War I Germany. Maps.

449. Smogorzewski, Każimierz M. POLAND'S ACCESS TO THE SEA. London: George Allen and Unwin, Ltd., 1934. 468p. 35-3410.

    An exhaustive account of the Polish claims, mainly historical, to the area of Pomorze. Author recognizes that the Versailles Conference intended that Poland should have access to the Baltic Sea but through an area which linguistically, if not culturally, was Polish. Chapter dealing with the Kaszuby. Maps. Bibliographical notes at the end of each chapter.

450. Sobański, Wacław, ed. WESTERN AND NORTHERN TERRITORIES OF POLAND; DEMOGRAPHIC PROBLEMS. Poznań: Wydawnictwo Zachodnie, 1960. 2v. 61-27267.

    Series of ten essays about the areas and peoples obtained from Germany as a result of World War II. Maps.

451. Super, Donald E. THE BACKGROUND OF POLISH-GERMAN RELATIONS IN CHARTS AND FIGURES. New York: Ellner Company, Publishers, 1932. unpaged. 44-17057.

    Maps, charts and figures dealing almost exclusively with Pomorze and the other sensitive border points with interwar Germany. No documentation. Maps.

*Special Works*

452. Szaz, Zolton M. GERMANY'S EASTERN FRONTIERS; THE PROBLEM OF THE ODER-NEISSE LINE, with a foreword by Harold Zink. Chicago: Henry Regnery Company, 1960. 256p. 60-14059.

    Covers Polish western frontiers, the so-called "Oder-Neisse" boundary, from its role in international affairs, particularly the United States and Britain vis-à-vis the problem of Germany after World War II. Defines territory and people; historical background; wartime; Russian role in creating the Oder-Neisse Line; German attitudes. Bibliography, pp. 223-247.

453. Terry, Sarah M. POLAND'S PLACE IN EUROPE. Princeton, N.J.: Princeton University Press, 1983. 394p. 82-47617.

    A scholarly discussion of the role played by General Sikorski in Polish history and how the western boundary had already been foreseen by the Polish Government-in-Exile back in 1943. Based upon material from Polish archives.

454. TRANSFER OF THE GERMAN POPULATION FROM POLAND: LEGEND AND REALITY. Warszawa: Western Press Agency, 1966. 54p. 67-9636.

    Polish refutation of "West German propaganda" accusing Poland "of crimes committed in connection with the resettlement of the German population from Poland." Illustrations. Map.

455. Wagner, Wolfgang. THE GENESIS OF THE ODER-NEISSE LINE; A STUDY IN THE DIPLOMATIC NEGOTIATIONS DURING WORLD WAR II. Stuttgart: Brentano Verlag, 1957. 168p. A58-4091.

    Distinctively pro-German view of the problem. Author refers to "Polish pressure towards the West." Maps. Bibliography, pp. 156-159.

456. Weinstein, J. UPPER SILESIA; A COUNTRY OF CONTRASTS. Paris: Gebethner and Wolff, 1931. 104p. SD 32-28.

    A Polish defense of Upper Silesia as belonging to Poland. Includes a brief historical sketch of the area of all Silesia. Maps.

457. Wiepert, Friedrich von. THE ODER-NEISSE PROBLEM; TOWARDS FAIR PLAY IN CENTRAL EUROPE. Bonn: Edition Atlantic-Forum, 1964. 163p. 65-5018.

   German point of view on loss of territories to Poland and the attempt to look at this loss objectively recognizing at the same time that many Germans were displaced. A problem is stated and then there follows a discussion of Polish-German relations through the centuries, how the Oder-Neisse line came to be. Illustrations. Portraits. Maps.

458. Wiewióra, Bolesław. POLISH-GERMAN FRONTIERS FROM THE STANDPOINT OF INTERNATIONAL LAW. Poznań: Wydawnictwo Zachodnia, 1959. 2d rev. ed. 224p. 59-46118.

   Originally a doctoral thesis. Author outlined the matters with regard to the frontier between Poland and Germany: Territorial changes after World War II, the Yalta and Potsdam Agreements, transfer of German population, the question of recognition and the peace treaty with Germany. Bibliography, pp. 216-224.

459. Wilder, Jan A. THE POLISH REGAINED PROVINCES; A SURVEY OF A YEAR'S ACHIEVEMENT. London: William Hodge and Company, Ltd., 1948. 109p. 48-26225.

   Covers economic and political aspects of territory acquired from Germany after World War II. Also covers first year of Polish administration of territory. Map.

460. Zachodnia Agencja Prasowa. WESTERN AND NORTHERN TERRITORIES OF POLAND: MARITIME PROBLEMS. Poznań: Wydawnictwo Zachodnia, 1960. 47p. 61-21811.

   Brief discussion of the maritime economy, achievements and development prospects of the shipbuilding industry and Polish sea fishing. Illustrations. Maps.

461. Żółtowski, Adam. BORDER OF EUROPE; A STUDY OF THE POLISH EASTERN PROVINCES. London: Hollis and Carter, 1950. 348p. 51-219.

   History of eastern Poland from 1596 to 1939. Interpretation of this area as Polish based upon historical principles. Includes Russian outlook on this region. Map. Bibliography, pp. 329-333.

Special Works 107

Cities and Towns

GENERAL

462. Adamczewski, Jan. THE TOWNS OF COPERNICUS. Warszawa: Interpress Publishers, 1972. 189p. 74-157795.

Principally illustrations, mostly black-and-white, but some colored of the cities of Toruń, Kraków, Lidzbark, Olsztyn, Frombork, Lubawa, Grudziądz, Elbląg, Pieniężno, Gdańsk.

463. Fisher, Jack C., ed. CITY AND REGIONAL PLANNING IN POLAND. Ithaca, N.Y.: Cornell University Press, 1966. 491p. 65-23997.

Written by Polish authorities and a Polish interpretation of that country's postwar planning process. A compilation of unusually detailed presentations by prominent Polish planners of the inner workings of their organization. Illustrations. Maps. Charts.

464. McBride, Robert M. TOWNS AND PEOPLE OF MODERN POLAND. New York: Robert M. McBride and Co., 1938. 302p. 38-27505.

Extremely valuable retrospective work dealing with interwar Poland. Author describes principal Polish cities including Gdynia, Warszawa, Wilno, Lwów, Kraków, Częstochowa and Poznań. Many fine photographs of scenes from these cities in sepia. Contains an index. Maps.

465. Stolica. POLISH CITIES IN PHOTOGRAPHS. Warszawa: Stolica, 1955. 95p. 56-21805.

Photographs with some textual material which are reprints from the weekly magazine STOLICA. Cities covered are Kraków, Stalinogrod, Wrocław, Poznań, Gdańsk, Białystok, Lublin and Warszawa. City life c. 1955. Maps.

GDAŃSK

466. Fuchs, Karl H. DANZIG--WHAT IS IT ALL ABOUT. n.p., 1939. 55p. 41-14384.

A collection of eight short essays about the critical
position the "Danzig issue" was in the months preceding
the outbreak of war in September, 1939, between Germany
and Poland. Authors are Danzigers. Six black-and-
white illustrations of the city and its people.

467. Gartner, Margarete. comp. DANZIG AND THE CORRIDOR:
WORLD OPINION ON THE TOPIC OF TO-DAY, with a preface
by Albert Brackmann. Berlin: Volk and Reich Verlag,
1939. 72p. A40-1582.

A collection of statements by prominent world statesmen about Gdańsk (Danzig) and the so-called interwar
Polish Corridor. Index to authors precedes collection.

468. Mason, John B. DANZIG DILEMMA; A STUDY IN PEACEMAKING
BY COMPROMISE. Palo Alto, Calif.: Stanford University Press, 1946. 377p. A46-2759.

An objective and scholarly account of Gdańsk (Danzig),
with particular emphasis upon political and economic
problems presented at the Paris Peace Conference and
administrative problems which arose while Gdańsk
(Danzig) was under the protection of the League of
Nations. Many facsimiles of documents. Maps on lining
papers. Bibliography, pp. 308-322.

469. Morison, George H. DANZIG'S YESTERDAY--AND TO-MORROW.
Danzig: Danziger Verlagsgesellschaft, 1932. 62p.
NjP: 16378.653.

An historical sketch of the city of Gdańsk (Danzig)
complete with illustrations in black-and-white of the
principal sites. A defense of the concept of free city
states. List of important dates in the history of
Gdańsk (Danzig), p. 58. Maps.

470. Polish Research Centre. London. POLAND AND DANZIG.
London: Cornwall Press, Ltd., 1942. 32p. 43-8723.

Brief sketch of the question of Gdańsk (Danzig's)
place in Poland's history from a Polish point of view.
Bibliographical footnotes.

GDYNIA

471. Borowik, Józef, ed. GDYNIA, POLAND'S GATEWAY TO THE
SEA. Toruń: Baltic Institute, 1934. 97p. 38-1312.

Covers reason why city was built, description of harbor and installations, commercial development, tourist attractions, general information and addresses. Includes description of Kaszuby region in which city is situated. Illustrations. Maps.

472. Poland. Ministerstwo Przemysłu i Handlu. THE PORT OF GDYNIA, trans. by Arthur Osborne. Gdynia: Ministry of Industry and Commerce, 1936. 54p. 44-45062.

Detailed description of the port of Gdynia and a collection of illustrations and statistical data. Maps.

KRAKÓW

473. Adamczewski, Jan. IN CRACOW, trans. by Christina Cenkalska. Warszawa: Interpress Publishers, 1973. 298p. 75-505361.

Exhaustive history of and description of Kraków and its immediate environs. Includes an historical chronology and a discussion of the royal road, Wawel, Każimierz, Zwierzyniec, University district, Nowa Huta, museums, Lenin in Kraków, theatres in Kraków, etc. Illustrations. Maps.

474. Dużyk, Józef. CRACOW AND ITS UNIVERSITY, by J. Dużyk and Stanisław Salmonowicz. Kraków: Wydawnictwo Artystyczno Graficzne, 1964. 67-59331.

Description of the city of Kraków with particular emphasis on the Jagiellonian University. Illustrations.

475. Hartwig, Edward. CRACOW, trans. by Krystyna Kęplicz. Warszawa: "Sport i Turystyka" Publications, 1964. 2d ed. 65-96686.

Chiefly illustrations, mostly black-and-white, some colored of scenes of Kraków with explanatory notes.

476. Humphrey, Grace. COME WITH ME THROUGH KRAKÓW. Kraków: S.A. Krzyżanowski, 1934. 107p. 34-37036.

More than merely a guide-book, this work describes historically each of the major sites in Kraków as the author saw them c. 1934. Several black-and-white photographs of the principal sites are included.

477. Kupiecki, Edmund. CRACOW: LANDSCAPE AND ARCHITECTURE, trans. by Marek Łatynski. Warszawa: Arkady, 1967. 55p. 72-821.

Almost all black-and-white photographs, both exterior and interior, of buildings and landscapes with identifying captions. Text covers brief history of the city.

478. Lepszy, Leonard. CRACOW, THE ROYAL CAPITAL OF ANCIENT POLAND, ITS HISTORY AND ANTIQUITIES, trans. by Roman Dyboski. London: T.F. Unwin, 1912. 210p. 13-89.

An abridgement of a work commissioned by the Austrian government. Classic work on the history and development of the city. Includes attention to architecture, painting, sculpture and the applied arts in Cracow. Illustrations.

479. Saysse-Tobiczyk, Każimierz. CRACOW. Warszawa: Polonia Publishing House, 1961. 147p. 62-1634.

Mainly illustrations, some colored, which provide a rich historical introduction to the prospective tourist.

LWÓW

480. Bailly, Rose. A CITY FIGHTS FOR FREEDOM: THE RISING OF LWÓW IN 1918-1919; AN EPISODE IN THE HISTORY OF POLAND, trans. by Samuel S.B. Taylor. London: Publishing Committee Leopolis, 1956. 396p. 56-13980.

Numerous illustrations and portraits. Detailed account of the struggles of the city of Lwów towards the end of the Polish Great War to remain. Includes a history of the city, description of the city, many maps and plans of the city. Bibliography, pp. 365-367.

481. Rudnicki, Józef. A PAGE OF POLISH HISTORY: LWÓW, trans. by W.A. Massey. London: Polish Research Centre, 1944. 76p. A44-2190.

History of Lwów with black-and-white photographs of the principal buildings as they looked in the interwar period. Bibliographical footnotes. Scholarly written.

## SZCZECIN

382. Białecki, Tadeusz. SZCZECIN, by T. Białecki et al. Warszawa: Arkady, 1977. OL: DK4800.S9343B53.

Chiefly illustrations, black-and-white, some colored, of the landscape and architecture of the city. Maps.

## WARSZAWA

483. Bartoszewski, Władysław. WARSAW DEATH RING, 1939-1944, trans. by Edward Rothert. Warszawa: Interpress Publishers, 1968. 450p. 77-7668.

First thoroughly documented attempt in Polish historical literature to record the losses suffered by the people of Warszawa in 1939-1945. Concerned chiefly with the main executions of the Polish residents of Warszawa. The tragedy of the Jewish population has been outlined in a special chapter. Contains numerous lists of persons executed. Illustrations. Portraits. Maps. Bibliographical footnotes.

484. Bielecki, Tadeusz. WARSAW AFLAME: THE 1939-1945 YEARS YEARS, by T. Bielecki and Leszek Szymanski. Los Angeles, Calif.: Polamerica Press, 1973. 188p. 73-76000.

Popular history of Warszawa during German occupation divided chronologically into years through 1939-1945. Propagandistic. No documentation. Numerous illustrations. Maps.

485. Braun, Andrzej. THE PAVING STONES OF HELL, trans. by H.C. Stevens. London: Putnam, 1959. 151p. ScU: PG7158.B655.G43.

Novel set in contemporary Warszawa, depicts what happened to Poles who abandoned their Stalinist ideals.

486. Bryan, Julien H. SIEGE. New York: Doubleday Doran Company, 1940. 64p. 40-7614.

Story of Warszawa in September, 1939. Collection of photographs taken by author during the siege. Text of 64 pages by Maurice Hindus.

487. Bryan, Julien H. WARSAW: 1939 SIEGE, 1959 WARSAW REVISITED. Warszawa: Polonia Publishing House, 1960. 177p. 61-46301.

    Comparative study of the people of Warszawa as the author knew them and how they managed to survive. Numerous black-and-white illustrations.

488. Budrewicz, Olgierd. INCREDIBLE WARSAW, trans. by Christina Cenkalska. Warszawa: Interpress Publishers, 1972. 376p. 73-124732.

    Comprehensive, humorous account of all aspects of life in Warszawa: places and events, city districts and city streets and people. It is not intended to be a guidebook; it is merely the author's impressions of the city. Illustrations.

489. Ciborowski, Adolf. WARSAW, A CITY DESTROYED AND REBUILT. Warszawa: Polonia Publishing House, 1964. 322p. 65-4233.

    Extremely detailed picture and map book of Warszawa. Before and after (destruction of 1939-1945) photographs. Of special interest is calendar from January 13, 1945 to 1963. Includes many maps and city plans.

490. Ciborowski, Andrzej. WARSAW REBUILT, by A. Ciborowski and S. Jankowski, trans. by Agnieszka Glinka. Warszawa: Polonia Publishing House, 1962. 137p. 64-67550.

    Concentrates mainly on the destruction and rebuilding of Warszawa. Text followed by numerous before-and-after photographs showing scenes in 1945 juxtaposed with those in 1962.

491. Humphrey, Grace. COME WITH ME THROUGH WARSAW. Warszawa: M. Arct Publishing Co., 1934. 140p. 34-37035.

    More than merely a guidebook, this work describes historically each of the major sites in Warszawa as the author saw them c. 1934. Black-and-white photographs of the principal sites.

*Special Works*

492. Jankowski, Stanisław. WARSAW 1945 AND TODAY, by S. Jankowski and Adolf Giborowski, trans. by Jan Aleksandrowicz. Warszawa: Interpress Publishers, 1971. 119p. 74-173467.

    A series of black-and-white illustrations juxtaposed depicting scenes in 1945, after the city's destruction, and as the same site looked in 1971. Also added colored photographs. Includes a history of the city. Maps.

493. Przypkowski, Tadeusz. WARSAW. Glasgow: Książnica Polska, 1941. 15p. 43-37898.

    Selected photographs of scenes of Warszawa during the interwar period, 1918-1939, preceded by a narrative briefly describing the city.

494. WARSAW. Warszawa: "Polonia" Foreign Languages Publishing House, 1955. unpaged. MiD: 914.38W265.

    Mostly photographs of Warszawa including some reproductions of paintings of Warszawa by Canaletto and others.

495. Wynot, Edward D. WARSAW BETWEEN THE WORLD WARS. New York: Columbia University Press, 1983. 375p. 82-83527.

    History of the city of Warszawa after it was chosen to become the capital of the new Polish state. Emphasizes the main trends and events during the interwar period. Finally, topical examinations of the economy, society, politics, urbanization process, municipal services, and cultural life, are presented. Bibliography, pp. 357-372.

\*   Cohen, Israel. VILNA. Cited below as item 943.

496. Polish Research Centre. London. THE STORY OF WILNO. London: Polish Research Centre, 1944. rev. ed. 30p. 44-33109.

    A brief historical sketch of the city of Wilno. Attempts to prove its essentially Polish character. Contains many black-and-white illustrations of important buildings. Maps.

## Commerce

497. Polska Izba Handlu Zagranicznego. INFORMATION FOR BUSINESSMEN TRADING WITH POLAND. Warszawa: Polish Chamber of Foreign Trade, 1975. 167p. 76-368523.

    Contains concise information and advice concerning trade with Poland presenting the framework and patterns of Poland's foreign trade, its service network, etc. as well as all kinds of useful addresses. Maps.

## Cookery

498. Cantrell, Rose. POLISH COOKING. New York: Crown Publishers, Inc., 1977. 80p. 77-99186.

    The intent of this cookbook is to provide the reader and chef with a cross section of the cuisine found in the finest restaurants in Warszawa and that found on rural farms. Colored full-page illustrations.

499. Culinary Arts Institute. POLISH COOKBOOK. Chicago: Culinary Arts Institute, 1976. 96p. 76-14648.

    Traditional recipes tested for today's kitchens. How to prepare a Polish feast, history of famous Polish foods. Tested menus and recipes. Glossary of Polish food terms. Section also dealing with foods for Easter and Christmas. Illustrations, some in color. Titles of foods given in English and Polish.

500. Czerny, Zofia. POLISH COOKBOOK, trans. by Christina Cęnkalska and May Miller. Warszawa: Panstwowe Wydawnictwo Ekonomiczne, 1975. 494p. 76-383564.

    A Polish cookbook compiled by a native Pole covering her interpretation of contemporary Polish cuisine. Contains many colored illustrations.

501. Lemnis, Maria. OLD POLISH TRADITIONS IN KITCHEN AND AT THE TABLE, by M. Lemnis and Henryk Vitry, trans. by Eliza Lewandowska. Warszawa: Interpress Publishers, 1981. 303p.

    Not only a cookbook but also a "tale where typical Polish recipes are interwoven with a briefly outlined

*Special Works* 115

history of Polish culinary customs." Includes explanations of Polish holiday customs. Illustrations.

502. Ochorowixz-Monatowa, Marja. POLISH COOKERY, trans. and adapted by Jean Karsavina. New York: Crown Publishers, Inc., 1958. 314p. 58-8317.

English version of the basic Uniwersalna Książka Kucharska, (THE UNIVERSAL COOK BOOK), first published by the author in 1911. This work was considered the Bible of Polish cookery. Translator-adapter has chosen only those items usable to an average cook. Omits such items as "Turkey Garnished with Two Dozen Thrushes."

503. Polanie Club. Minneapolis. TREASURED POLISH RECIPES FOR AMERICANS, illus. by Stanley Legun. Minneapolis: Polanie Publishing Company, 1948. 148p. 49-1585.

A cookbook of Polish recipes collected through the years by a group of Polish-American women. Contains a two-page sketch of Polish Christmas customs. Editors state that all recipes are copies of Polish ones published in Poland prior to World War I. Illustrations.

504. Rysia, pseud. OLD WARSAW COOK BOOK. New York: Roy Publishers, 1958. 304p. 56-8468.

Comprehensive coverage of Polish cuisine divided into appetizers, soups, fish, meat, sauces, dairy dishes, mushrooms, vegetables, salads, desserts, cookies, drink drinks, liqueurs and preserves, holiday foods and customs, Christmas and Easter. Illustrations.

505. West, Karen. THE BEST OF POLISH COOKING: RECIPES FOR ENTERTAINING AND SPECIAL OCCASIONS. New York: Hippocrene Books, 1983. 132p.

"Delightful compilation of traditional Polish fare in easy-to-use menu format."

506. Żeranski, Alina. ART OF POLISH COOKERY. Garden City, N.Y.: Doubleday and Company, 1968. 366p. 68-27142.

Polish customs and favorite menus described followed by recipes. Illustrations.

## Culture

507. Gielżyński, Wojciech. CULTURE IN POLAND. Warszawa: Interpress Publishers, 1975. 93p. 80-485107.

Text covers monuments, museums, music, theatres, fine arts, folk culture in Poland, literature, cinema, schooling in the arts, culture in the press, radio and TV; cultural cooperation with foreign countries; organization of cultural activity in Poland. Numerous illustrations, many in color. Portraits.

## Częstochowa

508. THE GLORIES OF CZĘSTOCHOWA AND JASNA GÓRA. Worcester, Mass.: Our Lady of Częstochowa Foundation, 1955. 155p. OL: 232.931.G514.

Originally published in Polish in Poland. History of the picture and miracles associated with the shrine. Translated, edited and compiled by the Polish Roman Catholic clergy of the Diocese of Worcester, Massachusetts.

509. Rozanow, Zofia. THE CULTURAL HERITAGE OF JASNA GÓRA, by Zofia Rozanow and Ewa Smulikowska. Warszawa: Interpress Publishers, 1974. 179p. 76-361479.

Mainly colored photographs of the collection of the major art works of the Monastery of Our Lady of Częstochowa by the two persons assigned to catalog these works. The authors provide an outline of the history of the Monastery and then give information on the most interesting historical heirlooms and works of art accumulated over the centuries in the Monastery collection. Portraits.

## Dance

510. Wolska, Helen. DANCES OF POLAND. New York: Crown Publishers, 1972. 38p. 51-12276.

Description of dances followed by instructions on how to dance the Krakowiak, Mazur, Goralski and Oberek. Illustrations. Maps.

## Decorations of Honor

511. Wesolowski, Zdzisław P. POLISH ORDERS, MEDALS, BADGES
AND INSIGNIA MILITARY AND CIVILIAN, 1705-1985.
Miami: Printing Services, Inc., 1987. 404p.

    Principally illustrations, some in color, of every
    order, cross, medal, regimental breast badge and military insignia issued from the Commonwealth era of the
    Polish-Lithuanian Kingdom of 1705-1794, the Duchy of
    Warsaw, 1807-1813, the Congress Kingdom, 1815-1831, the
    Polish Republic, 1918-1939, the Polish Government-in-
    Exile, 1939-1945, and the Polish People's Republic,
    1943-1985. Material also includes civilian decorations, orders of the Catholic Church and paramilitary
    decorations and insignia. Description includes purpose, date of establishment, size, color of enamels and
    ribbons and number of classes.

## Description and Travel

512. Anderson, Herbert F. WHAT I SAW IN POLAND--1946.
Slough, Eng.: Windsor Press, 1946. 194p. 47-471.

    Based upon diary kept by author. Describes cities
    and towns visited. Impressions of a 57-year-old
    Englishman between January 10, 1946 and April 6, 1946.

513. Appleton, Edward T. YOUR GUIDE TO POLAND. New York:
Funk and Wagnalls, 1968. 263p. 68-18174.

    Informative, practical, friendly, lively travel
    guide. Contains maps of major cities. Includes short
    history of Poland together with information vital to
    the traveler. Illustrations are up-to-date.

514. Baerlein, Henry P.B. NO LONGER POLES APART, with an
introduction by the Polish Ambassador. London:
Longmans, Green and Co., 1936. 37-15776.

    Map of Poland on front and back lining papers. Fourteen illustrations. Account of impressions gained by a
    British traveler in Poland of late middle years in the
    early 1930s.

515. Bajcar, Adam. POLAND, A GUIDEBOOK FOR TOURISTS, trans. by Stanisław Tarnowski. Warszawa: Interpress Publishers, 1972. 226p. 72-170457.

The "official" tourist guide. Includes motoring map of Poland showing the routes. Amply illustrated. Discusses land and people.

516. Boswell, Alexander B. POLAND AND THE POLES. New York: Dodd, Mead and Company, 1919. 313p. 20-26318.

Based upon a study of Poland extending over many years and on personal contact with the Poles during five years residence in the country. Attempt at an unprejudiced account of the Poles and to combat some of the false ideas that were inspired by the enemies of the Polish people. Illustrations. Maps.

517. Boyd, Louise A. POLISH COUNTRYSIDES: PHOTOGRAPHS AND NARRATIVES. New York: American Geographical Society, 1937. 235p. 37-1719.

Part one is a narrative and photographs and maps while the second part is photographs grouped by topics.

518. Brandes, Georg M.C. POLAND; A STUDY OF THE LAND, PEOPLE, AND LITERATURE. New York: Macmillan Company, 1903. 310p. 7-16761.

Observations and appreciations of Poland, its life and culture in a series of impressions, 1885, 1886, 1894 and 1899. Also, a description of the romantic literature of the nineteenth century. Lively and thoughtful foreign evaluation.

519. Bristol, Helen O. AFTER THIRTY YEARS; POLAND REVISITED. Rutland, Vt.: House of Tuttle, 1939. 224p. 39-22130.

Result of a summer visit to Poland. Very intimate account of things remembered. Author's parents of Polish extraction. Contains a glossary of Polish words and phrases including biographical and historical notes. Illustrations. Maps.

*Special Works* 119

520. Budrewicz, Olgierd. POLAND FOR BEGINNERS, trans. by Edward Rothert. Warszawa: Interpress Publishers, 1974. 174p. 76-381343.

    Basic introduction to Poland for persons who have never been there and plan a visit. Divided into "What to know," "What to understand," "What to discover," and "What to see." Illustrations.

521. Cazin, Paul. POLAND, trans. by Virgil Burnett. Paris: Librairie Hachette, 1961. 125p. 62-2357.

    Chiefly illustrations, mostly black-and-white, with a few colored, of Polish scenes, mainly urban. First 31 pages are a geographical and historical sketch of the country. Maps.

522. Czarnowski, Adam. IN THE LOW BESKID MOUNTAINS: A TOURIST GUIDE, with text by Marian Sobański. Warszawa: Interpress Publishers, 1968. 143p. 76-263248.

    Mostly illustrations, mainly black-and-white, some colored, of the Beskid range of the Carpathian mountains.

523. Dowie, Menie M. A GIRL IN THE KARPATHIANS. New York: Cassell Publishing Company, 1891. 301p. 3-5223.

    A description of a grip through Eastern Galicia taken during the last decade of the nineteenth century when the region was part of the Austro-Hungarian Empire. References to Huculi, defined as "Ruthenian highlanders." Illustrations. Maps. Several editions published.

524. THE ENGLISH ATLAS CONTAINING A DESCRIPTION OF POLAND. New York: Polish Institute of Arts and Sciences in America, 1943. 28p.

    Reprint of only that portion of the atlas dealing with Poland. Introduction by Oskar Halecki. Textual material from early Polish sources. Maps.

525. Filipowicz, Tytus. POLAND, PAST AND PRESENT, by Stefan Karski, pseud. Warszawa: Drukarnia Krajowa, 1927. 160p. 29-28192.

Presents a picture of modern Poland upon the background of her ancient history, traditions and institutions. Illustrations. Portraits. Maps.

526. Firsoff, Valdemar A. THE TATRA MOUNTAINS. London: Lindsay Drummond, 1942. 127p. 42-50467.

Author lived in region for several years. Includes materials not only of Polish Tatra but also of the Slovak Tatra. Description of the flora and fauna. Illustrations. Maps.

527. Fournier, Eva. POLAND, trans. by Alis Joffa. New York: Viking Press, 1964. 191p. 64-3292.

Written as a pre-travel guide to Poland covering that country's history with special emphasis on World War II and the post-war aftermath. Published originally in French and subsequently translated into English. Illustrations. Maps. Bibliography, p. 190.

528. Gardner, Monica M. POLAND. London: Adams and Charles Black, Ltd., 1942. 87p. 43-5622.

Reprint edition of a work originally published in 1917. The author presents personal impressions of Poland, the Polish people and Polish customs as she experienced them after World War I. Illustrations. Maps.

529. Gronowicz, Antoni. POLISH PROFILES: THE LAND, THE PEOPLE AND THEIR HISTORY. Westport, Conn.: Lawrence Hill and Co., 1976. 320p. 75-23929.

Popular portrait of Poland based upon three trips by a native-borne Pole turned American citizen. One-third of the book is a brief sketch of Polish history; the other two-thirds covers contemporary life. Illustrations. Maps.

530. Heine, Mark E. POLAND. New York: Hippocrene Books, Inc., 1979. 182p. 79-92828.

Book designed to acquaint the prospective visitor to Poland with its principal tourist features. Many black-and-white illustrations.

## Special Works

531. Hine, Daryl. POLISH SUBTITLES: IMPRESSIONS FROM A JOURNEY. New York: Abelard Schuman, 1962. 159p. 63-7366.

    Author and illustrator traveled in Poland during the fall of 1961. Illustrations.

532. Humphrey, Grace. POLAND THE UNEXPLORED. Indianapolis: Bobbs-Merrill Company, 1931. 332p. 31-9127.

    Author took a trip to Poland in 1930 and wrote this account of her visit. Several illustrations. Contains a chapter entitled, STRAIGHTENING OUT POLISH HISTORY.

533. Humphrey, Grace. POLAND TODAY. Warszawa: M. Arct Publishing Co., 1935. 178p. 36-27078.

    Particularly valuable for numerous photographs depicting Poland as author found it in 1934-1935. Covers Gdynia, schools, railroads and roads, sports, health matters, industry, agriculture, social service, art and culture, Polish women of that day. Interesting is fact that Old Town in Warszawa also had been "restored" after World War I. Illustrations. Portraits.

534. Hutchinson, Alexander H. TRY CRACOW AND THE CARPATHIANS. London: Chapman and Hall, 1872. 256p. NjP: 1638.488.

    Engraved illustrations. Since area covered did not have political independence at the time book was written, observations of Czech and Hungarian scenes also are included. Appendices include list of Carpathian flora, heights of mountains, lakes, etc. Maps.

535. Izbicki, Roman. IN THE BIESZCZADY MOUNTAINS: TOURIST GUIDE, trans. by Tadeusz Sumiński. Warszawa: Interpress Publishers, 1968. 142p. 78-5903.

    Principally illustrations, mostly black-and-white, some colored, of the area known as the Polish Bieszczady range in southeastern Poland. It is essentially a tourist guide, as the sub-title suggests. Illustrations. Maps.

## Special Works

536. Kish, George. POLAND. Garden City, N.Y.: Doubleday and Co., 1960. 64p. 60-51330.

    Prepared with the cooperation of the American Geographical Society. A clear and simple description of contemporary Poland along with a bit of history. Illustrations. Maps.

537. Kostrowicki, Jerzy. POLAND: NATURE, SETTLEMENT, ARCHITECTURE, trans. by Doreen H. Potworowska. Warszawa: Arkady, 1973. 545p. 75-307268.

    Principally photographs, mostly black-and-white, some colored, of the Polish countrysides, buildings, people, monuments, with accompanying notes. Divided into geographical regions with maps of each region covered. Illustrations.

538. Krzyżanowski, Lech. GDAŃSK-SOPOT-GDYNIA: A GUIDE TO THE TRIUNE CITY. Warszawa: "Sport i Turystyka" Publications, 1974. 147p. OL: DK651.G34K77.

    Tourist guide to cities as of 1974. Illustrations. Maps.

539. Lewitt, Jan. POLISH PANORAMA. London: M.I. Kolin, Ltd., 1941. 140p. 42-6911.

    Chiefly illustrations with commentary. Divided into geographical regions. Retrospective value for conditions in Poland just prior to World War II. Wilno and Lwów included as "Polish" cities and described as such. Illustrations. Maps on lining papers.

540. Little, Frances Delancy. SKETCHES IN POLAND, written and painted by Frances Delancy Little. London: A. Melrose, Ltd., 1914. 344p. A15-511.

    Contains map of Poland with pre-Partition boundaries. Narrative of author's journey in Poland and a "truthful record of what was seen with her own eyes and heard with her own ears, descriptions of the places visited, the people met and the impressions that they made on her." Illustrations. Maps.

541. McLaren, Moray. A WAYFARER IN POLAND. London: Methuen and Co., Ltd., 1934. 205p. 35-6026.

*Special Works* 123

One big answer to those questions which every traveller receives upon his return home, "How did you enjoy yourself?" and, "What is the country like?" Valuable for retrospective, British view of Poland during the interwar period. Many valuable black-and-white snapshots taken during the trip. Maps.

542. Mason, Violet. THE LAND OF THE RAINBOW: POLAND AND HER PEOPLE. London: Minerva Publishing Co., Ltd., 1941. 322p. A42-1307.

A book about Poland: "Things that foreigners usually miss; things any traveller might see if he were lucky; and an historical sketch." Author travelled extensively throughout Poland c. 1932 and writes her impressions. Illustrations are not photographs but pen and ink sketches and rotogravures of sites. Maps.

543. Murray, Michael, ed. POLAND'S PROGRESS, 1919-1939. London: John Murray, 1944. 152p. 44-7865.

Visual account of Poland as seen by a British visitor. Illustrations. Maps on lining papers.

544. Newman, Bernard. THE NEW POLAND. London: Robert Hale, 1968. 256p. 71-365383.

Sensible account by a seasoned traveller about the country of Poland and the Polish people. Some information about Polish history and some uniquely Polish problems. Illustrations. Maps.

545. Newman, Bernard. PEDALLING POLAND. London: Herbert Jenkins, Ltd., 1935. 308p. 35-32813.

Impressions of the author's cycle tour of Poland and what "he learned on the spot, from Poles and Poland's minority races." Illustrations. Maps.

546. Newman, Bernard. PORTRAIT OF POLAND. London: Robert Hale, Ltd., 1959. 221p. 59-2443.

Polish history and background and description of various parts of Poland. Portraits of prominent Poles c. 1958. Illustrations. Maps.

547. Orłowicz, Mieczysław. SOUTHWESTERN POLAND, ILLUSTRATED GUIDE, trans. by A. Domaniewska. Warszawa: Ministry of Communications, 1927. 157p. A28-573.

   Government-sponsored tourist guide to southwestern Poland. Gravure illustrations. Two folded maps. Particularly explicit on railway lines. Retrospective value.

548. Pember-Devereux, Margaret R.R. POLAND REBORN. New York: E.P. Dutton Co., 1922. 256p. 23-1851.

   Account of Poland as seen through author's eyes after she had spent a summer in Poland in 1921. Covers a variety of topics ranging from the question of Silesia to the Jewish problem. Illustrations. Maps.

549. Phillips, Charles J.M. THE NEW POLAND. London: George Allen and Unwin, Ltd., 1923. 383p. 23-701.

   Author's impressions of Poland as a member of the American Red Cross Commission to Poland. Of special note are two chapters dealing with Jews in Poland entitled, THE JEW AND THE POLES and THE POLE AND THE JEW.

550. POLAND. Prepared by a group of Polish University Teachers, under the General Supervision of Paul Nagret. New York: McGraw-Hill Book Co., 1964. 383p. 65-286.

   Maps and plans of the cities. Includes history of the country and Warszawa, geography, economy and people people, cultural life, folk art. Description of various regions for the sophisticated tourist.

551. POLAND, FACTS AND FIGURES. Warszawa: Polonia Publishing House, 1960. OL: DK404.S8813.1960.

   Survey of all aspects of Polish life and culture by numerous writers as they perceived the country c. 1960. Designed for the prospective tourist. Illustrations. Portraits. Maps.

552. POLAND: FROM THE BALTIC TO THE CARPATHIANS. Warszawa: Arkady, 1975. unpaged. 76-362616.

   Mostly illustrations, some in color, of the country. Divided into regions.

## Special Works

553. POLAND: THE COUNTRY AND ITS PEOPLE, by Maciej Bielecki et al. Warszawa: Interpress Publications, 1970. 167p. 72-177535.

    Government-sponsored travel book on Poland with numerous authors participating. Includes sketch of history, system of government, social and political life, economy, education, science, culture, sport and tourism. Numerous illustrations mostly black-and-white, some colored. Some statistics.

554. POLAND; TRAVEL GUIDE. Warszawa: Sport i Turystyka, 1970. 439p. 78-27966.

    Contains 28 itineraries, 61 alternative routes and diversions, 52 schematic plans of towns, 6 diagrams of the regions, 30 diagrams of historical monuments, 27 schemes of itineraries, car map of Poland, about 8,500 miles of described routes, 877 localities. Illustrations.

555. Poland. Rada Ochrony Pomników Walki i Meczeństwa. SCENES OF FIGHTING AND MARTYRDOM; GUIDE: WAR YEARS IN POLAND, 1939-1945, trans. by George Bidwell. Warszawa: Sport i Turystyka Publications, 1968. 416p. 79-11830.

    Guide to monuments erected to memory of countless Poles killed by Germans during World War II. Divided by voivodships with each monument and its historical import described. Illustrations. Maps.

556. Sadowski, Michał. THIS IS POLAND. Warszawa: Interpress Publishers, 1974. 53p. 76-352035.

    Purpose of this brochure is to present a picture of contemporary Poland. Illustrations in color. Includes chapters on Polish history and one entitled, POLAND AND THE UNITED STATES. Illustrations.

557. Saysse-Tobiczyk, Kaźimierz. IN WESTERN POMERANIA, trans. by Jan Rusiecki. Warszawa: Polonia Publishing House, 1963.

    Mainly illustrations, some colored, which provide an historical introduction to the region known as Western Pomerania, or the area along the Baltic coast from the mouth of the Oder River to Gdańsk. Maps.

558. Saysse-Tobiczyk, Kazimierz. POLISH HEALTH RESORTS. Warszawa: Polonia Publishing House, 1961. 133p. OL: 914.304.S275.

A profusely illustrated guidebook to the principal health resorts in Poland.

559. Styczyński, Jan. VISTULA: THE STORY OF A RIVER. Warszawa: Interpress Publishers, 1973. 135p. OL: DK511.V5S95.

Mainly black-and-white illustrations of sites along the Wisła River.

560. Super, Paul. TWENTY-FIVE YEARS WITH THE POLES. New York: Paul Super Memorial Fund, 1947. 368p. 51-35231.

Account of time spent in Poland and with the Polish people. Of particular interest is the author's account of the Polish refugees in Romania after the war as well as space devoted to Poles in the Middle East and Africa. Map shows Polish refugee settlements in East Africa in 1944. Illustrations. Portraits.

561. Surdykowski, Jerzy. POLAND'S BALTIC COAST. Warszawa: Interpress Publishers, 1975. 253p.

Narrative but mostly black-and-white illustrations. Candid shots. Important for data on the Slovincians and Kaszuby.

562. THIS IS POLAND. Warszawa: Interpress Publishers, 1972. 216p. MCC: DK443.T45.

Collection of articles chosen from the monthlies, POLAND, NASZA OJCZYZNA and MAGAZYN POLSKI. Covers all aspects of Polish life and culture around 1972. Illustrations.

563. Trzeciak, Przemysław. ACROSS POLAND, trans. by Krystyna Cękalska. Warszawa: Polonia Publishing House, 1960. 219p. 61-4739.

Brief description of Poland's past and present is followed by a detailed description of the Baltic coast, the Lake district, the central lowlands, the southern uplands and the mountains. Illustrations. Maps.

564. Uszynska, Zofia, ed. POLAND, TRAVEL GUIDE, trans. by
     Irena Dobosz et al. Warszawa: AGPOL, 1960, 7v.

   Aimed to help foreigners from abroad who intend to
   visit Poland during 1966, the millenium year. Contains
   section on Polish folk culture. Other items covered
   are touring routes, essential information concerning
   regulations and formalities, and water sports data.
   Illustrations. Maps.

565. van Norman, Louis E. POLAND, THE KNIGHT AMONG NATIONS,
     with an introduction by Helene Modjeska. New York:
     Fleming H. Revell Company, 1907. 359p. 7-32871.

   Picture of Poland written by an American of Polish
   extraction. Includes many photographs of Poland taken
   during period when the book was written, i.e. 1907.
   Portraits. Maps.

566. Wassermann, Charles. EUROPE'S FORGOTTEN TERRITORIES.
     Copenhagen: R. Roussell, 1960. 272p. MCC:
     DD801.035.W363.

   An account of the then current conditions of former
   German territories which were incorporated into the
   post-World War II Polish state based upon a 4000-mile
   long journey through these territories in 1957. Illustrations. Maps on lining papers.

567. Winter, Nevin O. POLAND OF TO-DAY AND YESTERDAY.
     Boston: L.C. Page and Company, 1913. 349p.
     13-21031.

   Popular study of the history of Poland and conditions
   still existing in the land c. 1912. Contains a brief
   section on the Poles in America. Illustrations. Portraits. Maps. Bibliography, pp. 342-343.

568. Winter, Nevin O. THE NEW POLAND. Boston: L.C. Page
     and Company, 1923. 369p. 23-16677.

   A description of the land and people of Poland as
   viewed by a sympathetic admirer of the Polish people.
   Emphasizes immediate post-World War I conditions in
   Poland. Contains numerous illustrations of Polish
   scenes c. 1923. Interesting sidelights upon the characteristics of the Polish Jew.

569. Zieliński, Adam K., ed. POLAND. Warszawa: League for Promotion of Tourism in Poland, 1939. 160p. A40-2457.

Description of the country and its people. Has retrospective value as some of the cities and territory described, e.g. Wilno, are no longer Polish. Illustrations. Portraits. Maps, including one of the Polish railways.

## Economic Conditions

570. Alton, Thad P. POLISH NATIONAL INCOME AND PRODUCT IN 1954, 1955, AND 1956, by T.P. Alton et al. New York: Columbia University Press, 1965. 252p. 65-13617.

Purpose is to show the structure of the Polish economy in the years 1954, 1955 and 1956, first, in current market prices and, second, at factor cost. Concerned with the relative shares contributed to the gross national product by the various sectors of production--industry, agriculture, construction, forestry, transportation, and various other services--and with the allocation of the product to final uses--personal consumption, government consumption, and gross investment. Bibliography, pp. 235-242.

571. Alton, Thad P. THE POLISH POSTWAR ECONOMY. New York: Columbia University Press, 1955. 330p. 55-5751.

Study seeks to appraise the character of Polish economic planning and its success in solving problems of economic development. The inquiry is focused on developments after World War II, especially after 1946; however, for purposes of background and comparison, Polish economic development up to 1939 and the effects of World War II are included. Bibliography, pp. 307-315.

572. Bierut, Bolesław. THE POLISH NATION IN THE STRUGGLE FOR PEACE AND THE 6-YEAR PLAN, by B. Bierut and Hilary Minc. Warszawa: Czytelnik, 1951. 150p. 54-15452.

English translations of three articles written by the authors on economic conditions in Poland immediately after the Second World War.

573. Bożyk, Paweł. THE ECONOMY OF MODERN POLAND. Warszawa: Interpress Publishers, 1975. 161p. NjP: HC337.P7B7.

A brief, undocumented, sketch of economic life in contemporary Poland at the time of publication written for popular consumption. Some illustrations and tables.

574. Bożyk, Paweł. POLAND AS A TRADING PARTNER, trans. by Witold Kmiecik. Warszawa: Interpress Publishers, 1972. 134p. NjP: HF3637.B69.I3.

Popular description of Poland's foreign trade picture from the close of World War II to the time the book was written, c. 1972. Illustrations.

575. Bujak, Franciszek. POLAND'S ECONOMIC DEVELOPMENT: A SHORT SKETCH, trans. by K. Żuk Skarzewska. London: George Allen and Unwin, Ltd., 1926. 67p. 30-8749.

Author was professor at the Jan Każimierz University, Lwów. Book is a sketch of the economic history of Poland from its beginnings to 1914. Tables. Maps.

576. CO-OPERATIVE SELF-GOVERNMENT IN PEOPLE'S POLAND: STRUCTURE AND FUNCTIONS. Warszawa: Publishing House of the Central Agricultural Union of Co-Operatives, 1967. 81p. 78-244643.

The book deals with the aims and substance of the activity of co-operatives, the structure of the Polish co-operative movement and membership affairs.

577. Douglas, Paul F. THE ECONOMIC INDEPENDENCE OF POLAND: A STUDY IN TRADE ADJUSTMENTS TO POLITICAL OBJECTIVES. Cincinnati: The Reeter Press, 1934. 134p. 34-35097.

Author attempts to present a story of the Polish economy as it has been shaped in the pattern of political objectives: to trace, then, the development of Poland's economic life and to the study of adjustment of trade to political objectives is the purpose of this monograph. Numerous charts. Maps.

578. THE ECONOMIC DEVELOPMENT OF POLAND'S WESTERN AND NORTHERN REGIONS, a joint work by Edmund Męclewski et al. Warszawa: Państwowe Wydawnictwo Ekonomiczne, 1961. 326p. 62-3242.

Celebrates "return" of territory to Poland. By Polish scholars. Many illustrations particularly significant

of cities before and after restoration. Many tables.
Some charts. Bibliography, pp. 323-326.

579. Falkowski, Mieczysław, ed. STUDIES ON THE THEORY OF
REPRODUCTION AND PRICES. Warszawa: PWN-Polish
Scientific Publishers, 1964. 437p. 66-50157.

A series of essays by Polish economists. Includes:
construction of a model devised to account for the
actual process of Polish post-World War II industrial
growth, elements of growth, problems of growth and of
investment, investment efficiency, financial aspects of
planning, Polish views on the economics of socialism,
sectoral economics. Glossary of economic terms.
Bibliography, pp. 415-434.

580. Feiwel, George R. INDUSTRIALIZATION AND PLANNING UNDER
POLISH SOCIALISM. New York: F. Praeger, 1971. 2v.
79-145951.

Contents: Volume I-Poland's industrialization policy;
a current analysis--sources of economic growth and
retrogression. Volume II-Problems in Polish economic
planning; continuity, change and prospects. Tables.
Charts. Bibliography, Vol. II, pp. 413-454.

581. Górecki, Roman. POLAND AND HER ECONOMIC DEVELOPMENT.
London: George Allen and Unwin, Ltd., 1935. 124p.
36-27266.

Examination of the economic situation in Poland in
1935. Contains numerous photographs of buildings,
bridges, etc. Portraits. Maps.

582. Jędrychowski, Stefan. THE FUNDAMENTAL PRINCIPLES OF
ECONOMIC POLICY IN INDUSTRY. Warszawa: Polonia
Publishing House, 1957. 35p. 59-23900.

English translation of a stenographic report of lecture delivered in February, 1957 by the author.

583. Karpiński, Andrzej. POLAND AND THE WORLD ECONOMY,
trans. by Leon Szwajcer and Harry Yaris. Warszawa:
Polonia Publishing House, 1960. 131p. 61-65026.

An analysis of Poland's economic indices as compared
with those of the world economy. Many tables comparing
Poland to other countries including western Europe and
the U.S.A.

## Special Works

584. Karpiński, Andrzej. 20: TWENTY YEARS OF POLAND'S ECONOMIC DEVELOPMENT, 1944-1964, trans. by Eugene Lepa. Warszawa: Polonia Publishing House, 1964. 153p. 65-29383.

   An undocumented popular account of Poland's economic development between 1944 and 1964 as seen by a native Pole.

585. Klarner, Czesław. SILESIA AND POMERANIA; BASIC ELEMENTS OF POLAND'S ECONOMIC INDEPENDENCE. Toruń: Baltic Institute, 1934. 77p. 38-32827.

   A defense of the position "that the basic functions of the free development of Poland's economical life are the two Polish provinces of Silesia and Pomerania." Includes many tables and charts and a map entitled, SILESIAN-POMERANIAN COMMUNICATIONS.

586. Kula, Witold. AN ECONOMIC THEORY OF THE FEUDAL SYSTEM: TOWARDS A MODEL OF THE POLISH ECONOMY, 1500-1800, trans. by Lawrence Garner. Atlantic Highlands, N.J.: Humanities Press, 1976. 191p. 77-351876.

   This book is not so much a study of the Polish economy in the modern era but "rather an attempt to develop methods which enable us to study the history of economic life." Maps.

587. Kwiatkowski, Eugenjusz. THE ECONOMIC PROGRESS OF POLAND. Warszawa: The Polish Economist, 1928. 72p. AGR28-1230.

   The subject of this book is "how Poland has employed the nine-year period, 1919-1928, of her independence for the consolidation of its national life." Charts. Tables. Graphs.

588. Landau, Zbigniew. THE POLISH ECONOMY IN THE TWENTIETH CENTURY, by Z. Landau and Jerzy Tomaszewski, trans. by Wojciech Roszkowski. New York: St. Martin's Press, 1984. 346p. 84-13328.

   An economic history of Poland since 1900 with special emphasis on contemporary "People's" Poland. Bibliography, pp. 323-332.

589. Leszczycki, Stanisław. LONG-TERM PLANNING AND SPATIAL STRUCTURE OF POLAND'S NATIONAL ECONOMY. Wrocław: Zakład Narodowy im. Ossolińskich, 1971. 66p. 72-195010.

One of a series of lectures delivered at the Rome Centre of the Polish Academy of Sciences in May, 1969 and at the Universities of Turin, Padua, Bologna and Verona between 1969 and 1970. Discussion of Poland's national economy between 1961 and 1965. Maps. Includes bibliographical references.

590. Łychowski, Tadeusz. GENERAL PREMISES OF ECONOMIC POLICY; TEN YEARS OF PEOPLE'S POLAND. Warszawa: "Polonia" Foreign Languages Publishing House, 1955. 62p. 56-24713.

Description of the general premises of economic policy in the early part of post-World War II Poland by a professor at the Central School of Planning and Statistics.

591. Młynarski, Feliks J. THE INTERNATIONAL SIGNIFICANCE OF THE DEPRECIATION OF THE ZŁOTY IN 1925. Warszawa: The Polish Economist, 1926. 89p. 27-5207.

Although the book focuses on the issue of the Polish złoty, it is also useful for an understanding of economic conditions during Poland's first seven years of independence.

592. Montias, John M. CENTRAL PLANNING IN POLAND. New Haven, Conn.: Yale University Press, 1962. 410p. 62-8256.

This book surveys, analyzes, and appraises the Polish experience with central planning in an institutional framework adopted from the Soviet model. Material gathered, in part, from interviews with Polish officials and economists. Charts. Tables. Graphs. Bibliography, pp. 375-392.

593. Podolski, T.M. SOCIALIST BANKING AND MONETARY CONTROL: THE EXPERIENCE OF POLAND. Cambridge: Cambridge University Press, 1972. 392p. 72-76088.

594. Rybczynski, Mieczysław. THE POMERANIAN VISTULA.
Toruń: Baltic Pocket Library, 1934. 79p. 38-10479.

Author discusses the economic history of the Wista, the current status of the lower Wista, the lower Wista under Polish administration, navigation on the lower Wista, and the economic importance of the lower Wista to Poland. Maps.

595. Secomski, Każimierz. PREMISES OF THE FIVE-YEAR PLAN IN POLAND, 1956-1960. Warszawa: Polonia Publishing House, 1958. 59-19613.

Discussion of Poland's post-war economic development and then of the plan as listed in title by a professor at the Central School of Planning and Statistics in Warszawa.

596. Sołdaczuk, Józef, ed. INTERNATIONAL TRADE AND DEVELOPMENT, THEORY AND POLICY, trans. by S. Breford et al. Warszawa: PWN-Polish Scientific Publishers, 1966. 345p. NjP: HF81.S65.

A collection of essays by Polish scholars on the problems of the theory and policy of foreign trade chiefly the Polish experience. Aim is to help the foreign reader to understand Poland's foreign trade problems more fully. Illustrations.

597. Stankiewicz, W.J. INSTITUTIONAL CHANGES IN THE POSTWAR ECONOMY OF POLAND, by W. Stankiewicz and J.M. Mantias. New York: Mid-European Studies Center, 1955. 125p. 55-5453.

Purpose of study was to provide accurate and thorough information concerning satellite Europe and to analyze developments in Communist Poland through the summer of 1954. It concentrates upon the study of institutional developments in the economic sphere. Bibliography, pp. 114-125.

598. Taylor, Jack. THE ECONOMIC DEVELOPMENT OF POLAND, 1919-1950. Ithaca, N.Y.: Cornell University Press, 1952. 222p. 52-8541.

The book deals in some detail with the economic affairs of Poland between 1919 and 1950, i.e. economic development based on official statistics of the Polish government, League of Nations publications and UN publications. Of particular importance is a chapter dealing with the Polish economy under Nazi-Soviet occupation. Bibliography, pp. 209-214.

599. Wąsowicz, Józef. OUTLINE OF ECONOMIC GEOGRAPHY. Warszawa: "Polonia" Foreign Languages Publishing House, 1955. 57p. 56-1138.

    Review of country and its people, industry, agriculture, transportation and communications, foreign trade by a Professor of Cartography at the University of Wrocław. Maps.

600. Wellisz, Leopold. FOREIGN CAPITAL IN POLAND. London: George Allen and Unwin, Ltd., 1938. 281p. 39-1380.

    An examination of the part played by foreign capital in Poland and the reasons why it entered the country, conditions under which it works, further prospects for foreign capital in Poland. Charts. Bibliography, pp. 265-272.

601. Woodall, Jean. THE SOCIALIST CORPORATION AND TECHNOCRATIC POWER. New York: Cambridge University Press, 1982. 282p. 82-1271.

    Chronologically covers period 1958-1980 and a scholarly interpretation of the nature of the Polish working class, industrial management, the Polish United Worker's Party (PZPR) and the basic unit of economic production, the industrial enterprise. Bibliography, pp. 265-274.

602. Zielinski, Janusz G. ECONOMIC REFORMS IN POLISH INDUSTRY. New York: Oxford University Press, 1973. 333p.

    One in a series of monographs on economic reforms in East European industry. Scope confined to economic reforms in centrally-planned industries. Includes a brief statistical profile and a glossary of main political events, 1956-1971. Tables. Charts. Maps.

603. Zweig, Ferdynand. POLAND BETWEEN TWO WARS: A CRITICAL STUDY OF SOCIAL AND ECONOMIC CHANGES. London: Secker and Warburg, 1944. 176p. A45-940.

### Education

604. Liberska, Barbara. EDUCATION AND YOUTH EMPLOYMENT IN POLAND. Berkeley, Calif.: Carnegie Council on Policy Studies in Higher Education, 1979. 83p. 79-50704.

    One of seven publications dealing with education and youth employment in contemporary societies. Description of Polish youth in the years 1960 to 1975 on the basis of changes in the demographic structure of the 15-to-24 age groups as well as education and employment policies for this age group.

605. Singer, Gusta. TEACHER EDUCATION IN A COMMUNIST STATE: POLAND, 1956-1961. New York: Bookman Associates, Inc., 1965. 282p. 64-14450.

    Deals with teacher education in Poland from 1956 to 1961, including analysis of the organization and curricula of teacher education institutions for primary and secondary school teachers, and for those who intend to teach general subjects in the vocational school system. Bibliography, pp. 247-275.

### Fiction

606. Dennis, Geoffrey P. HARVEST IN POLAND. New York: Alfred A. Knopf, Publisher, 1925. 340p. 25-8314.

    Concerns itself with the supernatural, being the battle between a young man and a giant who strives to win his soul for the devil.

607. Eschstruth, Nataly von. POLISH BLOOD; A ROMANCE, trans. by Cora L. Turner. New York: John B. Alden, 1889. 367p. 6-38152.

    A refugee Polish nobleman finds refuge with a Prussian noble, Count Dynar. Dynar adopts the infant son of the Pole and the plot revolves around the boy, Janek, and his rivalry and love with the daughter of Dynar, Xenia.

608. Korbonski, Stefan. BETWEEN THE HAMMER AND THE ANVIL, trans. by Marta Erdman. New York: Hippocrene Books, 1982. 224p. 80-9065.

Fifteen short stories about Poles and how they fared during World War II. Very heart-warming and filled with pathos, these stories portray a vivid picture of everyday life.

609. Kuncewiczowna, Maria. THE FORESTER. New York: Row Publishers, 1954. 208p. 54-8162.

    Novel set in Poland during nineteenth century about Casimir, a healthy boy with a deep instinct for love, a boy growing up in an atmosphere of hatred, trying to find out what he wants his life to be.

610. Kuniczak, Wiesław. VALEDICTORY. Garden City, N.Y.: Doubleday & Co., 1983. 389p. 79-8022.

    Novel about Polish airmen set during World War II. First these Polish fliers go to England then encounter frustration when Soviet domination of Poland occurs.

611. Lourie, Richard. SAGITTARIUS IN WARSAW. New York: Vanguard Press, 1973. 185p. 73-83036.

    Fiction but really a series of essays, impressions of Polish life as encountered by an American of Polish ancestry who meets an assorted group of Polish citizenry. A critical commentary on daily life in Poland during the 1970s.

612. Mackiewicz, Józef. ROAD TO NOWHERE, trans. by Lew Sapieha. Chicago: Henry Regnery Company, 1964. 381p. 64-16796.

    Story opens in August, 1940 and closes in June, 1941. Characters try to adjust themselves to the new order of things in Poland. Characters are fictitious; the people, animals, things, events, etc. are authentic.

613. Morgan, S.R. THE POLISH ORPHAN; OR VICISSITUDES, A TALE. Baltimore, Armstrong and Berry, 1938. 2v. CtY: PS646.F5.M675P6.1838.

    Story of a young Polish orphan girl's new life in the United States in the Jacksonian era, the daughter of a fictional count Laniski, a Polish Patriot.

614. Nałkowska, Sofja R. KOBIETY, WOMEN; A NOVEL OF POLISH
LIFE, trans. by Michael H. Dziewicki. New York:
G.P. Putnam's Sons, 1920. 324p. 21-492.

Self-revelations of a beautiful, intellectual and
self-centered girl--the transitional woman. Story of
Polish life.

615. Parizeau, Alice. THE LILACS ARE BLOOMING IN WARSAW,
trans. by A.D. Martin-Sperry. New York: New
American Library, 1985. 303p. 84-27322.

Story of a family re-united in Warszawa in 1945 and
how this family coped through the birth and rise of the
Solidarność movement. Author wrote the book originally
in French and lives in Canada. As an expatriate, she
displays an insight not always possible to a native.

616. Romanski, Andrzej K. PRISONERS OF THE NIGHT, trans. by
Walter M. Besterman. Indianapolis: Bobbs-Merrill
Company, 1948. 260p. 47-12218.

Novel based on the life and death in a labor camp in
the northern part of Russia. The central character is
Wolski, a Polish doctor, who has an affair with a beautiful Russian woman doctor, also imprisoned because her
father was a landowner. In the end, the doctor is released but the woman has to stay.

617. Serrailler, Ian. ESCAPE FROM WARSAW. New York:
Scholastic Book Service, 1963. 218p. 74-95605.

This is the story of a Polish family and of what happened to them during the Second World War and immediately thereafter. Written for teen-agers. Illustrations.

618. Todd, Mary I. VIOLINA OR POLAND AND LIBERTY. New
York: John L. Strus, 1904. 268p.

Novel about Poland set during the latter part of the
nineteenth century. Portraits. Illustrations.

619. Trevor, Elleston. THE WARSAW DOCUMENT, by Adam Hall,
pseud. Garden City, N.Y.: Doubleday, 1971. 304p.
77-139027.

A novel of intrigue and suspense set in Warszawa. A Cold War spy story which gives a realistic picture of life in Poland at the time that the book was written.

### Folklore

620. Czarnecka, Irena, comp. FOLK ART IN POLAND. Warszawa: Polonia Publishing House, 1957. 234p. OL: NK976.P6C854.

    All photographs, some colored, of landscape, buildings, interiors and furnishings, ceramics, weaving, embroidery and lace, costumes, leather and metalcraft, paper-cuts and decorations, paintings, sculptures, musical instruments.

\*   Elgoth-Ligocki, Edward. LEGENDS AND HISTORY OF POLAND. Cited above as item 14.

621. Gawalewicz, Marjan. THE QUEEN OF HEAVEN, trans. by Lucia B. Szczepanewicz and Kate B. Miller. New York: Dial Press, 1929. 234p. 29-28072.

    Collection of legends about the Mother of God in Polish folk tales. Illustrations.

622. Koszałki Opałki. English and Polish. TREASURED POLISH FOLK RHYMES, SONGS AND GAMES, trans. by Polanie Editorial Staff. Minneapolis: Polanie Publishing Company, 1976. 56p. 76-55897.

    Rhymes, songs and games compiled from the folk research and childhood reminiscences of Zofia Rogoszowna. Includes musical notation.

623. Pawlowska, Harriet M. MERRILY WE SING. 105 POLISH FOLKSONGS. Collected and edited by H.M. Pawlowska. Detroit: Wayne State University Press, 1961. 263p. M61-1024.

    Polish and English words. Musical notation. Contains an analysis of the Polish folksongs by Grace L. Engel.

*Special Works* 139

## Foreign Relations

624. Beck, Józef. FINAL REPORT. New York: Robert Speller and Sons, Publishers, Inc., 1957. 278p. 57-11887.

 Many portraits of author during his life. Covers his activities from 1926 to 1939. Book a history of Polish foreign policy. Last section is, in effect, fragments of a study concerning twenty years of international politics. Illustrations.

625. Biddle, Anthony J.D. POLAND AND THE COMING OF THE SECOND WORLD WAR: THE DIPLOMATIC PAPERS OF A.J. DREXEL BIDDLE, JR. Columbus: Ohio State University Press, 1976. 358p. 75-45433.

 Author was U.S. Ambassador to Poland, 1937-1939. Papers edited by P.V. Connistrow et al. Bood divided into an introductory essay, based on Polish as well as western sources, that discusses Biddle's role and the atmosphere in which he worked; a lengthy report being an eyewitness account of the collapse of the Polish Republic; and diplomatic documents. Illustrations. Portraits.

626. Brackmann, Albert, ed. GERMANY AND POLAND IN THEIR HISTORICAL RELATIONS, trans. by S. Miles Bouton. Berlin: R. Oldenbourg, 1934. 266p. 35-2096.

 Series of articles by German historians about historical relations between the Poles and the Germans. Apparently published to counteract unfavorable Polish and French interpretation of Polish history. No bibliographies. Few articles contain any documentation. Illustrations. Maps.

627. Budurowycz, Bohdan B. POLISH-SOVIET RELATIONS, 1932-1939. New York: Columbia University Press, 1963. 229p. 63-7509.

 Purpose of this study is to trace the course of Polish-Soviet relations from the conclusion of the non-aggression pact between the two nations in July, 1932 until the fourth partition of Poland in September, 1939 and to assess the nature of that relationship. Revision of thesis at Columbia University, 1958. Maps. Bibliography, pp. 199-218.

628. Ciechanowski, Jan. DEFEAT IN VICTORY. Garden City, N.Y.: Doubleday and Company, Inc., 1947. 397p. 47-966.

A true picture of events and trends in American foreign policy towards Poland as the author saw them developing during the four and one-half years of his last diplomatic mission as Ambassador of Poland to the United States. It is a personal record of his observations and opinions. It is not an official presentation of the Polish problem.

629. Cienciala, Anna M. FROM VERSAILLES TO LOCARNO: KEYS TO POLISH FOREIGN POLICY, 1919-1925, by A.M. Cienciala and Tytus Komarnicki. Lawrence: University of Kansas Press, 1984. 384p. 84-2302.

Provides the vital historical background and the full European setting for a central European diplomatic issue. It demonstrates above all the failure of the British and French to understand Poland's position. Maps. Bibliography, pp. 347-364.

630. Cienciala, Anna M. POLAND AND THE WESTERN POWERS, 1938-1939: A STUDY IN THE INTERDEPENDENCE OF EASTERN AND WESTERN EUROPE. Toronto: University of Toronto Press, 1968. 310p. 68-111458.

Object of this study is to explain the nature and historical roots of the problems facing Polish foreign policy in 1938-1939 and the manner in which they were approached by the men who shaped and directed Polish diplomacy. Secondly, to illustrate the political interdependence in these years of eastern and western Europe. Basic sources were Polish, German, British and American foreign policy documents. Portraits. Maps. Bibliography, pp. 264-291.

631. Coates, William P. SIX CENTURIES OF RUSSO-POLISH RELATIONS, by W.P. Coates and Zelda K. Coates. London: Lawrence and Wishart, 1948. 235p. 49-2685.

This book is a history of Russo-Polish relations, not a history of Soviet-Polish relations, because it deals with Russo-Polish relations stretching back for over six centuries. Distinctly pro-Soviet version of this relationship. Contains documentation in footnotes. Maps.

*Special Works* 141

632. Dębicki, Roman. THE FOREIGN POLICY OF POLAND, 1919-1939, FROM THE REBIRTH OF THE POLISH REPUBLIC TO WORLD WAR II. New York: F. Praeger, 1962. 192p. 62-13732.

The purpose of this book is to provide the reader with a concise account of the diplomatic activity of successive Polish governments between 1919 and 1939 as observed by a close witness and to present the general trends of Polish foreign policy against a background of the domestic and international circumstances that motivated them. Bibliography, pp. 179-184.

633. Federowicz, J.K. ENGLAND'S BALTIC TRADE IN THE EARLY SEVENTEENTH CENTURY: A STUDY IN ANGLO-POLISH DIPLOMACY. Cambridge: Cambridge University Press, 1980. 334p. 79-11406.

This book constitutes a substantially revised revision of a doctoral dissertation submitted at Cambridge in the autumn of 1975. Objective is a description of the commercial relationship between England and the Polish Commonwealth and an explanation of the decline in that relationship. Illustrations. Maps. Bibliography, pp. 311-325.

634. Gajda, Patricia A. POSTSCRIPT TO VICTORY: BRITISH POLICY AND THE GERMAN-POLISH BORDERLANDS, 1919-1925. Washington, D.C.: University Press of America, 1982. 232p. 81-40634.

This is a study of Great Britain's relationship with the new Republic of Poland, tracing this relationship in the first half-decade following World War I concentrating on British interest in the status of Gdańsk (Danzig) and the fate of Upper Silesia. Maps. Bibliography, pp. 217-227.

635. Garland, John S. INDUSTRIAL COOPERATION BETWEEN POLAND AND THE WEST. Ann Arbor, Mich.: UMI Research Press, 1985. 200p. 84-28070.

A research paper which grew out of the author's participation in a collaborative research project undertaken by a United States team of researchers based at Indiana University and a Polish team based at the Foreign Trade Research Institute in Warszawa. Illustrations. Bibliography, pp. 191-198.

636. GERALD FORD'S VISIT TO POLAND, 28-29 JULY 1975.
     Warszawa: Interpress Publishers, 1975. 43p. OL:
     E183.8.P7.G3.

   A description of the President's visit written and
   published in Poland thereby presenting a Polish point
   of view. Illustrations. Portraits.

637. Grabski, Stanisław. THE POLISH-SOVIET FRONTIER. New
     York: Polish Information Center, 1944. 35p.
     44-33393.

   A discussion of the Polish-Russian frontier established by the Treaty of Riga in 1921. As a member of
   the Polish delegation at the peace conference in Minsk
   and Riga, the author was a participant in the events he
   discusses. Illustrations. Portraits. Maps.

638. Gromada, Thaddeus V., ed. ESSAYS ON POLAND'S FOREIGN
     POLICY, 1918-1939. New York: Józef Piłsudski
     Institute of America, 1970. 71p. OL: DK418.G73.

   Reprint of papers delivered at Piłsudski Institute on
   November 11, 1968 to commemorate Polish independence's
   50th birthday. Six separate papers by six separate
   scholars.

639. Gronowicz, Antoni. PATTERN FOR PEACE; THE STORY OF
     POLAND AND HER RELATIONS WITH GERMANY. New York:
     Paramount Publishing Co., 1951. 215p. 51-13248.

   A Polish apologia for her claims to the western territories after World War II told through the Polish-
   German conflicts through a thousand years. No documentation. Maps.

640. Henderson, H.W. AN OUTLINE OF POLISH-SOVIET RELATIONS.
     Glasgow: Polish Information Center, 1944. 36p.
     44-8428.

   Brief survey of Russo-Polish relations with emphasis
   on the period from 1918 onwards. Attempts to justify
   Polish claims to territories taken from Poland by
   Russia in 1939. Illustrations. Maps.

641. Horak, Stephan. POLAND'S INTERNATIONAL AFFAIRS, 1919-
     1960; A CALENDAR OF TREATIES, AGREEMENTS, CONVENTIONS,
     AND OTHER INTERNATIONAL ACTS, WITH ANNOTATIONS,

REFERENCES, AND SELECTIONS FROM DOCUMENTS AND TEXT OF TREATIES. Bloomington: Indiana University Press, 1964. 248p. 64-63009.

Purpose of this volume is to help students of international affairs and of Polish affairs identify the international agreements in which Poland participated. Bibliography, pp. xi-xviii.

642. Jędrzejewicz, Wacław. POLAND IN THE BRITISH PARLIAMENT, 1939-1945. New York: Józef Piłsudski Institute of America for Research in the Modern History of Poland, 1946. 3v. 48-702.

Contents: Vol. I-British guarantees to Poland to the Atlantic Charter, March 1939-August 1941; Vol. II-Fall, 1941-Spring, 1944; Vol. II-Summer, 1944-Summer, 1945. Stenographic reports of British Parliamentary debates on the subject of Anglo-Polish relations. Illustrations. Maps. Bibliography, Vol. III, pp. 701-716.

643. Karski, Jan. THE GREAT POWERS AND POLAND, 1919-1945; FROM VERSAILLES TO YALTA. Washington: University Press of America, 1985. 697p. 84-22000.

The main theme of the study deals with the policies of the Great Powers toward Poland during the years 1919-1945. Based upon documentary and archival records, memoirs of the main statesmen and various fragmentary studies by recognized scholars in the field. Bibliography, pp. 627-671.

644. Kennedy, John Fitzgerald, President, United States, 1917-1963. JOHN F. KENNEDY AND POLAND; SELECTION OF DOCUMENTS, 1948-1963. New York: Polish Institute of Arts and Sciences in America, 1964. 140p. 64-9016.

Contains texts of Kennedy's addresses and writings directly or indirectly pertaining to Poland and the Poles. It covers his public activity from 1948 until November 1963. Illustrations.

645. Kokot, Józef. THE LOGIC OF THE ODER-NEISSE FRONTIER, trans. by Andrzej Potocki. Poznań: Wydawnictwo Zachodnie, 1959. 289p. OL: 943.043.K79.

Author discusses the question of the western frontiers of Poland as established on the Oder-Neisse line in the

light of international law, demography and economy.
Tables. Bibliography, pp. 269-280.

646. Konovalov, Serge. RUSSO-POLISH RELATIONS: AN HISTORICAL SURVEY. Princeton, N.J.: Princeton University Press, 1945. 102p. A45-4172.

Mostly historical narrative plus appendices which contain documents which explain and illustrate points made in the historical survey. Maps.

647. Korbel, Józef. POLAND BETWEEN EAST AND WEST; SOVIET AND GERMAN DIPLOMACY TOWARD POLAND, 1919-1933. Princeton, N.J.: Princeton University Press, 1963. 321p. 63-9993.

Study of Soviet and German diplomacy toward Poland. Polish foreign policy, per se, is here analyzed only to the extent to which it reflected Moscow's and Berlin's diplomatic moves toward Warszawa. Bibliography, pp. 290-309.

648. Korczynski, Alexander, ed. POLAND BETWEEN GERMANY AND RUSSIA, 1926-1939; THE THEORY OF TWO ENEMIES, ed. by A. Korczynski and Tadeusz Swiętochowski. New York: Piłsudski Institute of America, 1975. 72p. NjP: 1069.23405 no. 29.

Collection of papers delivered at Columbia University in 1974 on the apparent dilemma which Poland faced during the fateful thirteen-year period just prior to the outbreak of World War II.

649. Kot, Stansław. CONVERSATIONS WITH THE KREMLIN, AND DISPATCHES FROM RUSSIA, trans. by H.C. Stevens. London: Oxford University Press, 1963. 285p. 64-263.

Chiefly translations of reports of various conversations which the author had with various members of the Soviet Government while ambassador to Russia from Poland during the period 4 September 1941 to 13 July 1942. Also contains translations of other reports to General Sikorski and of other conversations with members of the Soviet Government.

## Special Works

650. Kulski, Władysław W. GERMANY AND POLAND: FROM WAR TO PEACEFUL RELATIONS. Syracuse: Syracuse University Press, 1976. 336p. 75-42453.

 An analysis of both the Polish and German points of view regarding their mutual relations not only during the interwar period but also after World War II. It also covers West German-Polish relations through the 1970s. This book places German-Polish relations in the context of the broader issues of European security, East-West detente, and German reunification. Bibliography, pp. 313-325.

651. Kuśnierz, Bronisław. STALIN AND THE POLES: AN INDICTMENT OF THE SOVIET LEADERS. London: Hollis and Carter, 1949. 315p. 50-2548.

 A detailed account of what the author describes as "the crimes of Soviet imperialism." Covers period from 1939 to 1948 and describes the Sovietization of Polish territory and later the postwar Polish state.

652. Lane, Arthur B. I SAW POLAND BETRAYED; AN AMERICAN AMBASSADOR REPORTS TO THE AMERICAN PEOPLE. Indianapolis: Bobbs-Merrill Co., 1948. 344p. 48-5435.

 Report by the U.S. Ambassador to Poland from July, 1945 to his resignation on January 19, 1947 after elections in Poland. Takes the position that Poland was abandoned to Russia by the West. Illustrations. Portraits. Maps.

653. Lerski, Jerzy Jan, comp. HERBERT HOOVER AND POLAND: A DOCUMENTARY HISTORY OF A FRIENDSHIP. Stanford, Calif.: Hoover Institution Press, 1977. 124p. 77-72051.

 Author relates the story of Hoover's activities in behalf of Poland beginning with his role as head of the American Relief Administration after World War I, then through Hoover's election campaign, presidency and later years. Illustrations.

654. Lipski, Józef. DIPLOMAT IN BERLIN, 1933-1939; PAPERS AND MEMOIRS OF JÓZEF LIPSKI, AMBASSADOR OF POLAND, ed. by Wacław Jędrzejewicz. New York: Columbia University Press, 1968. 679p. 67-25871.

Not intended to be a history of Polish-German relations but reports, reminiscences, notes, and articles written while the author was Polish Ambassador to Germany during the six years prior to World War II. Illustrations. Portraits. Bibliography, pp. 653-660.

655. Lukas, Richard C. BITTER LEGACY: POLISH-AMERICAN RELATIONS IN THE WAKE OF WORLD WAR II. Lexington: University of Kentucky Press, 1982. 191p. 82-1972.

Book deals with the political and economic relations between the United States and Poland and also explores the impact of these relations on such post-World War II issues as relief, repatriation, Polish-American opinion and the origins of the Cold War. Maps. Bibliography, pp. 170-181.

656. Lukas, Richard C. THE STRANGE ALLIES: THE UNITED STATES AND POLAND, 1941-1945. Knoxville: University of Tennessee Press, 1978. 230p. 77-8585.

Scholarly, up-to-date account of United States policy toward Poland during the Second World War. Includes a chapter entitled, POLONIA AND THE POLISH QUESTION, which attempts to ascertain the role played by so-called Polish-Americans in the determination of U.S. foreign policy. Maps. Bibliography, pp. 209-221.

657. Łukasiewicz, Juliusz. DIPLOMAT IN PARIS, 1936-1939; PAPERS AND MEMOIRS OF JULIUSZ ŁUKASIEWICZ, AMBASSADOR OF POLAND; ed. by Wacław Jędrzejewicz. New York: Columbia University Press, 1970. 408p. 79-83530.

Materials used for writing this book are in Piłsudski Institute of America in New York City. Primarily memoirs covering period from middle of March to end of September, 1939, and two articles on the Rambouillet loan and on Teschen Silesia question. Illustrations. Portraits. Maps. Bibliography, pp. 385-397.

658. Mackiewicz, Stanisław. COLONEL BECK AND HIS POLICY. London: Eyre and Spottiswood, Ltd., 1944. 139p. 44-7868.

The author herein presents a complete picture of the foreign policy of Poland as handled by Colonel Józef Beck from his accession as Vice-Minister for Foreign

*Special Works* 147

Affairs in November of 1932 until the invasion of
Poland in September of 1939. It is an analysis of the
policy, not of the man. No documentation.

659. Matuszewski, Ignacy. GREAT BRITAIN'S OBLIGATIONS
TOWARDS POLAND AND SOME FACTS ABOUT THE CURZON LINE.
New York: National Committee of Americans of Polish
Descent, 1945. 85p. 45-7824.

Presents with fairness the reciprocal obligations of
Great Britain and Poland as based upon the Agreement of
Mutual Assistance of August 25, 1939. Illustrations.
Maps.

660. Montanus, B. POLISH-SOVIET RELATIONS IN THE LIGHT OF
INTERNATIONAL LAW. New York: University Publications, 1944. 54p. 45-2096.

Analysis of Polish-Soviet relations from the legal
viewpoint. Purpose of the study is to present the
problem of Polish-Soviet relations from the legal point
of view completely omitting any elements of politics,
history, etc. Covers period from 1921 to 1944. Illustrations. Maps.

661. Newman, Simon. MARCH 1939: THE BRITISH GUARANTEE TO
POLAND: A STUDY IN THE CONTINUITY OF BRITISH FOREIGN
POLICY. Fairlawn, New Jersey: Oxford University
Press, 1976. 263p. 77-351888.

Purpose of this book is to examine the origins of the
British guarantee to Poland made by Prime Minister
Chamberlain on 31 March 1939. Bibliography, pp. 226-237.

662. O'Konski, Alvin E. AMERICA ON POLAND. Swantantrapur,
Awanh State, India: M. Frydman, 1945. 63p.
46-20245.

Extension of remarks of A.E. O'Konski of Wisconsin in
the U.S. House of Representatives, Thursday, February
1, 1945. Remarks were directed towards the question of
Polish-Soviet relations.

663. Ortmayer, Louis L. CONFLICT, COMPROMISE AND CONCILIATION: WEST GERMAN-POLISH NORMALIZATION, 1966-1976.
Denver: University of Denver Graduate School of
International Studies, 1975. 162p. 76-374221.

An analysis of the transition of West German-Polish relations "over the past two decades," i.e. 1960-1980. Stresses domestic political variables. Contains English text of treaty between the Federal Republic of Germany and the People's Republic of Poland of 1971.

664. Ploss, Sidney I. MOSCOW AND THE POLISH CRISIS: AN INTERPRETATION OF SOVIET POLICIES AND INTENTIONS. Boulder, Colo.: Westview Press, Inc., 1986. 182p. 85-31504.

Author writes about the Russian reaction to the declaration of martial law in Poland in 1981 using propaganda analysis to trace the Kremlin's policy decisions and its internal leadership debates during the crisis.

665. POLISH-U.S. INDUSTRIAL COOPERATION IN THE 1980s; FINDINGS OF A JOINT RESEARCH PROJECT, ed. by Paul Marer and Eugeniusz Tabaczynski. Bloomington: Indiana University Press, 1982. 409p. 81-47884.

Results of a three-year joint project between teams of Americans and Polish specialists on East-West trade. Integrates American and Polish academic, business and government perspectives.

666. Potichnyj, Peter J., ed. POLAND AND THE UKRAINE, PAST AND PRESENT. Edmonton, Alta.: Canadian Institute of Ukrainian Studies, 1980. 365p. UW: DK4185.R9P64.

Seventeen studies originally presented at the eleventh annual McMaster Conference devoted to Communist and East European Affairs. Object was to survey 1,000 years of relations between Poland and the Ukraine. Contributors were well-known respected scholars of both Polish and Ukrainian and non-Slavic descent.

667. Poznański, Czesław. THE FLAMING BORDERS, preface by Adam Ciolkosz. London: Hutchinson and Company, Ltd., 1944. 92p. A45-1095.

A Polish Socialist analyzes the conditions in Poland from 1914 to the outbreak of the Second World War. A critique of Polish foreign policy, especially towards Germany.

## Special Works

668. PRESIDENT NIXON'S 24 HOURS IN WARSAW. Warszawa: Interpress Publishers, 1972. 134p. OL: DK443.5.I5.

    Mainly a photographic record of the visit of President Richard M. Nixon of the United States of America to Poland, specifically, Warszawa, on May 31, 1972. Illustrations. Portraits.

669. Przezdziecki, Rajnold, hrabia. DIPLOMATIC VENTURES AND ADVENTURES: SOME EXPERIENCES OF BRITISH ENVOYS AT THE COURT OF POLAND, translated by Prince and Princess Alexander Sapieha. London: Polish Research Centre, Ltd., 1953. 262p. 53-37748.

    Carefully documented study from the beginnings of the Polish state through the reign of Sanisław August Poniatowski. Contains many portraits of the kings of Poland. Illustrations.

670. Rachwald, Arthur R. POLAND BETWEEN THE SUPERPOWERS: SECURITY VS. ECONOMIC RECOVERY. Boulder, Colo.: Westview Press, 1983. 154p. 83-6758.

    Examines the foreign and domestic policies of Poland since World War II in light of the country's relations with the Soviet Union and the United States. Author focuses on security, guaranteed by both alliance with the Soviet Union and by support for the idea of European collective security. Bibliography, pp. 137-152.

671. Rakowski, Mieczysław F. THE FOREIGN POLICY OF THE POLISH PEOPLE'S REPUBLIC. Warszawa: Interpress Publishers, 1975. 210p. 77-351062.

    An undocumented, popular discussion of the subject: historical reminiscences; Poland's entry into the international arena; on the threshold of the Cold War; world peace in danger; first signs of slackening in international tension; a decade of struggle against the concept of the Cold War; and Polish foreign policy in the years, 1971-1974.

672. Rhode, Gotthold, ed. THE GENESIS OF THE ODER-NEISSE LINE IN THE DIPLOMATIC NEGOTIATIONS DURING WORLD WAR II: SOURCES AND DOCUMENTS, comp. and ed. by G. Rhode and Wolfgang Wagner. Stuttgard: Brentano Verlag, 1959. 2v. 60-569.

Interpretation, as well as documentation, of the question of the western boundaries of Poland from the German viewpoint. Maps. Bibliography, Vol. I, p. 156.

673. Rosenthal, Harry K. GERMAN AND POLE: NATIONAL CONFLICT AND MODERN MYTH. Gainesville: University Presses of Florida, 1976. 175p. 76-2402.

Author wishes simply to trace the evolution of the German view of the Poles. An analysis both of the psychological and material bases of the German image of the Poles. Divided into historical periods. Bibliography, pp. 149-167.

674. Rozek, Edward J. ALLIED WARTIME DIPLOMACY: A PATTERN IN POLAND. New York: John Wiley and Sons, Inc., 1958. 481p. 57-13449.

Study of American foreign policy as regards the London Polish government's efforts to win and keep Polish freedom based upon Polish sources. It is also an analysis of Soviet foreign policy particularly the Soviet conquest of Poland. Maps. Bibliography, pp. 465-470.

675. Singer, Daniel. THE ROAD TO GDAŃSK: POLAND AND THE U.S.S.R. New York: Monthly Review Press, 1981. 256p. 80-39914.

Presents contemporary situation in the historical context of the post-World War II dissident movements in the Soviet Union and Poland. Based on thirty years of work as a dedicated socialist and journalist specializing in that region.

676. Skwarczynski, Pawel. A FATEFUL MEETING AT ELSINORE IN 1580, ed. by Waclaw W. Soroka. Stevens Point, Wisc.: University of Wisconsin-Stevens Point. Office of Academic Support Programs, 1982. pp. 82-171815.

Study of Polish-English relations in the second half of the sixteenth century. Centers on the persecution of a Catholic priest, James Bosgrove, S.J. and Polish intervention on his behalf resulting in his release.

677. Sulimirski, Tadeusz. POLAND AND GERMANY, PAST AND FUTURE. London: West-Slavonic Bulletin, 1942. 67p. 43-4210.

*Special Works*  151

Survey of Polish-German relations throughout history from the Polish viewpoint. Numerous maps covering all historical periods.

678. Super, Margaret L. POLAND AND RUSSIA: THE LAST QUARTER CENTURY. New York: Sheed and Ward, 1944. 251p. 44-5309.

 History of Polish-Soviet relations between 1918 and 1943. Based upon innumerable conversations, letters, and a mass of documentary material. Author lived in Poland with her husband from 1922 to 1939. Maps. Bibliography, pp. 197-200.

679. Umiastowski, Roman. POLAND, RUSSIA AND GREAT BRITAIN, 1941-1945: A STUDY OF EVIDENCE. London: Hollis and Carter, 1946. 544p. 47-22311.

 Covers the relations between Poland and Russia on the one hand and between Poland and Britain on the other during a period of four years beginning from the Russo-Polish Treaty of 1941 and the Crimean Agreement and the recognition by the Allies in the summer of 1945 of the Soviet-sponsored Lublin Committee as the Polish Provisional Government. Maps.

680. Umiastowski, Roman. RUSSIA AND THE POLISH REPUBLIC, 1918-1941, written with the assistance of Joanna Mary Aldridge. London: "Aquafondata," 1945. 319p. 46-2558.

 Account of the centuries-old dispute between the Russians and the Poles. Most of the book concentrates upon events from 1939 to 1941. Illustrations. Maps. Bibliographical footnotes.

681. von Riekhoff, Harald. GERMAN-POLISH RELATIONS, 1919-1933. Baltimore: Johns Hopkins University Press, 1971. 421p. 73-141999.

 Originally a doctoral dissertation at Yale University. Study of German-Polish relations between the 1918 armistice and Hitler's accession to power. Author has tried throughout this work to provide a truly objective assessment of events and personalities. Bibliography, pp. 391-403.

682. Wandycz, Piótr S.  CZECHOSLOVAK-POLISH CONFEDERATION AND THE GREAT POWERS, 1940-1943.  Bloomington: Indiana University Press, 1956.  152p.  60-3358.

Scholarly monograph by an expert which traces the history of Czechoslovak-Polish relations during the interwar period with special emphasis on the roles of the Great Powers in these relations.  Contains documents.  Note on sources, pp. 138-150.

683. Wandycz, Piótr S.  SOVIET-POLISH RELATIONS, 1917-1921. Cambridge, Mass.:  Harvard University Press, 1969. 403p.  69-18047.

Study attempts to present Soviet-Polish relations against the background of past centuries.  Emphasis is on Polish and Soviet, not Polish and White Russian, relations.  Scholarly and exhaustive account.  Maps. Bibliography, pp. 293-309.

684. Wandycz, Piótr S.  THE UNITED STATES AND POLAND. Cambridge, Mass.:  Harvard University Press, 1980. 465p.  79-11998.

Main thrust of this study is the relations between the United States and Poland.  Covers period from beginnings of the United States but major emphasis is on rebirth of Poland during World War I, the interwar period, the Second World War and post-war through Gierek.

685. Weyers, J.  POLAND AND RUSSIA.  London:  Barnard and Westwood, Ltd., 1943.  64p.  44-537.

Outline of Polish-Russian relations, 1921-1942, prior to break in relations between Polish government-in-exile and the U.S.S.R.  Anti-Russian viewpoint.  Illustrations.  Maps.

686. Zins, Henryk.  ENGLAND AND THE BALTIC IN THE ELIZABETHAN ERA, trans. by H.C. Stevens.  Totowa, N.J.: Rowman and Littlefield, 1972.  347p.  MiU: HF3508.P7.Z783.

Primarily concerned with England's trade with the Polish Commonwealth during the second half of the sixteenth century within the context of Anglo-Baltic

*Special Works* 153

commercial and political relations. Exhaustively documented. Illustrations. Bibliography, pp. 320-331.

### Genealogy

687. Gnacinski, Jan. POLISH AND PROUD: TRACING YOUR POLISH ANCESTRY, by Jan and Len Gnacinski. Indianapolis: Ye Olde Genealogie Shoppe, 1983. 78p. 79-84318.

A wealth of information for the beginner in genealogical research. Includes an incomplete list of Polish parishes in the U.D., maps of current 49 wojewodztwos in Poland, etc. Illustrations.

\* Obal, Thaddeus J. A BIBLIOGRAPHY FOR GENEALOGICAL RESEARCH INVOLVING POLISH ANCESTRY. Cited above as item 154.

688. Ortell, Gerald A. POLISH PARISH RECORDS OF THE ROMAN CATHOLIC CHURCH, THEIR USE AND UNDERSTANDING IN GENEALOGICAL RESEARCH. Buffalo Grove, Ill.: Genun Publications, 1984. 86p. OL: CS49.07.

Designed to help the novice researcher understand the information contained in the primary Polish records. Illustrations.

689. Wellover, Maralyn. TRACING YOUR POLISH ROOTS. Milwaukee: Author, 1985. 87p.

Purpose of the book is to instruct the reader on how to begin search for Polish-born ancestors by checking the home jurisdiction for helpful sources of information and how to proceed to the Civil and Printed sources to find the places of origin. Illustrations. Maps.

### Geographical Conditions

690. Gorczyński, Władysław. COMPARISON OF THE CLIMATE OF THE UNITED STATES AND EUROPE, WITH SPECIAL ATTENTION TO POLAND AND HER BALTIC COAST. New York: Herald Square Press, Inc., 1945. 288p. A45-3388.

Monograph devoted to the comparative description of the sunshine climate alone. Includes sunshine comparisons between the Polish coast and the remaining part of Europe. Many charts and maps. Illustrations.

691. Nałkowski, Wacław. POLAND AS A GEOGRAPHICAL ENTITY. London: George Allen and Unwin, Ltd., 1917. 63p. 17-16217.

   Gives a general survey of the geography of Poland c. 1912. Author wishes to give a geographical synthesis of the Polish territories. Illustrations. Maps.

692. Srokowski, Stanisław. EAST PRUSSIA. Toruń: Baltic Institute, 1934. 45p. 37-14909.

   Author was professor of geography at the School of Political Sciences at Warszawa. Covers geographical situation and natural conditions of East Prussia, the population, and the economic situation of the region as of 1934. Maps. Bibliography, p. 4.

Geography

693. Buczek, Karol. THE HISTORY OF POLISH CARTOGRAPHY FROM THE 15TH TO THE 18TH CENTURY, trans. by Andrzej Potocki. Wrocław: Polskiej Akademii Nauk, 1966. 135p. NjP: Map Room: 16379.219.1966.

   Originally published in Polish. A history of cartography in Poland. The sixty maps of Poland and/or Central Europe. Bibliographical footnotes.

694. Pertek, Jerzy. POLES ON THE HIGH SEAS, trans. by Alexander T. Jordan. Warszawa: Zakład Narodowy im. Ossolinskich, 1978. 372p. NjP: G277.5.P413.

   Intention of this book is to acquaint the reader with an overview of Poland's seafaring traditions. Covers Polish sea voyages all over the world from 960 to the late 19th and early 20th centuries. Illustrations. Maps.

695. Pounds, Norman J.C. THE UPPER SILESIAN INDUSTRIAL REGION. Bloomington: Indiana University Press, 1956. 242p. 59-62540.

   An economic history of Silesia with a geographical perspective. Begins with Silesia in the eighteenth

*Special Works* 155

century and finishes with the Second World War and immediately thereafter. Maps.

### German Occupation
### 1939-1945

696. Brzeska, Maria. THROUGH A WOMAN'S EYES: LIFE IN POLAND UNDER GERMAN OCCUPATION. London: Maxlove Publishing Co., Ltd., 1944. 92p. A45-1391.

    Title is self-explanatory. Many black-and-white illustrations of interest depicting life in German-occupied Poland during World War II. Some photographs showing samples of clandestine newspapers. A personal narrative about Poland.

697. Cyprian, Tadeusz. NAZI RULE IN POLAND, 1939-1945, by T. Cyprian and Jerzy Sawicki. Warszawa: Polonia Publishing House, 1961. 261p. 62-908.

    This book sets out the basic documentary material on the Nazi crimes committed in Poland, 1939-1945. Material collected and edited by Professors Cyprian and Sawicki, both lawyers specializing in criminal law and university professors. No bibliography. Documentation slight. Illustrations.

698. Evans, Jon. THE NAZI NEW ORDER IN POLAND. London: Victor Gollancz, Ltd., 1941. 184p. 41-25513.

    The primary purpose of this book is to display a working model of the Nazi "New Order," which the Nazi propaganda machine had been ceaselessly striving to persuade the world to be as desirable. Maps.

699. Gross, Jan T. POLISH SOCIETY UNDER GERMAN OCCUPATION: THE GENERAL GOUVERNEMENT, 1939-1944. Princeton, N.J.: Princeton University Press, 1979. 343p. 78-70298.

    Analysis of the occupation of Poland in the framework of sociologically significant questions. Main purpose is to identify the alternative forms of collective life that emerged in response to the social control exercised by the Germans. Bibliography, pp. 307-321.

700. Gumkowski, Janusz. POLAND UNDER NAZI OCCUPATION, by
J. Gumkowski and Kazimierz Leszczyński, trans. by
Edward Rothert. Warszawa: Polonia Publishing House,
1961. 219p. MiD: R940.94075.G953g.

Polish account of the Nazi occupation with many roto-
gravure photographs, many shocking, of atrocities per-
petrated by German occupation troops. Many facsimiles
of German documents and orders.

701. Korboński, Stefan. FIGHTING WARSAW, THE STORY OF THE
POLISH UNDERGROUND STATE, 1939-1945, trans. by F.B.
Czarnomski. New York: Macmillan, 1956. 495p.
MiD: 940.9485.K841k.

Author was last chief of the Polish Wartime Underground. Concerns various people and events, everything
which made everyday life and the climate of the Underground, especially of Warszawa. Author refers to the
text as reminiscences.

702. Korboński, Stefan. THE POLISH UNDERGROUND, A GUIDE TO
THE UNDERGROUND, 1939-1945, trans. by Marta Erdman.
New York: Columbia University Press, 1978. 268p.
77-82393.

A "description of Polish underground organization and
activities during the war." English version of Polish
account. Author well-qualified having been actively
engaged in underground activities during the period.

703. Korboński, Stefan. WARSAW IN CHAINS, trans. by Norbert
Guterman. New York: Macmillan Company, 1959. 319p.
MiD: 943.8.K841w.

Companion volume to the author's FIGHTING WARSAW.
Covers author's experiences from July 26, 1945 to
November 14, 1947. Diary form. Author escapes to
Sweden. Epilogue includes purge in 1951, Poznań
rebellion in June, 1956, and October, 1956, revolution.
Maps.

704. Korboński, Stefan. WARSAW IN EXILE, trans. by David J.
Welsh. New York: F. Praeger, 1966. 325p. 66-12476.

Continues personal narrative of author's life in Warszawa from July, 1945. Events and impressions the author registers day after day offering the reader a faithful picture of life in Poland at the turn of two epochs, separated by the Second World War. Ends with his escape from Poland first to Sweden and then to the United States. Second volume in the trilogy. Illustrations.

705. Kotowski, Monika. THE BRIDGE TO THE OTHER SIDE, trans. by Maia Wojciechowska. Garden City, N.Y.: Doubleday, 1970. 164p. 75-116264.

Unique little book by a Polish novelist. Nineteen episodes of children undergoing German occupation of Poland.

706. Lukas, Richard C. THE FORGOTTEN HOLOCAUST: THE POLES UNDER GERMAN OCCUPATION, 1939-1944. Lexington: University of Kentucky Press, 1986. 300p. 85-13560.

Carefully researched study of Poland under the Nazi Occupation emphasizing the sufferings of the Poles, often overlooked by Holocaust literature. Illustrations. Maps. Bibliography, pp. 273-286.

707. Pilichowski, Czesław. NO TIME-LIMIT FOR THESE CRIMES. Warszawa: Interpress Publishers, 1980. 186p. NjP: D804.G4P5413.

Deals with the entire Nazi treatment of Polish people, including the Jews. Covers deportation, persons, labor camps, concentration camps, etc. Facsimiles of posters, broadsides, etc. Illustrations.

708. Piotrowski, Stanisław, ed. HANS FRANK'S DIARY. Warszawa: Państwowe Wydawnictwo Naukowe, 1961. 320p. 61-3502.

Diarist Hans Frank was Governor General of Poland during the Second World War. This book presents a systematic record of the most important aspects of Frank's criminal activities while Governor General in Kraków. It is based on scientific, objective and impartial analysis of the vast amount of material contained in his diary and in documents which came to light during the Nuremberg Trial. Illustrations. Bibliography, pp. 181-201.

709. Polish Research Centre. London. GERMAN FAILURES IN
POLAND: NATURAL OBSTACLES TO NAZI POPULATION POLICY.
London: The Cornwall Press, Ltd., 1942. 30p.
43-7153.

A sketch of the state of affairs in German-occupied
Poland from 1939 up to publication of this work. Of
particular note is a map of "Western Poland: German
Administrative Divisions." Bibliographical footnotes.

710. Poland. Ministerstwo Spraw Zagranicznych. GERMAN
OCCUPATION OF POLAND; EXTRACT OF NOTE ADDRESSED TO
THE ALLIED AND NEUTRAL POWERS. New York: Greystone
Press, 1942. 240p. 42-12281.

Collection of documents enacted by German General
Gouvernement covering Poland. Also includes statements
regarding conditions in the occupied territory.

711. Popiołek, Kaźimierz. SILESIA IN GERMAN EYES, 1939-
1945, trans. by Andrzej Potocki. Katowice:
Wydawnictwo Sląsk, 1964. 238p. 67-61480.

An attempt to explain the Germanization of the Sląsk
region prior to and during the German occupation of
Poland between 1939 and 1945 and the Polish reaction to
these measures.

712. Przymanowski, Janusz. POLISH ROADS TO VICTORY.
Warszawa: Interpress Publishers, 1975. 181p.
76-358410.

A selective photographic record of Polish military
activities including the Underground throughout World
War II. Photographs are from the Historical Museum in
Warszawa. Brief text pp. 5-23.

713. Sagajllo, Witold. MAN IN THE MIDDLE: A STORY OF THE
POLISH RESISTANCE, 1940-45. London: Leo Cooper,
1984. 200p. 84-1357163.

A "true picture of underground life and of the associated problems faced by the Poles during the German
occupation." Description of problems containing the
German terror. Finally, a narrative of author's efforts
to survive the German occupation and "Russian liberation" and escape to the West after World War II.
Illustrations. Portraits. Maps.

*Special Works*  159

714. Segal, Simon. NAZI RULE IN POLAND. London: Robert Hale, Ltd., 1943. 214p. A43-3736.

    First book to describe in scientific detail Nazi rule in Poland. Nazis were deporting and exterminating Poles in order to make a new living space for German colonists. Covers organization of the regime, population, religious, cultural and economic life, ghettos and the Underground Movement. Map of interwar Poland delineating areas incorporated into Germany and General Gouvernement. Illustrations. Maps.

715. Winiewicz, Józef M. AIMS AND FAILURES OF THE GERMAN NEW ORDER. London: Polish Research Centre, 1943. 107p. A44-2072.

    Concerned with the importance of the relative biological strength of the German and Polish nations in connection with the German plans of world expansion. Author used mainly German sources. Maps. Bibliography, pp. 104-107.

### Heraldry

716. Peckwas, Edward A. COLLECTIONS OF ARTICLES ON POLISH HERALDRY. Chicago: Polish Genealogical Society, 1978. 20p.

    Purpose was to publish something on the subject of Polish heraldry. Much of the information and art work appeared originally in HERBARZ POLSKI by Kasper Niesiecki, 1845.

### History

717. Arnold, Stanisław. OUTLINE HISTORY OF POLAND; FROM THE BEGINNING OF THE STATE TO THE PRESENT TIME, by S. Arnold and Marian Żychowski. Warszawa: Polonia Publishing House, 1962. 245p. 65-40126.

    Emphasizes period from the Partitions to present. Accentuates the revolutionary movements, particularly socialist ones. Illustrations of the rotogravure type. No documentation. No bibliography.

718. Arthurton, Eileen A. POLAND, LAND OF THE WHITE EAGLE.
London: Maxlove Publishing Company, Ltd., 1944.
120p. 44-47546.

Author states that "her book was intended to give an outline picture of Poland." The thirty-one brief chapters range from "Legends of Long Ago" to the "Struggle of Polish Youth." Professor William J. Rose read and corrected first part of the book. Illustrations. Portraits. Maps on linging papers.

719. Beneś, Vaclav L. POLAND, by V.L. Beneś and Norman J.G. Pounds. New York: F. Praeger, 1970. 416p. 74-77306.

Divided into four parts entitled: History; Land and Resources; The Polish Republic; and, The People's Republic. Illustrations. Portraits. Maps. Bibliography, pp. 393-397.

720. THE CAMBRIDGE HISTORY OF POLAND, ed. by William F. Reddaway et al. Cambridge: The University Press, 1941-1950. 2v. A41-4089.

Volume I: From the Origins to Sobieski, 1696. Volume II: From Augustus II to Piłsudski, 1697-1935. Each chapter has been written by a specialist in the fields covered. Definitive work in English for period up to 1935. Illustrations. Maps.

721. Chołoniewski, Antoni. THE SPIRIT OF POLISH HISTORY, trans. my Mme. Jane Arctowska. New York: Polish Book Importing Co., Inc., 1918. 67p. 19-8570.

Brief sketches about Polish history but not presented in a chronological order.

722. Corsi, Edward C. POLAND: LAND OF THE WHITE EAGLE. New York: Wyndham Press, 1933. 224p. 33-22281.

Book written to bring before the reader data and facts about Poland. Covers history, Poles in America and a tour through Poland. Illustrations. Portraits. Maps.

723. Czechowski, Michael B. POLAND: SKETCH OF HER HISTORY. New York: Baker and Godwin, 1863. 58p. NN: C-2p.4619.

*Special Works* 161

>Subtitled "Treatment of the Jews, Laws Concerning Them; Polish Serfs and Their Freedom by the Czar Alexander II; Cause of the Present Polish Insurrection." Of particular value is chronological table of the sovereigns of Poland and the principal events in the reign of each, pp. 41-58. Contains statistics of Poland according to the limits established in 1772.

724.  Davies, Norman. GOD'S PLAYGROUND, A HISTORY OF POLAND. New York: Columbia University Press, 1982. 2v. 81-10241.

>Probably the best popular work on Polish history published in the English language. It is not merely a political narrative but covers other aspects of life as well. The second volume contains a section at the end entitled, "Solidarity, 1980-1981," pp. 720-725. Illustrations. Portraits. Maps. Bibliographical notes, pp. 644-679.

725.  Davies, Norman. HEART OF EUROPE: A SHORT HISTORY OF POLAND. New York: Oxford University Press, 1984. 511p. 83-22003.

>Emphasis is on those "elements of Poland's past which have had the greatest impact on present attitudes in Poland." Narrative moves from the present to the past. Appendix contains data on the Polish Armed Services as of 1982. Genealogical tables. Illustrations. Maps. Includes bibliographical references.

726.  Dunham, Samuel A. THE HISTORY OF POLAND IN ONE VOLUME. London: York: Longman, Brown, Green and Longmans, 1849. 324p. 6-13667.

>Covers history to 1831. Represents English viewpoint of the early nineteenth century. Order follows the reigns of the various kings of Poland. Includes a chapter entitled, "Society, Constitution, Manners, etc. of the Ancient Poles." Illustrations.

727.  Dyboski, Roman. OUTLINES OF POLISH HISTORY. London: G. Allen and Unwin, Ltd., 1931. 285p. MiD: 943.8.D98a.

>A course of lectures delivered at King's College, University of London, during two successive visits in 1923 and 1924. Map. Bibliography, pp. 275-278.

728. Dyboski, Roman. TEN CENTURIES OF POLAND'S HISTORY. Warszawa: Polish Institute for Collaboration with Foreign Countries, 1937. 33p. 38-18497.

 Brief survey of Polish history by the author when he was a professor in the University of Kraków. Contains one map of inter-war Poland.

729. Frankel, Henryk. POLAND: THE STRUGGLE FOR POWER, 1772-1939. London: Lindsay Drummond, Ltd., 1946. 191p. A47-157.

 Purpose was to fill certain gaps in the literature on Poland and her people by stressing the analysis of social and economic, rather than that of diplomatic and political factors. Concludes that the economic, social and political oppression of the population was largely responsible for Poland's backward development in all spheres and her helplessness in the face of foreign aggression both in 1772-1795 and in 1939. Illustrations. Maps.

730. Gieysztor, Aleskander. MILLENIUM: A THOUSAND YEARS OF THE POLISH STATE, by A. Gieysztor et al. Warszawa: Polonia Publishing House, 1961. 208p. 62-6849.

 A sketchy, illustrated story of Polish history commemorating the country's millenium. Illustrations. Maps.

731. Gieysztor, Aleksander. A THOUSAND YEARS OF POLISH HISTORY, by A. Gieysztor et al. Warszawa: Polonia Publishing House, 1961. 103p. 61-41661.

 Brief, illustrated history from Poland's beginnings to the present. Contains facsimile of sixteenth-century map of Poland.

732. Górka, Olgierd A. OUTLINE OF POLISH HISTORY, PAST AND PRESENT. London: Alliance Press, Ltd., 1945. 140p. A45-4809.

 Divided into two parts: Survey of Polish history and a survey of social life and customs. Maps.

733. Grimsted, Patricia K. THE "LITHUANIAN METRICA" IN MOSCOW AND WARSAW: RECONSTRUCTING THE ARCHIVES OF

THE GRAND DUCHY OF LITHUANIA. Cambridge, Mass.: Oriental Research Partners, 1984. 73p. 83-83094.

A description of the Lithuanian Metrica, chancery records of the Grand Duchy of Lithuania and other high-level archival materials. This is a republication of the Ptaszycki inventory with marginal indications of the location and current archival code of the materials listed. Illustrations. Maps.

734. Halecki, Oskar. A HISTORY OF POLAND, trans. by Monica M. Gardner and Mary Corbridge-Patkaniowska. New York: Roy Publishers, 1943. 336p.

Written and published by a Polish scholar who describes this work as "a simple manual of Polish history, more complete and more widely read ... and to make the reader reflect on the essential problems of Polish history." Maps on lining papers.

735. Halecki, Oskar. A HISTORY OF POLAND. New York: David McKay Company, Inc., 1976. 366p. 76-5560.

"New" edition of original history of Poland published in 1956 with maps and an up-to-date epilogue.

736. Harley, John H. POLAND PAST AND PRESENT. A HISTORICAL STUDY. London: George Allen and Unwin, Ltd., 1917. 255p. 17-20974.

Author sets forth in broad touches the memorable events of Polish history. He describes with very great precision and clearness the conditions of the diverse administrations imposed on Poland since its partition. Maps.

737. HISTORY OF POLAND, by Aleksander Gieysztor et al; trans. by Krystyna Cękalska et al. Warszawa: Polish Scientific Publishers, 1968. 783p. 68-6941.

A comprehensive historical study by five of Poland's leading historians. Covers the country's history only up to 1939. Reflects current historiographical scholarship in Poland. Illustrations. Portraits. Maps. Bibliography, pp. 727-740.

738. Jędlicki, Marjan Z. GERMANY AND POLAND THROUGH THE AGES. Cambridge: Galloway and Porter, Ltd., 1942. 23p. A42-5148.

Lecture given at Cambridge University on October 31, 1941. Maps.

739. Jedruch, Jacek. CONSTITUTIONS, ELECTIONS AND LEGISLATURES OF POLAND, 1493-1977: A GUIDE TO THEIR HISTORY. Washington, D.C.: University Press of America, 1982. 590p. 81-40301.

A survey of the parliamentary history of Poland. Contains biographical sketches of political personalities. Numerous lists. A treasure of information on Poland's constitutional history. Illustrations. Portraits. Bibliography, pp. 529-570.

740. Konopczyński, Władysław. A BRIEF OUTLINE OF POLISH HISTORY, trans. by Francis Benett. Geneva: Imprimerie Atar, 1920. 140p. 38-29277.

Part of the POLISH ENCYCLOPEDIA, published separately. Divided into two parts emphasizing modern history of Poland. No documentation. Maps.

741. Kraitsir, Charles V. THE POLES IN THE UNITED STATES OF AMERICA, PRECEDED BY THE EARLIEST HISTORY OF THE SLAVONIANS, AND BY THE HISTORY OF POLAND. Philadelphia: Kiderlen and Stollmeyer, 1837. 196p. 5-6792.

Bulk of this treatise deals with the early history of peoples who lived in eastern Europe from the time of the Greeks; the Poles and their history; and with the Poles in the United States. Especially valuable for discussion of pre-966 east European tribal peoples. No documentation.

742. Kryczynski, John N. THE RECOVERY OF POLAND. Philadelphia: Kryczynski and Wasilewski, 1847. 325p. 5-6793.

Short history prompted by Poland's fall. Part one, the larger and more important part, is entitled "The Recovery of Poland," which is, in effect, a history of Poland, Poniatowski. The second part deals with the secret police and sketches of the life of the Grand Duke Constantine of Russia. No documentation. Printed privately by the author.

743. Lewinski-Corwin, Edward H. THE POLITICAL HISTORY OF POLAND. New York: Polish Book Importing Co., 1917. 628p. 17-19703.

A cultural as well as political history with many little-known personalities outside Poland discussed, e.g. Elizabeth Drużbacka, 1695-1765, first Polish woman writer, with portrait. Especially valuable for illustrations, particularly portraits. Emphasizes the modern period. Maps.

744. Orvis, Julia S. A BRIEF HISTORY OF POLAND. Boston: Houghton Mifflin Co., 1916. 359p. 16-22948.

Covers all of Polish history with emphasis on modern period. Contains list of Jagiellonian dynasty. Maps. Annotated bibliography, pp. 335-336.

745. Patterson, Eric J. POLAND. London: J.W. Arrowsmith, Ltd., 1934. 152p. 34-39490.

One in a series of works devoted to presenting in a brief form the complete story of the development of the states of the world from their origin to the present day. Maps. Annotated bibliography, pp. 146-147.

746. Pogonowski, Iwo C. POLAND: A HISTORICAL ATLAS. New York: Hippocrene Books, 1987. 321p. 87-675198.

Collection of 180 rather poorly prepared maps of Polish history for the past two thousand years. Includes text with information about such things as the Polish Parliament (Sejm) and the evolution of the Slavic languages. Bibliography.

747. A REPUBLIC OF NOBLES: STUDIES OF POLISH HISTORY TO 1864, ed. and trans. by J.K. Fedorowicz et al. Cambridge: Cambridge University Press, 1982. 310p. 81-12284.

Collection of thirteen essays by some of Poland's most distinguished historians covering aspects of Polish history from the beginnings of the Polish state to the collapse of the Insurrection of 1863. Illustrations. Maps.

748. Rose, William J. POLAND. Harmondsworth, Middlesex, Eng.: Penguin Books, Ltd., 1939. 244p. 39-31850.

Extremely readable book on the history of Poland by an eminent scholar for popular consumption. Published in 1939 when western eyes were focused on the country. Illustrations. Maps. Bibliography, pp. 125 and 245.

749. Rose, William J. POLAND'S PLACE IN EUROPE: THREE LECTURES. London: Scottish-Polish Society. London Branch, 1945. 39p. 46-20556.

Lectures given in the summer of 1943: 1. Polish-Lithuanian-Ruthenian Commonwealth. 2. The Nineteenth Century. 3. Restored Poland. Maps.

750. Rose, William J. THE RISE OF POLISH DEMOCRACY. London: G. Bell & Sons, Ltd., 1944. 253p. 44-51599.

Purpose is to relate achievements of the Polish nation in the field of public affairs. Historical survey of political life in Poland with emphasis on democratic traditions. Illustrations. Maps.

751. Ross, M. of Durham. A HISTORY OF POLAND FROM ITS FOUNDATIONS AS A STATE TO THE PRESENT TIME. London: Pattison and Ross, 1835. 575p. NjP: 1638.785.

Both a history of Poland from the commencement of Polish history to the extinction of the monarchy as well as a retrospective description of Poland c. 1835. No documentation. Illustrations.

752. Siuchiński, Mateusz. AN ILLUSTRATED HISTORY OF POLAND, trans. by Stanisław. Warszawa: Interpress Publishers, 1979. 225p. 80-460137.

A profusely illustrated sketch of the history of Poland apparently directed to a secondary school-age audience. Illustrations. Portraits. Maps.

753. Slocombe, George E. A HISTORY OF POLAND. New York: T. Nelson & Sons, Ltd., 1939. 375p. 41-3880.

*Special Works* 167

A general history of Poland by an English scholar covering Slav origins through 1934. Illustrations. Portraits. Maps. Bibliography, pp. 367-368.

754. Slocombe, George E. POLAND. New York: Frederick A. Stokes Co., 1916. 316p. 17-21375.

 Covers history of the country beginning with the origin of the Slavs through the first part of World War I. Portraits. Maps. Bibliography, p. 309.

755. Super, Paul. EVENTS AND PERSONALITIES IN POLISH HISTORY. London: J.S. Bergson, 1936. 115p. 38-3460.

 A sketch of Polish history from 966 through the Piłsudski era. Divides the sketch by reigns of Polish kings and, at times, by events. Many portraits of historical personages. Illustrations. Maps.

756. Tennant, A.E. STUDIES IN POLISH LIFE AND HISTORY. London: George Allen and Unwin, Ltd., 1924. 254p. 24-28459.

 Gives a sufficient insight into things Polish as well as a general view of the country, its inhabitants and history. Contains facsimiles of music. Maps.

757. Tymieniecki, Każimierz, ed. HISTORY OF POLISH POMERANIA, trans. by Eileen Znaniecka. Poznań: Society of Lovers of Polish History, 1927. 181p. OL: D491.P791T9.

 Series of essays about the region by several scholars. Many references to the Kaszuby. Maps. Bibliography, pp. 165-167.

758. Whitton, Frederick E. A HISTORY OF POLAND, FROM THE EARLIEST TIMES TO THE PRESENT DAY. London: Constable & Co., Ltd., 1917. 302p. 18-7906.

 A clear, concise history of Poland. Most of the text devoted to period from the first partition in 1772. Maps.

759. Wojciechowski, Zygmunt. POLAND'S PLACE IN EUROPE, trans. by B.W.A. Massey. Poznań: Instytut Zachodni, 1947. 460p. 47-7208.

Collection of studies of history of German-Polish relations. Originally published clandestinely in Poland. Contains biographical sketches of authors. Maps.

760. Zaleski, August. LANDMARKS OF POLISH HISTORY. London: George Allen and Unwin, Ltd., 1916. 46p. 16-13394.

    A brief survey of Polish history.

761. Zamoyski, Adam. THE POLISH WAY. New York: Franklin Watts, Inc., 1988. 422p. 87-50290.

    "A lavishly illustrated history, from the tenth century to the present day, tells of Poland's achievements as a European nation. Illustrations. Maps. Bibliography, pp. 398-401.

History
962-1386. Piasts.

762. Czajkowski, Anthony P. POLAND AND THE GREGORIAN REFORM. New York: Fordham University Press, 1942. 332p.

    Doctoral dissertation at Fordham University. Attempts to trace the relationship of one of the Slav countries, Poland, to the religious, political and military phases of the reforms of Pope Gregory VII (1073-1085). Bibliography, pp. 323-332.

763. Dzięcioł, Witold. THE ORIGINS OF POLAND. London: Veritas Foundation Publication Centre, 1966. 311p. 67-77013.

    Attempts to synthesize historical findings up-to-date in order to explain the rise of Poland in relation to the great historical processes that transcended Polish history. Purpose is to make a comprehensive synthesis for foreign scholars as an introduction to the problems of the origin of Poland and the role of this country in the formation of Europe and to give to people of Polish ancestry an account of the origins of the Polish community from that spring. Maps. Bibliographical notes, pp. 265-300.

764. Gąsiorowski, Antoni, ed. THE POLISH NOBILITY IN THE
MIDDLE AGES, trans. by Aleksandra Rodzinska-
Chojnowska. Wrocław: Zakład Narodowy im.
Ossolińskich, 1984. 298p. MiU: HT653.P7P76.

Nine scholarly essays by experts in Polish medieval
history emphasizing the role of the aristocracy during
the Middle Ages in Poland.

765. Grudzinski, Tadeusz. BOLESLAUS THE BOLD, CALLED ALSO
THE BOUNTIFUL, AND THE BISHOP STANISLAUS: THE STORY
OF A CONFLICT. Warszawa: Interpress Publishers,
1985. 255p. NjP: DK4224.G7813.

More than a narrative of a period of Polish history,
it is also a sketch of the historiography of the
Bolesław-Św. Stanisław conflict. Includes many illustrations of ancient and contemporary renditions of the
principal characters. Bibliography, pp. 247-251.

766. Jasienica, Paweł. PIAST POLAND, trans. by Alexander
Jordan. New York: Hippocrene Books, 1985. 266p.
OL: DK4212.J3513.

Family saga of the House of Piast which ruled Poland
from the tenth to the fourteenth centuries. This essay
attempts to explain the national character of the
Poles. Author is a popular writer in his native
Poland. Illustrations. Portraits.

767. Knoll, Paul W. THE RISE OF THE POLISH MONARCHY: PIAST
POLAND IN EAST CENTRAL EUROPE, 1320-1370. Chicago:
University of Chicago Press, 1972. 276p. 77-187155.

Both a study in Polish history and an analysis of one
aspect of the history of east central Europe in the
fourteenth century as seen from Kraków. The book
focuses upon the re-emergence of the Polish state as a
factor in the affairs of the region and traces in a
roughly chronological manner the role which Łokietek
and Każimierz give Poland in this area and era. Maps.
Bibliography, pp. 249-266.

768. Manteuffel, Tadeusz. THE FORMATION OF THE POLISH
STATE--THE PERIOD OF DUCAL RULE, 963-1194, trans. by
Andrew Gorski. Detroit: Wayne State University
Press, 1982. 171p. 81-11583.

First published in Poland in 1976, this important history written by the foremost post-war Polish historian, describes the emergence of the Polish state. Maps. Includes bibliographical references.

769. Schedel, Hartmann. SARMATIA, THE EARLY POLISH KINGDOM: FROM THE ORIGINAL NURENBERG CHRONICLE, trans. by Bogdan Deresiewicz. Los Angeles: Plantin Press, 1976. 48p. 76-377530.

An extract from the Nurenberg Chronicle dealing with the beginnings of Polish history. Only 350 copies printed. Illustrations.

770. Wojciechowski, Zygmunt. MIESZKO I AND THE RISE OF THE POLISH STATE. Toruń: Baltic Institute, 1936. 233p. 38-1751.

Covers early history of Poland from the viewpoint of interwar Polish scholarship. Documentation with notes, pp. 174-224. Illustrations. Maps.

## History
### 1386-1573. Jagiellonians.

771. Bogucka, Maria. NICHOLAS COPERNICUS, THE COUNTRY AND TIMES, trans. by Leon Swajcer. Wrocław: Ossoliński State Publishing House, 1973. 201p. 74-157794.

A history of Poland during the period of Copernicus' life as well as a commentary on the man and his work. It comprehensively covers all aspects of Polish life and culture during this period ranging from the economy to the field of medicine. Illustrations. Portraits. Maps.

772. Evans, Sir Geoffrey C. TANNENBERG: 1410 and 1914. London: Hamish Hamilton, 1970. 182p. 74-550095.

Scholarly study of the two famous battles as symbolic of the animosity which has existed between Teuton and Slav since 1235. Includes battle maps for both battles, numerous illustrations, and short biographical notes on both German and Russian commanders in the 1914 battle. Bibliography, pp. 174-175.

*Special Works* 171

773. Jasienica, Paweł. JAGIELLONIAN POLAND, trans. by Alexander Jordan. Miami: American Institute of Polish Culture, 1978. 416p.

     An undocumented history of Poland during the Jagiellonian dynasty. Author states in a postscript that book was not intended to be scholarly but simply an essay, i.e. "literature using history for its subject." Portraits. Maps. No bibliography.

774. Krasinski, Walerjan S. HISTORICAL SKETCH OF THE RISE, PROGRESS, AND DECLINE OF THE REFORMATION IN POLAND AND OF THE INFLUENCE WHICH THE SCRIPTURAL DOCTRINES HAVE EXERCISED ON THAT COUNTRY IN LITERARY, MORAL, AND POLITICAL RESPECTS. London: Author, 1838-1840. 2v. 18-17398.

     Dedicated to the Protestants of the British Empire and of the United States by a Polish Protestant. Extensive coverage. No bibliography. Numerous explanatory footnotes. No documentation.

775. Omitted.

776. Laskowski, Otton. THE BATTLE OF GRUNWALD AND THE GERMAN "DRANG NACH OSTEN." London: Scottish-Polish Society, London Branch, 1942. 22p. NN: EAG-p.v.308.

     Brief account of the Battle of Grunwald. Written and published during the German occupation of Poland during World War II. Maps.

777. POLAND, THE LAND OF COPERNICUS, trans. by Bogusław Buczkowski et al. Warszawa: Ossolineum, 1973. 231p. 73-168096.

     A collection of several scholarly essays on Poland during the time of Copernicus. Covers all aspects of life. Illustrations. Portraits. Maps. Bibliographical notes, pp. 215-216.

History
1573-1795. Including Partitions.

778. Bain, Robert W. THE LAST KING OF POLAND AND HIS CONTEMPORARIES. London: Methuen and Co., Ltd., 1909. 296p. 9-35904.

Presents a picture of the social, moral and intellectual condition of Polish society at the moment when the Polish state was about to disappear forever from the map of Europe. Also, to explain how it was that Poland, by the end of the eighteenth century, had become a nuisance to her neighbors and an obstacle to the development of her own people. Illustrations. Portraits.

779. Boand, Nell H. LEWIS LITTLEPAGE. Richmond, Va.: Whittet and Shepperson, 1970. 290p. 75-139608.

Lewis Littlepage was first confidential secretary to the last king of Poland, Stanisław August II, 1786-1787. Deals with Polish history through author's autobiography. Portraits.

780. Coxe, William. TRAVELS INTO POLAND, RUSSIA, SWEDEN AND DENMARK INTERSPERSED WITH HISTORICAL RELATIONS AND POLITICAL INQUIRIES. New York: Arno Press, 1971. 210p. 76-135802.

Originally published in 1785, this is an English gentleman's recollections of his trip to Poland. First part covers a brief sketch of Polish history including first partition. Remainder is mainly description of his travels. Illustrations. Maps.

781. Eversley, George J.S. THE PARTITIONS OF POLAND. London: T. Fisher Unwin, Ltd., 1915. 328p. A15-2707.

History based on accounts spread over several chapters in their HISTORIES OF THE FRENCH REVOLUTION by von Sybel and A. Sorel with additional material from other sources. Illustrations. Portraits. Maps.

782. THE FALL OF POLAND IN 1794: AN HISTORICAL TRAGIC DRAMA IN FOUR ACTS. London: Longman, Brown, Green and Longmans, 1855. 90p. 20-8409.

A play in the English language about the disappearance of the Polish state from the map of Europe in 1795. Includes remarks by the patriot-author pleading for help to defeat Russian and Austrian despotism.

*Special Works* 173

783.  Haiman, Miecislaus, comp. THE FALL OF POLAND IN CON-
TEMPORARY AMERICAN OPINION. Chicago: Polish Roman
Catholic Union of America, 1935. 271p. 35-5999.

Commentary and augmentation of author's earlier work,
POLAND AND THE AMERICAN REVOLUTIONARY WAR, 1932. Periodical articles in American newspapers, reports of
correspondents. Illustrations.

784.  Horn, David B. BRITISH PUBLIC OPINION AND THE FIRST
PARTITION OF POLAND. London: Oliver and Boyd, 1945.
98p. 46-86.

An anthology of British public opinion reacting to
the First Partition of Poland in 1772. Includes reactions by government leaders. Illustrations.

785.  Kaplan, Herbert H. THE FIRST PARTITION OF POLAND. New
York: Columbia University Press, 1962. 215p. 62-
17550.

A new appraisal of the origins and first stages of
the first partition. Covers events between 1762 and
1773 which led to partition including interaction between European diplomacy and Poland's domestic history.
Maps. Bibliography, pp. 197-209.

786.  Lord, Robert H. THE SECOND PARTITION OF POLAND: A
STUDY IN DIPLOMATIC HISTORY. Cambridge, Mass.:
Harvard University Press, 1915. 586p. 15-25072.

Author's Ph.D. thesis in Harvard in 1910. As sub-
title suggests, book is a study of the diplomatic history of Europe as a whole with subject of the Second
Partition as a focal point. Bibliography, pp. 557-572.

787.  Marcinkowski, Karol. THE CRISIS OF THE POLISH-SWEDISH
WAR, 1655-1660. Wilberforce, O.: Ohio University
Press, 1951. 98p. 52-24117.

The subject of the present study is that period of
the Polish-Swedish War of 1655-1660 which became the
turning point of that struggle between the two Baltic
powers. Bibliography, pp. 85-98.

788.  Morton, John B. SOBIESKI, KING OF POLAND. London:
Eyre and Spottiswoode, 1932. 286p. 32-13049.

An attempt to reconstruct, for English readers, the last and highest moment of Poland's existence as a great European power before the complete chaos which led to the Partitions. Illustrations. Portraits. Maps. "A Notebook of Authorities," pp. xiii-xvi.

789. Saxton, Luther C. FALL OF POLAND. New York: C. Scribner, 1851. 2v. 5-35940.

Contains an analytical and a philosophical account of the causes which conspired to bring about the ruin of Poland with a history of the country from its origin. Portraits. Maps.

790. Stone, Daniel. POLISH POLITICS AND NATIONAL REFORM, 1775-1788. New York: Columbia University Press, 1977. 122p. 76-3926.

Revised and heavily abridged version of the author's doctoral dissertation. Although its subject deals directly with politics and government, it is equally a history of political conditions in Poland just prior to the Partitions. Bibliography, pp. 109-117.

791. Sutton, John L. THE KING'S HONOR AND THE KING'S CARDINAL. Lexington: University of Kentucky Press, 1980. 250p. 80-51021.

Although the book is a history of the war of Polish Succession, 1733-1738, a general European conflict, the history of Poland is the central object of the war and the book. Bibliographical note, p. 245.

792. Vajiravudh, King of Siam. THE WAR OF POLISH SUCCESSION. Oxford: B.H. Blackwell, 1901. 73p. 2-7531.

Object of this brief sketch is to lay before the student a few facts about the War of Polish Succession collected from various sources and selected with the idea of throwing light on the subject from as many aspects as possible. References, pp. v-vi.

793. Żółkiewski, Stanisław. EXPEDITION TO MOSCOW: A MEMOIR, trans. by M.W. Stephen. London: Polonica Publications, 1959. 167p. 60-33260.

Memoirs of Hetman Zołkiewski, hero of the Polish invasion of Russia in 1610. The account is a graphic

*Special Works* 175

one and gives a vivid picture of the fighting in those days. Illustrations. Portraits. Maps. Bibliography, p. 36.

## History
### 1795-1918. Partitioned Poland.

794. Betley, Jan A. BELGIUM AND POLAND IN INTERNATIONAL RELATIONS, 1830-1831. s'Gravenhage: Mouton and Co., 1960. 298p. 61-4349.

Deals with diplomatic activity brought about by the Belgian and Polish revolutions during the years 1830 and 1831. Maps. Sources, pp. 13-18.

795. Blanke, Richard. PRUSSIAN POLAND IN THE GERMAN EMPIRE (1871-1900). New York: Columbia University Press, 1981. 268p. 81-065162.

Study of the evolution of Prussian Polish policy between 1871 and 1900 and the evolution of the Polish minority in Germany with an emphasis on the impact of Prussian policies and the German context in general on the particular direction taken by Polish nationalism and the way an evolving Prussian-Polish society both called forth and largely frustrated various government measures. Maps. Bibliography, pp. 239-259.

796. Brock, Peter. NATIONALISM AND POPULISM IN PARTITIONED POLAND: SELECTED ESSAYS. London: Orbis Books, 1973. 219p. NjP: 1638.2117.

Seven separate articles on Polish history: Contours of Polish Nationalism under the Partitioning Powers; Struggle for Academic Freedom at the University of Kraków in the Early 1820's; Pacifist in Wartime; Political Programme of Polish Democratic Society; Ivan Vahylevych and the Ukrainian National Identity; Florjan Cenova and the Daszub Question; Bolesław Wysłouch, Pioneer of Polish Populism. Includes bibliographical references.

797. Coleman, Arthur P. A NEW ENGLAND CITY AND THE NOVEMBER UPRISING. Chicago: Polish Roman Catholic Union Archives and Museum, 1939. 64p. 39-30781.

A study of editorial opinion in New Haven, Connecticut, concerning the Polish Insurrection of 1830-1831. Study pertains to the record wave of pro-Polish sympathy in the United States. Chronological tables of the Uprising, pp. 63-64.

798. Coleman, Arthur P. THE POLISH INSURRECTION OF 1863 IN THE LIGHT OF NEW YORK EDITORIAL OPINION, by A. Coleman and M.M. Coleman. Williamsport, Pa.: Bayard Press, 1934. 131p. 35-7934.

Contains a checklist of editorials on the Polish Question in the leading New York dailies for 1863, pp. 125-131.

799. Edwards, Henry S. THE PRIVATE HISTORY OF A POLISH INSURRECTION, FROM OFFICIAL AND UNOFFICIAL SOURCES. London: Saunders, Otley and Co., 1865. 2v. A18-815.

An eyewitness account of the Insurrection of 1863 by a special correspondent of the TIMES of London in Poland. The second volume is made up almost entirely of letters addressed to the TIMES from Poland and Russia while the Insurrection was going on.

800. Gnorowski, S.J.B. INSURRECTION OF POLAND IN 1830-1831; AND THE RUSSIAN RULE PRECEDING IT SINCE 1815. London: James Ridgeway, 1839. 415p. 5-13107.

Sympathetic account by a contemporary Pole of the Polish Insurrection of 1830-1831 against Russia. No documentation.

801. Halicz, Emanuel. PARTISAN WARFARE IN 19TH CENTURY POLAND: THE DEVELOPMENT OF A CONCEPT, trans. by Jane Fraser. Odense, Denmark: Odense University Press, 1975. 220p. 76-381633.

Thesis of the book is the problem of the national liberation movement in 18th- and 19th-century Poland. This problem is dealt with from a military, social and political point of view. Also examines the interdependence between the method of conducting a national way and the socio-political situation. Portraits. Maps.

Special Works                                                    177

802.  Hordynski, Józef. HISTORY OF THE LATE POLISH REVOLU-
      TION AND THE EVENTS OF THE CAMPAIGN. Boston: Carter
      and Hendee, 1832. 406p. 1-18691.

      Work written in Polish, dictated to translator in
      French. Account of revolution of 1830. Detailed,
      directed at the American audience. Portraits. Maps.

803.  Kieniewicz, Stefan. THE EMANCIPATION OF THE POLISH
      PEASANTRY. Chicago: University of Chicago Press,
      1969. 265p. 79-92684.

      History of the Polish peasantry since 1800. Author
      traces with consummate skill the changes in Polish
      society that gradually brought the Polish peasants into
      the mainstream of national life. Maps. Bibliography,
      pp. 263-272.

804.  Kukiel, Marjan. CZARTORYSKI AND EUROPEAN UNITY, 1770-
      1861. Princeton, N.J.: Princeton University Press,
      1955. 354p. 54-6076.

      An essay, a sketch of a historical portrait of the
      statesman, Czartoryski, as perceived by the author after
      having lived several years among his relics and his
      papers, and after a study of his political ideas and
      activities. Illustrations. Portraits. Maps. Bibli-
      ography, pp. 323-334.

805.  Kulczycki, John L. SCHOOL STRIKES IN PRUSSIAN POLAND,
      1901-1907: THE STRUGGLE OVER BI-LINGUAL EDUCATION.
      New York: Columbia University Press, 1981. 279p.
      80-68445.

      Study of the conflict between the Protestant German
      governors of Prussian Poland and their Catholic Polish
      subjects over use of language in schools. Based upon
      exhaustive research. Maps. Bibliography, pp. 254-268.

806.  Leslie, Robert F. THE HISTORY OF POLAND SINCE EIGHTEEN
      SIXTY-THREE, by R.F. Leslie et al. Cambridge:
      Cambridge University Press, 1980. 494p. 78-73246.

      An account of the evolution of Poland from conditions
      of subjection to its reconstitution in 1918, develop-
      ment in the years between World Wars and reorganization
      after 1944-45. Chronologically, the text covers the

the period from 1863-1975. Fully documented. An update of the CAMBRIDGE HISTORY OF POLAND which ended the narrative with the year 1935.

807. Leslie, Robert F. POLISH POLITICS AND THE REVOLUTION OF NOVEMBER 1830. London: Athlone Press, 1956. 307p. A56-6712.

 Represents, in part, the work done for a Ph.D. thesis at the University of London: Author spent two terms in Poland. Title is self-explanatory. Maps. Bibliography, pp. 287-302.

808. Leslie, Robert F. REFORM AND INSURRECTION IN RUSSIAN POLAND, 1856-1865. London: Athlone Press, 1963. 272p. 63-3747.

 A short account of the Polish Insurrection of 1863 and its antecedents and the problem of how Poland was to achieve her passage from one form of social organization to another. Also discusses the political and economic emancipation of the Polish peasantry. Bibliography, pp. 252-266.

809. Thackeray, Frank W. ANTECEDENTS OF REVOLUTION, ALEXANDER I AND THE POLISH KINGDOM, 1815-1825. New York: Columbia University Press, 1980. 197p. 80-66053.

 Presents Tsar Alexander's concept of government and his attitude toward Poland, the role of Alexander's advisors, as well as the hopes and disillusions of the Poles which eventually led to the Revolution of 1830. Bibliography, pp. 181-192.

810. Tims, Richard W. GERMANIZING PRUSSIAN POLAND: THE H-K-T SOCIETY AND THE STRUGGLE FOR THE EASTERN MARCHES IN THE GERMAN EMPIRE. New York: Columbia University Press, 1941. 312p. 41-24159.

 Study is concerned with the particular aspect of the struggle between the Germans and the Poles: to describe the German reaction to the contest and particularly what happened to the H-K-T Society. Illustrations. Portraits. Maps. Bibliography, pp. 289-308.

811. Turczynowicz, Laura B. de Gozdawa. WHEN THE PRUSSIANS CAME TO POLAND. THE EXPERIENCES OF AN AMERICAN

*Special Works* 179

WOMAN DURING THE GERMAN INVASION. New York: G.P. Putnam's Sons, 1916. 281p. 17-207.

A description of what happened when the Germans invaded Poland in 1914 including her battle with typhus, the sufferings of the people, the ruin and the devastation of the country. Portraits.

812. Waliszewski, Każimierz. POLAND, THE UNKNOWN. London: W. Heinemann, 1919. 263p. 20-6295.

Re-evaluation of Polish history during the period 1772-1918 when her history was related only as part and parcel of the partitioning powers. Taken, in part, from author's work in Polish first published in Kraków in 1890.

813. Wandycz, Piotr S. THE LANDS OF PARTITIONED POLAND, 1795-1918. Seattle: University of Washington Press, 1974. 431p. 74-8312.

One volume in a series of books on the history of east central Europe. A history of the Polish nation in the nineteenth century. Emphasis is on the state territory of the Commonwealth. Includes discussion of Germans and Jews and their relations with the Poles. Maps. Bibliography, pp. 381-411.

814. Wieczerzak, Joseph W. A POLISH CHAPTER IN CIVIL WAR AMERICA. New York: Twayne Publishers, 1967. 264p. 67-25186.

Subtitled, THE EFFECTS OF THE JANUARY INSURRECTION ON AMERICAN OPINION AND DIPLOMACY. Doctoral dissertation. Bibliography, pp. 219-227.

815. Zielinski, Anthony J. POLAND IN THE WORLD OF DEMOCRACY. St. Louis: The Author, 1918. 262p. 19-15811.

An analysis of the causes and effects of the Partitions. Seems to have been written to further the cause of Polish independence.

History
1918-1939. First Polish Republic.

816. Bandrowski, Juliusz K., ed. THE GREAT BATTLE ON THE VISTULA, trans. by Harriet E. Kennedy. London: Sampson Low, Marston and Co., Ltd., 1921. 24p. 26-19790.

 Detailed account of the Battle of Warszawa, August 16-22, 1920, during the Russo-Polish War. Maps.

817. Brooks, Sidney. AMERICA AND POLAND, 1915-1925. New York: American Relief Administration, 1925. 111p. NN: TAA.

 The story of the rebirth and restoration of the Polish nation and America's participation therein. Data on actual financial assistance given to Poland by the United States. Illustrations.

818. Cornebise, Alfred E. TYPHUS AND DOUGHBOYS: THE AMERICAN POLISH TYPHUS RELIEF EXPEDITION, 1919-1921. Newark: University of Delaware Press, 1982. 188p. 81-70530.

 A "bit of military antiquarianism," well-researched, about the American Polish Relief Expedition that functioned in Poland from 1919 to 1921. As such, it sheds light on events in Poland during that time period. Illustrations. Bibliography, pp. 181-183.

819. D'Abernon, Edgar V. THE EIGHTEENTH DECISIVE BATTLE OF THE WORLD, WARSAW, 1920. London: Hodder and Staughton, Ltd., 1931. 178p.

 Author's observations while member of British mission to Poland to conclude armistice. Diary from July 22, 1920 to September 2, 1920. Portraits. Maps.

820. Davies, Norman. WHITE EAGLE, RED STAR; THE POLISH-SOVIET WAR, 1919-1920. New York: St. Martins Press, 1972. 318p. 70-185518.

 Special features include military maps of campaigns, biographical index with sketch of individuals prominent,

*Special Works* 181

both Poles and non-Poles. Illustrations. Portraits. Maps. Bibliography, pp. 289-293.

821. Fisher, Harold H. AMERICA AND THE NEW POLAND. New York: Macmillan Company, 1928. 403p. 28-10637.

Written in collaboration with Sidney Brooks. A sympathetic presentation of Polish history and how it was affected by the United States in modern times. Author states that the "relation of the status of the Polish nation to the political system of Europe: bond of sympathy between Poland and America established by Kościuszko and Pułaski and strengthened the participation of hundreds of thousands of Poles in our national life; and the world economic situation have determined the character of America's part in the restoration of Poland." Bibliography, pp. 369-380.

822. Grove, William R. WAR'S AFTERMATH, POLISH RELIEF IN 1919. New York: House of Field, Inc., 1940. 223p. A44-1402.

Story presented here is largely of personal experiences and contacts as recorded in a personal diary and the reports of associates and the author in the American Relief Administration. Pictures something of the plight of the unfortunate men, women and children who were left stranded in the war-torn area. Portraits. Maps.

823. Heymann, Frederick G. POLAND AND CZECHOSLOVAKIA. Englewood Cliffs, N.J.: Prentice-Hall, Inc., 1966. 181p. 66-22803.

Deals with the history of the peoples of Poland and Czechoslovakia essentially as one, i.e. to combine the developments of both countries in each chapter on a chronological basis. An attempt to sketch and interpret some of the dominant but complex issues which arose in the history of these nations. Maps. Suggested readings, pp. 163-171.

824. Korostovets, Vladimir K. THE RE-BIRTH OF POLAND. London: Geoffrey Bles, 1928. 317p. 29-8983.

Author was a correspondent for the NEW YORK WORLD. Book is a result of observations placed in a diary.

Covers the period from the beginning of World War I
through 1925. Illustrations. Portraits.

825. Kosćiuszko Foundation. New York. PADEREWSKI, HIS
COUNTRY AND ITS RECENT PROGRESS. New York:
Kośćiuszko Foundation, 1928. 46p. 29-4931.

A brief sketch of the conditions in Poland during the
twenties. Brief articles about Paderewski and Poland.
Portraits of Paderewski, Piłsudski and Moscicki, among
others.

826. Kukiel, Marian. THE POLISH-SOVIET CAMPAIGN OF 1920.
London: Oliver and Boyd, 1941. 23p.

Written as a review and summary of General Sikorski's
study of the Polish Campaign. Maps of the campaign.

827. Machray, Robert. POLAND, 1914-1931. New York: E.P.
Dutton, 1932. 447p. 32-26655.

Aims at presenting an historical account, in great
detail, of the new Poland which emerged from World War
I, constituted herself a state, fought and won a great
war on her own account, obtained definitive frontiers,
and developed into a great power. Portraits. Maps.
Bibliography, pp. 425-427.

828. Machray, Robert. THE PLAND OF PIŁSUDSKI. New York:
E.P. Dutton, 1937. 508p. 37-10660.

Incorporates previous book entitled, POLAND, 1914-
1931, much condensed, and carrying the history of
Poland up to mid-July, 1936. Contains text of the new
Constitution of Poland, translated by the Polish Committee for International Law Commission for International Law Co-Operation. Portraits. Map. Bibliography, pp. 487-489.

829. Piłsudski, Józef. THE YEAR 1920 AND ITS CLIMAX, BATTLE
OF WARSAW. London: Piłsudski Institute of London,
1972. 283p. 73-84491.

Historical description of political developments
affecting the Polish cause before World War I, during
the War and beyond to 1923. Also, an historical

*Special Works* 183

account of the military operations waged by Poland up
to the middle of 1919 on several fronts and from
February, 1919 to October 18, 1920 on the Soviet front.
Illustrations. Portraits. Maps.

830. Polonsky, Antony. POLITICS IN INDEPENDENT POLAND,
1921-1939; THE CRISIS OF CONSTITUTIONAL GOVERNMENT.
Oxford: Clarendon Press, 1972. 572p. 72-188451.

Describes the political life of the newly independent
Polish state from March, 1921 to September, 1939.
Investigation of the political development of the largest and most populous state. Based primarily on the
minutes of the Sejm and Senate, and other governmental
documents. Maps. Bibliography, pp. 524-560.

831. Rothschild, Joseph. PIŁSUDSKI'S COUP D'ÉTAT. New
York: Columbia University Press, 1966. 435p.
66-28266.

An inquiry into the causes, events, and consequences
of the crisis of May, 1926 in Polish political history.
An analysis of a significant period in the political
history of Poland and a case study of the preparation,
execution and attempted consolidation of a coup d'état
within a given set of historico-political and socioeconomic conditions. Maps. Bibliography, pp. 403-424.

832. Super, Margaret Low. THE CASE FOR POLAND. Ann Arbor,
Mich.: Michigan Committee of Americans for Poland,
1945. 92p. 46-149.

Description of Russia's treatment of Poland and how
the reconstructed Polish state of 1918-1939 had the
right to the same territories after World War II.
Illustrations. Maps.

833. Watt, Richard M. BITTER GLORY: POLAND AND ITS FATE,
1918 TO 1939. New York: Simon and Schuster, 1979.
511p. 79-12958.

A comprehensive, popular history of interwar Poland
seemingly based upon secondary sources. Illustrations.
Portraits. Maps on lining papers. Bibliography, pp.
475-479.

834. Zamoyski, Adam. THE BATTLE FOR THE MARCHLANDS. New York: Columbia University Press, 1981. 218p. 81-65952.

Purpose of this book is "to explain, as simply as possible, how and why Soviet troops were routed before Warsaw and what factors and personalities were responsible." Maps. Bibliography, pp. 206-213.

835. Żarnowski, Janusz. NOVEMBER 1918, trans. by Jan Sęk. Warszawa: Interpress Publishers, 1984. 231p.

One of a series designed to dispel myths surrounding Polish history. This book places events which occurred in November, 1918 into the perspective of the achievements and errors of the two interwar decades. Illustrations. Portraits.

History
1939-1945. World War II.

836. Bethell, Nicholas W. THE WAR HITLER WON: THE FALL OF POLAND. SEPTEMBER 1939. New York: Holt, Rinehart and Winston, 1973. 472p. 72-78122.

Author recounts Hitler's conquest of Poland in the light of a dual condemnation of the invader and those who permitted it. Suggests success was partially due to Hitler's charisma. Includes chronological list of major events, September 1, 1939 through November 9, 1939. Maps. Bibliography, pp. 450-453.

837. Coutouvidis, John. POLAND 1939-1947, by J. Coutouvidis and Jaime Reynolds. Leicester, Eng.: Leicester University Press, 1986. 393p. MiU: DK4410.C6811.

A history of Poland during the period, 1939-1947, with liberation from German occupation as the focal point. Also, examines way in which the perceived national interests of the liberating powers (Britain, the U.S.S.R., and the U.S.A.) were translated into policies in Poland. Two parts: Part One by John Coutouvidis examines the Polish government-in-exile from its formation to its disintegration and isolation; Part Two by Jaime Reynolds deals with the internal struggle in Poland during the German occupation and the immediate post-war years. Illustrations. Maps. Bibliography, pp. 372-382.

838. THE DARK SIDE OF THE MOON, with a preface by T.S. Eliot. New York: C. Scribner's Sons, 1947. 299p. 47-1221.

The book is the story of what happened to Poland and of what happened to innumerable Poles between 1939 and 1945. The aim of the book is to provide a background to state a case. Data obtained from prisons, penal camps and personal narratives.

839. Datner, Szymon. CRIMES AGAINST POWS: RESPONSIBILITY OF THE WEHRMACHT. Warszawa: Zachodnia Agencja Prasowa, 1964. 382p. 67-56868.

Story of those who after taken prisoner by the German Army were exterminated or died of maltreatment, hunger or exhaustion. Includes other than Poles but most of the book is devoted to the Polish prisoners. Illustrations. Portraits. Bibliography, pp. 369-370.

840. Datner, Szymon. GENOCIDE, 1939-1945, by S. Datner et al. Warszawa: Wydawnictwo Zachodnie, 1962. 334p. NN: D15.3371.

Present study proposed to acquaint the reader with the manner in which Poland's territory was to become German land and extermination of the Polish population. Based on documents assembled by the Central Commission for the Investigation of Nazi Crimes in Poland. Illustrations.

841. Jordan, Peter. FIRST TO FIGHT. New York: Roy Publishers, 1943. 48p. 43-6795.

A pamphlet-like little book which describes Poland's invasion by Germany, a brief history of the struggle, and the aftermath with Polish forces continuing the struggle overseas. Illustrations. Portraits. Maps.

842. Kacewicz, George V. GREAT BRITAIN, THE SOVIET UNION AND THE POLISH GOVERNMENT IN EXILE, 1939-1945. The Hague: Martinus Nyhoff, 1979. 255p. 78-31832.

An attempt to analyze the dilemmas confronting the Polish government-in-exile in London during the Second World War. Main objective is to investigate the actual operation of the Polish government-in-exile and the overall policies of the British government vis-à-vis the Soviet Union insofar as they had a direct bearing on Anglo-Polish relations. Bibliography, pp. 235-247.

843. Kennedy Robert M. THE GERMAN CAMPAIGN IN POLAND (1939). Washington, D.C.: Department of the Army, 1956. 141p. 56-61858.

One of a series of studies on German military operations in World War II against forces other than those of the United States. Designed principally as reference work for Army schools and colleges. Illustrations. Maps. Bibliography, pp. 136-137.

844. Korwin-Rhodes, Marta. THE MASK OF THE WARRIOR; THE SIEGE OF WARSAW, SEPTEMBER 1939. New York: Libra Publishers, Inc., 1964. 191p. 64-25187.

An account of the author's experiences in the siege of Warszawa, September 1-30, 1939. Gives a series of necessarily incomplete sketches showing the role of some individuals in an important historical event.

845. Listowel, Judith M.H. CRUSADES IN THE SECRET WAR. London: Christopher Johnson, 1952. 287p. 52-68128.

Although not primarily concerned with Poland, this story of a Polish-born secret agent does relate to the country. The author states that she relates the story of Colonel Nart, an account of his dealings with German's satellites and the results obtained by sheer logic.

846. Nadel, Norbert. BELLS OF DOOM, THE AUTOBIOGRAPHY OF A TWENTIETH-CENTURY EUROPEAN. New York: Hutchinson and Co., 1947. 271p. 47-29667.

Personal narrative. Spans author's life prior to World War I during that war, interwar Poland, and up to 1944. Author was a Polish Jew. Illustrations.

*Special Works* 187

847. Norwid-Neugebauer, Mieczyław. THE DEFENSE OF POLAND (SEPTEMBER 1939), trans. by Peter Jordan. London: M.I. Kolin, Ltd., 1942. 228p. 42-19730.

Present work is an extract from a military study, based mainly on the reports of participants in the campaign and such documents as are at present available. Author was a Lieutenant-General in the Polish Army. Maps. Sources, p. 228.

848. Nurowski, Roman, ed. WAR LOSSES IN POLAND, 1939-1945. Poznań: Wydawnictwo Zachodnie, 1960. 135p. MiU: D810.D6N97.

Essays by Janusz Gumkowski and others on the war against Poland in 1939. Maps. Documentation contained with text.

849. Poland. Ministerstwo Informacji. THE BLACK BOOK OF POLAND. New York: G.P. Putnam's Sons, 1942. 615p. 42-20476.

Published by the Polish Ministry of Information. Covers record of German barbarism from the close of the war in Poland, which ended October 6, 1939, until the end of June, 1941. Facsimiles. Illustrations. Maps.

850. Poland. Ministerstwo Informacji. THE GERMAN FIFTH COLUMN IN POLAND. London: Hutchinson and Co., Ltd., 1941. 157p. OL: 943.042.P757.

A revelation of the activities of the German spies and diversionist agents in Poland. Based on ample documents and eyewitness accounts, this highly interesting book shows up the Nazi subversive methods which also were employed by Germany in other countries. Maps on lining papers.

851. Poland. Ministerstwo Informacji. POLAND AFTER ONE YEAR OF WAR. London: George Allen and Unwin, 1940. 77p. OL: D765.A34.

A description of the situation in Poland from September 1, 1939 to September 1, 1940 including the German and Russian occupation and the establishment of a Polish government-in-exile. Maps.

852. Strzetelski, Stanisław. WHERE THE STORM BROKE: POLAND FROM YESTERDAY TO TOMORROW. New York: Roy Publishers, 1942. 257p. 42-50525.

An attempt to explain the diplomatic events which led to the invasion of Poland by Germany in 1939. Author also describes early period of the occupation and attempts to look into the future.

853. Westerby, Robert. THE POLISH GOLD, by R. Westerby and Robert M. Low. London: Methuen & Co., Ltd., 1940. 88p. 40-9960.

Authentic story of the transporting of the gold reserve from the Bank of Poland in Warszawa to the Bank of France in Paris. Written by a news reporter based on official report of the new Ministry of Finance to the Polish government in France in Paris, written by Adam Koc and Ignacy Matuszewski.

854. Wrzos-Glinka, Stanisław, ed. WE HAVE NOT FORGOTTEN, 1939-1945, ed. by S. Wrzos-Glinka et al. Warszawa: League of Fighters for Freedom and Democracy, 1959. 266p. MiU: D804.G3Z98.

Chiefly illustrations of occupation and war in Poland. Commentary also in Russian and French. Contains statistics on executions and military losses in all battles in which Polish troops fought. Many shots of atrocities.

## History
## 1945-

855. Ascherson, Neal. THE POLISH AUGUST: THE SELF-LIMITING REVOLUTION. New York: Viking Press, 1982. 320p. 81-52150.

An eyewitness account of the events in Poland since August, 1980 by a veteran observer of Polish affairs. Examines the role of the Polish Communist Party, the Solidarity union movement and the Catholic Church. Bibliography, pp. 301-302.

856. Blazynski, George. FLASHPOINT POLAND. New York: Pergamon Press, 1979. 415p. 79-15320.

*Special Works* 189

      This book tries to analyze the position of contemporary Poland between the years 1970 and 1979, the situation inside the country and to look into its future. Attempts to be comprehensive by relying on conversations with scores of individuals from all walks of life. Bibliography, pp. 397-400.

857. Bromke, Adam, ed. GIEREK'S POLAND, ed. by Adam Bromke and John W. Strong. New York: F. Praeger Co., 1973. 219p. 72-14208.

      Published in cooperation with Canadian Slavonic Papers. Jointly prepared by authors in Poland and outside observers of the Polish scene. Views of Polish and western authors on Poland in the 1970s. Includes bibliographical references.

858. Brumberg, Abraham, ed. POLAND: GENESIS OF A REVOLUTION. New York: Vintage Books, 1983. 322p. 82-40111.

      Series of essays on the situation in Poland in 1980. Contains nine commentaries by noted scholars and a section of readings on various contemporary problems. Contains also a complete English translation of the Gdańsk Agreement dated August 31, 1980, a list of Polish acronyms with English translations and notes for each chapter.

859. Cary, William H. POLAND STRUGGLES FORWARD. New York: Greenberg, 1949. 192p. 49-1252.

      Author wrote book after contact with Polish refugees while working in France in 1947. Visited Poland for approximately six months in same year. Set down what he found out about Poland. Illustrations. Portraits. Maps.

860. DeWeydenthal, Jan. THE POLISH DRAMA, 1980-1982, by J. DeWeydenthal, Bruce D. Porter, and Kevin Devlin. Lexington, Mass.: Lexington Books, 1983. 351p. 82-48527.

      This book is concerned with: Internal developments in Poland before the imposition of martial law; A description of Soviet policies toward Poland and east European responses related to the Polish situation;

The historical background of western communist reaction to events in Poland after the emergence of Solidarnosc; and, An analysis of political problems entailing the imposition of martial law. Includes bibliographical references.

861. Dziewanowski, Marian K. POLAND IN THE TWENTIETH CENTURY. New York: Columbia University Press, 1977. 309p. 76-51216.

    An attempt to interpret, to an intelligent Western reader, the complexities of a country that exists in a unique aura resulting from the mixture of grim geopolitical realities and the deeply rooted, historically conditioned yearnings of its people. Illustrations. Portraits. Bibliographical note, p. 295.

862. Forni, Luigi. THE DOVE AND THE BEAR, trans. by Tina Mattei. New York: Hippocrene Books, 1983. 160p. MiU: DK4440.F73.

    Author's interpretation of how Pope John Paul II prevented the Polish crisis of 1980 from degenerating into the third world war. Concludes that the Pope met secretly with Leonid Brezhnev.

863. Gibney, Frank B. THE FROZEN REVOLUTION; POLAND: A STUDY IN COMMUNIST DECAY. New York: Farrar, Straus and Cudahy, 1959. 269p. 59-9175.

    Travel in 1957 and a diary turned study of Poland's experiences under Communism. Influence of events of October, 1956 revealed. Author went to Poland as a reporter to tell what he had seen. Illustrations. Maps.

864. Karpiński, Jakub. COUNT-DOWN, THE POLISH UPHEAVALS OF 1956, 1968, 1970, 1976, 1980, trans. by Olga Amsterdamska and Gene M. Moore. New York: Karz-Cohl, 1982. 214p. 82-203.

    Book records the disintegration of the Polish Communist Party and the integration of Polish society, culminating in the birth of Solidarity in August, 1980. In the face of totalitarian dictatorship, Polish society has achieved independence, unity and democratic commitment that the Communist Party ignores at its own risk and that force cannot destroy.

*Special Works* 191

865. Kerstein, Edward S. RED STAR OVER POLAND, A REPORT FROM BEHIND THE IRON CURTAIN. Appleton, Wisc.: C.C. Nelson Publishing Co., 1947. 174p. 47-3296.

Author worked and lived with many of the average citizens of Poland and thus obtained first-hand information of conditions in Poland. Book consists of dispatches author wrote about his experiences in Poland. Illustrations.

866. Lewis, Flora. CASE HISTORY OF HOPE: THE STORY OF POLAND'S PEACEFUL REVOLUTIONS. New York: Doubleday, 1959. 267p. 58-12051.

An account of four years (1953-1957), during which Poland moved from unmitigated despair to qualified optimism. The author was an American correspondent who spent time in post-war Poland and traces the series of events that followed Stalin's death and shows how, little by little, the very worst Russian pressures have been taken off the country's economy and the very worst Communist pressures off her people.

867. Mikołajczyk, Stanisław. THE RAPE OF POLAND: THE PATTERN OF SOVIET AGGRESSION. New York: Whittlesey House, 1948. 309p. 48-9402.

A passionate and personal account of how the author viewed the communization of Poland, emphasis being not so much on communization as on Sovietization. Written after escape in late 1947 to the West. Illustrations. Portraits. Maps.

868. Ostaszewski, Jan, ed. MODERN POLAND BETWEEN EAST AND WEST. London: Polish School of Political and Social Science, 1971. 143p. 77-865708.

Main purpose of this book is to show, in a brief survey, that during the last fifty years of Polish history Poland has become a powerful, dynamic force in central and eastern Europe and should be given a proper part in the final organization of Europe based upon the principles of liberty, self-determination and free association of European nations.

869. Poland. Ministerstwo Spraw Zagranicznych. Departament Prasy i Informacji. FOREIGNERS ON POLAND. Warszawa:

Ministerstwo Spraw Zagraniczych, 1946. 219p. 51-15553.

A collection of 24 articles, favorable and unfavorable, reprinted just as they appeared in the foreign press on Poland in 1946.

870. THE REAL POLAND: AN ANTHOLOGY OF SELF-PERCEPTION, ed. by Alfred Bloch. New York: Continuum Publishing Company, 1982. 201p. 82-1559.

Selections from Polish writers. Panoramic views of Polish history. Selections from the writings of politicians who diagnosed the conditions that made Polish history so difficult.

871. Roos, Hans. A HISTORY OF MODERN POLAND, FROM THE FOUNDATION OF THE STATE IN THE FIRST WORLD WAR TO THE PRESENT DAY, trans. by J.R. Foster. New York: Alfred A. Knopf, 1966. 303p. 65-11131.

Tries to portray the period from the First World War to the present day, c. 1965. Depicts not only the political and diplomatic history of Poland, but also the pattern of Polish society and the political ideas associated with it. Maps. Bibliography, pp. 293-295.

872. Schaufele, William E. POLISH PARADOX: COMMUNISM AND SELF-RENEWAL. New York: Foreign Policy Association, 1981. 72p. 81-70157.

An attempt at an analysis of events in Poland at a time when Solidarność had just emerged as a legitimate movement. Author was U.S. Ambassador to Poland from June, 1977 to September, 1984. Illustrations. Maps. Bibliography, p. 72.

873. Sharp, Samuel L. POLAND, WHITE EAGLE ON A RED SHIELD. Cambridge, Mass.: Harvard University Press, 1953. 338p. 53-6034.

An attempt to present selectively, and primarily for the benefit of the intelligent non-specialist, those aspects of the Polish problem which are relevant to an understanding of the issue in its historical and contemporary setting. Maps. Bibliographical essay in preface, pp. vi-vii.

*Special Works*

874. Shneiderman, Samuel L. THE WARSAW HERESY. New York: Horizon Press, 1959. 253p. 59-14695.

    Author relates the story of the 1956 Uprising, the full story of Władysław Gomułka, and the powerful influences of the Catholic Church. Author was born, raised and educated in Poland and subsequently became a journalist. This book is a journalistic report written after many trips to Poland. Illustrations. Maps.

875. Stehle, Hansjakob. THE INDEPENDENT SATELLITE; SOCIETY AND POLITICS IN POLAND SINCE 1945. New York: F.A. Praeger, 1965. 361p. 65-18075.

    Tries to answer the question, "What, in fact, has survived from the legendary October which marked Poland's break with Stalinism in 1956?" Draws upon the author's first-hand observations of life in Poland between 1957 and 1962. Maps. Bibliography, pp. 339-340.

876. Stern, Harold P. THE STRUGGLE FOR POLAND. Washington, D.C.: Public Affairs Press, 1953. 79p. 53-10838.

    Gives an historical account of the struggle waged between East and West for the control of Poland and the position taken by the various governments and groups involved and their direct and indirect moves to further their objectives are discussed. Maps. Bibliography, pp. 77-79.

877. Syrop, Konrad. POLAND: BETWEEN THE HAMMER AND THE ANVIL. London: Robert Hale, Ltd., 1968. 208p. 68-119582.

    A popular history of Poland with an emphasis on contemporary life especially post World War II. Illustrations. Portraits. Maps. Bibliography, pp. 199-200.

878. Syrop, Konrad. POLAND IN PERSPECTIVE. London: Robert Hale, Ltd., 1982. 255p. NjP: DK4140.S97.

    Revised and enlarged edition of author's book entitled, POLAND: BETWEEN THE HAMMER AND THE ANVIL first published in 1968. Brings the story up to the military coup at the end of 1981. Maps.

879. Syrop, Konrad. SPRING IN OCTOBER; THE STORY OF THE POLISH REVOLUTION, 1956. New York. F.A. Praeger, 1958. 207p. 57-14803.

This book tells the story of a Polish revolution of 1956. It is a story, but not a history, having been written so shortly after the events which took place. Contains an historical introduction. Many quotations from Polish newspaper articles, poems and speeches, most of them not elsewhere available in English translation. Also, subject matter based on numerous conversations with people who have been to Poland recently and with Polish visitors to Britain. Chronology of events September/October, 1954 through January 20, 1957. Illustrations. Maps.

880. Weschler, Lawrence. THE PASSION OF POLAND, FROM SOLIDARITY THROUGH THE STATE OF WAR. New York: Pantheon Books, 1984. 263p. 83-24942.

Text originally appeared as a series of articles in the NEW YORKER on the rise and fall of Solidarity from its birth in Gdańsk through martial law. Author is a journalist. Illustrations. Maps.

881. Woods, William H. POLAND: EAGLE IN THE EAST; A SURVEY OF MODERN TIMES. New York: Hill and Wang, 1968. 272p. 68-30763.

British observer commissioned by the Polish Government to visit Poland and thereafter write a book about contemporary Poland. Spent 1967 in Poland and later revisited the country in 1968. Covers history from 1939 to 1968. Illustrations. Maps.

882. Żurawski, Joseph W. POLAND: THE CAPTIVE SATELLITE. Detroit: Endurance Press, 1962. 194p. 62-20289.

Presents the interplay of all forces as they now constitute and determine Poland's history. Sources used were secondary ones, articles in periodicals, newspaper accounts, accounts of visitors to Poland, U.S. government documents. Illustrations. Maps. Bibliography, pp. 161-171.

*Special Works* 195

History
Fiction

883. Babel, Isaak E. RED CAVALRY, trans. by Nadia Hilstein. New York: Alfred A. Knopf, 1929. 213p. 29-17889.

Story of Budyenny's famous Cavalry Army; the individuals in it in their role in the invasion of Poland during the Polish campaign of 1920-1921 in fictionalized form. Translator credits Anglo-French mission's intervention caused end of the war in favor of the Poles.

884. Baskerville, Beatrice C. PLAYGROUND OF SATAN. New York: W.J. Watt & Company, 1918. 308p. 19-3703.

Novel about Poland set during the First World War. Centers on an old Polish noble family and their English visitor and how they all became victims of German oppression.

885. Frischauer, Paul. A GREAT LORD, trans. by Phillis and Trevor Blewitt. New York: Random House, 1937. 371p. 37-39117.

Historical novel of Poland in Napoleonic times. In a note, the author reveals that the story is based on actual family papers. Names and some events are fictitious.

886. Gielgud, Val H. OLD SWORDS. Boston: Houghton Mifflin Co., 1928. 296p. 28-7325.

Set during World War and immediately thereafter. Descendents of a famous Polish noble become antagonists.

887. Gielgud, Val H. WHITE EAGLES, A STORY OF 1812. Boston: Houghton Mifflin Co., 1929. 279p. 29-23361.

Set during Napoleon's campaign in Russia. A Pole, Adam Konski, becomes a member of the French secret service. Romantic story woven around his adventures in that capacity.

888. Hutter, Catherine. ON SOME FAIR MORNING. New York: Dodd, Mead and Company, 1946. 403p. 46-7189.

Story of the relations between Poland and Germany during World War I and for some time after it. The central character is the broad-minded wife of a German nobleman who owns a large estate in Poland.

889. Jaron, Phillip. TWO ALONE. Boston: Houghton Mifflin Co., 1941. 240p. 41-5436.

   A Polish love story with a background of war. A young peasant soldier falls in love, leaves the army and both finally escape to neighboring Lithuania and are married there.

890. Karsavina, Jean. WHITE EAGLE, DARK SKIES. New York: Charles Scribner's Sons, 1974. 623p. 73-1113.

   An engrossing novel of Poland at the turn of the century. The country is seething with unrest. Young patriots yearn to be free from the heart of story but his novel vividly conveys whole fabric of Polish life. Hero is a Polish Jew.

891. Kelly, Eric P. THE TRUMPETER OF KRAKÓW, A TALE OF THE FIFTEENTH CENTURY. New York: Macmillan Company, 1928. 218p. 28-21739.

   An adventure story of a Tartar chieftain who covets a legendary crystal owned by the Charnetski family of the Ukraine. They take refuge in Kraków only to be followed by the Tartars. Story told through the eyes of a fifteen-year-old boy.

392. Kuniczak, Wiesław S. THE MARCH. New York: Doubleday and Company, 1979. 840p. 78-22598.

   The novel faithfully chronicles the initial German occupation of Poland in 1939, the voluntary relocation of hundreds of thousands of Poles, the infamous Katyn Forest massacre, and its little-known follow-up, the White Sea Massacre. Maps on lining papers.

893. Kuniczak, Wiesław S. THE THOUSAND HOUR DAY. New York: Dial Press, 1966. 628p. 66-24263.

   Novel set during first thousand hours of World War II, the time of the blitzkrieg in Poland.

*Special Works*

894. Michener, James A. POLAND. New York: Random House, 1983. 556p. 83-4477.

Novel about Poland following pattern established by the author in his earlier novels. A select group of events in Polish history, viz. the Mongol invasions, the battle with the Teutonic Knights, the Swedish invasion, Sobieski's victory over the Turks at Vienna and both world wars are scenes which form the background for the affairs of three main families, the Lubonski, the Bukowski and Buk, are enacted. Whatever sacrifices are made to historical accuracy, are compensated by an engaging story popularizing Poland and its people.

895. Poray, J.B. FINGER ON THE TRIGGER. London: Allan Wingate, 1952. 268p. OL: 893.63.P821.

Although a novel, the story is based on actual events which took place during the German occupation of Warszawa. Deals with two segments of society, the Underground and the Underworld.

896. Porter, Jane. THADDEUS OF WARSAW: A TALE FOUNDED ON POLISH HEROISM. New York: A.L. Burt Company, 1919. 461p. 20-19335.

Story of a young Pole, Thaddeus, descendent of Jan Sobieski, and his adventures during the second and third partitions of Poland. About two-thirds of the story is set in Poland where the hero finds refuge and adventure. Thaddeus is revealed ultimately to be the relative of an Englishman. Appeared in several editions spanning several years.

897. Read, Piers P. POLONAISE. New York: J.B. Lippincott Co., 1976. 347p. 76-15306.

Novel about the lives of a brother, Stefan, and his sister, Krystyna, descendents of Polish minor gentry and how the two survive interwar, war and postwar Poland, 1914-1950, with some interesting sidelights into the Poles as human beings.

898. Rudnicki, Adolf. ASCENT TO HEAVEN, trans. by H.C. Stevens. New York: Roy Publishers, 1951. 204p. 51-22490.

Innate human fears that are intensified under stress is the real theme of these stories of people of Warszawa, victimized by modern warfare, torn by inner conflicts which suddenly seem acute in times of destruction and struggles for survival--lovers who discover their allusions about each other, a Jewish boy who fears ridicule of his beard, more than death.

899. Skurzynski, Gloria. MANWOLF. New York: Houghton Mifflin Co., 1981. 177p. 80-22393.

Set in Poland in the Middle Ages this is a haunting tale of suspense and romance, of a mother and son whose destinies were both linked to a mysterious nobleman who always wore a leather mask.

900. Solski, Wacław. THE TRAIN LEAVES AT MIDNIGHT. New York: Crown Publishers, Inc., 1951. 287p. 51-12803.

Novel of suspense which takes us underground in Poland during the terrible occupation that followed World War II. The author, a writer of international reputation, was in Russia during the revolution in 1917, in Germany in the 1930s when Hitler rose to power, in France when Paris fell, in London during the Blitz. He was born in Poland and knows his people.

901. Styron, William. SOPHIE'S CHOICE. New York: Random House, 1979. 515p. 78-21835.

The story of ill-fated lovers, one of whom is a Polish survivor of the Holocaust, specifically Oświęcim, one Sophie Zawistowska. She lives in Brooklyn in the late 1940s and her experiences are told in flash-back. The "choice" is revealed towards the end of the story and is directly related to her tragic experiences in Poland.

902. Thomas, Frederick W. THE POLISH CHIEFS: AN HISTORICAL ROMANCE. New York: J.K. Porter, 1832. 2v.

The story of Pułaski and Kośćiuszko in fictional form. Includes references to U.S. military support for Polish revolutions in the early nineteenth century.

*Special Works* 199

903. Wnukowski, Joseph S. SUN WITHOUT WARMTH. London: Veritas Foundation Publications Centre, 1966. 376p. 68-86630.

 An emotional story based upon fact of the lives and hardships endured by a coterie of persons from a Polish village after the Fourth Partition of Poland in 1939. The Poles eventually all are exiled to Siberia and the story ends when Germany invades Russia and the Poles are freed.

### Industries

904. Bochenski, Aleksander. TRACING THE DEVELOPMENT OF POLISH INDUSTRY, trans. by Edmund Wiszniewicz. Warszawa: Interpress Publishers, 1971. 111p. 72-187672.

 Traces the successive steps marking the progress in science and research in various branches of knowledge and industry in post-war Poland: society and technology, science and research, chemistry, mining, power industry, iron works, engineering industry, electronics and measuring instruments, some electrical branches left out. Illustrations.

905. Iskra, Wiesław. THE INDUSTRIAL DEVELOPMENT OF POLAND, trans. by Eugene Lepa. Warszawa: Interpress Publishers, 1970. 90p. 72-21252.

 Popular account of the level, the rate, directions and factors of industrial development of Poland in the post-war period and up to 1985 in perspective. Author is a Polish economist. Illustrations. Bibliographical footnotes.

906. Majkowski, Karol. POLISH TEXTILES. Leigh-on-the-Sea, Eng.: F. Lewis, Publishers, Ltd., 1968. 14p. 74-356498.

 Black-and-white illustrations of contemporary Polish textiles with descriptive notes. Forty-eight plates.

907. World Power Conference. Polish National Committee. POWER SOURCES IN POLAND AND THEIR UTILIZATION. Warszawa: M. Arct, 1931. 175p. NjP: HC339.W89.

Report issued by the Polish National Committee of the power resources in Poland c. 1931 with maps indicating the distribution of these resources, as well as the high tension lines, etc. Black-and-white illustrations. Maps. Charts. Tables. Bibliography, pp. 167-176.

## Intellectual Life

908. Balicki, Stanisław W. CULTURAL POLICY IN POLAND, by S.W. Balicki et al. Paris: UNESCO, 1973. 67p. 73-79494.

Purpose of series is to show how cultural policies are planned and implemented in various member states. Studies deal with the principles and methods of cultural policy, the evaluation of cultural needs, administrative structures and management, planning and financing, etc. Contains a section entitled, "Polish Culture Throughout the World." Illustrations.

909. CULTURE IN PEOPLE'S POLAND, ed. by Tadeusz Galinski, trans. by Eugene Lepa and Olga Lepa. Warszawa: Państwowe Wydawnictwo Ekonomiczne, 1966. 440p. 68-7338.

Several authors wrote articles on literature, art, music, film, folk art, theater, museums, architecture, libraries, education and educational affairs. Comprehensive study of cultural conditions c. 1965. Cultural chronicle, 1944-1965. Illustrations. Maps. Portraits.

910. Fiszman, Joseph R. REVOLUTION AND TRADITION IN PEOPLE'S POLAND: EDUCATION AND SOCIALIZATION. Princeton, N.J.: Princeton University Press, 1972. 382p. 70-166369.

Analysis of the roles of education and of the teacher in a period of deep sociopolitical and economic transformation and a description of the patterns of recruitment and training of teachers who would fill the anticipated roles and perform the expected functions. Bibliography, pp. 329-365.

911. Goldfarb, Jeffrey C. ON CULTURAL FREEDOM, AN EXPLORATION OF PUBLIC LIFE IN POLAND AND AMERICA. Chicago: University of Chicago Press, 1982. 173p. 82-8325.

An analysis of the forces which determined artistic and academic expression in Poland and the United States from contemporary theatrical productions in New York City and Warszawa.

912. Harrell, Jean G., ed. AESTHETICS IN 20TH CENTURY POLAND; SELECTED ESSAYS, ed. by J.G. Harrell and A.C. Wierzbańska. Lewisburg, Pa.: Bucknell University Press, 1973. 285p. 78-38984.

    Primary aim is to present important Polish essays in aesthetics that are largely unknown to the English-reading public. Brief biographical sketches of writers. Includes bibliographical references.

913. Jordan, Zbigniew A. PHILOSOPHY AND IDEOLOGY; THE DEVELOPMENT OF PHILOSOPHY AND MARXISM-LENINISM IN POLAND SINCE THE SECOND WORLD WAR. Dordrecht, Neth.: D. Reidel, 1963. 600p. 63-5056.

    Purpose is to describe the development of philosophy in Poland since the end of the Second World War and the development of Marxist-Leninist philosophy in the intellectual life of contemporary Poland. Bibliography, pp. 538-590.

914. Kuncewiczowna, Maria, ed. THE MODERN POLISH MIND: AN ANTHOLOGY OF STORIES AND ESSAYS BY WRITERS LIVING IN POLAND TODAY. Boston: Little, Brown and Company, 1962. 440p. 62-10531.

    Collection of stories and essays by Polish authors. Each selection is preceded by a brief biographical sketch of the author. Anthology serves to show how the Polish mind worked under the pressure of communism as opposed to national tradition.

915. Lednicki, Wacław. POLAND AND THE WORLD. New York: Polish Institute of Arts and Sciences, 1948. 92p. 48-31451.

    Author's lectures on Polish and Russian literature which were originally printed in the quarterly bulletin of the Polish Institute of Arts and Sciences in America. Bibliography, p. 92.

916. Lednicki, Wacław. RUSSIA, POLAND AND THE WEST: ESSAYS IN LITERARY AND CULTURAL HISTORY. New York: Roy Publishers, 1954. 419p. 54-6541.

   Series of essays devoted to Poland's position in western European and Russian relations. Emphasis is placed on cultural development and relations. Much material on Dostoyevsky including an entire essay on Dostoyevsky and Poland. Illustrations. Portraits.

917. Litwiński, Leon. INTELLECTUAL POLAND. New York: Polish Book Importing Co., 1916. 61p. 16-22449.

   Lecture delivered at Cambridge University on May 19, 1916. Includes chronological outline of the history of the Polish universities. Weaves in conditions in 1915 with historical discussion. A "state of intellectual life" report.

918. POLISH SOCIOLOGY: SELECTION OF PAPERS FROM THE POLISH SOCIOLOGICAL BULLETIN. Wrocław: Ossolineum, 1974. 307p. 75-305824.

   Translation of a number of papers written for the Polish Sociological Bulletin on the occasion of the VIII World Sociological Congress in Toronto. Illustrations.

919. Pomian-Srzednicki, Maciej. RELIGIOUS CHANGES IN CONTEMPORARY POLAND: SECULARIZATION AND POLITICS. Boston: Routledge and Kegan Paul, 1982. 227p. 82-500.

   Author, daughter of Polish war-refugee parents, presents a critical appraisal of the documentary evidence for and against the process of secularization in Polish society and examines all the relevant Polish material on the subject. Bibliography, pp. 223-226.

920. Raina, Peter K. POLITICAL OPPOSITION IN POLAND, 1954-1977. London: Poets and Painters' Press, 1978. 584p. NjP: DK4436.R33.

   Presentation of Polish intellectuals who were in opposition to the authoritarian rule and dogmatic policies of the Communist Party. A detailed description of dissent in Polish intellectual circles during the stated period. Bibliography, pp. 553-569.

921. Simon, Brian. EDUCATION IN NEW POLAND. London: Lawrence and Wishart, 1955. 63p. 55-653.

A report written by the author after a visit to Polish schools and universities at the invitation of the country's Committee for Cultural Relations with foreign countries in Warszawa. Illustrations.

922. Skolimowski, Henryk. POLISH ANALYTICAL PHILOSOPHY. London: Routledge and Kegan Paul, 1967. 275p. 67-82250.

Work aims to trace the origins and describe the nature of analytical philosophy, to examine in detail the sources, development, and contributions of the Polish analytical movement, and to relate Polish to British analytical philosophy. Bibliography, pp. 262-265.

923. Skubała-Tokarska, Zofia. POLISH UNIVERSITIES. Warszawa: Polonia Publishing House, 1959. 174p. 61-21824.

Purpose is to give foreign readers an outline history of universities in Poland and some information about their present state. Many black-and-white photographs of sites and contains portraits of Hugo Kołłątaj and Stanisław Staszic, among others.

924. THE SOVIETIZATION OF CULTURE IN POLAND; COLLECTIVE work. Paris: Mid-European Research and Planning Centre, 1953. 207p. 53-39609.

Report based on studies written by Polish emigre authors living in Paris on various subjects ranging from philosophy to biology.

925. Super, Paul. ELEMENTS OF POLISH CULTURE AS SEEN BY A RESIDENT FOREIGNER. London: Baltic Institute, 1935. 74p. 37-14908.

Brief description of the culture of Poland, particularly the Wista-Baltic region, as viewed by the author, an Englishman residing in Poland. Illustrations. Bibliography, pp. 74-75.

926. Taras, Ray. IDEOLOGY IN A SOCIALIST STATE: POLAND, 1956-1983. New York: Cambridge University Press, 1984. 299p. 84-4970.

Examine the role of ideology in a socialist state and the way it may change. Focuses on ideological developments in Poland from October, 1956 to the end of 1983. Based upon research in Poland. Bibliography, pp. 289-292.

927. Walicki, Andrzej. PHILOSOPHY AND ROMANTIC NATIONALISM: THE CASE OF POLAND. New York: Oxford University Press, 1982. 415p. 81-18120.

An analysis of the philosophical currents which helped create and were shaped by Polish romantic nationalism between 1830 and 1850. Includes a study of Marx and Engel's views on the Polish national question. Bibliography, pp. 400-409.

928. Wepsiec, Jan. POLISH INSTITUTIONS OF HIGHER LEARNING. New York: Polish Institute of Arts and Sciences, 1959. 110p. 59-37794.

A handbook of Poland's universities, libraries, cultural institutions, research centers and learned societies. A tool for scholars, authors, librarians, and anyone interested in cultural exchange between the West and Poland. Bibliography, pp. 9-10.

929. Wiatr, Jerzy J. PAST AND PRESENT IN POLISH SOCIOLOGY. Warszawa: Polish Academy of Sciences, 1974. 23p. OL: HM22.P71W5.

Lecture given at the Polish Academy of Sciences Center in Rome in 1972. Covers the problems which confront Polish sociology at the time the lecture was given.

930. Zatko, James J., comp. THE VALLEY OF SILENCE; CATHOLIC THOUGHT IN CONTEMPORARY POLAND. Notre Dame, Ind.: University of Notre Dame Press, 1967. 391p. 67-12125.

Anthology of contemporary Catholic intellectual life in Poland being a collection of essays by various Polish Catholic scholars on various subjects. All were

*Special Works* 205

associated with the Catholic University of Lublin. Contains brief biographical sketches of contributors.

931. Ziffer, Bernard. POLAND: HISTORY AND HISTORIANS; THREE BIBLIOGRAPHICAL ESSAYS. New York: Mid-European Studies Center, 1952. 107p. 53-6596.

An attempt to present succinctly, but exhaustively, the remarkable Polish achievements in history up to World War II with special emphasis on the period of Polish independence, 1918-1939. Gives the English-speaking reader a general picture of Polish intellectual accomplishments and provides a bibliographical description of the main sources and more important works of the respective branches of Polish learning as well as a critical evaluation of them. Includes bibliographies.

### Jews In Poland

932. Apenszlak, Jacob, ed. THE BLACK BOOK OF POLISH JEWRY; AN ACCOUNT OF THE MARTYRDOM OF POLISH JEWRY UNDER NAZI OCCUPATION. New York: Roy Publishers, 1943. 343p. 44-1657.

Detailed account of the plight of the Jews in Poland from the beginnings of the German invasion. Chronological documentary text presenting the course of events, of the responsible affidavits of eyewitnesses, of official reports and statements, of excerpts of original letters, quotations from the Nazi press and of photographs smuggled out of Poland. Illustrations.

933. Bartoszewski, Władysław. THE BLOOD SHED UNITES US. PAGES FROM THE HISTORY OF HELP TO THE JEWS IN OCCUPIED POLAND. Warszawa: Interpress Publishers, 1970. 243p. 78-275305.

Attempts to pay tribute to victims murdered by Nazis on Polish soil. Largely based on documentary material contained in author's earlier publications. Concentrates mainly on the events which took place in Warszawa and the activities of the Council for Aid to Jews. Illustrations. Portraits. Bibliography, pp. 230-244.

934. Bartoszewski, Władysław, ed. RIGHTEOUS AMONG NATIONS: HOW POLES HELPED THE JEWS, 1939-1945, ed. by W. Bartoszewski and Zofia Lewin. London: Earlscourt Publications, Ltd., 1969. 834p. 77-416924.

   A collection of accounts of individual Jewish persons who were aided by Poles during the German occupation during World War II. Grouped under various subject headings, each of which comprises a chapter. Also contains a section entitled, "Documents," pp. 615-778, which illustrate chiefly the collaboration of Poles and Jews and various forms of aid given to Jews by Poles.

935. Bartoszewski, Władysław. THE SAMARITANS: HEROES OF THE HOLOCAUST, by W. Bartoszewski and Zofia Lewin; ed. by Alexander T. Jordan. New York: Twayne Publishers, Inc., 1970. 442p. 74-110706.

   More information about how the Poles aided the Jews in Poland during the Nazi occupation. Originally published in Polish.

936. Bartoszewski, Władysław. THE WARSAW GHETTO: A CHRISTIAN'S TESTIMONY. New York: Harper & Row, 1988. 160p.

   A Polish historian outlines here the efforts of Poles to help the Jews in Poland who remained after the 1942 purges in that country.

937. Bauman, Janina. WINTER IN THE MORNING: A YOUNG GIRL'S LIFE IN THE WARSAW GHETTO AND BEYOND, 1939-1945. London: Virago Press, 1986. 195p. MiU: DS135.P62W3B34.1986.

   An account written forty years later by a survivor of the Holocaust in Poland. Based upon author's diary and writings of author's mother. Illustrations. Portraits.

938. Berenstein, Tatiana. ASSISTANCE TO THE JEWS IN POLAND, 1939-1945, by T. Berenstein et al. Warszawa: Polonia Publishing House, 1963. 82p. 65-84756.

   Object is to rescue from obscurity the sacrifice of those Poles who, despite the raging terror and their own tragedies and misfortunes, risked their lives to bring relief to the most stricken members of the

*Special Works* 207

community--the Jews during the Nazi occupation of
Poland. Illustrations. Portraits. Bibliography, pp.
79-83.

939. Berg, Mary. WARSAW GHETTO, A DIARY, ed. by S.L.
Shneiderman. New York: L.B. Fischer, 1945. 253p.
45-2281.

Author was imprisoned in Warszawa Ghetto at age 15.
Daughter of an American citizen. Kept a diary, being
an eyewitness record. Notes written originally in
Polish. At age 20, she decided to publish the diary.
Covers period from October 10, 1939 to March 5, 1944.

940. Birenbaum, Halina. HOPE IS THE LAST TO DIE: A PERSO-
NAL DOCUMENTATION OF NAZI TERROR, trans. by David
Welsh. New York: Twayne Publishers, 1971. 246p.
77-167696.

Documentary account of author's experiences in
Warszawa Ghetto. First published in 1967, 28 years
after the end of World War II. Author was in concentration camps at Majdanek, Auschwitz, Ravensbruck, and
Neustadt-Glewe.

941. Borzykowski, Tuwie. BETWEEN TUMBLING WALLS, trans. by
Mendel Kohansky. Lokame Ha-Getaot, Israel: Ghetto
Fighters House, 1972. 229p. 72-950450.

Covers period between September, 1942 and January,
1945. Centers on author's own experiences, his description of the lives and the actions of the Jewish
Fighting Organization. Memoirs. Illustrations.

942. Bujak, Franciszek. THE JEWISH QUESTION IN POLAND.
Paris: Imprimerie Leve, 1919. 50p. 19-18651.

A brief discussion of the actual condition of Jews in
the reconstructured Polish state with special attention
given to their future, especially in the political and
economic life of Poland.

943. Cohen, Israel. VILNA. Philadelphia: Jewish Publication Society of America, 1943. 531p. 44-237.

Comprehensive history of the Jewish community of
Wilno from its earliest time, 1322, to the present.

Since so many of the residents of Wilno were Jewish, this book serves as a history of that city. Illustrations. Bibliography, pp. 517-519.

944. David, Janina. A SQUARE OF SKY; RECOLLECTIONS OF MY CHILDHOOD. New York: W.W. Norton, 1964. 221p. 65-25937.

 A personal account of life in occupied Poland. Author relates here childhood and adolescence as the only child of well-to-do Jewish parents in a Polish town to the changes after the German invasion as the family moved into the Warszawa Ghetto. A first-hand picture of everyday life in the Ghetto.

945. David, Janina. A TOUCH OF EARTH, A WARTIME CHILDHOOD. New York: Orion Press, 1969. 207p. 76-83402.

 Autobiographical memoir of the author from age 13 through age 16. Sequel to her A SQUARE OF SKY.

946. Dobroszycki, Łucjan. THE CHRONICLE OF THE ŁÓDZ GHETTO, 1941-1944, trans. by Richard Lourie et al. New Haven: Yale University Press, 1984. 551p. 84-3614.

 Story of the Ghetto where 240,000 Jews were crowded. An eerie and horrific scene told in terse entries. Illustrations. Portraits. Maps.

947. Dobroszycki, Łucjan. IMAGE BEFORE MY EYES: A PHOTOGRAPHIC HISTORY OF JEWISH LIFE IN POLAND, 1864-1939, by Ł. Dobroszycki and Barbara Kirshenblatt-Gimblett. New York: Schocken Books, Inc., 1977. 75-35448.

 Comprehensive account, both written and photographic, of Jews in Poland from the earliest days to the invasion of Poland in 1939. Illustrations. Maps. Bibliography, pp. 251-256.

948. Donat, Alexander. THE HOLOCAUST KINGDOM: A MEMOIR. New York: Holt, Rinehart and Winston, 1965. 361p. 64-21920.

 Personal narrative of a life in the Warszawa Ghetto during the German occupation. No documentation. No bibliography. Author was 34 in 1939; memoir written 25 years later. Maps.

*Special Works* 209

949. Dubnov, Semen M. HISTORY OF THE JEWS IN RUSSIA AND POLAND, FROM THE EARLIEST TIMES UNTIL THE PRESENT DAY, trans. by Israel Friedlaender. Philadelphia: Jewish Publication Society of America, 1920. 3v. 16-16352.

   Contents: Vol. I-From the beginning until the death of Alexander I, 1825. Vol. II-From the death of Alexander I until the death of Alexander III, 1825-1894. Vol. III-From the accession of Nicholas II, until the present day with bibliography and index. Emphasis on the Jews in Russia.

950. Eisner, Jack. THE SURVIVORS, ed. by I.A. Leitner. New York: Morrow, 1980. 320p. 80-13184.

   Describes one facet of life in the Warszawa Ghetto--that of the juvenile smugglers. The author, who founded the "Warsaw Ghetto Resistance Organization," at age 13, became the leader of such a gang, which sneaked across the Ghetto walls to obtain food for the starving Jewish inhabitants. Illustrations.

951. Folkmann, Adolf. THE PROMISE HITLER KEPT, as told to Stefan Szende. New York: Roy Publishers, 1945. 281p. 45-5961.

   Experiences of a Polish Jew in Nazi-dominated territories from September, 1930 to October, 1943, as told to Stefan Szende. First detailed eyewitness report on the extermination of Polish and other European Jews. Also contains first detailed account on conditions in east Poland during the Russian occupation from 1939 to 1941.

952. Friedman, Philip. MARTYRS AND FIGHTERS: THE EPIC OF THE WARSAW GHETTO. New York: Frederick Praeger, 1954. 325p.

   Main purpose is to demonstrate that although sheer physical force and oppression may accomplish an act of total genocide, they can never destroy faith, ideas and traditions. Annotated bibliography, pp. 313-320. Illustrations. Maps.

953. FROM A RUINED GARDEN; THE MEMORIAL BOOKS OF POLISH JEWRY, trans. and ed. by Jack Kugelman and Jonathan

Boyarin. New York: Schocken Books, 1983. 275p. 83-42717.

Condensation of more than 100 memorial books written during the past thirty years.

954. Glas-Wiener, Sheva. CHILDREN OF THE GHETTO, trans. by Shirley Young. Fitzroy, Victoria: Globe Press, 1983. 220p. NjP: DS135.P62L6434.

Story of Jewish children living in a small ghetto in the small Polish village of Marysin on the outskirts of Łódz by a woman who had been assigned to work there during the German occupation. Author wrote the book forty years after the fact so that it is largely reminiscences.

955. Glicksman, William M. IN THE MIRROR OF LITERATURE: THE ECONOMIC LIFE OF THE JEWS IN POLAND AS REFLECTED IN YIDDISH LITERATURE, 1914-1939. New York: Living Books, Inc., 1966. 254p. 66-17529.

Ph.D. dissertation for Dropside College for Hebrew and Cognate Learning, Philadelphia. An attempt to reconstruct and depict the economic aspect and milieu of the Jews in Poland between the two world wars. Aim is to show the economic activities of the big Jewish industrialist, as well as of the peddler trudging with his pack through the villages, of the storekeeper and market woman, the white collar worker, the professional class and the luftmensch, whose existence was most precarious. Bibliography, pp. 244-249.

956. Goetel, Ferdynand. FROM DAY TO DAY. New York: Viking Press, 1931. 292p. 31-11282.

Diary describes, day by day, the author's present spiritual state and material surroundings in the Polish city of Kraków, to which he has returned from the war, and the novel describes the past experiences as a Polish prisoner of war in Turkestan.

957. Goldstein, Bernard. THE STARS BEAR WITNESS. New York: Viking Press, 1949. 295p. 49-8564.

Story of the plight of the Jews in Warszawa during the Nazi invasion and subsequent occupation by a politically active Polish Jew. Covers period from September, 1939 through the spring of 1949. Map on lining papers.

958. Goodhart, Arthur L. POLAND AND THE MINORITY RACES. New York: Brentano's, 1920. 194p. 20-15472.

   Edited diary of author who was part of a group commissioned to ascertain facts regarding the reported wholesale killing of Jews in Poland. Primarily concerned with the Jews but also refers to Lithuanians, White Russians and Ruthenians. Map.

959. Grossman, Mendel. WITH A CAMERA IN THE GHETTO, ed. by Zvi Sner and Alexander Sened, with text from THE CHRONICLE OF THE ŁÓDZ GHETTO, ed. by Łucjan Dobroszycki and Danuta Dombrowska. New York: Schocken Books, 1977. 107p. 76-48815.

   Candid photographs of the Łódz Ghetto captioned chronologically February 28, 1941-December 3, 1942. Explanatory notes accompany photographs. Section covers life of Mendel Grossman, pp. 99-107.

960. Gutman, Yisrael. THE JEWS OF WARSAW, 1939-1943: GHETTO, UNDERGROUND, REVOLT, trans. by Ina Friedman. Bloomington: Indiana University Press, 1982. 512p. 81-47570.

   Considers the broader character of Jewish public life as it took shape during the occupation and ghettoization of what had been Europe's greatest Jewish urban center. While previous treatments of the subject have related events from a single point of view--Jewish or German--this remarkable book makes use of extensive primary and secondary materials from Jewish, German, and Polish sources to throw light on critical events. Illustrations.

961. Gwiazdowska, Marie Ż. IN THE CLUTCHES OF THE JEWS. Ann Arbor, Mich.: University Town Publishers, 1933. 176p. OL: DS135.P6G85.

   Impressions of an American female visitor on a trip abroad c. 1932 and her opinions on the status of the Jews in Germany and Poland particularly because of the extended visit there. An "eyewitness" account of the situation at that time. Illustrations. Portraits.

962. Heller, Celia S. ON THE EDGE OF DESTRUCTION: JEWS IN POLAND BETWEEN THE TWO WORLD WARS. New York: Columbia University Press, 1977. 369p. 76-22646.

 Conveys the situation of the Jews in interwar Poland as well as to reconstruct the main outlines of this complex community and to capture the dynamic and the complexity of the Jewish community. Discusses anti-Semitism in Poland during this period. Illustrations. Maps. Bibliographical footnotes.

963. Hilberg, Raul. THE WARSAW DIARY OF ADAM CZERNIAKOW: PRELUDE TO DOOM, ed. by R. Hilberg et al., trans. by Stanisław Staron and the staff of Yad Vashem. New York: Stein and Day, 1978. 420p. 78-9272.

 Translation of Polish manuscript of the diary which, in turn, was based upon Hebrew edition published in 1968. Map of Warszawa Ghetto, 1940-1942. Covers period from September 6, 1939 through July 22, 1940. Illustrations. Notations on Sources, pp. 408-411.

964. Hyams, Joseph. A FIELD OF BUTTERCUPS. Englewood Cliffs, N.J.: Prentice-Hall, Inc., 1968. 273p. 68-27840.

 Story of "Our Home," an orphanage for 200 children in the Warszawa Ghetto run by Janusz Korczak based upon Korczak's diary covering period May-August, 1942. Intimate details of orphanage and ghetto life. Author contacted orphans now adults and others for further information and based his story on all this documentation. Story of the search told in epilogue entitled, "On the Trail of Korczak."

965. Iranek-Osmecki, Każimierz. HE WHO SAVES ONE LIFE. New York: Crown Publishers, Inc., 1971. 336p. 72-108073.

 A complete documented story of the Poles who struggled to save Jews during World War II. No official bibliography but notes at end of book have bibliographical references, stated "official dispatches and documents drawn from many previously unpublished sources."

966. JEWS IN POLAND, YESTERDAY AND TODAY. London: White Eagle Press, Ltd., nd. 88p. OL: DS135.P6J46.

*Special Works* 213

No author given but at top of title page is "Polish
Association in Great Britain." Aim of book is to re-
fute claims that Poles facilitated and collaborated
with the Nazis in extermination of the Jews. Includes
English translations of articles in Polish newspapers
supporting evidence.

967. Johnpoll, Bernard K. THE POLITICS OF FUTILITY: THE
GENERAL JEWISH WORKERS BUND OF POLAND, 1917-1943.
Ithaca, N.Y.: Cornell University Press, 1967. 298p.
67-13044.

Object of this work is to explore the workings of a
particular political party in a specific setting and to
examine the party's approach to problems as they arose
and the solutions that were suggested. The work inves-
tigates the basic questions that confronted the Bund
and the way the Bund answered them. Bibliography, pp.
271-283.

968. THE KALISH BOOK. English version prepared by I.M.
Losk. Tel Aviv: Eylon Press, 1968. 327p. HE68-
2549.

A history of the Jews in Kalish. A memorial to the
30,000 Jews who perished under the Nazis. Profusely
illustrated.

969. Kaplan, Chaim A. SCROLL OF AGONY: THE WARSAW DIARY OF
CHAIM A. KAPLAN, ed. by Abraham I. Katsh. New York:
Macmillan Co., 1965. 350p. 64-12533.

It is not merely an echo of the death cries of the
Warszawa Ghetto, in it are woven the strands of a narrative of martyrdom of the Jews in Poland. It is also
a record of the Nazi conquest of Poland, the relationship of the Jews and their Polish neighbors, and of the
internal life of the Jews within the ghetto. Illustrations. Maps on lining papers.

970. Karsov, Nina. IN THE NAME OF TOMORROW, by N. Karsov
and Szymon Szechter. New York: Schocken Books,
1971. 285p. 70-161560.

A story of the relationship between Szymon Szechter,
a Polish Jew, an intellectual, and Nina Karsov, a
friend, confident and secretary, wife for awhile. It

is also a description of the treatment of political dissenters in Poland and analyzes Communism as a system of rule. Period covered is 1966-1970. Illustrations. Portraits.

971. Katz, Alfred. POLAND'S GHETTOS AT WAR. New York: Twayne Publishers, Inc., 1970. 175p. 78-120535.

    Main purpose of this study is to examine the role, exercised by the Jewish parties in the resistance movements in occupied Poland between the years 1939 and 1944. Concerned primarily with the five main ghettos created by the Germans in Warszawa, Białystok, Kraków, Wilno and Łódz. Bibliography, pp. 161-170.

972. Korenblit, Michael. UNTIL WE MEET AGAIN: A TRUE STORY OF LOVE AND WAR, SEPARATION AND REUNION, by M. Korenblit and Kathleen Janger. New York: Putnam, 1983. 298p. 82-24148.

    Written by Korenblit's son and an associate, the book vividly recalls experiences of World War II Poland. Personal recollection of history. Illustrations.

973. Krakowski, Shmuel. THE WAR OF THE DOOMED: JEWISH ARMED RESISTANCE IN POLAND, 1942-1944, trans. by Orah Blaustein. New York: Holmes and Meier Pubs., Inc., 1984. 340p. 83-18537.

    A "deep and informative account" of the reaction of the Jews to the murder of their people on foreign soil, specifically armed resistance. This resistance took place in the forests of Poland, in Polish partisan and commando units, in the cities and in prisoner-of-war and internment camps. Relies on primary Polish, Russian, Yiddish and German sources. Also, drew upon personal interviews with approximately 500 fighters. Maps.

974. Kukielko, Renya. ESCAPE FROM THE PIT. New York: Sharon Books, 1947. 189p. A48-6399.

    Story of author's life from outbreak of World War II in September, 1939 through her eventual escape to Palestine in 1944.

975. Laudynowa, Stefania. A WORLD PROBLEM: JEWS--POLAND-- HUMANITY; A PSYCHOLOGICAL AND HISTORICAL STUDY,

trans. by A.J. Zielinski et al. Chicago: American
Catalogue Printing Co., 1920. 2v. 20-13706.

This work has been written in order to fill the cry-
ing need of an impartial exposition of the relations
between the Poles and the Jews in Poland. It purports
to indicate how some Polish Jews had conspired to
undermine Polish treatment of them. Concentrates on
the Jewish situation in Poland during World War I.

976. Lewin, Isaac. THE JEWISH COMMUNITY IN POLAND: HISTORI-
CAL ESSAYS. New York: Philosophical Library, 1985.
247p. 84-16705.

Essays covering a thousand years of Jewish history in
Poland. Divided into several periods, e.g. "A Jewish
lawyer in Poland in the fifteenth century."

977. Litman, Jacob. THE ECONOMIC ROLE OF JEWS IN MEDIEVAL
POLAND: THE CONTRIBUTION OF YTZHAK SCHIPPER. Washington, D.C.: University Press of America, 1984.
306p. 84-15305.

Initially a doctoral dissertation submitted to New
York University in 1968. Covers the life and career of
the Jewish-Polish historian, Yitzhak Schipper, and history of Jews in Poland during medieval times. Origins
of Jewish settlement in Poland are of special interest.
Portraits. Maps. Bibliography, pp. 277-299.

978. Marcus, Joseph. SOCIAL AND POLITICAL HISTORY OF THE
JEWS IN POLAND, 1919-1939. New York: Mouton Publishers, 1983. 569p. 82-22420.

Book divided into two parts: A social history including schools, housing, etc. and a political history.
A thorough and exhaustive study. Bibliography, pp.
529-557.

979. Mendelsohn, Ezra. ZIONISM IN POLAND: THE FORMATIVE
YEARS, 1915-1926. New Haven: Yale University Press,
1982. 373p. 81-10301.

History of the Zionist movement in Poland between
1915, the year which ushered in a new era of political
freedom for Polish Jewry, and 1926, the beginning of a
new period in interwar Polish history. Maps.

980. Niezabitowska, Małgorzata. REMNANTS: THE LAST JEWS OF POLAND, trans. by William Brand and Hanna Dobosiewicz. New York: Friendly Press, 1986. 272p. 86-1468.

   A collection of colored illustrations with accompanying articles about the Jews still in Poland. Author devoted five years to this work and visited all the principal Jewish settlements. Maps.

981. Nirenstein, Albert. A TOWER FROM THE ENEMY; CONTRIBUTIONS TO A HISTORY OF JEWISH RESISTANCE IN POLAND. New York: Orion Press, 1959. 372p. 59-7897.

   History of what happened to the Jews in Poland from the beginning of the Nazi occupation and how they resisted. There is no documentation even for the illustrations which makes it difficult to determine objectivity. No bibliography. Map.

\* Piechotka, Maria. WOODEN SYNAGOGUES. Cited above as item 89.

982. Pinkus, Oscar. THE HOUSE OF ASHES. Cleveland: World Press, 1964. 243p. 64-12462.

   An account of the survival of the author and a small group of other Jews, some of them members of his family, from 1939-1945. Indicates that the author feared the victorious Poles and not the defeated Germans. Book first published in Israel under the title, OD MUTZAL.

983. Poland. Rada Ochrony Pomnikóow Walki i Meczeństwa. STRUGGLE, DEATH, MEMORY, 1939-1945. Warszawa: Wydawnictwo Artystyczne i Filmowe, 1963. unpaged. 64-43740.

   Chiefly illustrations of atrocities suffered at the hands of the Germans by the Jews in Poland. Album prepared by Stanisław Poznański. Book issued on the twentieth anniversary of the rising of the Warszawa Ghetto, 1943-1963.

984. Rabinowicz, Harry M. THE LEGACY OF POLISH JEWRY: A HISTORY OF POLISH JEWS IN THE INTER-WAR YEARS, 1919-1939. New York: Thomas Yoseloff, 1965. 256p. 65-11349.

*Special Works* 217

Relates the history of Polish Jewry during their fateful inter-war years, outlining basic trends and sketching a general picture of the Polish scene. Illustrations. Portraits. Bibliography, pp. 243-249.

985. Rashke, Richard L. ESCAPE FROM SOBIBOR. Boston: Houghton Mifflin, 1982. 389p. 82-12127.

 An account of the escape of prisoners from the Sobibor concentration camp in Poland. Based upon eyewitness recollections of 18 Sobibor survivors. Illustrations. Bibliography, pp. 369-371.

986. Ringelblum, Emanuel. NOTES FROM THE WARSZAWA GHETTO; THE JOURNAL OF EMANUAL RINGELBLUM, ed. and trans. by Jacob Sloan. New York: McGraw-Hill Book Co., 1958. 369p. 58-8048.

 Day-to-day eyewitness account by the man who was the best equipped to keep that account, Emanuel Ringelblum, archivist of the Warszawa Ghetto. Covers period January, 1940 through June, 1942. Maps.

987. Ringelblum, Emanuel. POLISH-JEWISH RELATIONS DURING THE SECOND WORLD WAR, trans. by Dafna Allon et al. Jerusalem: Yad Vashem, 1974. 76-1394.

 Polish attitudes and actions toward the Jews during the German occupation. Also a history of the Warszawa Ghetto. Includes an historical summary of the Polish-Jewish relations before the war. Contains portrait of the author.

988. Rochman, Leyb. THE PIT AND THE TRAP, A CHRONICLE OF SURVIVAL. New York: Holocaust Library, 1982. 271p. 82-084220.

 Chronicle of author's experiences in the Minsk-Mazowiecki Ghetto, a small town about 25 miles northeast of Warszawa, for period February 17, 1943 to the end of July, 1945. One portrait of author; a map of the immediate vicinity of the town.

989. Roiter, Howard. VOICE FROM THE HOLOCAUST. New York: William-Frederick Press, 1975. 221p. 75-19856.

 Covers the holocaust in general as well as the Janowska graveyard of Galician Jews, the Warszawa

Ghetto, Treblinka, the death factory, and the long road out of Treblinka and Majdanek.

990. Rothenberg, Jerome. POLAND, 1931. New York: Unicorn Press, 1960. unpaged. 69-11136.

    Poems presented here are the first installment of an ongoing series of ancestral poems begun in 1956. Unbound leaves printed on handmade Japanese paper. In a folio, limited ed. Map of Ostrów-Mazowiecka, two photographs, one montage.

991. Rubinstein, Erna F. THE SURVIVOR IN US ALL: A MEMOIR OF THE HOLOCAUST. Hamden, Conn.: Archon Books, 1983. 185p. 83-11813.

    Story of a Jewish family who had fled the Nazis when they invaded Poland in 1939 and what happened to its members. The author survived to tell her story.

992. Segal, Simon. THE NEW POLAND AND THE JEWS. New York: Lee Furman, Inc., 1938. 223p. 38-34569.

    A study of the confrontation of democracy and authoritarianism in the new Poland with special reference to the role of anti-Semitism. The study inquires not only how anti-Semitism is being used, but also why, what it is doing to the Jews and what it is doing to the non-Jews. Bibliography, pp. 217-219.

993. Shatyn, Bruno. A PRIVATE WAR, trans. by Oscar E. Swan. Detroit: Wayne State University Press, 1985. 285p. 84-21905.

    Account of the survival of a Polish Jew and how he outwitted the Nazis masquerading as a non-Jew armed with "Aryan papers" obtained with the help of Polish friends. Illustrations. Portraits. Maps.

994. Shneiderman, Samuel L. BETWEEN FEAR AND HOPE, trans. by Norbert Guterman. New York: Arco, 1947. 316p. 47-11676.

    An account of contemporary Poland by a Jewish journalist. Concerned primarily with Jewish affairs and in that sense this work is a "homecoming," a native's return. Good coverage of career and activities of Stanisław Mikołajczyk.

*Special Works*

995. Shneiderman, Samuel L. THE RIVER REMEMBERS. New York: Horizon Press, 1978. 192p. 77-93935.

    Not only the history of one man's heritage but also the complete panorama of Jewish shtetl life in Poland from the eleventh century to the present. The river of the title is the Wisła, or Vistula, along whose banks many of the Jewish communities were located. Illustrated. Bibliography, pp. 191-192.

996. Steiner, Jean F. TREBLINKA, trans. by Helen Weaver. New York: Simon and Schuster, 1967. 415p. 67-14236.

    Treblinka Camp story pieced together from written testimony and conversations with survivors of the camps. Tells how camp was first set up specifically to kill the Jews, how it was organized, how operated and how inmates revolted and destroyed the camp.

997. Tec, Nechama. WHEN LIGHT PIERCED THE DARKNESS: RIGHTEOUS CHRISTIANS AND THE POLISH JEWS. New York: Oxford University Press, 1986. 262p. 85-7261.

    Discusses the actions and motivations of Polish Christians who hid Jews from the Nazis. Written by a woman who pretended to be a Catholic for three years. Illustrations. Bibliography, pp. 237-253.

998. Tenenbaum, Joseph L. IN SEARCH OF A LOST PEOPLE: THE OLD AND NEW POLAND. New York: Beechhurst Press, 1948. 312p. 48-9518.

    Author went on a trip to Poland in 1946, spent two and one-half months there to collect facts and materials about conditions among the Jews at that time. Visited cities in Poland and former concentration camp sites. Includes an extensive bibliography of works in English and Polish pertinent to Jews in Poland and available at that time.

999. Tenebaum, Joseph L. UNDERGROUND, THE STORY OF A PEOPLE. New York: Philosophical Society, 1952. 532p. 52-7945.

    An unusually detailed description of the mass extermination of Jews in Poland, western Ukraine, Byelorussia and Lithuania. Also, the struggles of the Jewish underground. Illustrations.

1000. Turkow Kaminska, Ruth. I DON'T WANT TO BE BRAVE ANYMORE. Washington, D.C.: New Republic Books, 1978. 255p. 78-17417.

Personal narrative of a Polish Jewish couple who wound up in a Russian prison camp. The book deals with the author's imprisonment and eventual escape. Author was daughter of famous actress, Ida Kaminska. Illustrations. Portraits.

1001. Tushnet, Leonard. THE PAVEMENT OF HELL. New York: St. Martin's Press, 1972. 210p. 73-87395.

Historical and biographical accounts of the heads of the Jewish Councils: Adam Czerniakow of Warszawa; Mordecai Chaim Rumkowski of Łódz; and Jacob Geda of Wilno. Includes portraits of each man. Illustrations. Bibliography, pp. 209-210.

1002. Vinecour, Earl. POLISH JEWS: THE FINAL CHAPTER. New York: McGraw-Hill Book Co., 1977. 121p. 77-4405.

Author presents a brief sketch of the history of the Jews in Poland and then presents a photographic survey of the final chapter of Jewish life in Poland at the present time. Many illustrations of synagogues and other public buildings. Bibliography, p. 121.

1003. Vinocur, Ana. A BOOK WITHOUT A TITLE. New York: Vantage Press, 1976. 139p.

Reminiscences of the author, a survivor of the Łódz Ghetto, the concentration camps including Oświęcim. Written thirty years later when author lived in her new home made in Uruguay.

1004. Vishniac, Roman. POLISH JEWS: A PICTORIAL RECORD. New York: Schocken Books, 1947. 16p. 47-30584.

Consists mostly of portraits of pre-war Jewish types--schoolboys, rabbis, storekeepers. One of the last pictorial records of Jews in Poland before the Nazi invasion of 1939. Photographs taken in 1938.

*Special Works* 221

1005. THE WARSAW GHETTO IN PHOTOGRAPHS: 206 VIEWS MADE IN 1941, ed. by Ulrich Keller. New York: Dover Publications, Inc., 1984. 131p. 83-20540.

    Mainly photographs divided into following subject categories: internal ghetto administration, internal ghetto police, ghetto labor, forced labor outside the ghetto, amusements of the ghetto elite, worship, street scenes, market scenes and charity food programs, beggars, children, victims of hunger and typhus, burials, Łódz Ghetto.

1006. Wdowinski, David. AND WE ARE NOT SAVED. New York: Philosophical Library, 1963. 123p. 63-15723.

    An account of the life of the author in the Warszawa Ghetto including the 1943 uprising of which he was a survivor. Illustrations. Portraits.

1007. Weinryb, Bernard D. THE JEWS IN POLAND: A SOCIAL AND ECONOMIC HISTORY OF THE JEWISH COMMUNITY IN POLAND FROM 1100 to 1800. Philadelphia: Jewish Society of America, 1973. 424p. 72-12178.

    A comprehensive study of the Jews in Poland. Contains map on lining covers of Polish Jewry, 1667-1764. Bibliography, pp. 403-409.

1008. Wells, Leon W. THE JANOWSKA ROAD. New York: Macmillan Co., 1963. 63-16138.

    Personal narrative of a Polish Jew's ordeal in the Janowska concentration camp during the German occupation. Maps.

1009. Yanow, Leonard. LAZAR, THE AUTOBIOGRAPHY OF MY FATHER. New York: Viking Press, 1980. 212p. 79-22624.

    Biographical account of a boy growing up a Polish Jew in Russia during World War I. Maps.

1010. Ziemian, Joseph. THE CIGARETTE SELLERS OF THREE CROSSES SQUARE, trans. by Janina David. Mineapolis: Lerner Publications Company, 1975. 166p. 54-11900.

    A story of a small group of Jewish children in Warszawa during the German occupation and how they escaped from the Ghetto and lived in the non-Jewish section of the city. Some smuggled food and arms into the Ghetto. Others took part in both uprisings. Some went to Israel, others to Canada after the war. Illustrations. Portraits.

1011.  Zuckerman, Isaac, ed. THE FIGHTING GHETTOS, trans. and ed. by Meyer Barkai. Philadelphia: Lippincott, 1962. 407p. 62-11331.

Authentic documents written by eyewitnesses and participants in Jewish resistance movement during period of Nazis in the lands of eastern Europe. Mostly about the Jews in Poland. Extremely valuable for "Notes on the Camps." Maps.

1012.  Zuker-Bujanowska, Liliana. LILIANA'S JOURNAL; WARSAW, 1939-1945. New York: Dial Press, 1980. 162p. 80-139.

This is a journal written by the author in 1946. It tells the story of seven years in the life of a young Jewish girl. Originally written in Poland and translated by the author several years later. Illustrations.

1013.  Zylberberg, Michael. A WARSAW DIARY, 1939-1945. London: Vallentine, Mitchell & Co., Ltd., 1969. 220p.

Authentic story of one of the survivors of the Warszawa Ghetto and of an underground existence in the non-Jewish part of the city during the Second World War. Based on author's original diary which tells of the Ghetto Uprising and the Polish uprising of General Bor-Komorowski and of the moral conflict of the Poles who helped them and those who betrayed them. Illustrations. Portraits. Maps.

## Jews In Poland--Fiction

1014.  Glatstein, Jacob. HOMECOMING AT TWILIGHT, trans. by Norbert Guterman. New York: Thomas Yoseloff, 1962. 271p. 61-14963.

This stirring account of an American Jew's return to Poland for a visit after an absence of twenty years,

*Special Works*

captures the atmosphere of Jewish life in Poland just before the onset of World War II.

1015. Glatstein, Jacob. HOMEWARD BOUND, trans. by Abraham Goldstein. New York: Thomas Yoseloff, 1969. 142p. 68-10640.

A nameless American Jew returns to Poland by ship in the 1930s to visit his dying mother. This is a tragicomic, subtle autobiographical novel of the return home of the protagonist, a Jew from Poland, who has emigrated to America.

1016. Hersey, John R. THE WALL. New York: Alfred A. Knopf, 1950. 632p. 50-5697.

Fictional account of the systematic piecemeal extermination of the Jews of the Warszawa Ghetto and of the heroic resistance. Real story is the growth in spirit of a group of friends so that they emerge undismayed and triumphant in the face of physical annihilation.

1017. Moses, Adolf. LUSER, THE WATCHMAKER; AN EPISODE OF THE POLISH REVOLUTION, trans. by Mrs. A. de V. Chaudron. Cincinnati: Bloch and Co., 1883. 125p.

Although story is set during the 1830 Revolution, the characters are Jews.

1018. Shneur, Zalman. DOWNFALL. New York: Roy Publishers, 1944. 252p. 44-5462.

Set in Poland in 1915, it is the story of the rise and collapse of the Shatz family of Warszawa. Through the experiences of the Shatz family the novel recounts the details of Jewish life under the German occupation of Warszawa during World War I.

1019. Singer, Isaac B. THE FAMILY MOSKAT, trans. by A.H. Gross. New York: Alfred A. Knopf, 1966. 611p. 66-73418.

Biographical-fictional account of a Jewish family in Poland. Family tree in front.

1020. Singer, Isaac B. THE MAGICIAN OF LUBLIN, trans. by E. Gottlieb and Joseph Singer. New York: Noonday Press, 1960. 246p. 60-10006.

Tale about Yasha Mazur, who makes his living in the circuses and theaters of nineteenth century Poland. He can skate on the high wire, eat fire and above all charm any woman.

1021. Singer, Isaac B. THE MANOR, trans. by Joseph Singer and Elaine Gottlieb. New York: Farrar, Straus and Giroux, 1967. 67-25966.

First serialized in JEWISH DAILY FORWARD. Portrays epoch between the Polish Insurrection of 1863 and the end of the nineteenth century period when Jews began to play an important role in Polish industry, commerce, arts and sciences.

1022. Tomkiewicz, Mina. OF BOMBS AND MICE: A NOVEL OF WARTIME WARSAW, trans. by F. Gazel. New York: T. Yoseloff, 1970. 336p. 70-107106.

Novel about experiences of a Jewish family in Warszawa Ghetto during and including the 1943 Uprising.

### Juvenile Literature

1023. Brandys, Marian. POLAND. New York: Doubleday & Co., Inc., 1974. 156p. 74-108036.

Photographs illustrating brief survey of contemporary Poland by a native Polish author. Maps.

1024. Contoski, Joseph K. BOCHECK IN POLAND. Minneapolis: Polanie Publishing Co., 1983. 53p.

A children's story about the white storks, the fairy tale birds of the Old World. Illustrated by Karen Stombaugh.

1025. DeAngeli, Marguerite L. UP THE HILL. New York: Doubleday & Co., 1942. 88p. 42-24961.

Story of a little Polish-American girl, Aniela, growing up in a Pennsylvania mining town. Illustrated by drawings in black-and-white and in color. Brief glossary of Polish words and names.

1026. Elisofon, Eliot. WEEK IN AGATA'S WORLD: POLAND. New York: Macmillan Co., 1970. 48p. 73-107044.

A week in the life of a Polish girl as she finishes school, begins summer vacation, and travels on the family scooter to visit grandmother in the country. Illustrations.

1027. Estes, Eleanor. THE HUNDRED DRESSES. New York: Harcourt, Brace and Co., 1944. 80p. 44-8963.

Heroine is Wanda Petronski, a Polish-American girl. Illustrations.

1028. Gardner, Monica M. STORIES FROM POLISH HISTORY. London: Sheed & Ward, 1928. 177p. OL: 943.002.G175.

Written "for boys and girls" about the most dramatic and romantic events in the history of Poland, leaving aside what would be less likely to interest youthful readers. Illustrations. Portraits.

1029. Gebaroff, Ara J. STEFANIE WAS THE GOOD ONE. Caldwell, Idaho: Caxton Printers, 1949. 99p. 49-50104.

Story of Stefanie, young daughter of Polish immigrants, and their new life in America. Illustrations.

1030. Golawski, Michał. POLAND THROUGH THE AGES: AN OUTLINE OF POLISH HISTORY FOR YOUNG READERS, trans. by Paul Stevenson. London: Orbis Limited, 1971. 184p. 72-179212.

Originally published in Polish. Story ends in 1945. Many illustrations, chiefly black-and-white reproductions of Polish paintings of historical events. Portraits. Maps.

1031. Greene, Carol. POLAND. Chicago: Childrens Press, 1983. 126p. 82-19737.

Excellent general survey of the land and people of Poland for the juvenile reader. All illustrations in color. "Mini-facts at a glance," pp. 112-120. Portraits. Maps.

1032. Gronowicz, Antoni. BOLEK, trans. by Jessie McEwen. New York: Thomas Nelson and Sons, 1942. 240p. 42-23223.

Story of three Polish children from the country who are caught in the war of 1939 and who eventually escape via Romania and France to America. Illustrations.

1033. Gronowicz, Antoni. FOUR FROM THE OLD TOWN, trans. by Joseph Vetter. New York: Charles Scribner's Sons, 1944. 149p. 44-8098.

Story about Poland for the juvenile reader. Setting is Warszawa during World War II.

1034. Kelly, Eric P. THE BLACKSMITH OF VILNO: A TALE OF POLAND IN THE YEAR 1832. New York: Macmillan Co., 1930. 184p. 30-26879.

Story about the lost crown of Poland and how a young boy, Stefan, is involved in keeping it hidden from the Russians.

1035. Kelly, Eric P. FROM STAR TO STAR, A STORY OF KRAKÓW IN 1493. Philadelphia: J.P. Lippincott Co., 1944. 239p. 44-8026.

Story of Poland c. 1493 aimed at the young reader. Based upon the life of Copernicus. Illustrations.

1036. Kelly, Eric P. THE GOLDEN STAR OF HALICH, A TALE OF THE RED LAND IN 1362. New York: Macmillan Co., 1931. 215p. 31-23969.

An historical tale of Poland in the fourteenth century wherein a young boy saves the life of the kind and as a reward is sent on an adventure in search of the golden star of Halich. Illustrations. Maps.

1037. Kelly, Eric P. THE HAND IN THE PICTURE, A STORY OF POLAND, illustrated by Irena Lorentowicz. Philadelphia: J.B. Lippincott Co., 1947. 241p. 47-4735.

Although primarily written with the juvenile audience in view, this story of Poland has been gleaned "from the whole field of Polish history, from the early Chronicles of Długosz to the contemporary writings of Halicki."

1038. Kelly, Eric P. THE LAND OF THE POLISH PEOPLE. New York: Frederick A. Stokes, 1943. 72p. 43-14136.

Brief sketch of inter-war Poland (1918-1939) which includes history, description, social life and customs intended for the juvenile reader. Profusely illustrated. Contains one map of Poland.

1039. Kelly, Eric P. THE LAND OF THE POLISH PEOPLE. Philadelphia: J.B. Lippincott Co., 1952. 84p. 52-3743.

Revised edition of 1943 book with added chapters covering events since original publication. Illustrations.

1040. Kelly, Eric P. THE LAND AND PEOPLE OF POLAND, rev. by Dragos D. Kostich. Philadelphia: J.B. Lippincott Co., 1972. 143p. 73-37924.

Introduction to the geography, culture, and turbulent history of Poland. Revision of earlier works by Kelly. Illustrations. Maps.

\* Kelly, Eric P. THE TRUMPETER OF KRAKÓW. Cited above as item 891.

1041. Lenski, Lois. WE LIVE IN THE NORTH. Philadelphia: J.B. Lippincott Co., 1965. 152p. 65-21667.

Three short stories, one of which concerns a young Polish-American set in Hamtramck, Michigan. Illustrations.

1042. McKown, Robin. MARIE CURIE, illus. by Karl W. Swanson. New York: G.P. Putnam's Sons, 1971. 95p. 74-137990.

Biography of Maria Sklodowska Curie written for the young reader. Illustrations. Bibliography, p. 92.

1043. Mills, Lois. SO YOUNG A QUEEN. New York: Lothrop, Lee and Shepard, 1961. 172p. 60-12017.

Biographical sketch for juveniles. Lacks bibliographic references.

1044. Obojski, Robert. POLAND IN PICTURES. New York: Sterling Publishing Co., 1969. 64p. 71-90811.

Mainly black-and-white pictures accompanied by text about the land, history, government, people, economy.

Intended for use in elementary schools. Portraits. Maps.

1045. Pfeiffer, Christine. POLAND, LAND OF FREEDOM FIGHTERS. Minneapolis: Dillon Press, 1984. 175p. 83-15025.

Discusses the people, traditions, folkways, holidays, family life, food, schools, sports, recreation, and history of Poland for juvenile readers. Glossary of persons, places and things Polish, pp. 157-167. Illustrations. Portraits. Maps. Bibliography, pp. 170.

1046. Popescu, Julian. LET'S VISIT POLAND. London: Burke Publishing Co., 1984. 96p. OL: DK404.P699.1984.

Description of Poland, including history, designed for the young reader. Illustrations. Portraits. Maps.

1047. Porazinska, Janina. IN VOYTUS' LITTLE HOUSE, trans. by Lucia M. Borski. New York: Roy Publishers, 1944. 47p. 44-8334.

"In the house of Voytus, the cradle's two rockers want to rock in different ways. Painted figures on the clay pot call Voytus to dance and four skirts in the cupboard gossip of where they've been." BOOK REVIEW DIGEST, 1944.

1048. Serraillier, Ian. THE SILVER SWORD. New York: Criterion Books, 1959. 187p. 59-6556.

Novel based on fact, of three children cast adrift in Warszawa early in World War II after their home is blown up and their parents taken away by the Nazis to unknown destinations. Eventually children escape and wend their way to Switzerland where they are reunited with their parents.

1049. Szambelan-Strevinsky, Christine. DARK HOUR OF NOON. New York: Lippincott, 1982. 215p.

Story takes place during Nazi occupation. Grim picture of very young people's lives where they become killers of their occupiers.

1050. Terlikowska, Maria. A TREE UP TO THE SKY, trans. by Jerzy Brodzki. Warszawa: Krajowa Agencja Wydawnicza, 1975. 47p.

Translation of a Polish book published for juveniles. Illustrations.

1051. Turska, Krystyna. THE WOODCUTTER'S DUCK. New York: Macmillan Co., 1972. Unpaged. 72-85763.

Juvenile literature. Thirty pages with drawings in color for pre-schoolers to be related to them.

1052. Uminski, Sigmund H. URBAN'S BOYS. New York: Polish Publication Society of America, Inc., 1970. 47p. 70-131212.

A short episode of the activities of the Polish boys and girls in the Polish Underground during the German occupation of Poland between 1939 and 1945. Based on a personal story of a participant related to the author. Illustrations.

1053. Werstein, Irving. THE UPRISING OF THE WARSZAWA GHETTO. NOVEMBER, 1940-MAY, 1943. New York: W.W. Norton and Co., Inc., 1968. 151p. 68-16566.

For the juvenile reader, a graphic account of the 1943 Uprising by the Jewish community in the Warszawa Ghetto. The author wished "to present a shocking phase of not too distant history to my teen-aged readers." Illustrations. Maps. Notes on sources, pp. 149-150.

1054. Wojciechowska, Maia. TILL THE BREAK OF DAY. New York: Harcourt, Brace Jovanovich, 1972. 156p. 72-79145.

Memoirs of the author's adolescence during World War II, when her family escaped from Poland to temporary haven in France, Portugal, England, and finally, the United States.

1055. Wuorio, Eva Lis. CODE: POLONAISE. New York: Holt, Rinehart & Winston, 1971. 198p. 73-119094.

Author has drawn from wartime records and Polish government documents to tell the true story of a small

band of Polish children in occupied Warszawa working
for their country's freedom.

### Karaims

1056. Zajaczkowski, Ananiasz. KARAIMS IN POLAND: HISTORY,
LANGUAGE, FOLKLORE, SCIENCE. Warszawa: Państwowe
Wydawnictwo Naukowe, 1961. 114p. 62-5085.

A history of a small ethnic group of Turkic-speaking
people including a discussion of their religious beliefs. Illustrations.

### Kaszuby

1057. Giertych, Jędrzej. BALTIC TALES. London: Veritas
Foundation Press, 1955. 244p. 56-27615.

Four tales: A rat from the Far East. The rosary.
The sea nourishes, the sea destroys. Hannah. Stories
about the Kaszuby set in the early 1920s. Map of
Northern Cassubia, p. 180. Illustrations.

1058. Lorentz, Friedrich. THE CASSUBIAN CIVILIZATION, by
F. Lorentz et al. London: Faber and Faber, Ltd.,
1935. 407p. 36-10469.

Full descriptive account of Cassubian culture. An
extensive and exhaustive work. Contents: An outline
of Cassubian civilization, Cassubian and Polish ethnography, dialects of the Baltic Slavs. Includes
notes on authors. Illustrations. Maps. Bibliography,
pp. 396-397.

1059. Perkowski, Jan L. A KASHUBIAN IDEOLECT IN THE UNITED
STATES. Bloomington: Indiana University Press,
1969. 371p. 68-64529.

Results of a survey of Kashubian speakers in and
near Minnesota. Maps. Bibliography, pp. 353-371.

1060. Perkowski, Jan L. VAMPIRES, DWARVES AND WITCHES AMONG
THE ONTARIO KASHUBS. Ottawa: National Museum of
Canada, 1972. 85p. NIC: GR525.P458.

*Special Works* 231

The Kashubian people settled in Renfrew County,
Ontario, especially around the towns of Barry's Bay,
Paugh Lake and Wilno. This is their story with emphasis on the occult studied in relation to the Canadian
context. Contains many black-and-white photographs of
Kashubians in the area. Includes some Kashubian
texts. Maps. Bibliography, pp. 82-84.

1061. Topolińska, Zuzanna. A HISTORICAL PHONOLOGY OF THE
KASHUBIAN DIALECTS OF POLISH. The Hague: Mouton
and Co., 1974. 190p. 71-91484.

Principally a scholarly work concerned with the historical development of the language. Contains some
information on the Kaszuby themselves. Maps. Bibliography, pp. 136-137.

\* Wasilewski, Leon. NATIONALITIES IN POMERANIA. Cited
below as item 1112.

Katyn Forest Massacre, 1940

1062. FitzGibbon, Louis. KATYN. New York: Scribner's,
1971. 285p. 78-163499.

A dispassionate account of the Katyn murder in which
the reader is invited to trace the events as they
occurred. Many vivid photographs of corpses years
after event, bits and pieces of items found on victims.
Portraits. Maps. Bibliography, pp. 227-279.

1063. Furcolo, Foster. RENDEZVOUS AT KATYN. Boston: Marlborough House, Inc., 1973. 178p. 74-156175.

A novel based on one of the most shocking events in
modern history, the Katyn Massacres. Written by a
member of the U.S. Congressional Committee that investigated Katyn. Maps on lining papers.

1064. Komorowski, Eugenjusz A. NIGHT NEVER ENDING, with
Joseph L. Gilmore. Chicago: Henry Regnery Co.,
1974. 285p. 73-19870.

Purportedly the story of a sole survivor of the
Katyn Massacres. Journalistic in style. Two-thirds
of the book covers capture and imprisonment

of the Polish officers. Remainder of book covers author's escape and eventual restless existence as a refugee.

1065. Mackiewicz, Joseph. THE KATYN WOOD MURDERS. London: Hollis and Carter, Ltd., 1951. 252p. 51-38993.

Author, a Polish journalist born in Wilno, was present in 1943 when Germans unearthed graves. No documentation for narrative. An indictment of Soviet Russia for the murders. Contains twenty-one illustrations of graves and evidence unearthed. Authenticity of photographs not verified. Foreword by Arthur Bliss Lane, former U.S. Ambassador to Poland.

1066. Stahl, Zdzisław. THE CRIME OF KATYN; FACTS AND DOCUMENTS. London: Polish Cultural Foundation, 1965. 303p. 66-6706.

Narrative of the Polish prisoners-of-war who fell into Russian hands in 1939, the prisoners-of-war camp, deportation, discovery of the mass graves and official reports, stories from the scene, five weeks' work at Katyn, Soviet report. Illustrations. Portraits. Maps.

1067. Wittlin, Tadeusz. TIME STOPPED AT 6:30. Indianapolis: Bobbs-Merrill Co., 1965. 317p. 65-25653.

First full and factual account of thousands of Polish prisoners in concentration camps in the U.S.S.R. This is an historical account. Numerous references to Katyn Forest Massacre of 1940 including sections from U.S. House of Representatives, 82nd Congress, Final Report of the Select Committee to conduct an Investigation and Study of the facts, evidence, and circumstances of the Katyn Forest Massacre. Illustrations. Portraits. Maps. Bibliography, pp. 305-307.

1068. Zawodny, Janusz K. DEATH IN THE FOREST: THE STORY OF THE KATYN FOREST MASSACRE. Notre Dame, Ind.: Notre Dame University Press, 1962. 235p. 62-16639.

Reputedly researched and documented account. Documentation includes two interviews with two persons who were part of the group although not eyewitnesses. Illustrations. Bibliography, pp. 201-218.

## Language

1069. Bidwell, Charles E. OUTLINE OF POLISH MORPHOLOGY. Pittsburgh: University Center for International Studies, 1972. 137p. 73-43544.

    Author attempts to make available to English-speaking linguists and students of Slavic languages, a series of concise but relatively exhaustive structural descriptions of the grammatical structure and in particular the inflectional morphology of the principal standard Slavic languages, especially of such for which complete and modern linguistic descriptions are not readily avaiable. Bibliography, pp. 136-137.

1070. Fisiak, Jacek. AN INTRODUCTORY POLISH-ENGLISH CONTRASTIVE GRAMMAR, by J. Fisiak et al. Warszawa: Państwowe Wydawnictwo Naukowe, 1978. 160p. OL: PG6099.F5.

    A work on Polish-English contrastive grammar, giving a review of the most important subjects. Syntactic-semantic morphological and phonological problems are here examined by the authors from the viewpoint of transformative-generative linguistics. Bibliography, pp. 251-258.

1071. U.S. Library of Congress. Slavic and Central European Division. POLISH ABBREVIATIONS, A SELECTIVE LIST, compiled by Janina Wócicka. Washington, D.C.: Library of Congress, 1957. 164p. 57-60055.

    Second edition contains additional 600 abbreviations based on data located in a variety of Polish postwar monographs, periodicals and newspapers.

## Law

1072. Lasok, Dominik. POLISH FAMILY LAW. Leyden: A.W. Sijthoff, 1968. 304p. 71-406844.

    This book was written with the limited aim of providing a rudimentary exposition of the salient features of the system of family law now in force in the Polish People's Republic, set against their historical background. Bibliography, pp. 253-259.

1073. Poland. Laws, Statutes, etc. THE PENAL CODE OF THE
POLISH PEOPLE'S REPUBLIC, with an introduction by
William S. Kinney and Tadeusz Sadowski. South
Hackensack, N.J.: F.B. Rothman, 1973. 139p. 74-
182845.

1074. POLISH LAW THROUGHOUT THE AGES, ed. by Wenceslas
Wagner. Stanford, Calif.: Hoover Institution
Press, 1970. 476p. 76-115659.

Series of essays on Polish law including a discussion of the history and development. Fourteen essays by various Polish scholars. Includes bibliographical references.

## Learning and Scholarship

1075. Dobrowolski, Marian. POLISH SCHOLARS: THEIR CONTRIBUTION TO WORLD SCIENCE, trans. by Eugeniusz Lepa. Warszawa: "Polonia" Publishing House, 1960. 207p. 61-1470.

First work of its kind about Polish scientists, who have inscribed their names in the history of world science. It is intended as a popular book and therefore cannot take the place of more comprehensive works. Purpose is to acquaint readers with a selected group of Polish scholars and scientists throughout the history of Polish learning. Many portraits. Illustrations.

1076. EMPIRICAL SOCIOLOGY IN POLAND, comp. by Jan
Szczepański. Warszawa: PWN-Polish Scientific Publishers, 1966. 150p. 68-135098.

This book presents some aspects of the development of empirical sociology in Poland. Aim is to undertake a synthesized summary of the research findings in several important fields. Eight separate essays by Polish scholars.

1077. Kot, Stanisław. FIVE CENTURIES OF POLISH LEARNING.
Oxford: Basil Blackwood, 1941. 41-25152.

Three lectures delivered in the University of Oxford, May, 1941. English version by William J. Rose. Aim

*Special Works* 235

is to show how learning has always been a significant and vital element in the history of the Polish state. Author has sketched the history of Poland in the light of the transmission to the east and growth in the east of the learning of western Europe.

1078. Kuzawa, Mary Grace, Sister, C.S.F.N. MODERN MATHEMATICS: THE GENESIS OF A SCHOOL IN POLAND. New Haven, Conn.: College and University Press Publishers, 1968. 143p. 68-22383.

This book is intended primarily to trace the genesis and the evolving historical background of the Polish School of Mathematics which attained a zenith in world standing during the period 1918 to 1939. Bibliography, pp. 133-138.

1079. Mayewski, Paweł, ed. THE BROKEN MIRROR. New York: Random House, 1958. 209p.

A collection of writings from contemporary Poland. Purpose was to acquaint the American reader with what the more prominent Polish intellectuals and writers have to say about the system in which they live now that the opportunity to say it had come their way.

1080. POLISH RESEARCH GUIDE, 1964, ed. by Jerzy Kozłowski. Warszawa: Państwowe Wydawnictwo Naukowe, 1963. 419p. 64-2698.

Published once in 1964. List of schools and personnel engaged in research in Poland. Published for the National Science Foundation by Centralny Institut Informacji.

## Libraries and Librarianship

1081. Lewanski, Richard C., comp. A GUIDE TO POLISH LIBRARIES AND ARCHIVES. New York: Columbia University Press, 1976. 209p. 73-91484.

Purpose of work is to offer basic data on major library and archival collections in Poland. Arranged by location, provides data on library and a history of each. Bibliography, pp. 190-195.

1082. Łuczyńska, Alfreda, comp. LIBRARIES IN POLAND, INFORMATION GUIDE, trans. by Christina Cękalska. Warszawa: Polonia Publishing House, 1961. 108p. 61-4121.

   Very brief history of libraries in Poland followed by a description of the National Library in Warszawa and many important research, general and public libraries in Poland.

Literature--History and Criticism

1083. Dyboski, Roman. MODERN POLISH LITERATURE. London: Oxford University Press, 1924. 130p. 24-13479.

   A course of lectures delivered in the School of Slavonic Studies, King's College, University of London. Subject is Polish authors who were still alive either in the body or in spiritual influence upon the current generation. Discussion of the Polish novel, Polish dramatic literature, and Polish lyrical poetry.

1084. Dyboski, Roman. PERIODS OF POLISH LITERARY HISTORY. London: Oxford University Press, 1928. 163p. 33-33001.

   Lectures given February, 1923 to the University of Oxford. Covers Renaissance and Reformation; Polish literature in a century of wars; Political reform and literature in the era of Enlightenment; Evolution of Polish romanticism; Regional elements in Polish romanticism; and age of realism.

1085. Gardner, Monica Mary. POLAND, A STUDY IN NATIONAL IDEALISM. London: Burns and Oates, Ltd., 1915. 244p. War 15-56.

   Object is to give the English reader some faint conception of the idealism and the patriotism by which Poland has preserved her life through more than a hundred years of suffering and oppression. Discussion of literature and literary figures.

1086. Holewinski, Jan de. AN OUTLINE OF THE HISTORY OF POLISH LITERATURE. London: George Allen and Unwin, Ltd., 1916. 61p. 16-13393.

Explains with admirable clearness and brevity the part which literature has played in the life of the Polish race. Excellent outline of Polish literature.

1087. Kridl, Manfred. A SURVEY OF POLISH LITERATURE AND CULTURE, trans. by Olga Scherer-Virski. New York: Columbia University Press, 1956. 525p. 55-11748.

This book aims to present a general picture of the development of Polish literature from its beginnings in the Middle Ages to the end of the Second World War against a cultural background in which he describes historical and political events, the life of society, intellectual trade. Main purpose is to serve students and in part scholars not only in Polish but also in the other Slavic literatures and in comparative literature. Covers periods up to 1939. Bibliography, pp. 515-517.

1088. Krzyżanowski, Julian. A HISTORY OF POLISH LITERATURE. Warszawa: PWN-Polish Scientific Publishers, 1978. 807p. MiD: REF 891.85.K939h.

A comprehensive and complete work. Includes an essay entitled, THE LITERARY BOOKS OF THE POLISH NATION, a list of Polish literature in English translations, and black-and-white portraits or photographs of the principal literary figures.

1089. Krzyżanowski, Julian. POLISH ROMANTIC LITERATURE. London: George Allen and Unwin, Ltd., 1930. 317p. 30-32167.

First attempt to introduce the English reader to the whole of the most important section of Polish literature. Consists of part of lectures given in the School of Slavonic Studies, King's College, London, 1927-1928. Reprinted in 1968.

1090. Lednicki, Wacław. LIFE AND CULTURE OF POLAND AS REFLECTED IN POLISH LITERATURE. New York: Roy Publishers, 1944. 328p. 44-9167.

Series of lectures at Lowell Institute, Fall, 1943. Interpretative discourse about the most salient traits of the Polish nation and most important tendencies of its historical evolution. Polish literature,

literature in its broadest definition, is the theme. Bibliography, pp. 317-319.

1091. Levine, Madeline G. CONTEMPORARY POLISH POETRY, 1925-1975, ed. by Irene Nagurski. Boston: Twayne Publishers, 1981. 195p. 81-429.

Study of ten major contemporary Polish poets: Julian Przybos, Czesław Milosz, Krzysztof Kamil Baczyński, Tadeusz Gajcy, Zbigniew Herbert, Tadeusz Różewicz, Wisława Szymborska, Miron Białoszewski, Jerzy Harasymonowicz, Stanisław Grochowiak. Each chapter combines a study of the poet's career with a study of his poetry in terms of themes, philosophy and style.

1092. Maciuszko, Jerzy J. THE POLISH SHORT STORY IN ENGLISH: A GUIDE AND CRITICAL BIBLIOGRAPHY. Detroit: Wayne State University Press, 1968. 473p. 68-12253.

A revision of the author's thesis in Case Western Reserve University. Listing of principal writers with a brief biographical sketch of each one followed by titles of short stories, resume of the story and all extant English translations with imprints. Bibliography, pp. 465-471.

1093. Matuszewski, Ryszard. CONTEMPORARY POLISH WRITERS. Warszawa: Polonia Publishing House, 1959. 290p. A60-1153.

An introduction of some of Poland's leading contemporary writers. Biographical summaries and description of works of several. Includes a bibliography of works by contemporary Polish writers, translated into English and other languages. Compiled by Krystyna Jundzieł. Portraits.

1094. Miłosz, Czesław. THE HISTORY OF POLISH LITERATURE. New York: Macmillan Company, 1969. 570p. 69-10189.

Provides university students with as much information as possible within a limited number of pages. Stresses the fact that romanticism and Catholicism are of relatively recent origin in Polish literature. Begins with the Middle Ages. Includes passages from

*Special Works* 239

works. Illustrations. Portraits. Maps on lining papers. Bibliography, pp. 536-548.

1095. Rose, William J. POLISH LITERATURE. Birkenhead, Eng.: Polish Publication Committee, 1944. 27p. 45-3374.

Pamphlet survey of Polish literature with emphasis on the modern period. Contains list of English versions of Polish works, listing both British and American publications.

1096. Scherer-Virski, Olga. THE MODERN POLISH SHORT STORY. s'Gravenhage, Mouton and Co., 1955. 266p. A55-3712.

Analysis of the modern Polish short story, general classification of short stories into large structural types. Covers period from the beginning to outbreak of World War II. Contains portraits and biographical data on principal authors. Bibliography, pp. 249-254.

1097. Sobolewski, Paweł, ed. POETS AND POETRY OF POLAND. Milwaukee: Paul Soboleski Society, 1929. 464p. A31-77.

A collection of Polish verse, including a short account of the history of Polish poetry with sixty biographical sketches of Poland's poets and specimens of their composition, translated into the English language. Illustrations. Portraits.

1098. Weintraub, Wiktor. THE POETRY OF ADAM MICKIEWICZ. s'Gravenhage: Mouton and Co., 1954. 302p. 55-59147.

Aim of the book is to introduce to the English-speaking reader the great poet, Adam Mickiewicz. The book deals with Mickiewicz's poetry, and with poetry only. Included because it deals with a literary figure and to introduce his work. Bibliography, pp. 285-296.

Literature--Translations Into English

1099. Coleman, Marion M., comp. THE POLISH LAND. Cheshire, Conn.: Cherry Hill Books, 1974. 152p. 74-81566.

Sub-titled, A JOURNEY THROUGH POLAND FROM THE VISTULA TO THE POET'S LAND OF THE EASTERN BORDER: PERSONALITIES, POETRY, AN ANTHOLOGY. Tales, poems, legends arranged by region from which derived. Extension of first edition with added material.

1100. Coleman, Marion M. POLISH LITERATURE IN ENGLISH TRANSLATION; A BIBLIOGRAPHY. Cheshire, Conn.: Cherry Hill Books, 1963. 180p. 63-5711.

Mimeographed publication. Great writers and small have been covered in the bibliography, Nobel Prize winners, two of these, and obscure peasant scribblers from the southern mountains.

1101. Columbia University. Klub Polski. THE POLISH LAND, ZIEMIA POLSKA, AN ANTHOLOGY IN PROSE AND VERSE, ed. by Marion Moore Coleman. Trenton, N.J.: White Eagle Publishing Co., Inc., 1943. 43-18982.

An anthology of Polish prose and verse, mainly verse, translated into English. Poems and legends of various parts of Poland. Contains also a list of translators and an index of authors.

1102. Columbia University. Klub Polski. THE WAYSIDE WILLOW. Trenton, N.J.: White Eagle Publishing Co., Inc., 1945. 50p. 45-5096.

Prose and verse translated from the Polish by members of Klub Polski and edited by Marion Moore Coleman. Translators were former students of Polish at Columbia University during the academic sessions of 1944 and 1945.

1103. Filip, T.M., comp. A POLISH ANTHOLOGY, trans. by M.A. Michael. London: Duckworth, 1944. 405p. A44-3450.

Polish and English on opposite pages. Includes Polish literature translations into English and English literature translations into Polish. Includes also biographical sketches of famous Polish authors.

1104. Miłosz, Czesław, ed. and tr. POSTWAR POLISH POETRY: AN ANTHOLOGY. Garden City, N.J.: Doubleday and Co., 1965. 149p. 65-12373.

*Special Works* 241

Scope limited to living poets. Stress laid upon poems published since 1956. Biographical sketches of poets precede poetry.

1105. Segel, Harold B., ed. POLISH ROMANTIC DRAMA: THREE PLAYS IN ENGLISH TRANSLATION. Ithaca, N.Y.: Cornell University Press, 1977. 304p. 76-50264.

Contains analysis and description of three plays: FOREFATHER'S EVE, PART III, by Adam Mickiewicz; THE UNDIVINE COMEDY, by Zygmunt Krasinski; and FANTAZY by Juliusz Słowacki. Illustrations.

Military Techniques

1106. MILITARY TECHNIQUE: POLICY AND STRATEGY IN HISTORY. Warszawa: Ministry of National Defence Clearing House, 1976. 922p. 77-379006.

Series of sixteen articles by experts in the field of military strategy and history. Covers military affairs from the seventeenth century onwards. Illustrations.

Minorities

1107. Filinski, M. THE UKRAINIANS IN POLAND. London: Reynolds and Co., Ltd., 1931. 173p. 32-7696.

Published in response to complaints made by Ukrainians in Poland about their mistreatment as a minority group. Polish defense of the acquisition of this portion of Galacia of Ukrainian territory based on historical grounds. Discusses the current conditions ranging from general information, political life, economics, cultural, educational and social life and foreign influences upon Ukrainians in Poland. Contains tables and statistics. Maps.

\* Goodhart, Arthur L. POLAND AND THE MINORITY RACES. Cited above as item 958.

1108. Hagen, William W. GERMANS, POLES, AND JEWS: THE NATIONALITY CONFLICT. Chicago: University of Chicago Press, 1980. 406p. 80-10557.

A history of nationality conflict in the lands seized by Prussia in the Polish partitions. A study of the Prussian government's labors first to Prussianize and later to Germanize its Polish subjects, particularly in the province of Poznań. It focuses sharply on Polish resistance to Prussian rule. It does not neglect the Germans and Jews in the Poles' midst. Illustrations. Portraits. Maps. Bibliography, pp. 385-397.

1109. Horak, Stephen. POLAND AND HER NATIONAL MINORITIES, 1919-1939; A CASE STUDY. New York: Vantage Press, 1961. 259p. 60-15582.

An attempt on the part of the author to present in large outline an experiment in multinational relations within Poland. Covers period 1919-1939. Includes excerpts from the minorities treaty, the convention of Upper Silesia, the Constitution of 1921, the text of the statute of self-government, of voivodships Lwów, Tarnopol, Stanisławów. Polish viewpoint. Illustrations. Maps. Bibliography, pp. 232-254.

1110. Lengyel, Emil. THE CAULDRON BOILS. New York: Dial Press, 1932. 246p. 32-35037.

Account of Poland's minority problems identified as Wilno, Gdańsk, the Jews, Byelorussia, Upper Silesia and the Ukrainians. Book prepared following author's trip to Poland during the Summer of 1932. Author was a journalist. Illustrations. Maps.

1111. Revyuk, Emil, ed. POLISH ATROCITIES IN UKRAINE. Jersey City, N.J.: Svoboda Press, 1931. 512p. 32-342.

Collection of reports, some documents, mostly press reports, relating to the treatment of the Ukrainians in interwar Poland and particularly c. 1930. One map illustrates the ethnic composition of eastern Europe from the Ukrainian viewpoint.

1112. Wasilewski, Leon. NATIONALITIES IN POMERANIA. London: Baltic Pocket Library, 1934. 54p. 38-33715.

Discussion of the ethnical character of interwar Polish Pomerania. Chapter 7 covers the Kaszuby.

*Special Works*

Statistical data on Polish and non-Polish populations in Pomerania according to the Census of 1921 and the Census of 1931. Bibliography, p. 4.

Moving Pictures

1113. Butler, Ivan. THE CINEMA OF ROMAN POLANSKI. New York: A.S. Barnes & Co., 1970. 191p. 71-118773.

 A discussion of Polanski, three of his early shorts, and many of his other films. Each film is analyzed after a synopsis of the story line is given. Illustrations include portrait of Polanski and stills from the films. Bibliography, p. 191.

1114. CONTEMPORARY POLISH CINEMATOGRAPHY, by Władysław Banaszkiewicz et al. Warszawa: Polonia Publishing House, 1962. 173p. 63-5882.

 History of Polish cinematography including feature films, short films, the film industry, film clubs, amateur films, film press. Includes a list of films produced after the war, 1947-1961. Many illustrations including portraits, scenes from films, and advertisements.

1115. Fuksiewicz, Jacek. FILM AND TELEVISION IN POLAND. Warszawa: Interpress Publishers, 1976. 254p. 77-373227.

 Discussion of all aspects of post-war Polish cinematography. Includes information on television broadcasting in Poland. List of Polish filmmakers and actors with biographical sketches, awards for Polish films, etc. Illustrations, some in color. Includes scenes from films. Portraits.

1116. Kuszewski, Stanisław. CONTEMPORARY POLISH FILM, trans. by Bogna Piótrowska. Warszawa: Interpress Publishers, 1978. 126p. NjP: PN1993.5P55K813.

 Richly illustrated, black-and-white and colored, survey of contemporary films of all kinds, not merely full-length features. The prominent directors, e.g. Andrzej Wajda, are treated in individual chapters.

1117. Michałek, Bolesław. THE CINEMA OF ANDRZEJ WAJDA, trans. by Edward Rothert. South Brunswick, New Jersey: A.S. Barnes & Co., 1973. 175p. 72-7939.

Monograph which analyzes the appeal and significance of Wajda's work. Filmographies, pp. 159-171. Many illustrations which are scenes from the films.

Music

1118. Erhardt, Ludwik. MUSIC IN POLAND, trans. by Jan Aleksandrowicz. Warszawa: Interpress Publishers, 1975. 76-351223.

Survey of the history of music in Poland by demonstrating that Polish music did not start with Chopin and that it had many noteworthy composers before him. Illustrations. Portraits. List of foreign recordings of contemporary Polish music, pp. 161-162.

1119. Jarociński, Stefan, ec. POLISH MUSIC. Warszawa: PWN-Polish Scientific Publishers, 1965. 327p. 67-41752/MN.

Attempts to give to the foreign reader a possibly accurate story of Polish music, past and present. By design, Chopin has not been covered due to the numerous works about him and his work already available. Series of fourteen essays by experts. Illustrations. Portraits. Bibliography, pp. 297-314.

1120. Maciejewski, B.M. TWELVE POLISH COMPOSERS. London: Allegro Press, 1976. 229p.

Biographical sketches of twelve contemporary Polish composers. Portraits. List of works of Antoni Szałowski, pp. 207-209; list of works of Roman Maciejewski, pp. 210-212.

1121. Polanie Club. Minneapolis. TREASURED POLISH SONGS WITH ENGLISH TRANSLATIONS. Minneapolis: Polonie Publishing Co., 1953. 346p. M54-192.

Collection of Polish songs with musical notation and Polish and English lyrics. Contains an index of English titles and an index of Polish titles. Illustrations.

*Special Works*  245

1122. Rayson, Ethel. POLISH MUSIC AND CHOPIN, ITS LAUREATE. London: William Reeves, 1916. 64p. 17-11130.

    A sketch of the music of Poland with a special emphasis on the work of Chopin. Contains some facsimiles of music. Illustrations. Portraits.

1123. Sulikowski, Jerzy. POLISH MUSIC. Birkenhead, Eng.: Polish Publications Committee, 1944. 32p. 45-607.

    Brief survey of Polish music. Includes an alphabetical index of Polish composers. Some facsimiles of music. Bibliography, p. 33.

1124. Walaux, Marguerite. THE NATIONAL MUSIC OF POLAND: THE CHARACTER AND SOURCES. London: George Allen and Unwin, Ltd., 1916. 44p. 16-13391.

    Brief sketch of all types of music in Poland with special attention paid to Chopin.

## Oświęcim

1125. THE AUSCHWITZ ALBUM, text by Peter Hellman. New York: Random House, 1981. 167p. 80-53907.

    A book based upon an album of 188 photographs reportedly discovered accidentally in a vacated SS barracks. Portrays victims from their arrival through their selection for either slave labor or extermination. Text not of great value.

1126. Brewster, Eva. VANISHED IN DARKNESS. Edmonton, Alta.: NeWest Press, 1984. 143p. NjP: D805.P7B73.

    Author was a German Jewess imprisoned for a time in Oświęcim. She writes of those days in this personal narrative. Illustrations. Portraits.

1127. Broad, Pery. KZ AUSCHWITZ: REMINISCENCES OF PERY BROAD, SS-MAN IN THE AUSCHWITZ CONCENTRATION CAMP, trans. by Krystyna Michalik. Oświęcim: Państwowe Muzeum Oświęcima, 1965. 89p. 68-71107.

    Based upon a document purportedly written by the author describing the crimes perpetrated by the SS in Oświęcim. Illustrations. Portraits.

1128. FROM THE HISTORY OF KL-AUSCHWITZ, trans. by Krystyna
       Michalik. New York: Howard Fertig, 1982. 225p.
       81-5426.

   Contents: "The concentration camp Auschwitz; the
   Auschwitz sub-camps; The system of punishments used by
   the SS in the concentration camp at Auschwitz-
   Birkenau; Escapes of prisoners; Ethical and legal
   limits in experimentation in medicine in connection
   with Professor Clauberg's affair; Starvation in Auschwitz; The Singer; Days of horror; Most important
   events in the history of the concentration camp Auschwitz-Birkenau." Written by Polish scholars. Illustrations.

1129. Garliński, Józef. FIGHTING AUSCHWITZ, THE RESISTANCE
       MOVEMENT IN THE CONCENTRATION CAMP. London: Julian
       Friedman, Ltd., 1975. 327p. 75-309750.

   Given as a dispassionate, impartial and comprehensive account of the opposition by the inmates of
   Oświęcim and Birkenau concentration camps written
   thirty years after the fact by a former inmate. Contains numerous portraits of resistance leaders plus
   photographs of the camp. Maps. Bibliography, pp.
   298-311.

1130. Gilbert, Martin. AUSCHWITZ AND THE ALLIES. New York:
       Holt, Rinehart, and Winston, 1981. 368p. 80-28911.

   An account of "when and how the Allies in World War
   II learned of Nazi atrocities against Europe's Jewish
   population and of their reaction." Illustrations.
   Maps.

1131. Hart, Kitty. RETURN TO AUSCHWITZ: THE REMARKABLE
       STORY OF A GIRL WHO SURVIVED THE HOLOCAUST. New
       York: Atheneum, 1983. 178p. 81-61955.

   A personal narrative of a survivor of the Oświęcim
   concentration camp. The account which also covered
   the author's journies from Bielsko in southwestern
   Poland and eventually to England was written some
   forty years afterwards. Illustrations. Portraits.
   Maps.

Special Works 247

1132. KL AUSCHWITZ SEEN BY THE SS/HOSS, BROAD, KREMER, selected by Jadwiga Bezwińska and Danuta Czech, trans. by Constantine Fitzgibbon and Krystyna Michalik. New York: Howard Fertig, 1984. 331p. 83-16512.

Three documents written by SS men from the concentration camp at Oświęcim. Hoss wrote his memoirs while in a Polish prison. Kremer had kept a diary while at Oświęcim for three months. Broad wrote an account of crimes committed at Oświęcim. Illustrations. Portraits. Bibliography, pp. 319-320.

1133. Kielar, Wiesław. ANUS MUNDI: 1,500 DAYS IN AUSCHWITZ-BIRKENAU, trans. by Suanne Flatauer. New York: Times Books, 1986. 312p. 80-5129.

Personal account of time spent at Oświęcim by a survivor. Illustrations.

1134. Kulka, Erich. ESCAPE FROM AUSCHWITZ. South Hadley, Mass.: Bergin & Garvey Publishers, Inc., 1986. 150p. 85-22825.

Although primarily a personal narrative of how the author, a Czech Jew, actually escaped, the book describes conditions in Oświęcim rather graphically. Illustrations. Portraits.

1135. Lengyel, Olga. FIVE CHIMNEYS: THE STORY OF AUSCHWITZ. New York: Ziff-Davis Publishing Co., 1947. 213p. MiD: 940.947.L547f.

The story of the camp as told by the wife of a Hungarian physician. They were imprisoned in 1944 and survived the ordeal. They were finally freed when the Russians entered Poland early in 1945.

1136. Levi, Primo. SURVIVAL IN AUSCHWITZ AND THE REAWAKENING: TWO MEMOIRS, trans. by Stuart Woolf. New York: Summit Books, 1986. 397p. 85-27618.

A personal narrative by an Italian who had been deported to Oświęcim in 1944 (Survival in Auschwitz) and the author's journey back to Italy via a circuitous route including the U.S.S.R. (The Reawakening).

1137. Nomberg-Przytek, Sara. AUSCHWITZ: TRUE TALES FROM A GROTESQUE LAND, ed. by Eli Pfefferkorn and David Hirsch, trans. by Roslyn Hirsch. Chapel Hill: University of North Carolina Press, 1985. 185p. 84-17386.

 An account of the author's experiences in Oświęcim while a prisoner there for two years. Original Polish manuscript of journal kept by the author and found in 1980.

1138. Pawełczyńska, Anna. VALUES AND VIOLENCE IN AUSCHWITZ: A SOCIOLOGICAL ANALYSIS, trans. by Catherine S. Leach. Berkeley: University of California Press, 1980. 170p. 76-3886.

 Author "shows how ... the prisoners formed communities and sought to give social and moral structure to their lives." Maps.

1139. Pisar, Samuel. OF BLOOD AND HOPE. Boston: Little, Brown and Co., 1980. 311p. 80-10696.

 Reminiscences of the author's experiences as a youth in Oświęcim. Composed four decades later. Illustrations. Portraits.

1140. Poland. Główna Komisja Badania Zbrodni Hitlerowskich w Polsce. CONCENTRATION CAMP: OŚWIĘCIM-BRZEZINKA, BASED ON DOCUMENTARY EVIDENCE AND SOURCES, by Jan Sehn, trans. by Klemens Kęplicz. Warszawa: Wydawnictwo Prawnicze, 1957. 161p. 59-39123.

 Deals with the role and object of the Oświęcim camp against the general background of the Nazi concentration camp system. Illustrations. Portraits.

1141. Rudnicki, Adolf. LEST WE FORGET. Warszawa: Polonia Foreign Languages Publishing House, 1955. 170p. A55-10482.

 A collection of prose and poetry about Oświęcim. Excerpts from books, poems, by persons who experienced firsthand the horrors of the concentration camp.

1142. Smolen Kaźimierz. AUSCHWITZ 1940-1945, GUIDEBOOK THROUGH THE MESEUM, trans. by Krystyna Michalik. Oświęcim: Państwowe Muzeum, 1976. 118p. 73-151304.

Guidebook with an historical narrative. Numerous black-and-white illustrations of the camp and former inmates. Contains plan of the camp.

### Personal Narratives

1143. BEYOND HUMAN ENDURANCE: THE RAVENSBRUCK WOMEN TELL THEIR STORIES, trans. by Doris Ronowicz. Warszawa: Interpress Publishers, 1970. 181p. 76-30905.

    This book is a selection of reminiscences of twenty Ravensbruck ex-prisoners who had experimental operations performed on them. Each selection is preceded by a portrait and brief biographical sketch. Illustrations.

1144. Boleslavski, Richard. WAY OF THE LANCER, in collaboration with Helen Woodward. Indianapolis: Bobbs-Merrill Co., 1932. 316p. 32-26224.

    Author is known as a man of the theater. He began as an actor in the Moscow Art Theater. He is now a film director in Hollywood. For a few years in his life he was a lieutenant in the Polish Lancers, who were allies of the Russians fighting the Germans and the Austrians. Book is the story of the last days with the Russians and the rise of the Red Army which became their enemies. Maps on lining papers.

1145. Brandys, Kazimierz. A WARSAW DIARY, 1978-1981, trans. by Richard Lourie. New York: Vintage Books, 1985. 260p. 84-40052.

    A selection of passages from two volumes of author's journals, the complete text of which appeared in a Polish edition.

1146. Czapski, Józef. THE INHUMAN LAND, trans. by Gerard Hopkins. New York: Sheed and Ward, 1952. 301p. 52-8896.

    Covers period of a year, 1931-1942, spent in the Soviet Union. Includes a broad picture of the Soviet hinterland as well as a picture of the sufferings of a Polish exile. Illustrations.

1147. Czarnomski, Francis B., ed. THEY FIGHT FOR POLAND: THE WAR IN THE FIRST PERSON. London: George Allen and Unwin, Ltd., 1941. 284p. A42-543.

Personal stories of those who fought for Poland during the first two years of the Second World War. A collection of war stories. Illustrations. Portraits.

1148. Dragomir, V. IT STARTED IN POLAND. London: Faber and Faber, Ltd., 1941. 249p. A42-98.

Purpose was to tell author's friends in England what happened to him when the Nazis invaded Poland. Personal narrative of the author beginning with German invasion in September, 1939 through November when he escaped to Italy.

1149. Dyboski, Roman. SEVEN YEARS IN RUSSIA AND SIBERIA, 1914-1921, trans. and annotated by M.M. Coleman. Cheshire, Conn.: Cherry Hill Books, 1971. 177p. 79-137001.

Biography of a part of the life of a famous Polish Scholar, the period when he was exiled to Siberia between 1914 and 1921. A translation of his memoir. Portraits.

1150. Etchegoyen, Olivier, Comte d'. THE COMEDY OF POLAND, trans. by Nora Bickley. London: George Allen and Unwin, Ltd., 1927. 243p. 28-10538.

Author detailed to be placed to the French Military Mission to Poland. Interesting observations of immediate post-war era. Covers period 1920-1925.

1151. Ferderber-Salz, Bertha. AND THE SUN KEPT SHINING ... New York: Holocaust Library, 1980. 233p. 80-81684.

Memoir which describes author's experiences during the days of persecution of Jews in Poland during World War II. Includes her days spent in Oświęcim and Bergen Belsen concentration camps. Illustrations. Portraits. Maps.

1152. Gazel, Stefan F. TO LIVE AND KILL. London: Jarrolds, 1958. 215p. 59-31154.

Personal account of author's experiences after World War II broke out in Poland. He is at first captured by the Russians and later escaped to German-occupied Poland. From thence, he escaped to Hungary, then to Yugoslavia, finally to France by February, 1940, eventually to England. Served out the war in the British Navy. Illustrations. Portraits.

1153. Ginter, Maria. LIFE IN BOTH HANDS, trans. by P.C. Blauth-Muszkowski. London: Hodder and Stoughton, 1964. 254p. 66-33176.

Author's narrative of events as they occurred in her life in Poland from August 26, 1939 through December 28, 1944. Based on a record of facts as they occurred and thoughts as they came to mind. Illustrated by the author's own paintings.

1154. Halpern, Ada. CONDUCTED TOUR. New York: Sheed and Ward, 1945. 145p. 45-10375.

Description of a Polish exile's deportation to Siberia in Spring, 1940. Based on her diary to Spring, 1942 when she was permitted to return to Poland. Dispassionate account. Maps.

1155. Herling, Gustaw. A WORLD APART, trans. by Joseph Marek. London: Heinemann, 1951. 262p. 51-8066.

Fleeing from Nazi persecution, young Polish student Herling was caught by Russians in March, 1940 and spent two following years in Soviet prisons and in labor camp near Archangel, till he was finally released; later he joined the Polish Army and became a writer in London.

1156. Janta-Połczyński, Aleksander. BOUND WITH TWO CHAINS. New York: Roy Publishers, 1945. 234p. 45-37866.

Author's personal account of his experiences as a German prisoner-of-war during the Summer of 1941.

1157. Janta-Połczyński, Aleksander. I LIED TO LIVE: A YEAR AS A GERMAN FAMILY SLAVE, trans. by B.W.A. Marsey. New York: Roy Publishers, 1944. 312p. 44-47545.

Author was a cadet-officer in the Polish division fighting the Germans on the western front in June,

1940, unfolds in this book a little-known chapter in the history of this war. When France collapsed he was taken prisoner and throughout the year of has captivity he had to work on a German farm disguised as a French soldier.

1158. Johnston, Russell R. POLAND, 1945; A RED CROSS DIARY. Philadelphia: Dorrance and Co., 1973. 171p. 73-86340.

Story of author's year in Russia and Poland as a Red Cross field director attached to civilian relief. Diary format.

1159. Karski, Jan, pseud. STORY OF A SECRET STATE. Boston: Houghton Mifflin Co., 1944. 391p. 44-9776.

A purely personal story. Author tried to recall everything he had experienced, to tell about his own activities, and to recount the deeds of all those with whom he had actual contact. First member of the Polish Underground to publish some aspects of its story.

1160. Kmiecik, Jerzy. A BOY IN THE GULAG. New York: Quartet Books, 1983. 248p. NjP: (Dixon) HV8959. S65K54.

Actual account of the author's experiences after he had left home in 1939 at the age of sixteen to flee from the Germans ending up in Soviet-occupied Poland. This misadventure meant imprisonment in the U.S.S.R. and eventual escape and refuge in Great Britain after three years and 33,000 miles. Map.

1161. Knapp, Stefan. THE SQUARE SUN. London: Museum Press, 1956. 172p. 57-33776.

Illustrations are all of author's sculptures and his own portrait. Author states in the foreword that the book is purely and simply the narrative of a curious and adventurous life thrust upon him by reason of his capture by Russians, three years in labor camps in Siberia, escape to England where he joined the R.A.F.

1162. Korwin-Rhodes, Marta. IN SPITE OF EVERYTHING.
Kilmarnock, Eire: Dunlop and Drennan, 1942. 71p.
48-42744.

Diary of a nurse in military hospitals in Warszawa
at the very outset of the Second World War. It is a
personal account of the initial siege of Warszawa.
Many black-and-white photographs of the city and its
early destruction. Portraits. Maps.

1163. Kossak Szczućka, Zofia. THE BLAZE, REMINISCENCES OF
VOLHYNIA, 1917-1919, ed. by Francis B. Czarnomski.
New York: Polish Book Importing Co., 1927. 324p.
28-6001.

An emotional narrative of the experiences of the
author and her family during the period from the Treat
Treaty of Brześć-Litowsk to the summer of 1919 when
she managed to seek shelter and rejoin her family
among the Polish army.

1164. Kulski, Julian E. DYING WE LIVE: THE PERSONAL
CHRONICLE OF A YOUNG FREEDOM FIGHTER IN WARSZAWA,
1939-1945. New York: Holt, Rinehart and Winston,
1979. 304p. 78-31656.

A diary, beginning with August 24, 1939, of the author's experiences and so-called freedom fighter in
Warszawa during the German occupation. Profusely illustrated, photographs collected during the war. Portraits. Maps.

1165. Langer, Rulka. THE MERMAID AND THE MESSERSCHMIDT.
New York: Roy Publishers, 1942. 372p. 42-50798.

An account of a young woman, her mother and her two
children, caught in the bombardment of Warszawa in
1939. Story continues to February of 1940 when she
left to join her husband in the U.S. Describes life
in this city during the first few months of German
occupation.

1166. Maks, Leon. RUSSIA BY THE BACK DOOR, trans. by
Rosamona Batchellor. New York: Sheed and Ward,
1954. 264p. 54-3931.

The author was connected with the Polish Underground
from its beginning in 1939. In March, 1940, he and a
woman companion were sent into Russia to try to trace
the leader of the Underground who had been sent east.
This is the account of that very hazardous assignment.
Illustrations.

1167. Makucewicz, Peter. I ESCAPED FROM GERMANY, trans. by
 Patricia Woodward-Gottesman. London: Maxlove Publishing Company, Ltd., 1944. 125p. 44-6229.

 Story of a Polish soldier who after three attempts finally succeeded the fourth time to escape from a German prisoner-of-war camp during World War II. Illustrations. Maps..

1168. Meissner, Janusz. G-FOR GENEVIEVE: THE STORY OF A POLISH FLIER. New York: Roy Publishers, 1944. 254p. 44-5444.

 Sequel to author's L-FOR LUCY. Here he continues narrative when ordered to fly to Romania where internment leads to escape to England where he becomes a bombardier. Accounts of his missions bombing Germany.

1169. Meissner, Janusz. L-FOR LUCY. Edinburgh: Składnica Księgarska, 1945. 140p. 46-3413.

 Life and experiences of the crew of a Polish fighter plane named "Lucy." Continuation of the story, G-FOR GENEVIEVE which the author wrote previously. Black-and-white drawings.

1170. Młynarski, Bronisław. THE 79TH SURVIVOR, trans. by Każimierz Zdziechowski. London: Buchman and Turner, 1976. 246p. 77-350494.

 Authentic story of a Polish officer captured by the Soviet Army in September, 1939. The author was interned in the Starobyelsk camp. He remained there until October-November, 1941 when the camp and its prisoners were turned over to the Polish Army.

1171. Monat, Paweł. SPY IN THE U.S. New York: Harper and Row, 1962. 208p. 61-10211.

 A true story of espionage carried out against the United States by a Polish colonel during 1955-1958. Author eventually found asylum in the U.S.

1172. Mowrer, Lilian T. ARREST AND EXILE. New York: W. Morrow and Co., 1941. 274p. 41-21692.

 The true story of an American woman in Poland and Siberia, 1940-1941. Olga Kochanska is the person

*Special Works* 255

and her story was related to the author and written by her.

1173. Mur, Jan, pseud. A PRISONER OF MARTIAL LAW; POLAND, 1981-1982, trans. by Lillian Vallee. New York: Harcourt, Brace, Jovanovich, 1984. 311p. 84-15648.

Journal covering period from December, 1981 to August, 1982 while author interned in the Strzebielinek Camp near Gdańsk and also the months after he was released. Not only a book about prison conditions but also the attempt of a political activist to think through a year following the imposition of martial law. Illustrations. Portraits. Maps.

1174. MY NAME IS MILLION. New York: Macmillan Co., 1940. 284p. 40-34067.

Personal narrative of an anonymous Englishwoman, wife of a Polish army officer, relating her experiences from the date of the German invasion of Poland until her eventual return to England via Lithuania, Sweden and Germany in December, 1939.

1175. Nieścior, Leon. I SURVIVED HELL ON EARTH. Privately published, 1956. 179p. NjP: 14101.224.677.

Author's lurid account of his imprisonment in Oświęcim. Privately published. Numerous photographs whose sources were not given. Portraits.

1176. Nowak, Jan. COURIER FROM WARSAW. Detroit: Wayne State University, 1982. 477p. 82-8599.

Author was a postgraduate student of economics at Poznań University when war broke out. Became member of resistance movement. Was a courier bearing messages to the Polish authorities abroad. Made two journeys from Poland to Sweden, the second time going on to London for several months. He returned to Warszawa to take part in the rising of the capital against the Germans in the Summer of 1944. Returned to England after the uprising was suppressed. This is the story of his wartime experiences.

1177. Oreme, Alexandra. BY THE WATERS OF THE DANUBE, trans. by Norbert Guterman. New York: Duell, Sloan and Pearce, 1951. 360p. 51-10881.

Continuation of author's narrative of her self-imposed exile in Budapest. First book, entitled COMES THE COMRADE brought narrative up to March, 1945. This book begins the narrative in April of 1945 and includes author's return to Poland and re-exile in Hungary.

1178. Orme, Alexandra. COMES THE COMRADE, trans. by M.A. Michael and L. Meyer. New York: Morrow, 1950. 376p. 50-6729.

Life of a female Polish exile in Budapest. Author was a Pole who moved to Budapest in 1939 to escape Nazi occupation of her homeland. This book covers the period from December, 1944 to Spring of 1945 with the arrival of the "Comrade" from the East. Illustrations.

1179. Pawelek, Anne J. AN AMERICAN IN POLAND, ed. by Joseph A. Wytrwał. Detroit: Endurance Press, 1967. 285p. 66-28205.

The personal reminiscences of a Polish-American woman who spent a year studying at the Jagiellonian University in Kraków. It is a series of colorful sketches depicting Polish activities from every conceivable angle.

1180. Penzik, Irena. ASHES TO THE TASTE. New York: University Publishers, 1961. 378p. 61-8736.

An intimate picture of Poland's Communist elite in New York, Paris, Warszawa, by the niece and former secretary of a leading Polish diplomat.

1181. Phillips, Janine. MY SECRET DIARY. London: Shepheard-Walwyn, 1982. 152p. 82-180310.

A day-to-day account of the activities and thoughts of the author from May 16, 1939 to May 23, 1940.

1182. Piasecki, Victor, pseud. YOU'LL NEED A GUARDIAN ANGEL. London: Hamish Hamilton, 1979. 268p. NjP: D805.R9P46.

A "true story" of a Polish Army officer captured by the Soviets in 1939, his escape, recapture, time spent in Lubyanka until 1941 when the Soviet Union was

*Special Works* 257

> invaded by Germany and he was released. Story related to an English writer many years later.

1183. Piotrkowski, Rufin. MY ESCAPE FROM SIBERIA. London: Routledge, Warne, and Routledge, 1863. 386p.

> Narrative of a Pole who returning to Poland from Paris in 1843 is arrested and sent to prison in Siberia. Discusses his internment, other exiled Poles, his escape and subsequent return to Paris. Map traces his journey to and from Siberia from Paris. Portrait.

1184. Piotrowski, Marian. ADVENTURES OF A POLISH PRISONER, trans. by Louise L. Jarecka. London: L. Drummond, Ltd., 1943. 207p. 44-278.

> Account of experiences by author as a soldier in the Polish Army in France, as a prisoner in Germany. Period covered is July, 1939 to December, 1941. Illustrations.

1185. Polonius, Alexander, pseud. I SAW THE SIEGE OF WARSAW. London: William Hodge and Company, Ltd., 1941. 364p. A41-3725.

> Personal narrative, in diary form, of the Polish war from Monday, August 31, 1939 to Monday, October 23, 1939, in England. Route of exile followed was from Warszawa to Kovno to Riga thence by ship to Bergen and to England. Maps on lining papers.

1186. Pruszyński, Ksawery. RUSSIAN YEAR, THE NOTEBOOK OF AN AMATEUR DIPLOMAT. New York: Roy Publishers, 1944. 189p. 44-5170.

> A personal account of the author's visit to Russia from August, 1941 to 1942. Polish impression of the U.S.S.R. during the war years.

1187. Rawicz, Slavomir. THE LONG WALK: A GAMBLE FOR LIFE as told to Ronald Dowling. New York: Harper and Row, Publishers, 1956. 56-6906.

> A young Polish officer, arrested on charges of spying against Russia, was sentenced to twenty-five years hard labor in Siberia. With six fellow-convicts, and

later a girl found in the forests, he made his escape
and started his 3,000-mile walk to freedom. Maps on
lining papers.

1188. Rydel, W. LITTLE MAN'S STORY, trans. by Adam Truscoe.
Melbourne: Author, 1967. 395p. 68-75087.

An account of the author's life and experiences in
Poland up to the point when Germany invaded the country. Author was a teacher.

1189. Soltan, Christina. UNDER STRANGE SKIES. London:
George Allen and Unwin, Ltd., 1948. 480p. 49-15029.

This is the story of Christina, a young pianist.
Author narrates her experiences from November, 1938 as
she attempts to aid her Jewish piano teacher in
Berlin, then endures hardships during the invasion of
her country by Germany and Russia and eventually finds
refuge in Japan only to leave there when hostilities
between that country and the West broke out. Then to
Africa and finally to England.

1190. Stypułkowski, Zbigniew F. INVITATION TO MOSCOW.
London: Thames and Hudson, 1951. 359p. 51-4368.

Memoirs of the author's life as a prisoner-of-war
first in the U.S.S.R., then in Germany, as a member of
the Polish armed resistance, again as a prisoner in
the U.S.S.R. Spans the period from September 1, 1939
to 1945. Illustrations. Portraits.

1191. Swięcicki, Marek. SEVEN RIVERS TO BOLOGNA. London:
J. Rolls Book Co., Ltd., 1946. 115p. 46-20902.

A personal narrative by a young Polish journalist of
the activities of the Polish Second Corps during its
campaign in the Plains of Lombardy in the Spring of
1945. Illustrations. Portraits.

1192. Szalet, Leon. EXPERIMENT "E": A REPORT FROM AN
EXTERMINATION LABORATORY, trans. by Catherine B.
Williams. New York: Didier, Publishers, 1945.
284p. 46-1526.

A graphic fictionalized description of how the
mechanism of a concentration camp worked, how a

*Special Works* 259

prisoner's day was spent, how he worked, what he ate, what and how he suffered.

1193. Szmaglewska, Seweryna. SMOKE OVER BIRKENAU, trans. by Jadwiga Rynas. New York: Henry Holt, 1947. 386p. 47-30407.

The author was a university student in Warszawa in July, 1942, when the Gestapo caught and imprisoned her for her underground activities. For almost three years she lived through the horrors of Birkenau. This is her record of the sufferings of her fellow prisoners and herself during those terrible years.

1194. Szmaglewska, Seweryna. UNITED IN WRATH. Warszawa: "Polonia" Foreign Language Publishing House, 1955. 36p. 56-44476.

Personal recollections of author's internment in Oświęcim.

1195. Viomenil, Antoine Charles du Houx. THE PRIVATE LETTERS OF BARON DE VIOMENIL ON POLISH AFFAIRS, trans. by John F. Gough. Jersey, N.J.: Collins Doan Co., 1935. 275p. 35-6208.

Author was French military officer sent to Poland in 1771 and 1772. Reveals facts about the partition of Poland which took place in 1772. Portraits. Maps on lining papers.

1196. Virski, Fred. MY LIFE IN THE RED ARMY. New York: Macmillan Company, 1949. 260p. 49-8372.

Personal narrative of a twenty-one year old Pole drafted into the Soviet Army. A revealing account of a common soldier's life with the Red Army behind the Iron Curtain. Eventually, the author deserts the Soviet Army and joins the Polish Army.

1197. Warfield, Hania. CALL US TO WITNESS, A POLISH CHRONICLE, by Hania and Gaither Warfield. New York: Ziff-Davis Publishing Company, 1945. 434p. 45-5473.

Reminiscences by authors of their lives from August 20, 1939 to June 23, 1942. Some parts are written by Hania while others are written by Gaither.

1198.  Wasilewska, Eugenia. THE SILVER MADONNA, 1939-1945. New York: John Day, 1970. 216p. 75-143408.

This is a personal recollection of life in Russian-occupied Poland at the beginning of the Second World War and of Siberia as seen by a young Polish girl who describes her escape from Siberia, her capture in European Russia and subsequent imprisonment, her release at the height of the German offensive and finally the completion of her forced odyssey.

1199.  Węgierski, Dominik. SEPTEMBER 1939. London: Minerva Publishing Co., Ltd., 1940. 180p. A41-1988.

Account of personal "adventures" of the author during the so-called September Campaign of 1939.

\*      Wells, Leon W. THE JANOWSKA ROAD. Cited above as item 1008.

1200.  Wierzyński, Każimiera. THE FORGOTTEN BATTLEFIELD, trans. by Edmund Ordon. New York: Roy Publishers, 1944. 179p. 44-8528.

Illustrated by Zdzisław Czermonski. A series of accounts of the invasion of Poland in 1939. There are ten such accounts which the author stated were collected haphazardly. They were orally transmitted to the author. All of them deal with events which occurred during the short war between Germany and Poland.

1201.  Wittlin Tadeusz. A RELUCTANT TRAVELLER IN RUSSIA, trans. by Noel E.P. Clark. New York: Holt, Rinehart and Winston, 1952. 280p. 52-10041.

Account of author's travels in the U.S.S.R. when, fleeing from German-occupied Warszawa, he tried to get to France through the eastern part of Poland then occupied by the Russians.

1202.  Zawisza, Olgierd. ACROSS BURNING FRONTIERS. New York: Roy Publishers, 1943. 255p. 43-8045.

Personal narrative of Pole's adventures in Poland before World War II and how she survived war in Poland and in Europe eventually finding safety in the United States.

*Special Works* 261

1203. Żywulska, Krystyna. I CAME BACK, trans. by Krystyna Cenkalska. London: D. Dobson, 1951. 246p. 51-1236.

  The account of the author's experiences in prison in her native Poland during the Nazi occupation and in the terrible Auschwitz. The book ends with her escape.

Poles in Argentina--Fiction

1204. Marczyński, Antoni. THE RAVISHERS: A NOVEL OF WHITE SLAVERY IN ITS HEYDAY, by Anthony Kirkor, pseud. New York: The Ignis Co., 1955. 206p. 55-32177.

  Story of a young Polish girl forced into vice in Buenos Aires and how she is rescued from such a life and is returned to Poland.

Poles in Australia

1205. Johnston, Ruth. THE ASSIMILATION MYTH: A STUDY OF SECOND-GENERATION POLISH IMMIGRANTS IN WESTERN AUSTRALIA. The Hague: Martinus Nijhoff, 1969. 95p. 73-492825.

  A sociological study of the attitudes of the offspring of Polish immigrants in western Australia. Contains numerous charts and graphs. Bibliography, pp. 91-95.

1206. Johnston, Ruth. IMMIGRANT ASSIMILATION: A STUDY OF POLISH PEOPLE IN WESTERN AUSTRALIA. Perth: Paterson Brokensha Printery, Ltd., 1965. 289p. 67-73026.

  A scientific inquiry into the assimilation process as applied to Poles who emigrated to Western Australia after World War II. Aim is to study factors relating to the assimilation of selected groups of Polish immigrants in Western Australia. Concerned with the individual Polish immigrant. Bibliography, pp. 195-207.

## Poles In Canada

1207. Balawyder, Aloysius. THE MAPLE LEAF AND THE WHITE EAGLE. New York: Columbia University Press, 1980. 300p. 79-56525.

    Purpose is to demonstrate how the relations between Canada and Poland were largely determined by functional pragmatism; examines the Polish community in Canada as a basis for Canadian-Polish relations and to illustrate the importance of democratic values in Canadian-Polish relations. Illustrations. Bibliography, pp. 267-271.

1208. Hubicz, Edward M. POLISH CHURCHES IN MANITOBA: A COLLECTION OF HISTORICAL SKETCHES. London: Veritas Foundation Publication Centre, 1961. 239p. 63-23513.

    Really an historical sketch of the establishment of sixty-four Polish parishes in Manitoba. The story is divided into geographical regions. Some black-and-white illustrations of some of the church buildings. No interior shots. Maps.

1209. Kos-Rabcewicz-Zubkowski, Ludwik. THE POLES IN CANADA. Toronto: Polish Alliance Press, Ltd., 1968. 202p. 79-387843.

    Sub-titled, POLISH CONTRIBUTION TO THE DEVELOPMENT OF CANADA; OUTSTANDING POLISH CANADIANS. Depicts the achievements of outstanding individuals and to recall and to attempt to evoke the highlights of the Polish contribution to the development of Canada.

1210. Makowski, William B. HISTORY AND INTEGRATION OF POLES IN CANADA. St. Catherines, Ont.: Canadian Press Congress, 1967. 274p. 68-97440.

    An attempt to describe the history of Polish immigration in Canada but ends up as a fragmented discussion of various Polish settlements throughout the country. Loosely arranged geographically from east to west, the author discusses individuals, individual settlements, parishes, both Roman Catholic and Polish National Catholic, and organizations. Here and there are discussions of the Polish contributions to

Canadian life. Many tables, e.g. List by provinces of
the Polish Roman Catholic parishes in Canada. Chapter
VI is entitled, POLISH KASHOUBS IN THE RENFREW AREA.
Illustrations. Bibliography, pp. 231-239.

1211. Radecki, Henry. ETHNIC ORGANIZATIONAL DYNAMICS: THE
POLISH GROUP IN CANADA. Waterloo, Ont.: Wilfrid
Laurier University Press, 1979. 275p.

Revision of author's thesis, York University. Portrays the establishment and later developments of
Polish voluntary organizations limited to the metropolitan Toronto area.

1212. Radecki, Henry. A MEMBER OF A DISTINGUISHED FAMILY.
Toronto: McClelland and Stewart, 1976. 240p.

A history of Polish settlement in Canada topically
arranged: arrival, adjustment, organizations, language maintenance, the press, the family, religion,
work and occupational mobility, relationships, the
Canadian Polonia. Part of a series sponsored by the
Multiculturalism Program, Department of the Secretary
of State of Canada and the Publication Centre, Supply
and Services Canada. Illustrations. Bibliography,
pp. 223-235. OL: F1035.P6.R3.

1213. Turek, Wiktor. POLES IN MANITOBA. Toronto: Polish
Research Institute in Canada, 1967. 339p. 68-118525.

A history of Polonia in Manitoba, the broadest as
well as the most thoroughly researched study of the
Polish settlers. Bibliography, pp. 321-327.

1214. Turek, Wiktor. THE POLISH-LANGUAGE PRESS IN CANADA:
ITS HISTORY AND A BIBLIOGRAPHICAL LIST. Toronto:
Polish Alliance Press, 1962. 248p. 63-49091.

A scholarly and objective history of the Polish language press in Canada as well as the aims, struggles
and successes of the foreign language press in general.
Consists of two parts: an historical outline of the
growth of the Polish press, with a description of the
individual periodicals; and, a bibliographical list
arranged alphabetically of Polish periodicals. Maps.
Bibliography, pp. 210-216.

1215. Turek, Wiktor. THE POLISH PAST IN CANADA. Toronto: Polish Alliance Press, 1962. 138p. 65-36608.

A festaschrift consisting of some six contributions in honor of the seventy-fifth birthday of Professor William J. Rose. Five essays written in English, one in French. Illustrations. Portraits. Maps. Bibliographies included.

\*   Turek, Wiktor. POLONICA CANADIANA. Cited above as item 159.

1216. Wołodkowicz, Andrzej. POLISH CONTRIBUTION TO ARTS AND SCIENCES IN CANADA. London: White Eagle Press, 1969. 363p. 72-586326.

Documents the importance of the technical, intellectual and artistic fraction of the Polish ethnic group in the development of Canada. Includes a brief history of Polish immigration into Canada. Illustrations contain reproductions of paintings done by Polish-Canadians. Bibliography, pp. 15-17.

\*   Zolobka, Vincent, comp. POLONICA CANADIANA, 1958-1970. Cited above as item 161.

### Poles In Great Britain

1217. Pietrkiewicz, Jerzy. THE KNOTTED CORD, A NOVEL. New York: Roy Publishers, 1953. 267p. 53-9776.

Novel about a young Polish poet who comes to England in 1940 to continue a life interrupted by war.

1218. Poznanski, Czesław. POLISH ARTISTS IN GREAT BRITAIN. London: "Nowa Polska," 1944. 371p. A45-3131.

An album of Polish artists and a selection of the works which have been produced by the Poles in emigration. Illustrations.

1219. Pruszyński, Ksawery. POLISH INVASION, trans. by Peter Jordan. London: Minerva Publishing Co., 1941. 112p. A42-613.

*Special Works* 265

Deals with the Polish refugees in Scotland during
World War II. Although factual, book written in novel
form.

1220. Raczyński, Edward, hrabia. IN ALLIED LONDON. London:
Weidenfeld and Nicolson, 1962. 395p. 65-590.

Wartime diaries of the Polish Ambassador to the
Court of St. James. A continuous narrative of events
as seen through Polish eyes. More than just an
account of a Polish exile in Great Britain, it is also
an account of the activities of the Polish Government-
in-Exile. Contains an appendix with brief biographical sketches of principal Polish statesmen, commanders,
etc. Illustrations. Portraits.

1221. Zubrzycki, Jerzy. POLISH IMMIGRANTS IN BRITAIN. The
Hague: Martinus Nijhoff, 1956. 219p. 57-123.

Monographic study concerned mainly with settlement
of Poles in Great Britain. Also valuable for consideration of conditions in Poland and causes for emigration in general. Attempt to deal with the social
problems affecting the Poles in their new surroundings. Bibliography, pp. 216-219.

### Poles In New Zealand

1222. Gillis, Willie M. THE POLES IN WELLINGTON, NEW ZEA-
LAND, A PHENOMENOLOGICAL STUDY. Wellington: Dept.
of Psychology, Victoria University, 1954. 74p.
59-33567.

Problems of adjustment of Poles in Wellington as an
immigrant group. M.A. thesis for degree University
of New Zealand. Basically a scientific inquiry. It
is not an historical survey, although a brief sketch
is included.

1223. Skwarko, Krystyna. THE INVITED. Wellington, New
Zealand: Millwood Press, 1974. 96p. 75-332274.

The story of the travels of young Polish refugees
from southern Russia to a permanent home in New Zealand, written by a former schoolteacher who accompanied the children. Illustrations. Portraits. Maps.

Poles In The United States

1224. Babinski, Grzegorz, ed. POLES IN HISTORY AND CULTURE
OF THE UNITED STATES OF AMERICA, ed. by G. Babinski
and Mirosław Francic. Wrocław: Zakład Narodowy im.
Ossolinskich, 1979. 223p. OL: E184.P7P667.

A collection of fourteen papers delivered in June of
1976 in Warszawa at a conference dealing with the contributions of Poles and Polonia to the development of
the United States of America. Papers center on the
history of Polish settlement in the U.S., the history
of Polonia's activities in various spheres of the
American life and to contemporary changes and the part
played by American Polonia in the American society.

1225. Bakanowski, Adolf. POLISH CIRCUIT RIDER; THE TEXAS
MEMOIRS OF ADOLF BAKANOWSKI, 1866-1870, trans. and
annotated by Marion M. Coleman. Cheshire, Conn.:
Cherry Hill Books, 1971. 49p. 75-167938.

Translation of author's memoirs entitled MOJE
WSPOMNIENIA published in Lwów in 1916. Memoirs cover
period in Texas from 1866 to 1870 and does relate to
Polish settlements in Texas which he visited.

1226. Baker, T.L. THE EARLY HISTORY OF PANNA MARIA, TEXAS.
Lubbock: Texas Technical University, 1975. 69p.
OL: F394.Pi92B34.

A thoroughly documented and well-researched history
of the settlement of Panna Maria in Texas. Period
covered is 1855-1870. Contains portraits of Rev.
Leopold Moczygemba and Rev. Adolf Bakanowski. Bibliography, pp. 58-63.

1227. Baker, T.L. THE FIRST POLISH AMERICANS: SILESIAN
SETTLEMENTS IN TEXAS. College Station, Texas:
Texas A. and M. University Press, 1979. 78-6373.

An in-depth history of the Silesian Polish settlements in Texas. Chronologically, the study concentrates on nineteenth century. Illustrations. Portraits. Maps. Bibliography, pp. 232-255.

1228. Bernard, Richard M. THE POLES IN OKLAHOMA. Norman:
University of Oklahoma Press, 1980. 90p. 79-6714.

A comprehensive history of the relatively small groups of Polish immigrants who settled in Oklahoma around the time it attained statehood (1907). Brings the story up to 1976. Includes story and illustration of the only Polish Roman Catholic parish in the state. Illustrations. Maps. Bibliography, pp. 78-80.

1229. Blumer, Herbert. AN APPRAISAL OF THOMAS AND ZNANIECKI'S "THE POLISH PEASANT IN EUROPE AND AMERICA," with statements by William I. Thomas and Florian Znaniecki, a panel discussion and summary and analysis by Read Bain. New York: Social Science Research Council, 1939. 210p. 40-4813.

One of six books selected by Committee on Appraisal of Research of the Social Science Research Council to be subjected to critical appraisal. Critique is by Professor Herbert Blumer of the Department of Sociology, University of Chicago. Authors then furnished rejoinders.

1230. Bolek, Francis. THE POLISH AMERICAN SCHOOL SYSTEM. New York: Columbia Press Corporation, 1948. 108p. 49-2328.

Covers grammar schools, secondary schools, institutions of higher learning. Statistical summary of the state of education among Polish-speaking schools in the U.S. c. 1946. Sources are OFFICIAL CATHOLIC DIRECTORY.

1231. Bolek, Francis. WHO'S WHO IN POLISH AMERICA. New York: Harbinger House, 1943. 579p. 41-3350.

Third edition. A biographical directory of Polish-American leaders and distinguished Poles resident in the Americas. Contains 5,000 biographies not only of prominent living Americans of Polish descent, but also of historical figures whose contributions have been great. Includes an index of Polish-American organizations.

1232. Borkowski, Joseph A. PROMINENT POLISH PIONEERS OF THE U.S.A., 1770-1790. Pittsburgh, Penn.: Polish Falcon Museum, 1976. 65p. OL: E269.P6B67.

Vignettes. Not carefully researched. References, pp. 64-65.

1233. Borun, Thaddeus, ed. WE, THE MILWAUKEE POLES. Milwaukee: Nowiny Publishing Co., 1946. 290p. 48-14257.

The history of Milwaukeeans of Polish descent and a record of their contributions to the greatness of Milwaukee. Historical sketches, biographies of persons of prominence of Polish descent, sketches of Polish organizations. Illustrations. Portraits.

1234. Bridgeport, Conn. University. Sociology Colloquium. THE POLISH-AMERICANS OF BRIDGEPORT, A SOCIAL SURVEY by Ilona Aszody et al. Bridgeport, Conn.: University of Bridgeport, 1960. 47p. 60-3170.

An ongoing survey carried out by members of the Sociology Colloquium in cooperation with the Department of Sociology, University of Bridgeport, of the ethnic structure of assimilation process in the Greater Bridgeport area. Authors of report did their research while members of a class in social methods at the Univeristy. Bibliography, pp. 46-47.

1235. Brożek, Andrzej. POLISH AMERICANS, 1854-1939, trans. by Wojciech Worszyntowicz. Warszawa: Interpress Publishers, 1985. 274p.

An outstanding collection under one rubric of portraits of the most prominent Poles in America during the period. An outline of the basic questions concerning the Polish-American ethnic group up to the outbreak of the Second World War. Offers the perspective of Polish scholarship. Illustrations. Portraits. Maps. Bibliography, pp. 242-250.

1236. Budrewicz, Olgierd. THE MELTING-POT REVISITED, trans. by Edward J. Czerwinski and Andrzej Makarewicz. Warszawa: Interpress Publishers, 1977. 246p.

In addition to being a collection of sketches or biographies of well-known Americans of Polish background, the book attempts to answer the question, "What's become of the melting pot." Resulted from author's two journeys to the U.S. and what amounted to a couple of month's stay. Illustrations. Portraits.

1237. Bukowczyk, John J. AND MY CHILDREN DID NOT KNOW ME: A HISTORY OF THE POLISH AMERICANS. Bloomington:

*Special Works* 269

Indiana University Press, 1987, 190p. 85-45888.

Although entitled a "history," this work is really only a "concise, new interpretation of the Polish experience in America." Illustrations. Maps.

1238. Carpenter, Niles. A STUDY OF ACCULTURIZATION IN THE POLISH GROUP IN BUFFALO, 1926-1928. Buffalo: University of Buffalo, 1929. 31p. 29-22532.

Study conducted under the auspices of the Brown University study of ethnic in community life. Contains charts.

1239. Clowes, Florence W. POL-AM; A HISTORY OF THE POLISH-AMERICANS IN PITTSFIELD, MASSACHUSETTS, 1862-1945. Webster, Mass.: Economy Press, 1981. 144p.

A bit of local history, the subject being the Polish immigrants and their progeny who settled in the small city of Pittsfield, situated in western Massachusetts. Illustrations. Bibliography, p. 144.

1240. Coulter, Charles W. THE POLES OF CLEVELAND. Cleveland: Cleveland Americanization Committee. Mayor's Advisory War Committee, 1919. 42p. 19-16302.

One in a series describing various national groups in Cleveland. Purpose was to bring to Americans a knowledge of the life and customs of their foreign born neighbors. Illustrations. Maps.

1241. Dworaczyk, Edward J., comp. THE FIRST POLISH COLONIES OF AMERICA IN TEXAS. San Antonio: The Naylor Co., 1936. 201p. 36-20431.

A history of the Roman Catholic parishes in Texas. Traces establishment of parishes beginning with Panna Maria in 1854 and a parish in Richmond, Sacret Heart, in 1935. Illustrations of church buildings. Portraits of pastors. References, p. 201.

1242. Fox, Paul. THE POLES IN AMERICA. New York: George H. Doran Co., 1922. 143p. 22-14729.

One of the studies of racial groups, in the New American Series, made under the auspices of the

Interchurch World Movement. Maps. Bibliography, pp. 135-139.

1243. Friedel, Mieczysław W. THE POLISH BLOOD IN AMERICA'S VEINS. New York: Vantage Press, 1978. 99p. 78-109089.

Subtitled, SKETCHES FROM THE LIFE OF POLISH IMMIGRANTS AND THEIR DESCENDANTS IN AMERICA, ILLUSTRATING A PART OF AMERICAN HISTORY UNKNOWN TO MOST AMERICANS. Author himself emigrated to the U.S. from Poland in 1911 at age fourteen. Rambling sketches with no documentation whatsoever so that the accuracy of the statements and the statistics cannot be tested.

1244. Gelsavage, John J. HANDBOOK OF THE SARMATIAN HERITAGE: POLISH AMERICANS--WHO WE REALLY ARE. Warren, Mich.: Author, 1982. 90p.

A personal interpretation of the origins of Poles in the United States which deviates from the normally accepted one. Bibliography, pp. 80-82.

1245. Gerson, Louis L. WOODROW WILSON AND THE REBIRTH OF POLAND, 1914-1920. New Haven, Conn.: Yale University Press, 1953. 166p. 53-7774.

A study in the influence on American policy of minority groups of foreign origin. Purpose of the book is to show how the patriotic leaders of the movement for a new Polish nation worked on President Wilson through the Polish immigrant population of the United States and the Polish-American votes, to secure the rebirth of Poland. Illustrations. Bibliographical essay, pp. 140-145.

1246. Golab, Caroline. IMMIGRANT DESTINATIONS. Philadelphia: Temple University Press, 1977. 246p. 77-81334.

Although author states that her study represents an attempt to account for the geographic distribution of America's immigrants in the period 1870 to 1920, she uses the Polish experience in Philadelphia as her main focal point. Maps. Bibliographical footnotes.

1247. Grabowski, John J. POLISH AMERICANS AND THEIR COMMUNITIES OF CLEVELAND, by J.J. Grabowski et al.

*Special Works* 271

Cleveland: Cleveland State University, 1976, 256p.

Contains sketch of Polish history and culture, sketch of the Polish immigration to the United States, and a sketch of the Polish community of Cleveland. Illustrations. Maps. Includes bibliographies.

1248. Grzelonski, Bogdan. POLES IN THE UNITED STATES OF AMERICA, 1776-1865. Warszawa: Interpress Publishers, 1976. 240p. 78-104224.

Biographical sketches of individual Poles who were prominent in America make up the subject matter of this book. Portraits of them and of important contemporary Americans appear here. Maps. Bibliography, pp. 237-239.

1249. Haiman, Miecislaus. POLAND AND THE REVOLUTIONARY WAR. Chicago: Polish Roman Catholic Union of America, 1932. 208p. 32-17805.

Story of Poles in addition to Pułaski and Kościuszko who participated in the Revolutionary War. Includes an appendix entitled, WASHINGTONIANA IN POLAND. Bibliographical references in footnotes.

1250. Haiman, Miecislaus. POLES IN NEW YORK IN THE 17TH AND 18TH CENTURIES. Chicago: Polish Roman Catholic Union of America, 1938. 64p. 38-19810.

A brief historical-biographical sketch of the earliest Polish settlers in Manhattan. Bibliography, pp. 59-64.

1251. Haiman, Miecislaus. THE POLES IN THE EARLY HISTORY OF TEXAS. Chicago: Polish Roman Catholic Union of America, 1936. 64p. 36-17814.

A brief historical sketch of the first Polish settlements in Texas. Carries the story to 1855. Section includes the role of Poles in the war with Mexico.

1252. Haiman, Miecislaus. POLISH PAST IN AMERICA, 1608-1865. Chicago: Polish Roman Catholic Union of America, 1939. 178p. 39-20806.

A work briefly reviewing the Polish past in America from 1608 to 1865. Numerous illustrations. At the end of each chapter there are bibliographical references. Portraits. Maps.

1253. Haiman, Miecislaus. POLISH PIONEERS OF CALIFORNIA. Chicago: Polish Roman Catholic Union of America, 1940. 83p. 40-31601. OL: F870.P7.H3.

Purpose is to open the pioneer trail through California archives for future historians of the Polish immigration to the state, rather than to give a full and exact account of its beginnings. Story carried up to 1870. Portraits. Maps. Bibliography, pp. 79-82.

1254. Haiman, Miecislaus. POLISH PIONEERS OF PENNSYLVANIA. Chicago: Polish Roman Catholic Union of America, 1941. 72p. 41-14495.

A pioneer study in the early history of Poles in Pennsylvania. Discusses individual Poles and Polish families. Illustrations. Maps. Bibliography, pp. 66-72.

1255. Haiman, Miecislaus. POLISH PIONEERS OF VIRGINIA AND KENTUCKY. Chicago: Polish Roman Catholic Union of America, 1937. 84p. 37-23338.

Brief sketch of settlements by Poles in Virginia and Kentucky. Also includes NOTES ON GENEALOGY OF THE SADOWSKI FAMILY by A. Clay Sandusky. Illustrations. Bibliography, pp. 80-84.

1256. Hayden, Joal B. RELIGIOUS WORK AMONG POLES IN AMERICA. New York: Congregational Home Missionary Society, 1916. 48p. NN: ZAEp.v.787.

Author spent thirteen months in Austrian Poland in 1914-1915 where he lived among the Polish peasants and studied the language and the social and religious background of the Polish immigrant. Also visited chief Polish communities in the United States and interviewed many prominent Polish leaders and studied Protestant work among the Poles. Illustrations. Portraits.

*Special Works*

1257. Hill, Robert F. EXPLORING THE DIMENSION OF ETHNICITY. New York: Arno Press, 1980. 340p. 80-863.

    A study of status, culture and identity among Polish-Americans. Ph.D. dissertation in University of Pittsburgh, 1975. Author conducted sociological research among the Polish-Americans living in the Pittsburgh area and presented in his findings in this dissertation. Illustrations. Bibliography, pp. 320-340.

1258. Iwicki, John J. THE FIRST ONE HUNDRED YEARS: A STUDY OF THE APOSTOLATE OF THE CONGREGATION OF THE RESURRECTION IN THE U.S., 1866-1966. Rome: Gregorian University Press, 1966. 298p. 71-41828.

    A brief history of the work of the Resurrectionist Order divided into pastoral care of souls or history of parishes founded and or run by the Order; the Apostolate in education; and social and organizational work. Illustrations. Portraits. Bibliography, pp. 265-282.

1259. Kantowicz, Edward R. POLISH-AMERICAN POLITICS IN CHICAGO, 1880-1940. Chicago: University of Chicago Press, 1975. 260p. 74-16682.

    Ph.D. thesis, University of Chicago, 1972. Study presents a political history of Chicago's Polish-Americans from 1888 to 1940. It describes the political leaders of the Polish community, examines the voting patterns of Polish-Americans, explains the issues which Polish voters deemed significant and determines the economic and psychological functions which American politics served for Polish-Americans, and evaluates the successes and failures of the Polish-American community in Chicago politics and indicates what significance their political record holds for an understanding of ethnic politics in general. Covers period 1888-1940. Illustrations. Maps. Bibliographical references.

1260. Kowalik, Jan. THE POLISH PRESS IN AMERICA. San Francisco: R and E Research Associates, Inc., 1978. 76p. 77-90363.

    A review of the development of all periodical publications printed by and for Polish-speaking persons living in the United States. Contains a checklist of the Polish-American press as of 1974 and a geographical distribution of the Polish-American press in 1974. Sample mastheads from the publications included. Illustrations. Maps. References, pp. 45-50.

1261. Kuniczak, W.S. MY NAME IS MILLION: AN ILLUSTRATED HISTORY OF THE POLES IN AMERICA. Garden City, N.Y.: Doubleday and Co., 1978. 181p. 77-82954.

Admittedly a survey. Profusely illustrated in black-and-white. Many portraits of contemporary Polish-American figures. Maps.

1262. Kuzniewski, Anthony J. FAITH AND FATHERLAND, THE POLISH CHURCH WAR IN WISCONSIN, 1896-1918. Notre Dame, Ind.: University of Notre Dame Press, 1980. 171p. 80-233.

Originally a doctoral dissertation. The story of the heated debate, frustration, and dissidence involved in the attempt of the Poles in Wisconsin to gain the appointment of Polish-speaking bishops. Illustrations. Portraits. Bibliography, pp. 154-160.

1263. Lewski, Jerzy J. A POLISH CHAPTER IN JACKSONIAN AMERICA. Madison: University of Wisconsin Press, 1958. 242p. 58-6282.

Subtitled, The United States and the Polish Exiles of 1831. The purpose of this book is to revive a fascinating and almost forgotten fragment of American history on the basis of hitherto unused documentary data. The book will serve as a narration of the Polish exiles who were welcomed in the United States as heroes of universal freedom and will describe the deep interest and understanding of Europe shown by the leading intellectuals of Jacksonian America and their stand for the cause of enslaved Poland as though it were their own. Bibliography, pp. 221-230.

1264. Lopata, Helena Z. POLISH AMERICANS: STATUS COMPETITION IN AN ETHNIC COMMUNITY. Englewood Cliffs, N.J.: Prentice-Hall, Inc. 1976. 174p. 74-41401.

This book analyzes the life styles of Polish Americans and the history and current life styles of Polonia, the structurally complex ethnic community maintained by them for over a century with the help of

*Special Works* 275

changing ideologies and highly developed status competition. Several basic sociological concepts form the framework of this analysis: Polish Americans, national society, political state, ethnic community, life style, and status competition. Illustrations. Bibliography, pp. 157-168.

1265. Lunde, Karl. RICHARD ANUSZKIEWICZ. New York: Harry N. Abrams, Inc., Publishers, 1976. 207p. 76-28230.

Biographical sketch, notes, biographical outline, one-man exhibitions, group exhibitions, plates, both black-and-white and colored of this Polish-American artist. Bibliography, p. 200.

1266. Lyon, Norman T. HISTORY OF THE POLISH PEOPLE IN ROCHESTER. Buffalo: Polish Everybody's Daily, 1935. 180p. 35-13619.

Seeks to clarify the significance of local events in their relation to Polish-American development generally, and for the Polish-American reader, and to demonstrate the growth and fruition of the Polish cause in this country as exemplified in a typical community. Covers history through 1934. No documentation. Illustrations. Portraits. Maps.

1267. Majewski, Arthur J. WHEN HAMTRAMCK AND I WERE YOUNG. Detroit: Maryt Publishing Co., 1986. 120p. 86-62351.

A collection of personal reminiscences by the author concerning his childhood and adolescence as a Polish-American boy in Hamtramck, Michigan during the 1920s and 1930s.

1268. Mazur, Stella M. ROOTS AND HERITAGE OF POLISH PEOPLE IN LOWELL, MASSACHUSETTS. Lowell: Author, 1977. 117p. 76-369792.

A mixture of personal impressions, reminiscences and data about the author's family and others who live in Lowell. Includes biographical sketches of Poles who live in Lowell, a chronological history of the local Poles parish, Holy Trinity, among other things. Illustrations.

1269. Miąso, Józef. THE HISTORY OF THE EDUCATION OF POLISH
IMMIGRANTS IN THE UNITED STATES, trans. by Ludwik
Krzyżanowski. New York: Kośćiuszko Foundation,
1977. 295p. 76-26366.

An attempt to show the beginnings, development, and
functioning of the Polish schools in America over a
period of a hundred years. Concentrates on scholastic
institutions and their role in the life of the immigrants.
Illustrations. Bibliographical footnotes.

1270. Milostan, Harry. ENDURING POLES. Mt. Clemens, Mich.:
Masspac Publishing Co., 1977. 222p. 76-42844.

A series of brief articles about ephemeral aspects
of life among the Polish immigrants in the Great Lakes
region. Illustrations.

1271. Milostan, Harry. THE ERRANT NUN. Mt. Clemens, Mich.:
Masspac Publishing Co., 1978. 244p. 79-83634.

The life of Stanisława Lepszczynska, a woman born in
Poland and housekeeper to a priest in Manistee, Michigan, who was accused and convicted of murduring a nun,
Sister Mary Janina. Author attempts to present evidence to prove it was circumstantial. Illustrations.

1272. Milostan, Harry. GNIEŹNIKS: PIONEER POLONIANS, FACTS
AND FABLE. Mt. Clemens, Mich.: Masspac Publishing
Co., 1985. 292p. 83-060206.

A collection of curious essays on Poland and the
Poles and mainly the Polish settlements in northeast
Michigan. Includes some examples of fables told by
the Polonian pioneers. Illustrations. Portraits.
Maps.

1273. Milostan, Harry. PARISVILLE POLES, FIRST POLISH SETTLERS IN THE U.S.A. Mt. Clemens, Mich.: Masspac
Publishing Co., 1977. 269p. 77-77917.

An amply documented and well-illustrated account of
the settlement of Poles in Parisville, Michigan
including many curious and interesting facts about the
settlement's history. Illustrations. Portraits.
Maps.

*Special Works* 277

1274. Mizwa, Stephan P. THE STORY OF THE KOŚĆIUSZKO FOUNDA-
TION: HOW IT CAME ABOUT. New York: Kośćiuszko
Foundation, 1972. 134p.

Story of the Foundation by its first chief executive
officer. Author implies a personal story interwoven
with the story of the institution. Includes first
list of contributors, certificate of incorporation,
and by-laws. Illustrations. Portraits.

1275. Morawska, Ewa T. THE MAINTENANCE OF ETHNICITY, CASE
STUDY OF THE POLISH-AMERICAN COMMUNITY IN GREATER
BOSTON. San Francisco: R and E Research Associates,
1977. 161p. 76-56555.

Purpose was threefold: (1) to provide a socio-
historical outline of group's structural position and
cultural characteristics; (2) to analyze the influence
of selected factors such as educational status; and
(3) current social-cultural life of the community.
Author born in Poland and brings a European perspective to bear on ethnicity in the United States. Bibliography, pp. 141-159.

1276. Mostwin, Danuta. THE TRANSPLANTED FAMILY. New York:
Arno Press, 1980. 345p. 80-881.

Doctoral dissertation, Columbia University, 1971.
Subtitled, A Study of the Polish Immigrant Family to
the United States after the Second World War. Examination "of the patterns of the social adjustment of
the immigrant family to its new geographical, cultural
and national environment." Based upon responses from
over 2,000 Polish, post-World War II immigrants. Bibliography, pp. 1-6.

1277. Napolska, Mary Remigia, sister. THE POLISH IMMIGRANT
IN DETROIT TO 1914. Chicago: Polish Roman Catholic
Union of America, 1946. 110p. 46-6802.

Master's thesis, University of Notre Dame, 1943.
Brief historical sketch of Polish settlers in Detroit.
No attempt at comprehensiveness. Bibliography, pp.
103-110.

1278. Nesterowicz, Stefan. TRAVEL NOTES, trans. by Marion
M. Coleman. Cheshire, Conn.: Cherry Hill Books,
1970. 130p. 72-103602.

Author wrote some travel notes on a trip from St. Louis to New Orleans and Texas on which he visited Polish communities in the South central United States. These travels were undertaken while he lived in the United States. Illustrations. Portraits.

1279. Niemcewicz, Julian U. UNDER THE VINE AND FIG TREE, trans. by with an introduction and notes by M.J.E. Budka. Elizabeth, N.J.: Grossman Publishing Co., Inc., 1965. 398p. 65-15378.

 Travels through America in 1797-1799, 1805, with some further account of life in New Jersey. Illustrations. Portraits. Bibliography, pp. 365-373.

1280. Obidinski, Eugene E. ETHNIC TO STATUS GROUP: A STUDY OF POLISH AMERICANS IN BUFFALO. New York: Arno Press, 1981. 205p. 80-885.

 Doctoral dissertation, SUNY-Buffalo, 1968. Study of the "continued existence of the Polish Community in Buffalo and the transformation or change in subcommunity patterns." Based on observations made by the author during a period of residence in a Polish-American neighborhood and data obtained through "structured interviews with 99 persons comprising a random sample of members of six Polish-American organizations." Bibliography, pp. 199-205.

1281. Olszewicz, Bolesław. POLAND AND THE DISCOVERY OF AMERICA: A HISTORICAL AND BIBLIOGRAPHICAL ESSAY, trans. by Marjan Z. Arend. Poznań: Rolnicza Drukarnia i Księgarnia Nakładowa, 1931. 34p. NN: HAEp.v.224.

 A discussion of the references to America occurring in works published in Poland or by Polish authors abroad in the sixteenth and seventeenth centuries. Contains a chronological list of the Polish-Americans of the sixteenth and seventeenth centuries mentioned in the text. Illustrations. Maps.

1282. Olszyk, Edmund G. THE POLISH PRESS IN AMERICA. Milwaukee, Wisc.: Marquette University Press, 1940. 95p. 43-36902.

 M.A. thesis at Marquette University. Purpose of this book is to bring up-to-date and complete under

*Special Works* 279

one cover all information on the Polish-American press; to make available to English readers data on this subject which is written in Polish and has been hitherto inaccessible to them. Historical sketch, outstanding personalities. Bibliography, pp. 91-95.

1283. Paluszek, John L. AN AMERICAN JOURNEY. New York: American Ethnic Press, 1981. 122p. 81-65201.

This is a book about the ethnic heritage of three generations of a family which has its origins in Poland and now thrives on two continents. A story of a 1903 immigrant from Poland and what America has done for him, for his son and his grandson. Also the story of a pilgrimage to the old country by the son and the grandson.

1284. Parot, Joseph J. POLISH CATHOLICS IN CHICAGO, 1850-1920; A RELIGIOUS HISTORY. DeKalb, Ill.: Northern Illinois University Press, 1981. 298p. 81-11297.

First thorough account of the religious origins of Chicago's Polish community. Author used archival sources. Study begins with the stormy foundation of the Resurrectionist community-parishes, discusses in detail the development of one of the most serious religious schisms in American Catholic Church history, and climaxes with the dramatic conflict between the Polish clergy in Chicago, American Polonia and the American Catholic hierarchy. Includes list of "Polish Parishes in Chicago, 1867-1950," 57 in number as well as a list of them and their addresses. Illustrations. Portraits. Maps. Includes bibliographical references.

1285. PASTOR OF THE POLES: POLISH AMERICAN ESSAYS, by Stanislaus A. Blejwas and Mieczysław B. Biskupski. New Britain, Conn.: Central Connecticut State College, 1982. 223p. 82-072307.

Festschrift honoring Rt. Rev. Msgr. John P. Wodarski. Several articles divided among five principal subject areas: Poles and the Catholic Church in America; Polish Immigration to the United States; Polonia: Evolution and Structure; American Reaction to the Poles. One portrait of Wodarski. Biographical sketches of authors, pp. 219-223.

1286. Pienkos, Angela T., ed. ETHNIC POLITICS IN URBAN AMERICA: THE POLISH EXPERIENCES IN FOUR CITIES. Chicago: Polish American Historical Association, 1978. 108p.

Five separate essays by different scholars on the subject as stated in title. Cities covered are Buffalo, Detroit, Milwaukee and Chicago. Maps.

1287. Pienkos, Donald E. PNA, A CENTENNIAL HISTORY OF THE POLISH NATIONAL ALLIANCE OF THE UNITED STATES OF NORTH AMERICA. New York: Columbia University Press, 1984. 485p. 84-80619.

An exhaustive study of the Polish National Alliance relating how it grew from a tiny patriotic group to a massive insurance organization. Contains biographical sketches of the leaders of the PNA, pp. 367-405; and the text of speeches of the President of the United States to the PNA. Illustrations. Portraits. Maps. Bibliography, pp. 463-472.

1288. Pierce, Richard L. THE POLISH IN AMERICA. Chicago: Claretian Publications, 1972. 48p.

A cursory sketch of Polonia in the United States with the emphasis being on the achievements of famous Polish-Americans. Illustrations.

1289. POLES IN MICHIGAN. Detroit: Poles in Michigan Associated, 1953- v. 65-111.

A series of articles intended to present a variety of selected phases of the history of Polish pioneering in Michigan. First volume published January, 1955. Illustrations. Portraits.

1290. POLES IN AMERICA. BICENTENNIAL ESSAYS, ed. by Frank Mocha. Stevens Point, Wisc.: Worzalla Publishing Co., 1978. 781p. 78-060657.

A collection of nineteen individual essays covering a variety of topics ranging from first Poles in America to Polish contributions to America. Illustrations. Maps. Includes bibliographical references.

Special Works                                          281

1291.  THE POLES OF CHICAGO, 1837-1937, A HISTORY OF ONE CEN-
       TURY OF POLISH CONTRIBUTION TO THE CITY OF CHICAGO.
       Chicago:   Polish Pageant, Inc., 1937.  256p.  37-
       31245.

       Contents:  The Poles in Chicago, by M. Haiman. Hun-
       dred Years of Economic Contribution of the Poles to
       Chicago's Progress, by T.J. Lubera. The Rise of Poles
       in American Politics, by R.F. Lesset. Chicago Poles
       Share in City Art History, by J.J. Palczynska. Con-
       tributions of Americans of Polish Ancestry to the
       Development of Music in Chicago, by H.M. Glomski. The
       Amateur Theatre Among the Poles, by N. Kunka. The
       Polish Stage in Chicago, by H.J. Majewska. Polish
       Churches of Chicago and Vicinity. Polish Contributions
       to Social Welfare in Chicago by five separate authors.
       Polish Days and Other Demonstrations of Civil and
       National Character. Early Days of Sport Among Polish
       Americans in Chicagoland, by C.J.B. Wronski. Polish
       Organizations of Chicago.  Thrift Among Poles.  Biog-
       raphies of Prominent Polish Americans in the Chicago
       Area.

1292.  POLISH-AMERICAN COMMUNITY LIFE:  A SURVEY OF RESEARCH,
       by Irwin T. Sanders and Ewa J. Morawska. New York:
       Polish Institute of Arts and Sciences in America,
       1975.  300p.

       Purpose of this monograph was to review the extant
       literature on community studies involving Polish-
       Americans. Cooperative undertaking between Polish
       Institute of Arts and Sciences in America and Commu-
       nity Sociology Training Program at Boston University.
       Divided into residential patterns; structural positions
       of Polish-Americans; political participation and
       interethnic relations; Church and community; organiza-
       tional affiliation; the family; social relations; cul-
       ture and ethnic identity and identification. Bibliog-
       raphy, pp. 246-285.

1293.  Polish American Congress.  JAMESTOWN PIONEERS FROM
       POLAND, compiled by Francis W. Dziab, Karol Burke
       and Joseph Wiewiora. Chicago: Polish American
       Congress, 1958.  89p.  MiD: Burton-55.325.2438.P76j.

       Includes an historical sketch of the founding of
       Jamestown with an emphasis on the Polish settlers.  A

collection of articles, many from newspapers, about the Polish settlers. Numerous illustrations. Portraits. Maps.

1294. POLISH AMERICAN ENCYCLOPEDIA, prepared and compiled under the editorial direction of Francis Bolek and Ladislaus J. Siekaniec. Buffalo, N.Y.: Polish American Encyclopedia Committee, 1954- v. 56-42831.

Only one volume was published, the first A-B, of what was designed to present the contribuitons of Polish Americans or Americans of Polish descent to all phases of life in the U.S. Contains information on individuals as well as institutions. Illustrations. Portraits.

1295. POLISH-AMERICANS IN THE CITY OF NEW YORK, AN OUTLINE OF SOCIO-ECONOMIC AND CULTURAL NEED. New York: Polish and Slavic Center, Inc., 1979. 185p.

Book has as its primary goal providing governmental officials with information about the economic, social and cultural issues that Polish-American New Yorkers are concerned about as well as demonstrating that a gap does exist between the services available to Polish communities and those that are needed. Contains a bibliographical essay and guide to the Polish-American experience. List of works has been briefly annotated. List of Polish institutions of Greater New York area. Illustrations. Portraits. Maps. Bibliography, pp. 182-185.

1296. Polish Day Association. Chicago. POLES IN AMERICA; THEIR CONTRIBUTION TO A CENTURY OF PROGRESS. Chicago: Polish Day Association, 1933. 263p. NN: IEE.Poles.

Commemorative souvenir book completed and published on the occasion of the Polish week of hospitality, International Exposition, Chicago, 1933. Of particular value to persons interested in Chicago's Polonia. Contains numerous illustrations. History, some in Polish, some in English, of each Polish parish. Portraits.

1297. Polish Institute of Arts and Sciences in America. THE POLISH INSTITUTE OF ARTS AND SCIENCES IN AMERICA,

*Special Works*                                                    283

    by Stanisław Strzetelski, Director. New York:
    Polish Institute of Arts and Sciences in America,
    1960. 54p. 60-36044.

    This pamphlet has been prepared for the purpose of
    acquainting the public with the history of the Polish
    Institute of Arts and Sciences in America, its func-
    tions, services as well as with the people who took
    part in its development.

1298. Polzin, Theresita. THE POLISH-AMERICANS: WHENCE AND
    WHITHER. Pulaski, Wisc.: Franciscan Publications,
    1973. 282p.

    Attempt at a beginning to a type of sociological
    analysis of a mature Polish American type group, using
    the layman's language. An attempt to assemble socio-
    logical data, interpretations, and insights to per-
    ceive patterns and trends in the changes occurring
    within the Polish American community since its organi-
    zation. Bibliography, pp. 245-251.

1299. Przygoda, Jacek, ed. POLISH AMERICANS IN CALIFORNIA,
    1827-1977, AND WHO'S WHO. Los Angeles, Calif.:
    Polish American Historical Association, 1978. 372p.
    77-094170.

    Series of articles about Polish Americans in Cali-
    fornia. An exhaustive account covering all phases of
    Polish-American life with an emphasis on the present
    day. Illustrations. Portraits. Maps.

1300. Przygoda, Jacek. TEXAS PIONEERS FROM POLAND: A STUDY
    IN ETHNIC HISTORY. Los Angeles, Calif.: Author,
    1971. 171p. 72-158522.

    An historical sketch of the Polish settlements in
    Texas. Author used parish records, deeds, tax records,
    tax rolls and other public documents. Illustrations.
    Bibliography, pp. 106-110.

1301. Renkiewicz, Frank. FOR GOD, COUNTRY, AND POLONIA.
    Orchard Lake, Mich.: Center for Polish Studies and
    Culture, 1985. 177p. 85-72080.

    A literary account of the origins and development of
    the "Polish Seminary" located in the metropolitan

Detroit area written on the occasion of its centennial.
Illustrations. Portraits. Bibliography, pp. 151-153.

1302. Renkiewicz, Frank. THE POLES IN AMERICA, 1608-1972:
A CHRONOLOGICAL FACT BOOK. Dobbs Ferry, N.Y.:
Oceana Publications, Inc., 1973. 128p. 73-1879.

Chronologically traces the history and accomplishments of Poles in the United States from 1608 to 1972. Includes reproductions of documents pertinent to Polish-American history.

1303. Sandberg, Neil C. ETHNIC IDENTITY AND ASSIMILATION: THE POLISH-AMERICAN COMMUNITY; CASE STUDY OF METROPOLITAN LOS ANGELES. New York: F. Praeger, 1974. 88p. 73-10955.

Purpose of this study is to determine the relationship between different generational and social class groups within the Polish-American community and the salience of ethnicity in each group. Bibliography, pp. 78-84.

1304. Sanford, Albert H. THE POLISH PEOPLE OF PORTAGE COUNTY. Madison, Wisc.: State Historical Society of Wisconsin, 1908. 288p. 8-18589.

Includes an investigation into the early history and later development of this group and a description of conditions among them and such comments upon Polish characteristics as relate to the social and economic problems involved in their progress towards complete Americanization. Illustrations. Portraits. Maps.

1305. Serafino, Frank. WEST OF WARSAW. Hamtramck, Mich.: Avenue Publishing Co., 1983.

An attempt to place Hamtramck and its people in the news. Actually a series of statements about the Poles, the Polish immigrants in the Detroit area, particularly Hamtramck, and various incidents in its colorful past. Lacks organization and a central theme. Illustrations. Portraits. Maps. Bibliographical notes.

1306. Siekaniec, **Ladislaus J.** THE POLISH CONTRIBUTION TO EARLY AMERICAN EDUCATION, 1608-1865. San Francisco:

*Special Works* 285

  R and E Research Associates, 1976. 172p. 73-80719.

  The present study examines the educational opportunities of Poles in the United States from 1608 until about the time of the American Civil War, 1865. Concerned mainly with the field of liberal arts. Bibliography, pp. 165-172.

\*  Skendzel, Edward A. THE KOLASINSKI STORY. Cited above as item 257.

1307. Swastek, Joseph. THE FORMATIVE YEARS OF THE POLISH SEMINARY IN THE UNITED STATES. Orchard Lake, Mich.: Center for Polish Studies and Culture, 1985. 128p. 85-72080.

  Author traces the origins of the Seminary in the Polish immigrant experience of the 1860s and 1870s, the initial undertaking by Rev. Leopold Moczygemba, and the stewardship of the first rector, Fr. Joseph Dąbrowski, through 1903. Illustrations. Portraits. Bibliography, pp. 124-127.

1308. Thomas, William I. THE POLISH PEASANT IN EUROPE AND AMERICA, by W.I. Thomas and Florian Znaniecki. Chicago: University of Chicago Press, 1918-1920. 5v. 18-4821.

  First Scientific monograph seriously dealing with the Poles in the United States. Contains a wealth of autobiographical material originating from Polish immigrants themselves and scientifically analyzed.

1309. Uminski, Sigmund H. POLAND DISCOVERS AMERICA. New York: The Polish Publication Society of America, 1972. 117p. 72-88425.

  Real subject matter of this book is a discussion of the references to America occurring in works published in Poland or by Polish authors abroad in the fifteenth, sixteenth and seventeenth centuries. Chronological list of Polish Americans described in the text, pp. 101-102. Illustrations. Portraits. Bibliography, pp. 113-114.

1310. Uminski, Sigmund H. THE POLISH PIONEERS IN VIRGINIA. New York: Polish Publication Society of America, 1974. 139p. 73-89723.

   Concerned mainly with Poles who settled early in Virginia, dependent largely on Haiman's work which was revised and updated. Adequately documented with new and revised sources. Illustrations. Bibliography, pp. 130-133.

1311. Waldo, Arthur. TRUE HEROES OF JAMESTOWN. Miami: American Institute of Polish Culture, 1977. 256p.

   Purpose of this work is to present the influence of many centuries which led to the formation of the cradle of that nation of nations, Jamestown. Apparently well-researched but documentation not listed. Illustrations.

1312. Wiśniowski, Sygurd. AMERYKA: A GLOBETROTTER'S VIEW, trans. ed., and arranged by Marion M. Coleman. Cheshire, Conn.: Cherry Hill Books, 1972. 125p. 78-186272.

   Translation of a portion of Wiśniowski's works which included a trip to America from 1873 to 1875. A Pole's impressions of America. Not all the material directly pertains to the Poles in the U.S. because the author visited other than Polish communities. Portrait.

1313. Wloszczewski, Stefan W. HISTORY OF POLISH AMERICAN CULTURE. Trenton, N.J.: White Eagle Publishing Co., 1946. 150p. MCC: E184.P7.W55.

   Not a history of Polish-Americans per se but of a Roman Catholic priest in Southampton, Long Island, a representative of this culture. Parish is Mary, Queen of the Polish Crown. Also covers Poles in Connecticut Valley in Massachusetts. Illustrations. Portraits. Bibliography, pp. 147-150.

1314. Wood, Arthur E. HAMTRAMCK: A SOCIOLOGICAL STUDY OF A POLISH-AMERICAN COMMUNITY. New Haven, Conn.: College and University Press, 1955. 253p. 55-1518.

A history and a sociological analysis of the political community of Hamtramck up to c. 1955. Discusses local politics, the school system, delinquency and crime, cultural organizations and leisure, patterns of family life. Lacks bibliography. Occasional documentation throughout. Illustrations. Maps.

1315. Wrobel, Paul. OUR WAY: FAMILY, PARISH, AND NEIGHBORHOOD IN A POLISH-AMERICAN COMMUNITY with a foreword by Geno Baroni. Notre Dame, Inc.: University of Notre Dame Press, 1979. 192p. 78-62967.

A revised and expanded version of a doctoral dissertation completed in 1975 for the Anthropology degree at Catholic University of America. A sociological study of Transfiguration Parish in Detroit, Michigan. Notes, pp. 173-186.

1316. Wytrwal, Joseph A. AMERICA'S POLISH HERITAGE: A SOCIAL HISTORY OF THE POLES IN AMERICA. Detroit: Endurance Press, 1961. 350p. 60-15742.

In this social history an attempt has been made to give a faithful account of the contributions of two American Polish organizations to the development of the Polish immigrants in America, and of the general forces that have been and are at work in molding the destiny of the American-Polish element in American life. Maps. Bibliography, pp. 295-309.

1317. Wytrwal, Joseph A. BEHOLD, THE POLISH-AMERICANS. Detroit: Endurance Press, 1977. 667p. 77-84476.

Third major attempt to write a history of the Poles in the United States. Previous two histories carried the history to c. 1961 and then to c. 1969. An amplification of information previously covered plus additional information such as a sociological comparative study of how the Poles relate to Blacks, Jews, Indians and the Irish; Poles in the labor movement; and, a discussion of third-generation Poles.

1318. Wytrwal, Joseph A. THE POLES IN AMERICA. Minneapolis: Lerner Publications Co., 1969. 84p. 68-31506.

A review of the history of the Poles in America for the young reader. Part of "In America" series. Portraits. Maps.

1319. Wytrwal, Joseph A. POLES IN AMERICAN HISTORY AND TRADITION. Detroit: Endurance Press, 1969. 485p. 74-95272.

Survey of settlement, distribution of individual Poles and groups of Poles as they settled in the United States. Narrative divided into chronological periods beginning with the Colonial period and ending with immediate post-World War II settlement. Numerous individuals mentioned. Maps. Bibliography, pp. 443-458.

1320. Wytrwal, Joseph A. POLISH-BLACK ENCOUNTERS: A HISTORY OF POLISH AND BLACK RELATIONS IN AMERICA SINCE 1619. Detroit: Endurance Press, 1982. 558p. 81-71783.

Author has attempted to chronicle and describe Polish and Black encounters from remote historic time to the present. It also attempts to compile a picture of the involvement of European Poles in Africa. Emphasis appears to be on the past thirty-year period with a heavy reliance on journalistic accounts of areas of conflict where a Pole or a Polish-American comes into contact with Blacks, either individually or organizationally. Bibliography, pp. 507-529.

1321. Yarmolinsky, Avrahm. EARLY POLISH AMERICANS: A BIBLIOGRAPHICAL STUDY. New York: New York Public Library, 1937. 79p. 37-10131.

Present study on the Polish Americana of the sixteenth and seventeenth centuries is intended, however modest, to the bibliography of America and incidentally to the knowledge of how information about the New World spread in eastern Europe. Illustrations. Portraits.

## Poles In The United States--Fiction

1322. Abucewicz, John A. FOOL'S WHITE. New York: Carlton Press, 1969. 236p.

A simple tale of a Polish-American family in Lowell, Massachusetts. The heroine is Steffi Bicki, whose life from age six through womanhood leads her through personal tragedies to a career in nursing and then as a nun.

1323. Algren, Nelson. NEVER COME MORNING. New York: Harper, 1942. 284p. 42-11112.

"Story of poverty and crime among the Poles of Chicago's west side. The protagonist is Bruno Bicek, a young pugilist and near-gangster, whose poverty and code of "play straight with the gang" leads him into trouble, and he is arrested for murder in the midst of his first successful prize fight. Beside his story runs that of his girl, Steffie, who is forced by Bruno's code into becoming a member of Mama Tomek's brothel." BOOK REVIEW DIGEST, 1942.

1324. Allen, Frances N. THE INVADERS. Boston: Houghton-Mifflin Company, 1913. 370p. 13-5065.

"A story of a New England village in which foreigners--Slavs and Celts--are forcing out the old families and taking possession of historic places. Olivia Load, coming home from college, finds the old familiar life changed by the presence of the invading foreigners; finds her mother heavily in debt to one of their number, Irish Michael Joyce. Valiantly Olivia tries to meet the problem; teaches the district school; studies scientific farming in her efforts to make her worn-out acres pay. Gradually her race prejudice is overcome, partly through daily contact with her new neighbors, but largely through the influence of Patrick Joyce of Dublin University, charming, mannered and Irish-tongued." BOOK REVIEW DIGEST, 1913.

1325. Archer, Jeffrey. KANE AND ABEL; A NOVEL. New York: Simon and Schuster, 1979. 54p. 79-23311.

"William Lowell Kane and Abel Rosnowski--two men from widely different backgrounds, whose driving passions are overshadowed only by their obsession to destroy each other. One, a millionaire Boston Brahmin, the other, a penniless Polish immigrant--two men born on the same day in 1906, on opposite sides of the world, reaching the top in twentieth-century America. Spanning sixty years, Kane and Abel is the enormously compelling story of these two ruthless, powerful businessmen whose ultimate confrontation rocks the financial community--and their personal lives." BOOK REVIEW DIGEST, 1979.

1326.  Bankowsky, Richard. AFTER PENTECOST. New York: Random House, 1961. 302p. 61-6249.

"The characters are Polish-Americans in a New Jersey town. The narrative deals with the coming to the community of a Polish refugee woman, Magda. She is sponsored by Groszek, a politician at the request of his nephew, Roman, who wants to marry Magda even though she is nearly twice his age. The description of the lives of every person with whom Magda comes in contact and of many of whom she never meets drives the book on to its final moment of tragedy and violent death." BOOK REVIEW DIGEST, 1961.

1327.  Bankowsky, Richard. THE GLASS ROSE. New York: Random House, 1958. 308p. 58-5259.

"In the stream of consciousness manner, this novel recounts the rise and decline of a Polish immigrant family in New Jersey. The occasion is the seven-day wake of Stanisław Machek. The story is told through the thoughts and memories of the family and neighbors attending the wake." BOOK REVIEW DIGEST, 1958.

1328.  Cannon, Cornelia J. HEIRS. Boston: Little, Brown and Co., 1930. 309p. 30-4846.

"One of the chief social problems of modern New England life--that of the Americanization of incoming hordes of Europeans--is the main concern of Mrs. Cannon in this story of a New England schoolteacher in a New Hampshire mill town. Marilla Lamprey, who comes to Lovell to teach, marries Seth Walton, owner of the mill. She already recognizes the conflict between native and impoverished New England stock and the Polish newcomers who buy up the farms and in addition keep the mills going. Marilla's personal experiences are unfolded throughout against this background." BOOK REVIEW DIGEST, 1930.

1329.  Castle, William. HERO's OAK, by William Castle and Robert Joseph. New York: Reader's Press, 1945. 334p. 45-37861.

"The setting is Vermont, the time 1910-1936 and the people Polish immigrants; the story, strangely and hauntingly is primarily that of a woman and a tree--a beautiful, passionate, willful golden woman and a great towering oak about which clung a legend that the first man who came to a girl standing beneath its shade would be her husband. But this novel is more, much more, than just the story of beautiful Marja Javorska and the tree known as Krupa's Oak. It is the story of Alexander Krupa the immigrant, and his victory over the land he took up in the new world and his strange defeat. And it is the story of his son, Jan Krupa, who rose in station and became a doctor, only to meet defeat through the same strange cause." BOOK REVIEW DIGEST, 1945.

1330. Chase, Mary E. A JOURNEY TO BOSTON. New York: W.W. Norton, 1965. 114p. 64-23875.

One tragic event in the lives of the Polish settlers in the Upper Connecticut River Valley points up the strength and courage of these new Americans.

1331. Coons, Joan. WITHOUT PASSPORT, AN EVERYDAY NOVEL. New York: John Day, 1943. 436p. 43-7751.

"Two young children, studying music together under the same professor in a midwestern American town have equal chances to win fame and renown. The boy wins a scholarship and goes abroad to study, becomes famous as a violinist but misses happiness in life; the girl marries a farmer and puts aside her musical ambitions and is rewarded finally with the knowledge of her son's greatness." BOOK REVIEW DIGEST, 1943.

1332. DeVries, Peter. LET ME COUNT THE WAYS. Boston: Little, Brown and Company, 1965. 307p. 65-18130.

"Side-splitting story of Stan Waltz, furniture mover, unfaithful husband and atheist, who had an almost lifelong argument with his evangelistic wife, and son, Tom, as split a personality as was his home. He becomes an English professor, but inherits his father's attitudes until his conversion." BOOK REVIEW DIGEST, 1965.

1333. Driscoll, Paul F. MY FELICIA. New York: Macmillan Co., 1945. 275p. 45-8813.

"In his first novel, Paul Driscoll has chronicled the snobbery and petty antagonisms of a small New England mill town near Boston. Felicia, a beautiful second generation Polish girl, is caught between her loyalty to her background and her love for Mark Standler, second, scion of an eminent family. The problem is complicated by Faith Brimmer, a designing heiress, Steve O'Meara, an Irish lad irrepressibly in love with Felicia and Alec Marwick, a free-thinking Harvard Instructor." BOOK REVIEW DIGEST, 1945.

1334. Ferber, Edna. AMERICAN BEAUTY. New York: Doubleday and Co., 1931. 313p. 31-28323.

"Novel is set in Connecticut Valley and involves the Poles who farmed the land, eager, humble, land-loving Poles who were moving in, bringing fresh vigor to the earth and to the desiccated manless households." BOOK REVIEW DIGEST, 1931.

1335. Fineman, Irving. HEAR, YE, SONS. New York: Longmans, Green and Co., 1933. 306p. 33-23926.

"A successful New York lawyer, a Polish American Jew of 68 relates the story of his early years in the old world--his childhood in the ghetto overshadowed by fear of pogroms and persecution, his education, his betrothal and wedding, his enforced service in the Russian army and his escape to America at the age of 24. A brief prologue reviews hastily his life in America and the fortunes of his sons and daughter." BOOK REVIEW DIGEST, 1933.

1336. Girling, Zoë. POLONAISE. New York: Macmillan and Co., 1940. 273p. 40-2693.

A novel about a visit to Warszawa by three teen-age children of an English couple contemplating a divorce. The children are guests of a distant Polish relative who is employed in the Łazienki Palace as a cataloger. Story contrasts two civilizations and two ways of life during the late 1930s.

1337. Gray, Eunice. STEFFI, A NOVEL. New York: Exposition Press, 1951. 246p. 51-1931.

Steffi, a young Polish-American girl, works in a candy factory in Chicago. She is determined to leave her stifling home life and mundane job. She finds a better-paying job, lets an apartment, becomes a model, takes a lover, marries another, leaves her husband for

*Special Works* 293

        her ex-lover and ends up a waitress in and among the old neighborhood crowd.

1338.  Greely, John N. WAR BREAKS DOWN DOORS. Boston: Hale, Cushman and Flint, 1929. 278p. 29-25613.

        "A son of Polish immigrants living in the anthracite coal region of eastern Pennsylvania joins the United States Army, Jan Sincowiz. He learns about a life other than what he knew as a poor Polish-American youngster. He does well in the service, invests in his hometown's major employer, falls in love with the "poor little rich girl," obtains a commission, fights overseas in France, returns home victorious, marries Ellen and assimilates into the mainstream of bourgeois America." BOOK REVIEW DIGEST, 1929.

1339.  Harriman, Karl E. THE HOMEBUILDERS. Philadelphia: G.W. Jacobs and Company, 1903. 329p. 3-31025.

        Eight short stories about Poles in the United States.

1340.  Hayes, Florence. JOE-POLE, NEW AMERICAN. Boston: Houghton Mifflin Co., 1952. 244p. 52-5909.

        "The experiences of a sturdy Polish DP in a little New York state town. Joe's father worked on a farm and Joe found difficulty at first in making his way among his American schoolmates. But his integrity is not changed and he became Joe American instead of Joe Pole." BOOK REVIEW DIGEST, 1952.

1341.  Hełm-Pirgo, Marian. ROYAL DRAGOONS' IMMORTAL LOVE. Jersey City, N.J.: Bicentennial Publishing Corp., 1975. 313p.

        A novel about Polish settlers who arrived on American soil in 1608 and also those who took part in the Revolutionary War. Illustrations. Maps.

1342.  Hindus, Maurice G. MAGDA. Garden City, N.Y: Doubleday and Co., 1951. 314p.

        The story of a Polish immigrant, Mike Kozioł, who comes to America in 1910, starts as a farm worker and ends up a Texan landowner.

1343. Hughes, Rupert. ŻAL, AN INTERNATIONAL ROMANCE. New York: The Century Co., 1905. 346p. 5-34176.

"The tale of a young Polish pianist's battle for recognition in New York. There is the artist and dreamer's deathless enthusiasm which dominates Ladislav Moniusko and Rose Hargrave, a wealthy New York girl, whose father had set her apart for an English duke. The contrast between the Polish and American natures is excellently indicated." BOOK REVIEW DIGEST, 1905.

1344. Janney, Russell. THE MIRACLE OF THE BELLS. New York: Prentice-Hall, Inc., 1946. 497p. 46-2712.

"It is the story of a beautiful Polish-American girl from a Pennsylvania coal town who died just as she was about to make a name in Hollywood. The man who loved her, an ace publicity man, takes her body back to her native town, and attempts to carry out her last wishes for her funeral. It is then that the miracle of the bells occurs." BOOK REVIEW DIGEST, 1946.

1345. Krawczyk, Monica. IF THE BRANCH BLOSSOMS AND OTHER STORIES. Minneapolis: Polanie Publishing Co., 1950. 151p.

Stories of Polish-American life, presenting a quiet, frequently poignant account of a fine folk, struggling to make its way in an alien land, succeeding in its endeavor to the full, and finally adding its own particular spice and flavor to the composite culture of the United States. Illustrations.

1346. Kubiak, Wanda L. POLONAISE NEVERMORE. New York: Vantage Press, 1962. 210p. 63-43702.

Fictional story of Polish settlers in Berlin, Wisconsin during the period, 1866-1890.

1347. McAlpine, Dale K. MARIE NAIMSKA: A SAGA OF CHICAGO. Philadelphia: Dorrance and Company, 1954. 242p. 54-6754.

Novel depicting what happens to an established Polish family after leaving the homeland and settling in Chicago.

1348. Mikulski, John J. IN SENNAMAHONING UPLANDS: A NOVEL OF THE DEPRESSION DAYS IN CENTRAL PENNSYLVANIA. New York: Exposition Press, 1955. 93p. 55-11127.

A story of a Polish-American family in central Pennsylvania during the Great Depression, 1929-1939.

1349. Miniter, Edith M. OUT NATUPSKI NEIGHBORS. New York: Henry Holt and Co., 1916. 346p. 16-21054.

"The Natupskis from Poland settle in West Holly, Massachusetts having bought the Judson Buckland farm for two hundred dollars down and a large mortgage. The Natupskis bring West Holly its first experience of the immigration problem and the story is developed with considerable humor at the expense of both alien and American. The second part of the book has to do with the development of the Natupski children who all, in one way or another, become Americanized. While Statis Natupski learns American ways from Nancy Slocumb, Nancy and her husband, Abner, and the others learn that the Polanders have something to teach them." BOOK REVIEW DIGEST, 1916.

1350. Musial, Nellie. THE LITTLE WORLDS OF NELLIE MUSIAL. New York: Vantage Press, 1954. 81p. 54-7404.

"This book is an imaginative representation of American life as seen in the recollections of a Polish immigrant girl. It is presented to the reader as a work of fiction--true to life, but not an actual recording of fact." BOOK REVIEW DIGEST, 1954.

1351. Norris, Margaret. GYPSY BLOOD. New York: Hillman-Curl, Inc., 1939. 249p. 39-24925.

"Anna, to the immigration officials, was just another pretty Polish girl. To the polo-playing crowd on Long Island, a few years later she was the glamorous blonde whom wealthy Harry Baldwin fell in love with. The dramative story of how Anna emerged from the simple, diffident immigrant to an acknowledge glamour-girl with a fixed place in the social limelight, makes for exciting reading." BOOK REVIEW DIGEST, 1939.

1352. Pellowski, Anne. ANNA ROSE OF STAIRSTEP FARM. New York: Philomel Books, 1981. 176p.

Third in the series of books about the Korb family, a Polish-American family living in Wisconsin.

1353. Pellowski, Anne. BETSY'S UP-AND-DOWN YEARS. New York: Philomel Books, 1983. 157p. 82-22344.

Another addition to the series of books about the Korb family, a fictitious Polish-American rural family living in Wisconsin. Illustrated.

1354. Pellowski, Anne. FIRST FARM IN THE VALLEY: ANNA'S STORY. New York: Philomel Books, 1982. 192p. 82-5323.

First of the series of four books tracing four generations of a Polish-American family situated in the state of Wisconsin. Contains the author's family tree. Illustrated.

1355. Pellowski, Anne. WILLOW WIND FARM: BETSY'S STORY. New York: Philomel Books, 1981. 176p.

Concentrates on one member of the Polish-American family in Wisconsin, Betsy.

1356. Pellowski, Anne. WINDING VALLEY FARM: ANNIE'S STORY. New York: Philomel Books, 1982. 192p. 81-15908.

Third in the series of four works fictionalizing life of a Polish-American family in rural Wisconsin. Illustrated.

1357. Sienkiewicz, Henryk. AFTER BREAD: A STORY OF POLISH EMIGRANT LIFE TO AMERICA, trans. by Vatslaf A. Hlasko and Thomas H. Bullick. New York: R.F. Fenno and Co., 1897. 165p. 8-6886.

The tragic story of a Polish emigrant and his eighteen year old daughter who come to America with high hopes and both of whom meet untimely deaths.

1358. Tabrah, Ruth M. PULASKI PLACE. New York: Harper & Bros., Publishers, 1950. 280p. 50-5054.

"Of all the residents of Pulaski Place and Foundry Street, within the precincts of Our Lady's parish, only Steve Kowalski refuses to accept the traditions of the closely knit community. Back from service overseas,

Steve becomes the first citizen of Polish descent to win an appointment to the town's police force. The drama in the story lies in the conflict between Steve's broader concept of his job and the conviction of his mother and father, his neighbors, his parish priest, his younger brother and even his wife Irene, that Steve is our policeman." BOOK REVIEW DIGEST, 1950.

1359.  Vogel, Joseph. MAN'S COURAGE. New York: Alfred A. Knopf, 1938. 312p. 38-9836.

"Story of a Polish immigrant family in a small American city. Adam Wolak had come to America dreaming of a farm to call his own, but after 18 years as a day laborer, the depression puts the seal of defeat on his dream; the technicalities and red tape of the relief system bear down on his attitude of self-reliance and chaotic economic conditions finally bring his story to a tragic end." BOOK REVIEW DIGEST, 1938.

1360.  Waldo, Harold. STASH OF THE MARSH COUNTRY. New York: George H. Doran Company, 1921. 347p. 21-9516.

"The marsh country of the title is the region round Detroit and the Great Lakes where Poles and Bohemians have settled in numbers. Stashlaf Plazarski, or Stash, is one of the ambitious Polish boys who wants to get ahead and it's his story that is told. He follows various occupations, becoming in turn printer, violinist, actor, reporter, playwright, miner, army captain, yet he looks back on his life from an army training camp he has failed--failed in loyal return to his friends, and his disloyalty not only betrayed himself but it had brought tragedy to others. Looking back clearly now, he saw so clearly how these could have been averted. BOOK REVIEW DIGEST, 1921.

1361.  Wedda, Joseph. JASNA POLANA. New York: Doubleday, Inc., 1945. 293p.

A fictionalized account of reminiscences of life at Jasna Polana, a summer place for the author and his relatives and friends of Polish extraction. These people come from the Polish neighborhoods of Chicago. Author makes many philosophical comments about life via this story set somewhere in the 1930s and 1940s.

1362. Wylie, Ida A.R. STRANGERS ARE COMING. New York: Random House, 1941. 312p. 41-24081.

"Johnny-David Fenwick, son of a wealthy New Englander, was sent abroad by his father, in order to break up the boy's engagement. It was 1939, and Johnny-David was just in time for the invasion of Poland. When he came home, after some hair-raising experiences, he brought five refugees of assorted ages and stations in life. The way the refugees changed the life of the custom-ridden American college town's inhabitants is told in this book." BOOK REVIEW DIGEST, 1941.

Poles in Uruguay--Fiction

1363. Amorim, Enrique. THE HORSE AND HIS SHADOW, trans. by Richard L. O'Connell and James G. Lujan. New York: C. Scribner's Sons, 1943. 252p. 43-12146.

"A story of life on a large ranch in Uruguay. It is the story of the antagonisms of two brothers, the one the owner of the ranch, and the other a city man, a politician and a scholar. It is also the story of the servant girl, Bica, of the Polish refugees who have settled nearby, of Adelita, the beautiful mistress of the ranch, and of the great stallion, Don Juan which Marculo has brought to his brother as a gift. Essentially the story of the struggle of the Polish refugees against feudalistic owners of the great estancias in Uruguay c. 1940." Illustrations. BOOK REVIEW DIGEST, 1943.

Poles Outside Poland

1364. Juchniewicz, Mieczysław. POLES IN THE EUROPEAN RESISTANCE MOVEMENT, 1939-1945, trans. by Beryl Arct. Warszawa: Interpress Publishers, 1972. 177p. 74-168314.

Includes activities of Poles not only in Poland but also in other European countries such as Austria, Belgium, Bulgaria, Holland, Czechoslovakia, Yugoslavia, Rumania, Greece, France, Hungary and Germany. Includes portraits of many resistance leaders, including non-Poles. Author relied heavily on materials available in Poland only. Illustrations.

1365. Krolikowski, Łucjan. STOLEN CHILDHOOD: A SAGA OF POLISH WAR CHILDREN, trans. by Każimierz J. Rozniatowski. Buffalo, N.Y.: Father Justin Rosary Hour, 1983. 296p. OL: D810.C4K713.

Originally published in Polish. A description of the plight of thousands of Polish children deported to Soviet Russia and thereafter left homeless, some 380,000, between 1939 and 1941. Four parts: deportation to Russia, in Africa, through Europe and in Canada. Illustrations. Portraits. Maps.

1366. Mitchell, Harold. LECTURES: POLAND IN AFRICA AND ASIA. London: Scottish-Polish Society, 1943. 15p. NN: BZACp.v.347.

British military man visited the Polish Army and Polish refugees in the Middle East and various British colonies scattered throughout the continent of Africa and reported on what he had observed. Illustrations. Portrait.

1367. NINE MILLION POLES ABROAD. London: World League of Poles Abroad, 1943. 60p. NN: GLPp.v.135.

Interesting study of Poles abroad divided into geographical regions as well as a discussion of the diaspora. Particularly valuable are maps of the various regions denoting population density: Europe, U.S.A., Canada, South America and the Far East. Also includes tables showing number of Poles in the departements of France, states of the U.S. Unfortunately, no documentation. Maps.

Polish Jews in America--Fiction

1368. Yezierska, Anzia. ARROGANT BEGGAR. New York: Doubleday, Page and Co., 1927. 279p. 27-24899.

Story of an imaginative and rebellious girl from the tenements of New York who approaches the larger life promised by organized charity of the high hopes, of illusion and turns from it scarred by the experience and riches in trying to find her own place in the scheme of life.

1369. Yezierska, Anzia. BREAD GIVERS, A NOVEL. Garden City, New York: Doubleday, Page & Co., 1925. 297p. 25-18697.

"Skinny, half-starved, half-clothed tho she was, there was yet in the little Sara Smolinsky, the germ of stubborn strength that made her old Hebrew father call her Blut und Eisen. With fierce determination to know, to do and to be, she dragged herself up from the sordid Hester Street environment, away from the despotic temper of her father that had worked its disastrous will with her unhappy sisters, to work, to night school, to college, and at last--goal of her feverish ambition--to teach. Sara tells her own story. The traces of foreign idiom in her words lends vividness to spontaneity." BOOK REVIEW DIGEST, 1925.

1370. Yezierska, Anzia. CHILDREN OF LONELINESS: STORIES OF IMMIGRANT LIFE IN AMERICA. New York: Funk and Wagnalls Co., 1923. 270p. 23-16037.

Fictionalized form of life among Polish Jews in America as viewed by the author shortly after the turn of the century.

1371. Yezierska, Anzia. HUNGRY HEARTS. Boston: Houghton-Mifflin Co., 1920. 297p. 20-18936.

A novel set in New York about "Russian" Jews but author really depicts lives of Jews who came to this country from Russian-occupied Poland.

Polish National Catholic Church

1372. Andrews, Theodore H. THE POLISH NATIONAL CATHOLIC CHURCH IN AMERICA AND POLAND. London: Society for the Promotion of Christian Knowledge, 1953. 117p. A54-3735.

Author attempts to describe the Polish Church since the Reformation, the Polish people in the United States States, early independent movements, nature of the Polish National Catholic Church, beginnings and growth of the Church, its doctrines, its liturgical forms, church life, mission to Poland and relationships with other churches. Bibliography, pp. 115-117.

*Special Works* 301

1373. Bak, Bolesław R. SHORT HISTORY OF THE LIFE AND STRUG-
GLE OF BISHOP FRANCIS HODUR. Scranton, Penn.:
Author, 1954. 88p.

 A sympathetic biographical account of the founder of
 the Polish National Catholic Church by a member of that
 Church. Portrait.

1374. Fox, Paul. THE POLISH NATIONAL CATHOLIC CHURCH.
Scranton, Penn.: School of Christian Living, 1964.
144p. MiD: R284.8.F833p.

 Popular history of the Polish National Catholic
 Church. Includes history, appendixes which include
 Holy Mass, Confession of Faith, Constitution of the
 Church and a directory of churches in the United States
 and Canada. Also a list of clergy and parishes of the
 church in Poland. Illustrations. Portraits.

1375. Janowski, Robert W. THE GROWTH OF A CHURCH: A HIS-
TORICAL DOCUMENTARY. Scranton, Penn.: Straz Printery, 1965. 130p. 66-4330.

 A history of the Polish National Catholic Church in
 the United States based upon journal articles and other
 documents. Numerous black-and-white photographs of
 persons and places in this religious movement. Large
 section devoted to life of the founder, Francis Hodur.
 Portraits.

1376. Orzell, Laurence. ROME AND THE VALIDITY OF ORDERS IN
THE POLISH NATIONAL CATHOLIC CHURCH. Scranton,
Penn.: Savonarola Theological Seminary Alumni
Association, 1977. 49p. 77-75372.

 This book was originally a research paper prepared
 by the author while a student at the University of
 Scranton, a Jesuit institution, in 1976. As such, it
 is a sketch of the Roman Catholic view on the validity
 of Polish National Catholic Church orders. Bibliography, pp. 46-49.

1377. Włodarski, Szczepan. THE ORIGIN AND GROWTH OF THE
POLISH NATIONAL CATHOLIC CHURCH. Scranton, Penn.:
Polish National Catholic Church, 1976. 239p. 74-
33165.

A scholarly work about the Polish National Catholic Church, its origins, development, and achievements. Includes portraits of Bishop Hodur and others. Illustrations. Bibliography, pp. 227-231.

## Polish Question

1378. Benson, Edward F. THE WHITE EAGLE OF POLAND. New York: George H. Doran Company, 1919. 243p. 19-1284.

    Contains reconstruction of Poland, the German occupation of Poland, internal conditions of Russian Kingdom of Poland between 1914 and 1918. Maps.

1379. Chmielewski, Edward. THE POLISH QUESTION IN THE RUSSIAN STATE DUMA. Knoxville: University of Tennessee Press, 1970. 187p. 77-100411.

    "This study is intended to view the Polish Question in the Russian State Duma as a critical aspect of Russian domestic history and the constitutional experiment of the early twentieth century.... This book is based heavily on the stenographic reports of the State Duma and the State Council." Maps. Bibliography, pp. 175-182.

1380. THE GREAT POWERS AND THE POLISH QUESTION, 1941-1945: A DOCUMENTARY STUDY IN COLD WAR ORIGINS, ed. by Antony Polonsky. London: London School of Economics and Political Science, 1976. 282p. 76-376549.

    A collection of documents which describe the way in which the Great Powers handled the Polish Question leading to the Potsdam and Yalta Agreements. The reader is to make up his own mind on this question based upon these documents. Maps.

1381. Gurney, Arthur E. THE POPULATION OF THE POLISH COMMONWEALTH. London: George Allen and Unwin, 1916. 30p. MiU: DK402.5.P77 Pt. 2.

    A most accurate and vivid account of the population of the former Polish Commonwealth, a nation which notwithstanding its indisputable right to existence. Includes chart entitled, "Extent and Population of

*Special Works* 303

Polish Territories and Total Number of Poles in 1909 and 1910.

1382. Hill, Ninian. POLAND AND THE POLISH QUESTION: IMPRESSIONS AND AFTERTHOUGHTS. New York: Frederick A. Stokes Company, 1915. 340p. 15-18756.

Author visited Poland during summer of 1913. Book resulted from a study of Polish history (Morfil's POLAND and Lelewel's HISTOIRE DE POLOGNE). History and description of conditions of Poles in Prussia, Russia and Austria. Appendices include documents of Congress of Vienna relative to Poland. Chronological table of events in Polish history. British accounts of Insurrections of 1830 and 1863. Illustrations. Map.

1383. Jasienski, Alexander M. REBORN POLAND. New York: Lisiegki Press, 1919. 43p. 19-12088.

A short discussion on liberated Poland and what provinces should be given her by an instructor and company commander of the Royal School of Infantry at Halifax, Nova Scotia. Maps.

1384. Kowalczyk, Jan J. PRUSSIAN POLAND, A STRONGHOLD OF GERMAN MILITARISM. Copenhagen: Egmont H. Peterson Company, 1917. 66p. 17-32199.

Subtitled, "If Reunited with the Whole Polish Nation as an Independent State, One of the Strongest Pillars of Future European Peace." An accurate and impartial account of all facts and events with Prussian Poland by a journalist. Maps.

1385. Kubrakiewicz, Michał. REVELATIONS OF AUSTRIA. London: T.C. Newby, 1846. 2v. 5-42012.

A detailed account of how Galicia fared under Austrian rule, that is the character and effects of the Austrian depotism. Personal narrative and reminiscences through date of publication. Author was a functionary in the Austrian government. Highly critical.

1386. Kucharski, Rajmund. POLAND'S STRUGGLE FOR INDEPENDENCE, with a foreword by Lord Weardale. London: George Allen and Unwin, Ltd., 1916. 48p. MiU: DK402.5.P77 Pt. 2.

Historical sketch of Polish Question from Duchy of Warsaw to 1914. A defense of position of Polish independence.

1387. Leslie, Robert F. THE POLISH QUESTION: POLAND'S PLACE IN MODERN HISTORY. London: Historical Association, 1964. 39p. 65-3414.

A contemporary interpretation of the Polish Question by a professor of history at the University of London. Select bibliography, pp. 38-39.

1388. Lind, John. LETTERS CONCERNING THE PRESENT STATE OF POLAND. London: T. Payne, 1773. 393p. 19-2298.

Subtitled, "Together with the Manifesto of the Courts of Vienna, Petersburgh, and Berlin. And the Letters Patent of the King of Prussia." A collection of four essays written in the form of letters by the author postmarked Danzig in 1772 and Brussels in the same year. Retrospective view of the First Partition.

1389. Livinsky, Isidore. REMINISCENCES OF POLAND, HER REVOLUTIONS AND HER RIGHTS. London: Charles Gilpin, 1848. 96p. NN: GMF.

Subtitled, "A Brief Sketch of the Causes of the Revolutions from 1830 to the Incorporation of Cracow with the Austrian Empire; with a short Local Description of the City of Cracow." History of the revolution of 1830 and its aftermath. History of the insurrection of 1846 in Cracow and aftermath.

1390. Lundgren-Nielsen, Kay. THE POLISH PROBLEM AT THE PARIS PEACE CONFERENCE, trans. by Alison Borch-Johansen. Odense: Odense University Press, 1979. 603p. NjP: D651.P7L84.

Subtitled, "A STUDY OF THE POLICIES OF THE GREAT POWERS AND THE POLES, 1918-1919." Purpose of this exhaustive study is to deal with the position a new Polish state was to occupy in the new relationships between the nations and to take a new perspective in examining the problem and answering the question why the decision at the Peace Conference took the form that they did. Period covered is October, 1918 to 28 June, 1919. Maps. Bibliography, pp. 580-592.

1391. Lutosławski, Wincenty. THE POLISH NATION. Paris: Boyveau et Chevielet, 1917. 59p. NN: GLP P.V. 15, No. 5.

A lecture delivered at the Lowell Institute in Boston on October 21, 1907, and at the University of California on March 9, 1908. Deals with the question of nationality in Poland. The author seems concerned with the matter of establishing Polish nationalism. A defense or apologia for the reconstruction of the Polish state.

1392. Noailles, Emmanuel Henri V. de, marquis. WHAT IS POLAND? trans. by Edward E. Johnstone. London: Effingham Wilson, Royal Exchange, 1863. 80p. NN: GMF p.v.2, No. 2.

A consideration of the Polish Question. Not so much factual as speculation on Poland's demise from a sympathetic French viewpoint. Bound with other works under general title: POLAND AND HER FRONTIERS. Map.

1393. Phillips, Walter A. POLAND. New York: Henry Holt and Co., 1915. 256p. 16-12564.

Most of the book deals with the history of Poland from the Partitions through World War I. Object was not to retell the whole history of Poland but to collect out of that history and present in logical sequence those factors which have a direct bearing on the Polish Question in all its phases down to the present time. Bibliographical essay, pp. 251-253. Maps.

1394. Pitkiewicz, Józef. LETTER FROM A POLISH PATRIOT TO THE NATIONAL GOVERNMENT OF ENGLAND, trans. by C. Sharp. London: W. Jefs, 1864. 92p. NN: GMF p.v.2, No. 6.

Letter written by author from Lwów in 1863 and published in England to clarify position of the Poles on the Polish Question.

1395. THE POLISH QUESTION AND GENERAL MOURAVIEFF, by an Englishman. London: Joseph Causton and Sons, 1863. 93p. NN: GMF p.v.2, No. 4.

One of several small monographs dealing with the
Polish Question, this one anonymously written in its
defense.

1396. THE POLISH QUESTION AS AN INTERNATIONAL PROBLEM.
London: George Allen and Unwin, Ltd., 1916. 63p.
MiU: DK402.5.P77, pt. 2.

As title suggests, a discussion of the Polish Question written by a number of distinguished authorities, none of whom are identified.

1397. Posner, Stanisław. POLAND AS AN INDEPENDENT ECONOMIC
UNIT. London: George Allen and Unwin, Ltd., 1916.
40p. MiU: DK402.5.P77, pt. 2.

A lecture delivered at the École des Hautes Études Sociales, Paris, January 29, 1916. An impressive account of the material resources of Poland. Bibliography, p. 40.

1398. Sarolea, Charles. LETTERS ON POLISH AFFAIRS. Edinburgh: Oliver and Boyd, 1922. 140p. 11-16891.

Author attempts to show how the Polish Question is not a national problem but an international problem. Takes an anti-German stand toward newly-created Polish state.

1399. Wenkstern, Otto. PRUSSIA AND THE POLES. London:
Mann Nephews, 1862. 91p. NN: GMF, p.v.2, No. 1.

A consideration of the Polish Question as it pertains to the area taken by Prussia.

Polish Roman Catholic Church--U.S.

1400. Buczek, Daniel S. IMMIGRANT PASTOR: THE LIFE OF THE
RIGHT REVEREND MONSIGNOR ŁUCJAN BÓJANOWSKI OF NEW
BRITAIN, CONNECTICUT. Waterbury, Conn.: Hemingway
Corp., 1974. 184p. 74-81981.

Life of Msgr. Bójanowski which is an attempt to relate one story of the history of the Catholic Church among the Poles in the United States. Tribute to a leader. Illustrations. Bibliography, pp. 174-176.

## Politics and Government

1401. Allen, Julian. AUTOCRACY IN POLAND AND RUSSIA. New York: John Wiley, 1854. 200p. 5-15206.

   Subtitled, "Or, a Description of Russian Misrule in Poland, and an Account of the Surveillance of Russian Spies at Home and Abroad Including the Experience of an Exile." Author was born in Poland. While attending university in Grodno in 1844, he became a member of a Polish secret society. He escaped from possible Russian imprisonment and eventually sought asylum in the United States whence he wrote this account. Concentrates on Russo-Polish relations.

1402. BACKGROUND TO CRISIS; POLICY AND POLITICS IN GIEREK'S POLAND, ed. by Maurice D. Simon and Roger E. Kanet. Boulder, Colo.: Westview Press, 1981. 418p. 80-24168.

   A collection of essays examining the policy in relevant developments in Poland since the accession to power by Gierek in late 1970. Includes bibliographical references.

1403. THE BLACK BOOK OF POLISH CENSORSHIP, trans. and ed. by Jane L. Curry. New York: Random House, 1984. 451p. 83-47813.

   A set of official guidelines smuggled out of Poland in 1977 stolen from the main office for Control of the Press, Publications and Public Performance in Kraków by Tomasz Stryjewski. The regulations revealed here can now be used as a chart of what the Gierek administration knew and how they thought from 1974 to 1977. They also provide the most in-depth view of the inner workings and failings of a political apparatus.

1404. Blejwas, Stanislaus A. REALISM IN POLISH POLITICS. Boulder, Colo.: Slavica Publishers, Inc., 1984. 312p. 83-05814.

   Subtitled, "Warsaw Positivism and National Survival in Nineteenth Century Poland." Author's doctoral dissertation at Columbia University in 1974. A study, an assessment of the merits of the criticism of the development of the period, as well as a survey of the society, politics and economic development which constitute the history of this period. Bibliography, pp. 283-301.

1405. Bromke, Adam. POLAND'S POLITICS: IDEALISM VS. REALISM. Cambridge, Mass.: Harvard University Press, 1967. 316p. 66-21331.

Foreign policy has become a fundamental issue in Polish politics, overshadowing all other matters. In the endless debate over the course of this foreign policy, the Poles have split along psychological lines between those who imagine the world to suit their policy, and those who arrange their policy to suit the world. Bibliography, pp. 293-304.

1406. Buell, Raymond L. POLAND: KEY TO EUROPE. New York: Alfred A. Knopf, 1939. 406p. 40-3066.

A report on the problems confronting the country. Also, an analysis and survey of the problems of modern Poland. Author sympathetic to Polish problems. Both a history of inter-war Poland and a series of essays on Polish social, political, and economic problems. Map.

1407. Checinski, Michael. POLAND: COMMUNISM, NATIONALISM, ANTI-SEMITISM, trans. in part by Tadeusz Szafar. New York: Karz-Cohl Publishing Co., 1982. 289p. 82-266.

Study of the rise of the security service in postwar Poland. As the author states in his preface, this book covers three intertwining strands in postwar Polish history: the Communist Party, the security forces, and and the Jews. Based upon 80 interviews which the author conducted with former Communist Party officials, former security and military officers, leaders of Jewish cultural and economic institutions in Poland, and former Polish journalists. Also based upon the author's twenty years' experience in the Polish Army.

1408. Cieplak, Tadeusz N., ed. POLAND SINCE 1956. New York: Twayne Publishers, Inc., 1972. 482p. 79-125262.

Readings and essays on Polish government and politics since 1956. Readings reprinted from scholarly journals

Special Works 309

published in the West. Other reprints are translations of articles which appeared in Polish scholarly journals. Bibliography, pp. 459-467.

1409. COMMUNISTS ON COMMUNISM: READINGS ON THE POLISH "THAW." West New York, N.J.: Intercontinental Press Service, 1958. 67p. NjP: 1638.263.

Collection of readings from Polish press covering period from mid-1955 to late 1956. Readings range from poems to articles and short stories. All materials are from official publications. Includes biographical sketches of authors of articles. Illustrations.

1410. Day, William A. THE RUSSIAN GOVERNMENT IN POLAND. London: Longmans, Green, Reader and Dyer, 1867. 333p. 5-6356.

Continues, With a Narrative of the Polish Insurrection of 1863, materials for this Narrative collected during three visits to Russia and Poland in the years 1863, 1864 and 1865. Description of political structure of Russian-occupied Poland during latter part of the nineteenth century and a brief history of area since and including the Insurrection of 1863. Appendices include documents and diplomatic correspondence.

1411. DeWeydenthal, Jan B. THE COMMUNISTS OF POLAND: AN HISTORICAL OUTLINE. Stanford, Cal.: Hoover Institution Press, 1978. 217p. 78 59465.

Book is concerned exclusively with an organized group of Communists who came to power in Poland. Concise and informative. Bibliography, pp. 203-210.

1412. DeWeydenthal, Jan B. POLAND: COMMUNISM ADRIFT. Beverly Hills, Calif.: Sage Publications, 1979. 88p. 79-67732.

Author attempts an analysis of the political situation in Poland after the changes which came about under Edmund Gierek's leadership. Suggests internal changes emanate from disillusionment with Party politics and the increasing demands of the Catholic Church. References, pp. 87-88.

1413. Dziewanowski, Marian K. THE COMMUNIST PARTY OF POLAND: AN OUTLINE OF HISTORY. Cambridge, Mass.: Harvard University Press, 1959. 369p. 58-7500.

   Systematic history of the Communist Party of Poland. Extension of Ph.D. thesis for Harvard University. The book focuses on the Communist movement as a social and political force and not upon the internal functioning of the party machinery. Bibliography, pp. 293-314.

1414. FOR YOUR FREEDOM AND OURS: POLISH PROGRESSIVE SPIRIT FROM THE FOURTEENTH CENTURY TO THE PRESENT, ed. by Krystyna M. Olszer. New York: F. Ungar Pub. Co., 1981. 367p. OL: DK4110.F6.1981.

   A selection of documents, speeches and manifestoes. An update of the first edition which appeared in 1943. Includes items for Solidarność.

1415. Grosz, Wiktor. THE POLISH DEFEAT, SEPTEMBER 1939. Warszawa: Czytelnik, 1950. 91p. 52-36227.

   Author intended to interpret Poland's defeat in 1939 as the result of a capitalistic economic policy, a reactionary policy at home and an anti-Soviet reactionary foreign policy.

1416. Groth, Alexander J. PEOPLE'S POLAND: GOVERNMENT AND POLITICS. San Francisco: Chandler Publishing Co., 1972. 155p. MiD: 320.9438.J915p.

   Purpose is to provide an introduction to the politics of Communist Poland in the 1970s. It is a survey of the background, the major institutions, problems and personalities of the Polish regime since World War II. Also covers political development, political culture, the distributive impact of Communist power, the interplay of international and domestic politics. Map. Bibliographical essay, pp. 147-149.

1417. Hiscocks, Richard. POLAND, BRIDGE FOR THE ABYSS? AN INTERPRETATION OF DEVELOPMENTS IN POST-WAR POLAND. New York: Oxford University Press, 1963. 359p. 63-23578.

   Author made annual visits to Poland from 1957 to 1961. He was associated with the University of

*Special Works*  311

Manitoba. A study of post-war Poland. Emphasizes
development of Communism in Poland and political
affairs. Map. Bibliography, pp. 335-344.

1418. Hotchkiss, Christine. HOME TO POLAND. New York:
Farrar, Strauss, and Cudahy, 1958. 247p. 58-7837.

Author's observations of Polish life by a woman who
left Poland in 1939 and was returning for a first
visit since then in 1957. Author was married to an
American living in New York. Visit significantly
occurred after Uprising of Autumn 1956. Personal view
of the condition of politics in Poland during that
time. Map.

1419. Karol, K.S. VISA FOR POLAND, trans. by Mervyn Savill.
London: Macgibbon and Kee, 1959. 259p. 62-42403.

A former Pole, born and raised in Poland and who
spent several years in the U.S.S.R., a correspondent
living in France, returns to Poland in October, 1956
and travels throughout the country. He writes about
the changes which 1956 brought about and also makes
some observations on the future of the country.

1420. Komarnicki, Tytus. REBIRTH OF THE POLISH REPUBLIC.
London: William Heinemann, Ltd., 1957. 776p.
57-3573.

A study in the diplomatic history of Europe, 1914-
1920. The primary object of this book is to ascertain
the role played by Polish problems in world policy,
and in particular, in the policy of the Western Powers,
France, Great Britain and the United States during the
First World War, at the Paris Peace Conference and
immediately after; that is to say in the course of the
Polish-Soviet War in 1919-1920. Relied heavily on
British and American sources. Some Polish sources
also used. Maps. Bibliography, pp. 749-762.

1421. Korbonski, Stefan. THE POLISH UNDERGROUND STATE: A
GUIDE TO THE UNDERGROUND, trans. by Marta Erdman.
New York: Columbia University Press, 1979. 268p.
77-82393.

It is the task of the present work to give a brief,
almost encyclopedic account of the sum total of efforts

leading to the creation of the underground state. This book is intended to serve as a guide to the underground.

1422. Kridl, Manfred, ed. FOR YOUR FREEDOM AND OURS, trans. by Ludwik Krzyzanowski. New York: Frederick Unger Publishing Co., 1943. 359p. 43-9073.

Subtitled, POLISH PROGRESSIVE SPIRIT THROUGH THE CENTURIES. Collection of translated excerpts from Polish political writings to give the American reader a true picture of Polish though on moral, cultural, political and social problems. Some documents. Biographical sketches precede selections.

1423. Krzesinski, Andrew J. POLAND'S RIGHTS TO JUSTICE. New York: Devin-Adar Co., 1946. 120p. A49-33.

Author shows the great injury done to Poland and its consequences for the Allies and the whole world. The Yalta decision means an unprecedented betrayal of a nation by her allies and is contrary not only to the principle of justice and to the Atlantic Charter but also to natural and international laws. Bibliography, p. 117.

1424. Lipski, Jan J. KOR: A HISTORY OF THE WORKERS' DEFENSE COMMITTEE IN POLAND, 1976-1981, trans. by Olga Amsterdamska and Gene M. Moore. Berkeley: University of California Press, 1985. 561p. 84-16353.

A book about the efforts of a group of people who called themselves the Komitet Obrony Robotnikow and its activities. Author professes work not scholarly. Based on documents.

1425. Małcużynski, Karol. THE GOMUŁKA PLAN FOR A NUCLEAR ARMAMENTS FREEZE IN CENTRAL EUROPE. Warszawa: Zachodnia Agencja Prasowa, 1964. 108p. OL: JX1974.7.M25.

Story of Polish government's plan for a nuclear armaments freeze in central Europe--a memorandum submitted to all European and non-European governments on 29 February 1964.

*Special Works* 313

1426. Mason, David S. PUBLIC OPINION AND POLITICAL CHANGE
IN POLAND, 1980-1982. New York: Cambridge University Press, 1985. 275p. 85-5280.

Drawn on public opinion surveys conducted in Poland
during the Solidarity era to examine popular attitudes
on fundamental issues of political power and on the
dramatic political events of 1980-1982. A fresh look
at Solidarity from the public point of view. Bibliography, pp. 253-263.

1427. Morrison, James F. THE POLISH PEOPLE'S REPUBLIC.
Baltimore: Johns Hopkins University Press, 1968.
160p. 68-18209.

Part of a series of monographs dealing with integration and community building in the Communist Party
status of eastern Europe. Divided into five historical parts. Contains bibliographical footnotes.

1428. Myant, Martin. POLAND: A CRISIS FOR SOCIALISM.
London: Lawrence and Wishart, 1982. 254p. 82-238513.

Author attempts to explain how the crisis of August,
1980 can be understood and how the imposition of military rule came about. The first four chapters trace
the development of the crisis against the background
of Polish history. Contains bibliographical notes at
the end of each chapter.

1429. Narkiewicz, Olga A. THE GREEN FLAG: POLISH POPULIST
POLITICS, 1867-1970. Totowa, N.J.: Rowman and
Littlefield, 1976. 314p. 76-981.

A history of Polish populism. Bibliography, pp.
294-303.

1430. Oertzen, Freidrich W. von. SO THIS IS POLAND, trans.
by R.F. Clark. London: George Allen and Unwin,
Ltd., 1932. 288p. OL: 943.041.037.

Author was a political journalist, a German authority on Polish affairs. Describes the establishment of
the Piłsudski regime in Poland beginning with the
Miracle on the Vistula. Also describes the workings
of the regime with emphasis on the bad features.
Highly critical.

1431. Piekałkiewicz, Jarosław. COMMUNIST LEGAL GOVERNMENT: A STUDY OF POLAND. Athens, Ohio: Ohio University Press, 1975. 282p. 72-85539.

   A study of Communist local politics covering the period in 1958 when the Polish local government was reformed as a result of the anti-Stalinist limited revolution of 1956, to the end of 1972. Numerous diagrams and tables accompany this text. Illustrations. Bibliography, pp. 267-275.

1432. POLAND TODAY: THE STATE OF THE REPUBLIC, comp. by the Experience and the Future Discussion Group, with an introduction by Jack Bielasiak. Armonk, N.Y.: M.E. Sharpe, Inc., 1981. 231p. 81-8782.

   Two recent documents which the Poles themselves dissect their country's social, political, and economic systems, diagnose their current ills, and suggest cures for the sick man of socialism. Material based on survey questionnaires answered by more than 200 Polish intellectuals--members and nonmembers of the Communist Party, government officials, academics from a variety of fields, writers, journalists, and artists, the Catholic faithful and the nonreligious.

1433. POLAND UNDER JARUZELSKI: A COMPREHENSIVE SOURCEBOOK ON POLAND DURING AND AFTER MARTIAL LAW, ed. by Leopold Labedz and the Staff of SURVEY magazine. New York: Charles Scribner's Sons, 1984. 432p. 83-20324.

   A collection of addresses, essays and lectures by various writers, principally Polish, on Solidarność, martial law, resistance to it and various reactions to conditions in Poland after Jaruzelski came to power. Illustrations.

1434. POLISH POLITICS: EDGE OF THE ABYSS, ed. by Jack Bielasiak and Maurice D. Simon. New York: Praeger, 1984. 366p. 83-24759.

   Purpose of book is to explain the sixteen months of the Polish renewal by concentrating on reasons for the 1980-1981 upheavals, analyzing the economic, social and political developments between the outburst of the strikes and the state of war declaration, and

## Special Works

exploring the aftermath of these developments in martial law Poland. Fifteen articles. Biographical sketches of authors, pp. 367-369.

1435. Raina, Peter K. POLAND 1981: TOWARDS SOCIAL RENEWAL. London: George Allen and Unwin, Ltd., 1985. 472p. 84-21590.

Deals with the serious attempts made by both Solidarity and the government to initiate urgently needed socioeconomic reforms which would have helped overcome the crisis of political and economic stagnation. Bibliography, pp. 465-466.

1436. REVOLUTIONARY MARXIST STUDENTS IN POLAND SPEAK OUT, 1964-1968, by Jacek Kuron et al. New York: Merit Publishers, 1968. 96p. 68-8837.

Open letters by "voices of dissent," Jacek Kuron, Karol Modzelewski, Antoni Zambrowski and Isaac Deutscher, to various groups.

1437. Rousseau, Jean-Jacques. THE GOVERNMENT OF POLAND, trans. by Willmoore Kendall. Indianapolis: Bobbs-Merrill Co., 1972. 116p. 70-165184.

Author commissioned to provide the country with solutions to its constitutional problems. Author was a first to apply principles of democratic theory to a concrete political regime. Work is a clarification and criticism of the political teaching of the SOCIAL CONTRACT.

1438. Rozmaryn, Stefan. THE SEJM AND PEOPLE'S COUNCILS IN POLAND. Warszawa: Polonia Publishing House, 1958. 153p. 59-34180.

The purpose of this book is to acquaint the reader with the organization and activity of the representative bodies which constitute the political foundation of the system of the People's Democracy in Poland.

1439. Sanford, George. MILITARY RULE IN POLAND: THE REBUILDING OF COMMUNIST POWER, 1980-1981. London: Croom Helm, Ltd., 1986. 288p. MiU: DK4442.S2611. 1986.

Seeks to explain why it was possible for the Polish military to take power in December, 1981 and how it was done and the consequences. Bibliography, pp. 277-285.

1440. Sanford, George. POLISH COMMUNISM IN CRISIS, THE POLITICS OF REFORM AND REACTION, 1980-1981. New York: St. Martin's Press, 1983. 249p. NjP: HX315.7. A6S26.

An attempt to explain the Polish Reform Movement of 1980-1981 by presenting the values, presumptions, aims and discourses of the Polish Communist reformers themselves. Aimed to produce an uncommitted academic account based largely on Polish sources of the realities of Communist reform politics. Bibliography, pp. 229-241.

1441. Scaevola, pseud. A STUDY IN FORGERY. London: J. Rolls Book Co., Ltd., 1945. 123p. 45-6898.

A study of the Lublin Committee and its rule over Poland. Author presents to the reader the doings of a handful of Communists who seized power in Poland, i.e. the Lublin Committee. Undocumented. Authorship spurious. Portraits.

1442. Staar, Richard F. POLAND, 1944-1962: THE SOVIETIZATION OF A CAPTIVE PEOPLE. Baton Rouge, La.: Louisiana State University Press, 1962. 300p. 62-15027.

Covers governmental dynamics, including analyses and comments on the various aspects of the people's democracy in Poland, the legislative foundations of the state, and a description of elections; domestic, foreign and defense policies; the dominant political party and its youth auxiliaries and pressure groups which comprise the two subordinate and quasi-political organizations, the Roman Catholic Church, and finally anti-church movements. Contains many tables of election results, Communist Party membership, etc. Maps. Bibliography, pp. 277-290.

1443. Strong, Anna L. I SAW THE NEW POLAND. Boston: Little, Brown and Co., 1946. 280p. 45-11107.

A journalistic account of the visit to Poland of the author from November 1944 to July 1945. The author analyzes political conditions in the country which became complicated as a result of the Russian-Polish antipathy and subsequent modus vivendi reached after it became evident that an independent Poland was to be sponsored by the U.S.S.R.

1444. STUDIES IN POLISH POLITICAL SYSTEM, ed. by Jerzy J. Wiatr. Warszawa: Ossolineum, 1967. 242p. 68-35421.

The present volume includes a collection of papers written recently in various contexts by scholars from the institute as well as from the Sociology Department, University of Warszawa. It has been prepared and published to enable foreign scholars to get acquainted with representative examples of theoretical and empirical works in political sociology conducted in Poland. Bibliographical footnotes.

1445. Szczypiorski, Andrzej. THE POLISH ORDEAL: THE VIEW FROM WITHIN, trans. by Celina Wieniewska. London: Croom Helm, Ltd., 1982. 154p. 83-132725.

Essays which attempt at setting down the experiences of the author's life. They are reflections of a Pole, a novelist and a radio dramatist, who relates his country's political history during his lifetime.

1446. Toranska, Terea. "THEM:" STALIN'S POLISH PUPPETS, trans. by Agnieszka Kolakowska. New York: Harper & Row, 1987. 384p. 86-44364.

Author worked for KULTURA from 1975 to 1981 as a reporter. She has presented here a description of the inner circle of power in Poland immediately after World War II. Consists of a series of interviews with five of the highest officials in Stalinist Poland from 1945 to 1956: Julia Minc, Edward Ochab, Roman Werfel, Stefan Staszewski and Jakub Berman. Includes brief biographical sketches of prominent persons, both Polish and Russian, who were referred to in the text. Portraits.

1447. Weit, Erwin A. AT THE RED SUMMIT: INTERPRETER BEHIND THE IRON CURTAIN, trans. by Mary Schofield. New York: Macmillan Co., 1973. 226p. 72-88151.

Brings reader directly into the normally hidden
world of the Communist leaders. Covers author's experiences in the first few months of 1970. Originally
written in German. Intent is to bring book up-to-date
in view of latest developments and present situation
in eastern Europe. Deals with Polish affairs mostly
but also includes East German and Czech matters.
Illustrations.

1448. Woytak, Richard A. ON THE BORDER OF WAR AND PEACE.
New York: Columbia University Press, 1979. 168p.
78-63277.

Covers Polish intelligence and diplomacy in 1937-
1939 and the origins of the Ultra-Secret. Bibliography, pp. 119-133.

1449. Wynot, Edward D. POLISH POLITICS IN TRANSITION.
Athens: University of Georgia Press, 1974. 294p.
73-85024.

This book is divided into three distinct yet related
parts. The first discusses the general economic,
social and political scene in Poland during the period
in question, stressing the various problems facing the
regime. The second portion examines in detail the
genesis and substance of the ideology, policies, and
programs selected by the government to resolve these
pressing issues, while the final segment of the work
chronicles the attempts of the regime to enact its
programs and the obstacles it encountered within the
Polish community. The result is a case study of how a
developing nation in the late 1930s increasingly moved
toward the model of a Fascist state. Originally a
doctoral dissertation. Bibliography, pp. 269-285.

Population

1450. Murdzek, Benjamin P. EMIGRATION IN POLISH SOCIAL
POLITICAL THOUGHT, 1870-1914. New York: Columbia
University Press, 1977. 396p. 77-071391.

A broad statistical study of the multi-directional
population movements in historical Poland during the
period 1870 to 1914. Discusses this problem in Prussian Poland, Russian Poland and Austrian Poland,

*Special Works*

individually, and then the attitudes of the Poles themselves on emigration. Numerous tables and charts. Bibliography, pp. 277-304.

1451. Pietrucha, Jerzy. THE POPULATION OF WESTERN AND NORTHERN POLAND, trans. by Stanisław Tarnowski. Warszawa: Interpress Publishers, 1972. 139p. 72-191264.

A study, for popular consumption, of the demographic conditions in the territories acquired from Germany after World War II. Emphasis is on the permanency of the population changes after twenty-five years of occupation. Many tables, charts. Maps.

1452. Zielinski, Henryk. POPULATION CHANGES IN POLAND, 1939-1950. New York: Mid-European Studies Center, 1954. 101p. 54-7562.

Reviews selected aspects of the changes in the demographic structure of Poland caused by the war, the joint occupation of her territory by Germany and the U.S.S.R. and subsequent shifts in her boundaries. Bibliography, pp. 95-101.

### Public Opinion

1453. Radio Free Europe. Audience and Public Opinion Research Dept. THE POLISH SELF-IMAGE AND THE POLISH IMAGE OF AMERICANS, RUSSIANS, CHINESE, GERMANS AND CZECHS. Munich: Radio Free Europe, 1969. 64p. 78-387177.

Report based on a survey of 839 Polish nationals interviewed between October, 1966 and April, 1967. Most were either tourists or guests. Illustrations.

### Religious Conditions

1454. Braun, Jerzy, comp. and ed. POLAND IN CHRISTIAN CIVILIZATION. London: Veritas Foundation Publication Centre, 1985. 633p. MiU: HN39.P7P6411.

Collective work of 32 studies. Many black-and-white illustrations of important events from paintings; also portraits. Articles written by Polish scholars in

Polish. Name of translator appears at end of each article. All topics covered are concerned with the Catholic Church throughout Polish history. Maps.

1455. Bujak, Adam. JOURNEYS TO GLORY--A CELEBRATION OF THE HUMAN SPIRIT, with text by Marjorie Young. New York: Harper and Row, 1976. 203p. 76-9953.

Photographs by Adam Bujak of celebrations of religious cults in Poland. A pictorial record of religious pilgrimages as they were recorded by Bujak, a professional photographer from Poland. Bibliography, p. 203.

1456. Divine Word Missionaries. THE WORD IN THE WORLD: POLAND AND THE MISSIONS, ed. by Patrick Connor. Techny, Ill.: Society of the Divine Word, 1980. 207p. OL: BV2240.P7D5.

A long personal narrative of the work of the Polish members of the Divine Word Missionaries' activities throughout the world. Numerous photographs in black-and-white and color. Portraits.

1457. Edwards, Charles E. PROTESTANTISM IN POLAND. Philadelphia: Westminster Press, 1901. 61p. 45-28090.

A brief sketch of the history of the Protestant Revolt in Poland. Includes a description of Protestant groups at the turn of the century. Some bibliographical references throughout the text.

1458. Fox, Paul. THE REFORMATION IN POLAND: SOME SOCIAL AND ECONOMIC ASPECTS. Baltimore: Johns Hopkins University Press, 1924. 153p. 35-1665.

Attempts to gather material of social and economic nature and to point out the underlying causes of the rise and spread of the Reformation in Poland were chiefly social and economic rather than religious or even purely political. Bibliography, pp. 149-150.

1459. Godden, Gertrude M. POLAND YESTERDAY, TODAY AND TO-MORROW. London: Burns, Oates, 1940. 129p. A41-878.

An interim account of conditions existing in Poland under Nazi and Soviet rule set in the necessary perspective of the past thousand years of Polish national life. Seemingly concerned with religious persecution. Contains a foreword by Cardinal Hinsley of Westminster.

1460. Graham, Robert Andrew, S.J. THE POPE AND POLAND IN WORLD WAR TWO. London: Veritas Foundation Publications Centre, 1968. 62p. 79-372136.

Scholarly summary of documents in Vatican archives entitled THE RELIGIOUS SITUATION IN POLAND AND THE BALTIC STATES, 1939-1945. Throws light on the situation of the Catholic Church in Poland during the German occupation, 1939-1945.

1461. Hełm-Pirgo, Marian. VIRGIN MARY, QUEEN OF POLAND, HISTORICAL ESSAY. New York: Polish Institute of Arts and Sciences in America, 1966. 32p. 66-3586.

A brief discussion of the role of the Virgin Mary in the history of the Polish nation. Contains a black-and-white illustration of Our Lady of Grace in Lwów of Józef Szalc-Wolfowicz. Illustrations. Portraits. Maps. Bibliography, p. 33.

1462. Kot, Stanisław. SOCINIANISM IN POLAND, trans. by Earl Morse Wilbur. Boston: Starr King Press, 1957. 226p. 57-12746.

The social and political ideas of the Polish Anti-Trinitarians in the sixteenth and seventeenth centuries. Book deals with one important phase of the history of a religious body.

1463. Lanckorońska, Karolina. STUDIES ON THE ROMAN-SLAVONIC RITE IN POLAND. Rome: Pontifical Institute of Oriental Studies, 1961. 194p.

Covers several aspects of the problem of the use of the Slavonic language in the Roman rite in Poland with a special stress on the traces of a struggle between Latin and Slavonic rites in Poland. Covers an eight-year period. Illustrations. Maps. Bibliography, pp. 173-183.

1464. McLaren, Moray. POLAND'S THOUSAND YEARS, THE VANGUARD OF CHRISTENDOM. London: Catholic Institute for International Relations, 1965. 62p. 67-53473.

To celebrate the birth of the Polish nation in the tenth century and turning of her people to Christianity and to the West and to give English-speaking readers in the United Kingdom a brief study for the theme of the Christian and Catholic Poland that developed from that huge date in her history. Highlights of religious history, i.e. Catholicism in Poland. Illustrations.

1465. Peszkowski, Zdzisław. POLAND'S ADVENTURE IN GRACE: ONE THOUSAND YEARS, 966-1966. Orchard Lake, Mich.: Orchard Lake Schools, 1966. 63p. 72-33970.

An historical review of the role of Christianity in Poland. Ranges far afield and includes a brief discussion of Polish Catholicism in the United States. Contains portraits of all Polish kings and queens. Unique feature is a hagiographical study of Polish saints and beati. Portraits of most of these saints and beati with list of their feast days. No date of publication given. Illustrations. Portraits. Maps. Bibliography, pp. 61-63.

1466. Piekarski, Adam. THE CHURCH IN POLAND: FACTS, FIGURES, INFORMATION. Warszawa: International Publication Service, 1978. 238p. 79-307380.

Sole aim is the systematic presentation of the activity of the Church in People's Poland and its historical conditioning. Written by a Polish layman. Illustrations. Bibliographical note, pp. 236-238.

1467. Pietrkiewicz, Jerzy M. THE THIRD ADAM: THE MARIAVITE EXPERIMENT IN MYSTICAL MARRIAGE. London: Oxford University Press, 1975. 243p. 76-350380.

An exhaustive account, well illustrated with black-and-white photographs of the Mariavite sect. Centers on the one responsible for the founding of the sect, Archbishop Kowalski. A sympathetic account of a very touchy subject. Illustrations. Portraits. Bibliography, pp. 233-234.

1468. POLAND'S MILLENIUM OF CATHOLICISM. Lublin: Scientific Society of the Catholic University, 1969. 626p.

*Special Works* 323

An historical development of the Polish Christian community over a thousand years. In English, French, and German. Illustrations.

1469. Polish Research Centre. London. THE ORTHODOX EASTERN CHURCH IN POLAND: PAST AND PRESENT. Ditchling, Hassocks, Sussex, Eng.: Ditchling Press, Ltd., 1942. 49p. 43-4080.

An historical sketch of the Orthodox Church in Poland up to 1939. Bibliography facing p. 1.

1470. Polish Research Centre. London. THE PROTESTANT CHURCHES IN POLAND. London: Polish Research Centre, 1944. 66p. A44-2348.

A short and unvarnished account of the rise of the Reformation movement in Poland at the middle of the sixteenth century, of its sudden decline, of the vicissitudes through which the Lutheran and Calvinist Churches went during three and a half centuries, and of the position they enjoyed in the restored commonwealth in our own day, i.e. 1944. Bibliography, pp. 64-66.

1471. Pollard, Albert F. THE JESUITS IN POLAND. New York: Haskell House Publishers, 1971. 98p. 76-116799.

Reprint of the 1892 edition. An historical essay about the work of the Society of Jesus in Poland from the time of the Counter-Reformation to the suppression of the order in 1773. Documented. Includes bibliographical references.

1472. Radio Free Europe. Research and Analysis Department. THE POPE IN POLAND. Munich, West Germany: Radio Free Europe Research, 1979. 128p.

This booklet contains analyses of and reports on Pope John Paul II's visit to Poland in June, 1979. Illustrations.

1473. Strzelec, Karol W. THE BURNING BUSH: TRIALS AND HOPE OF THE POLISH PEOPLE. Chicago: Church Publishing House, 1917. 36p. 18-8655.

Mostly a pamphlet describing the birth, growth and development of the Baptist Church among the Poles in

Poland but principally in the United States. Numerous black-and-white illustrations. Describes modern Protestantism in Poland including the Mariavites. Portraits.

1474. Szajkowski, Bogdan. NEXT TO GOD--POLAND; POLITICS AND RELIGION IN CONTEMPORARY POLAND. London: F. Pinter, 1983. 264p. 83-40151.

An analysis of church and state relations in Poland since 1945. Centers on Polish Roman Catholic hierarchy, especially the Polish Primates, Wydzynski and Glemp, and Pope John Paul II. Bibliography, pp. 249-251.

1475. Tazbir, Janusz. A STATE WITHOUT STAKES: POLISH RELIGIOUS TOLERATION IN THE SIXTEENTH AND SEVENTEENTH CENTURIES, trans. by A.T. Jordan. New York: Twayne Publishers, 1967. 232p.

Translation of essays published in Polish in 1966 and treats the subject of religious tolerance during the sixteenth and seventeenth centuries. It also presents political, social and economic aspects. Special attention to Polish ideas of religious tolerance, particularly the doctrine of the Polish Anti-Trinitarians. Contains bibliographical references. Illustrations.

1476. Walicki, Jerzy. RELIGIOUS LIFE IN POLAND, trans. by Lech Zembrzuski. Warszawa: Interpress Publishers, 1970. 82p. 79-278334.

A brief review of religious conditions in Poland, all religions are treated from the Roman Catholic Church to the Muslims. Illustrations.

Russian Occupation, 1939-1945

1477. Grudzinska-Gross, Irena, ed. WAR THROUGH CHILDREN'S EYES: THE SOVIET OCCUPATION OF POLAND AND THE DEPORTATIONS, 1939-1941, ed. and comp. by Irena Grudzinska-Gross and Jan Tomas Gross; trans. by Ronald Strom and Dan Rivers. Stanford, Cal.: Hoover Institution Press, 1981.

Consists of 120 essays selected from compositions written by students from the Bialystok, Lwów,

Nowogród, Polesie, Stanisławów, Tarnopol, Wilno and Wołyn Wojewodships all situated in that part of interwar Poland invaded and occupied by the Soveit Russians in 1939. The essays describe their experiences vividly. Based on documents contained in Hoover Institution on War, Revolution and Peace at Stanford, California. Contains facsimiles of essays. Illustrations. Maps. Bibliography, pp. 255-256.

Social Conditions

1478. Ehrlich, Stanisław, ed. SOCIAL AND POLITICAL TRANSFORMATIONS IN POLAND. Warszawa: PWN-Polish Scientific Publishers, 1964. 329p. 65-56481.

A collection of essays on the social and political changes which have occurred in Poland during the postwar years. All essays were written by Polish scholars.

1479. Galeski, Bogusław. BASIC CONCEPTS OF RURAL SOCIOLOGY, trans. by H.C. Stevens. Manchester, Eng.: Manchester University Press, 1972. 209p. 73-82603.

Deals with post-war experiences; influences of Russian and Marxist writing. Includes basic characteristics of peasant farming followed by an outline of the main types of farming to be found in contemporary Poland. Occupational activity of peasant farmer is examined; peasant family and village community; status; changes; new attitudes towards farming. Concludes with an examination of the adequacy of traditional Marxist theory for an understanding of contemporary Polish rural society.

1480. Gorecki, Jan. DIVORCE IN POLAND: A CONTRIBUTION TO THE SOCIOLOGY OF LAW. The Hague: Mouton, 1970. 156p. 77-102956.

Considerations are of a monographic character; they are based mainly on an examination of a part of the practices of the Kraków Court and of some fragments of the practice of their divorce courts.

1481. Gross, Feliks. THE POLISH WORKER, A STUDY OF A SOCIAL STRATUM. New York: Roy Publishers, 1945. 274p. 45-5734.

Aim of this book is to contribute to a knowledge of the labor movements in Poland within the framework of Europe. The first chapter deals with the social history of the Polish proletariat. The subsequent chapters discuss the sociological structure of the Polish proletariat, its economic condition, Polish labor legislation, and the social milieu of Polish workers, as illustrated in excerpts from workers' memoirs. A special chapter is devoted to the situation of the Polish proletariat under Nazi occupation, while the concluding chapter surveys the present-day situation of the Polish working class.

1482. Grot-Kwasniewski, Jerzy. SOCIETY AND DEVIANCE IN COMMUNIST POLAND, trans. by Margaret Wilson. Warwickshire: Berg Publishers, 1984. 210p. MiU: HM291. G683.

A collection of studies about social deviance in contemporary Poland. Studies based upon sociological data collected and listed in the bibliography. Contains a chapter entitled "Do the Italians have a different attitude to deviance from the Poles?" Bibliography, pp. 201-210.

1483. Hann, C.M. A VILLAGE WITHOUT SOLIDARITY, POLISH PEASANTS IN YEARS OF CRISIS. New Haven: Yale University Press, 1985. 208p. 81-52242.

Study of life in the small village of Wisłak situated in the foothills of the Lower Beskid mountains of southeastern Poland. Covers history of the village, the public sector, administration and politics, religion, secular ideology and socialization, and family, neighbourhood and village. Illustrations. Portraits. Maps. Bibliography, pp. 203-204.

1484. Kąkol, Każimierz. SOCIAL RIGHTS AND FACILITIES IN POLAND. Warszawa: Polonia Publishing House, 1959. 91p. 59-51199.

A survey of workers' rights at work, the rights of women and young people, the system of insurance and social assistance and family rights as of the end of 1958. Illustrations.

1485. Kąkol, Każimeirz. THE SOCIAL SECURITY SYSTEM IN PO-
LAND. Warszawa: Polonia Publishing House, 1966.
59p. 68-48982.

Survey of development of a system from social insurance to a system of social security. Discusses social insurance, social assistance, socialized medical care and prospects of the social security systems as of 1966. Includes tables and charts. Illustrations.

1486. Kolaja, Jiri T. A POLISH FACTORY; A CASE STUDY OF WORKERS' PARTICIPATION IN DECISION MAKING. Lexington: University of Kentucky Press, 1960. 157p. 60-13713.

On the basis of interview data we see how the workers regard their work, factory management, and the agencies theoretically designed to serve their interests. Author's observational reports on workers' council meetings.

1487. Kozicki, Stanisław. THE SOCIAL EVOLUTION OF POLAND IN THE NINETEENTH CENTURY. London: Hodder and Stoughton, 1918. 40p. 18-22143.

Lectures delivered at University College, London, on May 10, 17 and 24, 1918. Titles of lectures were: Social Structure of Independent Poland; Rise of the Peasantry; Growth of the Middle and Working Classes.

1488. Lane, David S., ed. SOCIAL GROUPS IN POLISH SOCIETY, ed. by David Lane and George Kolankiewicz. New York: Columbia University Press, 1973. 380p. 73-158030.

The subject of this book is the study of social groups in Poland. Includes a general introduction to the changing social, political and economic structure of Poland, both before and after the foundation of the People's Republic of Poland. Follows a series of studies of individual social groups, i.e. working class, peasantry and intelligentsia. Illustrations. Maps. Bibliography, pp. 349-365.

1489. Majkowski, Władysław. PEOPLE'S POLAND: PATTERNS OF SOCIAL INEQUALITY AND CONFLICT. Westport, Conn.: Greenwood Press, 1985. 234p. 84-15689.

An examination of the problem of class in a Soviet-type society, i.e. Poland. Analysis concentrated on four Polish workers' upheavals: June, 1956 in Poznań; December, 1970 in the northern cities of the Baltic coast; June, 1976 in Radom and Ursus; and August, 1980 in Gdańsk and then throughout the country. Illustrations. Bibliography, pp. 215-226.

1490. Matejko, Alexander.   SOCIAL CHANGE AND STRATIFICATION IN EASTERN EUROPE:   AN INTERPRETATIVE ANALYSIS OF POLAND AND HER NEIGHBORS.  New York:  Praeger, 1974.  272p.  74-9424.

Book based not only on sociological investigations done by author, his students, and professional colleagues, but also on personal experience. Bibliography, pp. 225-264.

1491. Ossowski, Stanisław.  CLASS STRUCTURE IN THE SOCIAL CONSCIOUSNESS, trans. by Sheila Patterson.  New York: Free Press of Glencoe, 1963.  202p.  63-13183.

A sociological treatise which reflects in various respects the conditions prevailing in Poland which affected the manner in which the problems were presented.

1492. Pirages, Dennis.   MODERNIZATION AND POLITICAL-TENSION MANAGEMENT:  A SOCIALIST SOCIETY IN PERSPECTIVE; CASE STUDY OF POLAND.  New York:  F. Praeger, 1972. 260p.  70-180850.

Study of the effects of industrialization on Polish society using contemporary Poland as a laboratory. Author collected data while enrolled in University of Warszawa, Department of Sociology.  Contains many tables.  Study is one product of a collective research effort by Stanford University Studies of the Communist system.  Bibliography, pp. 253-260.

1493. Radio Free Europe.  Audience Research Department. POLAND'S NEW GENERATION; AN ATTEMPT AT A SOCIOLOGICAL DESCRIPTION AND ANALYSIS.  Munich:  Radio Free Europe, 1963.  213p.  63-42715.

Sociological analysis of a defined group as it existed at the time the research was done in 1963 and prior thereto. In mimeographed form. Bibliographical references throughout.

1494. Sebastian, Tim. NICE PROMISES. London: Chatto & Windus, 1985. 225p. NjP: HN537.5.S42.

 Author is BBC correspondent. Writes of his impressions of social conditions in Poland from May, 1979 to 1981 while stationed there.

1495. Słomczynski, Każimierz, ed. CLASS STRUCTURE AND SOCIAL MOBILITY IN POLAND, ed. by K. Słomczynski and Tadeusz Krauze. White Plains, N.Y.: M.E. Sharpe, 1978. 211p. 78-56273.

 Ten contributions by Polish sociologists on transformation of class structure, social mobility and class consciousness and class interests. Also a bibliography on stratification processes in Poland from 1956-1976.

1496. Sokal, Franciszek. SOCIAL INSURANCE IN POLAND. Geneva: A. Kundig, 1925. 106p. 25-21303.

 A summary of what was done both legislatively and administratively in the sphere of social insurance in Poland between 1920 and 1925 by the then Minister of Labour and Social Welfare of the Republic of Poland. Includes 23 black-and-white illustrations of health care facilities and a map entitled, "Progress of Organization of Sickness Funds and Proportion of Beneficiaries to Total Population on 1st January 1925."

1497. THE STRIKES IN POLAND: AUGUST 1980, by Jan B. de Weydenthal et al; ed. by William F. Robinson. Munich: Radio Free Europe Research, 1980. 447p. NjP: HD5397.7.A6S78.

 A chronological description of the strikes beginning July 16, 1980 with a conflict between the workers and the government and ending on September 23, 1980. Includes biographical sketches of leading figures, e.g. Lech Wałęsa and documents related to the negotiations and the settlements.

1498. Szczepanski, Jan. POLISH SOCIETY. New York: Random House, 1970. 214p. 73-108924.

Intended as a guide to Polish society around 1970 for American undergraduate students who are interested in sociology and political science. Author compiled data from research done in Poland over last 23 years and from personal experiences in administration and political activity in the Polish Sejm and the People's Council. Written in the United States. Includes a sketch of Polish history. Illustrations. Maps. Includes bibliographical references.

1499. TOWARDS POLAND 2000, PROBLEMS OF SOCIAL DEVELOPMENT, ed. by Jan Danecki. Wrocław: Zakład Narodowy Imienia Ossolinskich, 1980. 281p. NjP: HN537.5. T68.

A panorama of views on social aspects of social development in Poland by various authors. Divided into four parts: social forecasting in Poland; social and cultural framework; selected monographic studies; e.g. baby boom in Poland; and, spatial problems.

1500. Znaniecki, Florian. THE SOCIOLOGY OF THE STRUGGLE FOR POMERANIA. Toruń: Baltic Institute, 1934. 58p. 38-32313.

Author discusses the thousand years' conflict between the Poles and the Germans in Pomorze from a sociological point of view. He then goes on to discuss Poland's new social forces.

## Social Life and Customs

1501. Adams, Dorothy. WE STOOD ALONE. New York: Longmans, Green and Co., 1944. 284p. 44-6780.

An American woman, wife of the son of the rector of Kraków University, describes her European studies, her marriage, the death of her husband in a plane accident and her return to America with her young son at the beginning of the Second World War. The book also gives a picture of the life and customs in Poland during the period between the two wars. Illustrations. Portraits.

1502. Benet, Sula. SONG, DANCE, AND CUSTOMS OF PEASANT POLAND. London: D. Dobson, 1951. 247p. 52-1358.

Life of the Polish peasantry in its ritual and symbolic aspects by an ethnologist up through World War II as seen from the intellectual life at a Polish university, Warszawa, and from the life of an American university, Columbia. Author did field work among peasants 1930-1931. Illustrations.

1503. Chrypinski, Anna, ed. POLISH CUSTOMS. Detroit: Friends of Polish Art, 1972. 40p.

A rudimentary survey of Polish holiday customs as interpreted by members of the Friends of Polish Art. Attempts to describe only the most familiar Polish holidays. No real historical context so reader unable to determine whether customs relate to old Poland, contemporary Poland or to practices among Polish Americans. Illustrations.

1504. Heine, Marc E. THE POLES: HOW THEY LIVE AND WORK. New York: Praeger Publishers, 1975. 167p. 75-27494.

Comprehensive study including historical introduction to modern Poland and covers all aspects of life in contemporary Poland: People, language, religion, government, industry, agriculture, trade, housing, education, welfare services, culture, leisure activities, food and drink. Illustrations. Maps. Bibliography, pp. 164-165.

1505. Konopko, Jona. DUST OF OUR BROTHERS' BLOOD; A TALE OF POLAND, ed. by Earle C. Calhoun. Washington, D.C.: White Eagle Press, 1941. 307p. 41-6797.

Reminiscences in the form of vignettes depicting the author's childhood and early adult life in Poland before World War II, during the Republic as well. Illustrations.

1506. LePlay Society. POLISH STUDIES, ed. by A. Davies. London: LePlay Society, 1934. 66p. NN: BAC p.v. 251.

Study of Polish peasants particularly in the Tatra Mountain region. Rather scholarly observations made and included in text are valuable charts, e.g. anthropological survey of peasants of Biały Donajec. Numerous candid photographs of peasants and their life styles. Bibliography, pp. 66.

1507. Lorenc-Kot, Bogna. CHILD-REARING AND REFORM: A STUDY OF THE NOBILITY IN EIGHTEENTH-CENTURY POLAND. Westport, Conn.: Greenwood Press, 1985. 170p. 84-25203.

A scholarly account of men, women, and children in their roles as family members of the nobility in eighteenth-century Poland. Bibliography, pp. 148-158.

1508. Newman, Bernard. THE PEOPLE OF POLAND. London: Polish Publications Committee, 1943. 32p. CtY.

A brief description of inter-war Poland by a popular lecturer. Written for the British public. Illustrations. Portraits.

1509. Pack, Martin A. COSTUMES AND DANCES OF POLAND. Grosse Pointe Park, Mich.: American Council of Polish Cultural Clubs, 1978. Unpaged.

Booklet of six selected costumes and dances representing both national and regional considerations: polonez, Mazur, Kujawiak, oberek, Krakowiak and taniec goralski. Contains scores with libretti in Polish. Colored and black-and-white illustrations. Maps.

1510. Peterson, Virgilia. POLISH PROFILE. New York: Carrick and Evans, 1940. 319p. 40-9195.

A pessimistic tale of interwar Poland as viewed by the wife of a Polish prince, her adjustment to a feudal society, and finally the coming of the war and flight across the border.

1511. Polanie Club. Mineapolis. TREASURED POLISH CHRISTMAS CUSTOMS AND TRADITIONS, CAROLS, DECORATIONS AND A CHRISTMAS PLAY. Minneapolis: Polanie Club, 1972. 198p. 72-83746.

Collection of descriptions of the various Polish Christmas customs and how their observations are made, Christmas music including words and plans of decorations. Illustrations. Bibliography, p. 198.

1512. Slomka, Jan. FROM SERFDOM TO SELF-GOVERNMENT: MEMOIRS OF A POLISH VILLAGE MAYOR, 1842-1927, trans. by William J. Rose. London: Minerva Publishing Co., Ltd., 1941. 274p. A41-4956.

*Special Works* 333

Memoirs of the mayor of Dzików, a peasant village near Tarnobrzeg. An insight into the daily lives of the peasants during the period, 1842-1927. Author was born in 1842.

1513. Wedel, Janine. THE PRIVATE POLAND: A CONTEMPORARY SOCIAL HISTORY. New York: Facts on File Publications, 1986. 230p. 84-24731.

Impressions of Poland and her people gathered while the author was a member of a music group which toured Poland, later as a tourist and finally as a doctoral candidate in anthropology at the University of Warszawa, a total of three years, between 1977 and 1986. Illustrations. Bibliography, pp. 223-226.

1514. Zand, Helen S. POLISH PROVERBS. Scranton, Penn.: Polish American Journal, 1961. 54p. 61-1289.

A collection of proverbs in Polish with their English translations. Included are only those proverbs which are of purely Polish origin or which constitute an interesting variant of a universal proverb. Sources are author's own recollections, Polish authors, Polish language textbooks and newspapers and friends. Biographical sketch of author and her portrait appears at the beginning of the book.

## Socialism

1515. Blit, Łucjan. THE ORIGINS OF POLISH SOCIALISM. Cambridge: Cambridge University Press, 1971. 160p. 70-152642.

The history and ideas of the first Polish Socialist Party, 1878-1886. This book tells the story of the pioneers of Polish Marxism and international socialism based mainly on the manifestoes, political tracts and the three periodicals which they published during their short period of activity. Documentation of their activities prepared by gendarmerie for the Third Department in St. Petersburg and memoirs of leaders and members who escaped. First part of a large work to be a history of the Polish Marxist movement. Bibliography, pp. 154-155.

1516. Brock, Peter. POLISH REVOLUTIONARY POPULISM: A STUDY IN AGRARIAN SOCIALIST THOUGHT FROM THE 1830S TO THE 1850S. Toronto: University of Toronto Press, 1977. 113p. 77-2840.

This monographic study describes the activities and conflicting ideologies of the various organizations, abroad and in partitioned Poland, which were struggling for national independence and for agrarian and social reform. An historical study of an aspect of socialist thought in Poland known as populism. Bibliography, pp. 115-119.

1517. Kowalak, Tadeusz, ed. CO-OPERATIVES IN PEOPLE'S POLAND: SELECTED SOCIO-ECONOMIC PROBLEMS. Warszawa: Publishing House of the Central Agricultural Union of Co-Operatives, "Peasant Self-Aid," 1970. 171p.

This book contains summaries of articles included in a large collective work that was published in 1969 and successive tenth volume of the Library of Co-Operative Research Institute.

1518. Naimark, Norman M. A HISTORY OF THE "PROLETARIAT:" THE EMERGENCE OF MARXISM IN THE KINGDOM OF POLAND, 1870-1887. New York: Columbia University Press, 1979. 329p. 78-75248.

This book reconstructs the history of the "Proletariat" 1882-1886 and explores the national history of Poles in the Kingdom of Poland, in European Russia and in the borderlands of the Ukraine, Belorussia and Lithuania between 1863 and the early 1890s and how the Polish industrial revolution recast the social and economic life of the Congress Kingdom to the point where the working class would stand at the center of any subsequent internal solution to the Polish Question. Bibliography, pp. 311-324.

1519. Trepczynski, Stanisław. SOCIALISM AND NATIONAL DEVELOPMENT. Warszawa: Interpress Publishers, 1971. 129p. 73-163399.

A discussion of the evolution of socialism in Poland: Polish experiences, history of the controversy on the essence of democracy and realities of socialist development in Poland.

*Special Works* 335

## Solidarność

1520. Albright, Madeleine K. POLAND, THE ROLE OF THE PRESS IN POLITICAL CHANGE. New York: Praeger Scientific, 1983. 147p. 83-16144.

   Author's insights about forces at work during Solidarity period. Analysis of the Polish press during the days of dual power in Poland. Bibliographical notes, pp. 134-147.

1521. Andrews, Nicholas G. POLAND 1980-1981: SOLIDARITY VERSUS THE PARTY. Washington, D.C.: National Defense University Press, 1985. 351p. 84-601067.

   A portrayal of the events which led to martial law and the banning of Solidarity by a senior Foreign Service Officer of the United States government stationed in Poland at the time. Focus is on the struggle between Solidarność and the Polish Communist Party. The roles of the Catholic Church, the U.S.S.R., and other nations are also considered. Includes a chronology for period July 1, 1980 to December 13, 1981. Illustrations. Portraits. Maps.

1522. Craig, Mary. THE CRYSTAL SPIRIT: LECH WAŁĘSA AND HIS POLAND. London: Hodder and Stoughton, 1986. 320p. 87-B8945.

   Author attempts "to present the story of Poland in the last troubled half-century in an easy-to-read form" and "to give some idea of what the Polish experience has been this most troubled of centuries" and "to clear up some of the many misunderstandings which prevail in the West." Emphasizes Wałęsa and his Poland. Illustrations. Portraits. Maps. Bibliography, pp. 308-310.

1523. Dobbs, Michael. POLAND: SOLIDARITY: WAŁĘSA, by M. Dobbs, K.S. Karol and Dessa Trevisan. New York: McGraw-Hill Book Co., 1981. 128p. 81-6063.

   An account of the development of the Solidarność movement divided into three parts: Why Poland? Background to Crisis' The Peaceful Revolution; and Lech Wałęsa, Symbol of the Polish. August. Journalistic in style. Illustrations. Portraits. Maps.

1524. Eringer, Robert. STRIKE FOR FREEDOM: THE STORY OF LECH WAŁESA AND POLISH SOLIDARITY. New York: Dodd, Mead & Co., 1982. 177p. 81-12978.

Story of the sixteen months during which Solidarność predominated over Polish politics. It is also the story of Solidarność's leader, Lech Wałęsa. Written by an American journalist based in London. Illustrations. Portraits. Maps.

1525. Garton Ash, Timothy. THE POLISH REVOLUTION: SOLIDIARITY. New York: Charles Scribner's Sons, 1984. 388p. 83-20335.

Author was present at the Lenin shipyards in Gdańsk during the 1980 strike which preceded the creation of a Solidarity movement. Presents a scholarly narrative history of the movement. Includes a chronology which covers Polish history from 966 to 1980 and then a rather detailed list of events beginning with February, 1980 and ending on December 13, 1982 when martial law was suspended. Maps. Bibliography, pp. 371-374.

1526. MacShane, Denis. SOLIDARITY: POLAND'S INDEPENDENT TRADE UNION. Nottingham: Spokesman, 1981. 172p. 81-165158.

An account which explains the trade union work of Solidarność. Concentrates on industrial Solidarity and the industrial working class. Information obtained from Polish workers themselves.

\* Mur, Jan, pseud. A PRISONER OF MARTIAL LAW; POLAND, 1981-1982. Cited above as item 1173.

1527. POLICY AND POLITICS IN CONTEMPORARY POLAND, REFORM, FAILURE AND CRISIS, ed. by Jean Woodall. New York: St. Martin's Press, 1982. 200p. 81-47980.

The central theme of this book is to provide the reader with some logical explanation of the turbulent sequence of events in Poland since the summer of 1980 and to evaluate their significance in the context of the political reform and policy innovation that took place in Poland after 1970. Consists of a series of essays by specialists in Polish political, social and economic life.

*Special Works* 337

1528. Potel, Yean-Yves. THE SUMMER BEFORE THE FROST: SOLI-
DARITY IN POLAND, trans. by Phil Markham. London:
Pluto Press, 1982. 229p. MiU: DK4440.P843.

Presents an eye-witness rendering of the early moments of revolution in 1980 in Poland. Also includes author's personal assessment of the defeat of this revolution with the army take-over in December, 1981. Contains "Notes on People and Organization, pp. 221-226; and a Chronology of Events, pp. 227-228." Maps.

1529. SOLIDARITY: THE ANALYSIS OF A SOCIAL MOVEMENT:
POLAND, 1980-1981, by Alan Touraine et al, trans. by
David Denby. Cambridge: Cambridge University
Press, 1983. 203p. 83-1859.

Study is a sociological intervention. Result of a dialogue between self-analysis of militant members of the Solidarność movement and interpretations of the Franco-Polish team of researchers. Covers period with April-November, 1981. Map. Bibliography, pp. 202-203.

1530. Staniskis, Jadwiga. POLAND'S SELF-LIMITING REVOLUTION.
Princeton, N.J.: Princeton University Press, 1984.
325p. 82-61387.

Author, a consultant to the Gdańsk strike leaders during the August 1980 negotiations, offers an explanation of the political dynamics that led to the Polish revolution and the birth of Solidarity in 1980 and 1981 along with an extremely important analysis of postwar East Central Europe.

1531. Starski, Stanisław. CLASS STRUGGLE IN CLASSLESS
POLAND. Boston: South End Press, 1982. 263p. 82-80691.

Author was invited by the publisher to write a book describing and analyzing the events surrounding the Polish workers' struggle in 1980. Covers events from a Polish perspective in journalistic style up to the declaration of martial law in December 1981. Purpose was to provide an analysis of what was actually taking place in Poland. Illustrations. Portraits.

1532. Szymański, Leszek. CANDLE FOR POLAND, 469 DAYS OF SOLIDARITY. San Bernardino, Calif.: Borgo Press, 1982. 128p. 81-1231.

Critical look at the situation in Poland through December, 1981. Also, collection of basic documents, many translated into English from the original Polish texts. Includes brief biographical sketches of important personages, pp. 120-121. Bibliography, p. 119.

1533. Teschner, Józef. THE SPIRIT OF SOLIDARITY, trans. by Marek B. Zaleski and Benjamin Fiore. San Francisco: Harper & Row, 1984. 126p. 83-48988.

The author, a Polish priest, shows the reader the roots and principles of Solidarność and suggests that the movement spans geographic, religious, national, and economic borders.

1534. Weschler, Lawrence. SOLIDARITY, POLAND IN THE SEASON OF ITS PASSION. New York: Simon and Schuster, 1982. 221p. 81-671.

An American journalist's vivid report of the events in Poland between May, 1981 through December 27, 1981. Contains a chronology and the "21 demands which the Interfactory Strike Committee presented to government representatives on August 23, 1980 in Gdańsk, and which formed the basis for the negotiations in the agreements of August 31, 1980." Originally a series of reports for the NEW YORKER. Illustrations. Portraits. Maps.

Sports

1535. Sieniarski, Stefan. SPORT IN POLAND. Warszawa: Interpress Publishers, 1976. 179p. 73-121647.

A general description of all aspects of sports and athletic competition with particular attention being paid to Olympic material. Contains numerous photographs, some in color. Also includes various statistical tables, e.g. "Best Polish Sportsmen and Women," pp. 14-15. Portraits.

## Statistics

1536. Poland. Central Statistical Office. CONCISE STATIS-
TICAL YEARBOOK OF POLAND. Warszawa: International
Publications Service, 1949. v. 49-25078.

Contains the basic information on the country's
socioeconomic development. Also covers all aspects of
national life with the exception of religion.

## Tales

1537. Anstruther, Fay S. OLD POLISH LEGENDS. Glasgow: The
Polish Library, 1945. 66p. A47-388.

English translation of eleven old Polish tales.
Illustrations.

1538. Benecke, Else C.M., trans. MORE TALES BY POLISH AU-
THORS, trans. by E.C.M. Benecke and Marie Busch.
New York: Longmans, Green and Co., 1916. 288p.
A17-369.

Contents: MACIEJ THE MAZUR, by Adam Szymanski. TWO
PRAYERS by Adam Szymanski. THE TRIAL by Władysław
Reymont. THE STRONGER SEX by Stefan Żeromski. THE
CHUKCHEE by W. THE RETURNING WAVE by Bolesław Prus.

1539. Benecke, Else C.M., trans. SELECTED POLISH TALES,
trans. by E.C.M. Benecke and Marie Busch. New York:
Oxford University Press, 1921. 348p. 22-11595.

Contents: THE OUTPOST by Bolesław Prus. A PINCH OF
SALT by Adam Szymanski. KOWALSKI THE CARPENTER by
Adam Szymanski. FOREBODINGS by Stefan Żeromski. A
POLISH SCENE by Władysław Reymont. DEATH by Władysław
Reymont. THE SENTENCE by J. Kaden-Bandrowski.

1540. Bobak, Anna H. THE TRUMPET CALL FROM POLAND. Detroit:
Friends of Polish Art, 1984. 33p.

Six vignettes of Polish history incorporating the
legendary Hejnał. Illustrations.

1541. Borski, Lucia M., comp. GOOD SENSE AND GOOD FORTUNE,
and OTHER POLISH FOLK TALES, comp. and trans. by

L.M. Borski. New York: David McKay Co., 1970. 83p. 71-97804.

Twenty-three delectable tales from the most representative sources of Polish folklore depicting the humor, wit and cleverness of the people. Illustrations. Bibliography, p. 83.

1542. Borski, Lucia M., trans. THE GYPSY AND THE BEAR AND OTHER FAIRY TALES, trans. by L.M. Borski and Kate B. Miller. New York: Longmans, Green and Co., 1933. 129p. 33-27251.

Translation of Polish folklore for the juvenile reader but all can be appreciated by readers of all ages.

1543. Borski, Lucia M., trans. THE JOLLY TAILOR AND OTHER FAIRY TALES, trans. by L.M. Borski and Kate B. Miller. New York: Longmans, Green and Co., 1928. 28-25565.

Ten most representative of Polish folklore and fairy tales. Illustrations.

1544. Borski, Lucia M., trans. POLISH FOLK TALES. New York: Sheed & Ward, 1947. 123p. 47-12388.

A collection of Polish legends which the translator first heard in Poland where she spent her childhood. Later she told the stories to groups of children at the New York Public Library. These are sixteen tales, all known to Polish children, and all of a deeply religious nature. Illustrations.

1545. Brill, Edith. THE GOLDEN BIRD. New York: Frederick Watts, 1970. 151p. 69-14457.

A Polish fairy tale. Illustrations. Written and illustrated for the juvenile reader.

1546. Byrde, Elsie, trans. THE POLISH FAIRY BOOK. New York: J.B. Lippincott Company, 1925. 226p. 26-26142.

Free translation of twenty-three tales purportedly gleaned from oral traditions obtained from Polish sources. Illustrations.

Special Works                                                              341

1547. Coleman, Marion M. A BRIGAND, TWO QUEENS, AND A
      PRANKSTER; STORIES OF JANOSIK, QUEEN BONA, QUEEN
      KINGA AND SAWIZDRZAL. Cheshire, Conn.: Cherry Hill
      Books, 1972. 77p. 72-80394.

      Several Polish folk tales as told by the author in
      English translation.

1548. Coleman, Marion M. THE MAN ON THE MOON: THE STORY OF
      PAN TWARDOWSKI. Cheshire, Conn.: Cherry Hill Books,
      1971. 54p. 77-155638.

      An English version by the author of the Polish man
      on the moon known as Pan Twardowski.

1549. Coleman, Marion M. VISTULA VOYAGE; LORE OF THE POLISH
      MOTHER OF WATERS. Cheshire, Conn.: Cherry Hill
      Books, 1974. 92p. 73-82795.

      A collection of fifteen legends associated with the
      Wisła River. The book is divided into four sections
      and each section deals with a particular region
      through which the river flows.

1550. Coleman, Marion M., comp. A WORLD REMEMBERED: TALES
      AND LORE OF THE POLISH LANGUAGE. Cheshire, Conn.:
      Cherry Hill Books, 1965. 299p. 65-23439.

      Collection of several short tales based on oral
      accounts from Poles in the United States who heard
      them in Poland.

1551. Girling, Zoë, ed. POLISH FAIRY TALES. Chicago:
      Follett Publishing Company, 1968. 190p. 68-13806.

      Contains seventeen tales selected and retold for
      English-speaking children. Illustrated.

1552. Glinski, Antoni J. POLISH FAIRY TALES, trans. by
      Maude A. Biggs. New York: John Lane Company, 1920.
      96p. 21-658.

      Tales representing folklore of the eastern provinces
      of Poland and White Russia of extreme age, some of
      them dating back to primitive Aryan times. There is
      an apparent likeness between them and the folklore of
      other European nations and they are taken from a

larger collection made by A.J. Glinski. Explanatory appendix added by translator. Illustrations.

1553. Goldszmit, Henryk. MATTHEW, THE YOUNG KING. New York: Roy Publishers, 1945. 256p. 45-3237.

The author wrote this tale while director of an orphanage in Warszawa. It is a contemporary fable with a moral directed at the young reader. Illustrated.

1554. Gorska, Halina. PRINCE GODFREY, KNIGHT OF THE STAR OF NATIVITY, trans. by Roman Braun. New York: Roy Publishers, 1946. 206p. 46-7452.

Twelve wondrous stories of a Polish hero, Prince Godfrey, Knight of the Star of the Nativity, as told by the astrologer of his father's court. Twelve strange prophecies were made when the child was born. Twelve times they came true and none who was oppressed or in need of help ever failed to receive that help from Prince Godfrey. Illustrations.

1555. Kelly, Eric P. THE CHRISTMAS NIGHTINGALE: THREE CHRISTMAS STORIES FROM POLAND. New York: Macmillan and Company, 1932. p. 32-24676.

Three juvenile Christmas folk tales from Poland. Illustrated.

1556. McCrea, Lilian. POLISH FOLK TALES AND LEGENDS. London: Pitman & Sons, Ltd., 1959. 88p.

Seventeen of the most well-known and popular Polish tales and legends including Pan Twardowski. Illustrations.

1557. Maldzewski, Antoni. MARYA, A TALE OF THE UKRAINE, trans. by Arthur P. Coleman and Marion M. Coleman. Schenectady, N.Y.: Electric City Press, Inc., 1935. 75p. 36-3684.

A narrative poem of Poland.

1558. Uminski, Sigmund H. TALES OF EARLY POLAND. Detroit: Endurance Press, 1968. 100p. 67-30549.

A collection of legends. Illustrated.

*Special Works* 343

1559. Vencenz, Stanisław de. ON THE HIGH UPLANDS: SAGAS, SONGS, TALES AND LEGENDS OF THE CARPATHIANS, trans. by H.C. Stevens. New York: Roy Publishers, 1955. 344p. 55-9310.

Selections from Polish poetic prose. Illustrations.

1560. Wojciechowska, Maia. WINTER TALES FROM POLAND. Garden City, N.Y.: Doubleday and Co., 1973. 65p. 72-79885.

Includes eight tales, some original, some adapted from the folklore of Poland. Illustrations.

## Theater

1561. Csato, Edward. THE CONTEMPORARY POLISH THEATRE, trans. by Christina Cenkalska. Warszawa: Interpress Publishers, 1968. 34p. 69-129654.

A brief sketch of contemporary Polish theater that is twentieth century plays and playwrights with emphasis on the post-World War II period.

1562. Csato, Edward. THE POLISH THEATRE, trans, by Christina Cenkalska. Warszawa: Polonia Publishing House, 1963. 172p. 65-3833.

Some history. Directors and theaters, actors. Index of names and plays mentioned in text. Emphasis on development of directors and actors. Illustrations include portraits and scenes from plays. Especially useful retrospectively.

1563. Filler, Witold. CONTEMPORARY POLISH THEATRE. Warszawa: Interpress Publishers, 1977. 127p. 78-366672.

A history of Polish theater up to the end of the second world war. Also a discussion of theater in Poland during modern times. Includes a discussion of personalities as well as all aspects of theater. Numerous black-and-white photographs of scenes from plays. Bibliography, pp. 125-128.

1564. Goldfarb, Jeffrey C. THE PERSISTENCE OF FREEDOM: THE SOCIOLOGICAL IMPLICATIONS OF POLISH STUDENT THEATER. Boulder, Colo.: Westview Press, Inc., 1980. 159p. 79-5342.

A study of cultural freedom in a Polish Communist society. Based upon the author's participation in Polish student theater. Bibliography, pp. 153-159.

1565. Grotowski, Jerzy. TOWARDS A POOR THEATRE. New York: Simon and Schuster, 1968. 262p. 73-92200.

Articles by Grotowski, interviews with him and other supplementary material presenting his method and training. Description of style of Grotowski with plays and numerous illustrations.

1566. Szydłowski, Roman. THE THEATRE IN POLAND, trans. by Christina Cenkalska. Warszawa: Interpress Publishers, 1972. 176p. 72-169269.

Style of the Polish theatre, historical outline, the theater-yesterday and today, stage directors, stage designers, actors, theatrical geography, experiments and explorations, theatrical grass-roots, TV and radio theatre, and drama criticism. Illustrations. Portraits. Bibliography, pp. 173-176.

1567. TWENTIETH-CENTURY POLISH AVANT-GARDE DRAMA: PLAYS, SCENARIOS, CRITICAL DOCUMENTS ed. by Daniel Gerould. Ithaca, N.Y.: Cornell University Press, 1977. 287p. 76-13657.

Although the bulk of the work is devoted to translation of the plays and scenarios, the introduction is a description of avant-garde Polish drama. Includes works by Stanisław Ignacy Witkiewicz, and others. Illustrations. Bibliography, pp. 281-287.

### Transportation

1568. Taplin, Michael R. TRAMWAYS OF CZECHOSLOVAKIA AND POLAND. London: Light Railway Transport League, 1975. 44p.

A contemporary, popular, but thorough description of the various streetcar systems, with maps of Poland.

Includes cities of Bydgoszcz, Częstochowa, Elbląg, Gdańsk, Gorzów, Grudziądz, Katowice and environs, Kraków, Łodz, Poznań, Szczecin, Toruń and Warszawa, Wrocław. Contains streetcar rosters and route maps. Bibliography, p. 44.

## Warszawa--History--Uprising of 1943

1569. Ainsztein, Reuben. THE WARSAW GHETTO REVOLT. New York: Schocken Books, 1979. 238p. 79-118411.

    The first objective history of the Warsaw Ghetto revolt in the English language by one of the outstanding experts on the Jewish resistance in eastern Europe. Illustrations. Portraits of major participants. Maps. Bibliography, pp. 231-232.

1570. Kurzman, Dan. THE BRAVEST BATTLE: THE 28 DAYS OF THE WARSAW UPRISING. New York: G.P. Putnam's Sons, 1976. 386p. 76-2694.

    First attempt at a full-scale account of the 28-day armed uprising in the Warsaw Ghetto in 1943. Tried to tell the story through the participants focusing in particular on General Stroop and Mordechai Anielewicz. Extensive research and documentation. Illustrations. Portraits. Maps. Bibliography, pp. 369-386.

1571. Mark, Ber. UPRISING IN THE WARSAW GHETTO, trans. by Gershon Freidlin. New York: Schocken Books, 1975. 209p. 74-26913.

    Originally published in Poland in 1959. Author attempts to provide an historical background to the Uprising itself plus a day-by-day account of its actual unfolding. Contains documents of the Uprising. Illustrations. Maps. Bibliography, pp. 201-202.

1572. Shoskes, Henry. NO TRAVELER RETURNS, ed. by Curt Reiss. Garden City, N.Y.: Doubleday, Doran Co., Inc., 1945. 267p. 45-2282.

    An eyewitness account of the 1943 Uprising in Warszawa in the Ghetto based on the author's own experiences as well as documentary evidence by participants collected by the author. A history of the Ghetto from the beginning of occupation in 1939 to its destruction in 1943.

1573. Tushnet, Leonard. TO DIE WITH HONOR: THE UPRISING OF THE JEWS IN THE WARSAW GHETTO. New York: Citadel Press, 1965. 128p. 65-15488.

A survey of the Uprising of the Jews in 1943 in the Warsaw Ghetto based upon many sources, some secondary. It is not an eyewitness account. Author said he tried to simplify a complex situation. Maps. Bibliography, pp. 127-128.

Warszawa--History--Uprising of 1944

1574. Białoszewski, Miron. A MEMOIR OF THE WARSAW UPRISING, trans. by Madeline G. Levine. Ann Arbor, Mich.: Ardis, 1977. 234p. 78-300379.

A non-fictional work of literature which is deeply revisionist both in its presentation of the Warsaw Uprising and in its approach to the memoir genre. Portraits.

1575. Bogusławska, Anna. FOOD FOR THE CHILDREN, trans. by Ewa Barker. London: Leo Cooper, 1975. 201p. 76-266893.

The author's daughter translated the work written in Polish in 1947. It is the story of the lives of the people in a few streets on the boundary between the City Centre and the Riverside District during the moments of struggle. Maps.

1576. Bruce, George L. THE WARSAW UPRISING, 1 AUGUST--2 OCTOBER, 1944. London: Rupert Hart-Davis, Ltd., 1972. 224p. 72-195940.

The purpose of this book is to present the story of the Warsaw Uprising of 1 August 1944 and also to give some idea of the policies and of the people responsible for the events which made a heap of rubble out of one of Europe's finest cities and killed 250,000 people. Illustrations. Portraits. Maps. Bibliography, pp. 217-218.

*Special Works* 347

1577. Bytniewska, Irena. SILENT IS THE VISTULA: THE STORY
OF THE WARSAW UPRISING, trans. by Marta Erdman.
New York: Longmans, Green and Co., 1946. 275p.
46-5354.

    An account of the Warsaw Uprising of 1944 by a nurse.
    No documentation.

1578. Ciechanowski, Jan. THE WARSAW UPRISING OF 1944. New
York: Cambridge University Press, 1974. 332p. 73-
79315.

    Abridged and revised version of doctoral thesis for
    University of London. Purpose of study is to examine
    the political and ideological background of the Warsaw
    Rising and to trace the course of events which led to
    its outbreak. Not concerned with the rising itself.
    Study based primarily upon unpublished Polish docu-
    ments relating to the plans, aims and activities of
    the exiled authorities and leaders of the Underground
    state. It is also based on the author's interviews
    with and letters from highly-placed witnesses of the
    events and questions under examination. Through the
    Polish documents it is possible to trace the decisions
    and actions of the highest Polish authorities which
    culminated in the outbreak of the insurrection and to
    analyze their motives. Maps. Bibliography, pp. 316-
    325.

1579. Deschner, Gunther. WARSAW UPRISING. New York:
Ballantine Books, 1972. 157p. 72-183096.

    Illustrated history of the rising. Maps. Bibliog-
    raphy, p. 160.

1580. Hanson, Joanna K.M. THE CIVILIAN POPULATION AND THE
WARSAW UPRISING OF 1944. New York: Cambridge University Press, 1982. 345p. 81-15545.

    Based partly on primary sources in Poland and Great
    Britain. New look from a different angle. Includes
    an historical sketch of Warsaw during the Nazi occupa-
    tion, October, 1939 to July, 1944. Scholarly, careful
    approach. Illustrations. Portraits. Maps. Bibliog-
    raphy, pp. 322-336.

1581. Orpen, Neil. AIRLIFT TO WARSAW: THE RISING OF 1944.
Norman, Okla.: University of Oklahoma Press, 1984.
184p. 84-40277.

Story by a retired South African military officer
about the attempt of the Allied forces to arm and supply the Warsaw nationalists by an airlift. The author
also described the actual uprising. Illustrations.
Portraits.

1582. Rogala, Tadeusz. SEWERS OF WARSAW. New York:
Vantage Press, 1973. 215p.

A novel about the Warsaw Uprising of 1944. The
struggle of the Polish resistance and their prolonged
battle with the German army for the control of Warsaw.
Contains six major maps of areas under siege. Based
upon the author's recollection of the Warsaw Uprising
of 1944.

1583. Zagórski, Wacław. SEVENTY DAYS, trans. by John Welsh.
London: Frederick Muller, 1957. 276p.

An English translation of a Polish personal narrative of the activities of Captain Zagórski as member
of the Polish Home Army ordered to commence fighting
on August 1, 1944. Covers period from 30 July to
7 October 1944. Illustrations. Portraits. Maps.

1584. Zawodny, Janusz K. NOTHING BUT HONOUR: THE STORY OF
THE WARSAW UPRISING, 1944. Stanford, Calif.:
Hoover Institution Press, 1978. 328p. 76-51880.

Not only a history of the 1944 Warsaw Uprising but
also a comprehensive discussion of the origin and
development of the Polish Underground Army and the
complex factors leading to the decision by the Poles
to start an uprising. Illustrations. Portraits.
Bibliography, pp. 296-317.

## Wycinanki

1585. WYCINANKI/POLISH CUT-OUTS. Grosse Pointe, Mich.:
Friends of Polish Art, 1978. Unpaged.

*Special Works*

An explanation, history and description of Wycinanki, or Polish cut-outs. Includes many descriptions and patterns. Illustrations.

# AUTHOR INDEX

Abodaher, David J.   269, 354
Abrahall, Clare C.D.H.   214
Abucewicz, John A.   1322
Adamczewski, Jan   204, 462, 473
Adams, Dorothy   355, 1501
Agatstein, Mieczysław   301
Ainsztein, Reuben   1569
Albright, Madeleine K.   1520
Alcuin, pseud.   1
Algren, Nelson   1323
Allen, Frances N.   132-
Allen, Julian   1401
Alton, Thad P.   570, 571
Amorim, Enrique   1363
Anders, Władysław   93
Anderson, Herbert F.   512
Andrews, Nicholas G.   1521
Andrews, Theodore   1372
Anstruther, Fay S.   1537
Apenszlak, Jacob   932
Appleton, Edward T.   513
Archer, Jeffrey   1325
Arct, Bohdan   94, 95
Armitage, Angus   205, 206
Arnold, Stanisław   717
Arski, Stefan   404
Arthurton, Eileen A.   718
Ascherson, Neal   855
Askenazy, Szymon   405
Aszody, Ilona   1234
Augur, pseud.   See Poliakoff, Vladimir

Babel, Isaak E.   883
Babinski, Grzegorz   1224
Badura-Skoda, Paul   199
Baerlein, Henry P.B.   514
Baginski, Henryk   406, 407
Bailly, Rose   480

Bain, Robert N.   778
Bajcar, Adam   515
Bak, Bolesław   1373
Bakanowski, Adolf   1225
Baker, T.L.   1226, 1227
Balawyder, Aloysius   1207
Balicki, Stanisław W.   66, 908
Banach, Jerzy   125
Banasiewicz, Czesław Z.   See also Bielecki, Tadeusz
Bandrowski, Juliusz K.   816
Bankowsky, Richard   1326, 1327
Barbarski, Krzystztof   122
Barbey, Bruno   50
Barnett, Clifford R.   2
Bartelski, Lesław M.   400
Bartoszewski, Władysław   483, 933, 934, 935, 936
Baskerville, Beatrice C.   884
Batcheller, Tryphosa   300
Bates-Batcheller, Tryphosa. See Batcheller, Tryphosa
Bauman, Janina   937
Baxter, James H.   144
Beck, Józef   624
Benecke, Else C.M.   1538, 153 1539
Beneś, Vaclav L.   719
Benet, Sula   1502
Benson, Edward F.   1378
Berenstein, Tatiana   938
Berg, Mary   939
Bernard, Richard M.   1228
Bethell, Nicholas   230, 836
Betley, Jan A.   794
Betteridge, Don, pseud.   See Newman, Bernard
Bezwińska, Jadwiga   1132
Białecki, Tadeusz   482

Białoszewski, Miron 1574
Biddle, Anthony J.D. 625
Bidou, Henry 173
Bidwell, Charles E. 1069
Biegański, Witold 96, 97
Bielak, Stanisława Kostka,
 siostra 292
Bielasiak, Jack 1432, 1434
Bielecki, Maciej 553
Bielecki, Tadeusz 484
Bienkowska, Danuta. See
 Meeting Polish Writers
Bierut, Bolesław 572
Bigland, Eileen 215
Bilainkin, George 408
Birenbaum, Halina 940
Biskup, Marian 207
Biskupski, Mieczysław B.
 1285
Blanke, Richard 795
Blazynski, George 240, 856
Blejwas, Stanislaus A.
 1285, 1404
Blit, Łucjan 340, 1515
Blumer, Herbert 1229
Boand, Nell H. 779
Bobak, Anna H. 1540
Bochenski, Aleksander 904
Bochnak, Adam 124
Bogucka, Maria 771
Bogusławska, Anna 1575
Bolek, Francis 372, 1230,
 1231, 1294
Boleslavski, Richard 1144
Bor-Komoroski, Tadeusz. See
 Komorowski, Tadeusz
Borkowski, Joseph A. 1232
Borowik, Józef 471
Borski, Lucia M. 1541, 1542,
 1543, 1544
Borun, Thaddeus 1233
Borzykowski, Tuwie 941
Boswell, Alexander 516
Boucourechliev, Andre 174
Boyd, Louise A. 517
Bozyk, Paweł 573, 574
Brackmann, Albert 616

Brandes, Georg M.C. 518
Brandys, Kazimierz 1145
Brandys, Marian 1023
Brant, Irving 3, 4
Braun, Andrzej 485
Braun, Jerzy 1454
Brewster, Eva 1126
Bridgeport, Conn. University.
 Sociology Colloquium 1234
Brill, Edith 1545
Bristol, Helen O. 519
Broad, Pery 1127
Brock, Peter 796, 1516
Bromke, Adam 857, 1405
Bronowicz-Chylinska, Teresa
 384
Brooks, Sidney 817
Brożek, Andrzej 1235
Bruce, George L. 1576
Brumberg, Abraham 858
Bryan, Julien H. 486, 487
Brzeska, Maria 696
Buczek, Daniel S. 1400
Buczek, Karol 693
Budrewicz, Olgierd 5, 488,
 520, 1236
Budurowycz, Bohdan B. 627
Buell, Raymond L. 1406
Buffalo. University 302
Bujak, Adam 1455
Bujak, Franciszek 575, 942
Bulowczyk, John J. 1237
Burton, Katherine K. 366
Busch, Marie 1538
Bushnell, George H. 270
Butler, Ivan 1113
Bużiński, Józef 409
Byrde, Elsie 1546
Byron, May C. 175
Bytniewska, Irena 1577

Cameron, Charles O. 6
Cannon, Cornelia J. 1328
Cantrell, Rose 498
Cardwell, Ann Sue, pseud.
 See Super, Margaret Low
Carpenter, Niles 1238

Cary, William H.   859
Castle, William   1329
Cazin, Paul   521
Cegielka, Francis A.   387
Chase, Mary E.   1330
Checinski, Michael   1407
Chmielewski, Edward   1379
Chołoniewski, Antoni   721
Chrościcki, Juliusz A.   83
Chrypinski, Anna   1503
Ciborowski, Adolf   489
Ciborowski, Andrzej   490
Ciechanowski, Jan   628, 1578
Cienciala, Anna M.   629, 630
Cieplak, Tadeusz N.   1408
Clowes, Florence W.   1239
Coates, William P.   631
Coates, Zelda K.   631
Cohen, Israel   943
Coleman, Arthur P.   303, 312, 797, 798
Coleman, Marion M.   303, 304, 312, 313, 1099, 1100, 1547, 1548, 1549, 1550
Colonna, Bertram de.   See De Colonna, Bertram
Columbia University. Klub Polski.   1101, 1102
Contoski, Josepha K.   1024
Cook, Mabel   314
Coons, Joan   1331
Cornebise, Alfred E.   818
Corsi, Edward C.   722
Cortot, Alfred   176
Cottam, Kazimiera J.   297
Coulter, Charles W.   1240
Coutouvidis, John   837
Coxe, William   780
Craig, Mary   241, 1522
Csato, Edward   1561, 1562
Culinary Arts Institute   499
Curie, Eve   216
Curry Jane L.   1403
Cwikliński, Jan   219
Cynarski, Stanisław   208
Cynk, Jerzy B.   70, 71
Cyprian, Tadeusz   697
Czajkowski, Anthony P.   762

Czapski, Józef   1146
Czarnecka, Irena   620
Czarnecki, Jan   73
Czarnomski, Frances B   1147
Czarnowski, Adam   522
Czartoryski, Adam J.   220
Czech, Danuta   1132
Czechowski, Michael B.   723
Czerny, Zofia   500

D'Abernon, Edgar V.   819
Danecki, Jan   1499
Danilewicz, Maria   158
Datner, Szymon   839, 840
David, Janina   944, 945
Davies, Norman   145, 724, 725, 820
Day, William A.   1410
DeAngeli, Marguerite L.   1025
Debicki, Roman   632
De Colonna, Bertram   8
De Holewinski, Jan.   See Holewinski, Jan
Dennis, Geoffrey P.   606
Deschner, Gunther   1579
Detroit. Institute of Arts   126
Devlin, Kevin   860
DeVries, Peter   1332
Dewar, Diana   258
De Weydenthal, Jan   860, 1411, 1412, 1497
Divine Word Missionaries   1456
Dmochowski, Zbigniew   84
Dobbs, Michael   1523
Dobroszycki, Łucjan   946, 947
Dobrowolski, Marian   1075
Dobrowolski, Tadeusz   127
Dobrzycki, Jerzy   207
Dobrzynski, Wacław T.   9
Donald, Robert   410
Donat, Alexander   948
Doorly, Eleanor   217
Douglas, Paul F.   577
Dowie, Menie M.   523
Dragomir, V.   1148
Driscoll, Paul F.   1333

Drogosław, pseud. 10
Drożdżyński, Aleksander 411
Drzewieniecki, Walter M. 146, 412
Dubnov, Semen M. 949
Dumnicki, Juliusz 82
Dunham, Samuel A. 726
Dworaczyk, Edward J. 1241
Dużyk, Józef 474
Dyboski, Roman 11, 12, 13, 727, 728, 1083, 1084, 1149
Dzięcioł, Witold 763
Dziewanowski, Marian K. 342, 861, 1413

Edwards, Charles E. 1457
Edwards, Henry S. 799
Ehrlich, Stanisław 1478
Eisner, Jack 950
Elgoth-Ligocki, Edward 14, 15
Elisofon, Eliot 1026
Erhardt, Ludwik 1118
Eringer, Robert 1524
Eschstruth, Nataly von 607
Estes, Eleanor 1027
Etchegoyen, Olivier, comte d' 1150
Evans, Anthony W.W. 271
Evans, Geoffrey C. 772
Evans, Jon 698
Eversley, George J.S. 781

Faczyński, Jerzy 85
Falkowska, Maria 226
Falkowski, Mieczysław 579
Federowicz, J.K. 633
Feiwel, George R. 580
Feldman, Józef 413
Fenn, Ross S. 102
Ferber, Edna 1334
Ferderber-Salz, Bertha 1151
Fiedler, Arkady 99
Filinski, M. 1107
Filip, T.M. 1103
Filipowicz, Tytus 525
Filippi, Mary 186
Filler, Witold 1563

Fineman, Irving 1335
Firsoff, Valdemar A. 525
Fischer, LeRoy H. 232
Fisher, Harold H. 821
Fisher, Jack C. 463
Fisiak, Jacek 1070
Fiszman, Joseph R. 910
Fitzgibbon, Louis 1062
Folejewski, Zbigniew 221, 302
Folkmann, Adolf 951
Forni, Luigi 862
Fountain, Alvin M. 222
Fournier, Eva 527
Fox, Paul 1242, 1374, 1458
Francic, Miroslaw 1224
Frankel, Henryk 729
Friedel, Mieczysław W. 1243
Friedman, Philip 952
Frischauer, Paul 885
Fryde, Matthew M. 147
Fuchs, Karl H. 466
Fuchs, Werner 414
Fuksiewicz, Jacek 1115
Furcolo, Foster 1063

Gajda, Patricia A. 634
Galeski, Bogusław, 1479
Gardner, Monica M. 235, 273, 286, 305, 368, 528, 1028, 1085
Garland, John S. 635
Garliński, Józef 100, 1129
Gartner, Margarete, 467
Garton Ash, Timothy 1525
Gąsiorowski, Antoni 764
Gavoty, Bernard 177
Gawalewicz, Marjan 621
Gayre, George R. 74
Gazel, Stefan F. 1152
Gebaroff, Ara J. 1029
Gelsavage, John J. 1244
Gerould, Daniel 391, 1567
Gerson, Louis L. 1245
Gibney, Frank B. 863
Gide, André P.G. 178
Gielgud, Val H. 886, 887
Gielżyński, Wojciech 507

Giergielewicz, Mieczysław
  17, 369
Giertych, Jędrzej 18, 19,
  415, 1057
Gieysztor, Aleksander 730,
  731, 737
Gilbert, Martin 1130
Gilfond, Henry 322
Gillington, May Clarissa.
  See Byron, May C.
Gillis, Willie M. 1222
Ginter, Maria 1153
Girling, Zoë 1336, 1551
Giroud, Francoise 218
Glas-Wiener, Sheva 954
Glatstein, Jacob 1014, 1015
Glicksman, William M. 955
Glinski, Antoni J. 1552
Glinski, Matteo 179
Gnacinski, Jan 687
Gnorowski, S.J.B. 800
Godden, Gertrude M. 1459
Goetel, Ferdynand 956
Golab, Caroline 1246
Golawski, Michał 1032
Goldfarb, Jeffrey C. 911,
  1564
Goldstein, Bernard 957
Goldszmit, Henryk 227, 1553
Gömöri, George 327
Goodhart, Arthur L. 958
Gorczyński, Władysław 690
Gordon-Smith, Maria 189
Górecki, Jan 1480
Górecki, Roman 581
Górka, Olgierd A. 732
Gorska, Halina 1554
Gotlib, Henryk 128
Grabowski, John J. 1247
Grabski, Stanisław 637
Graham, Robert A. 1460
Gray, Eunice 1337
Great Britain. Foreign
  Office 20, 21, 22
Grace-Dąbrowska, Claire 186
Greely, John N. 1338
Grimsted, Patricia K. 733
Greene, Carol 1031

Gronowicz, Antoni 23, 180,
  274, 315, 316, 328, 529,
  639, 1032, 1033
Gross, Feliks 1481
Gross, Jan T. 699, 1477
Grossman, Mendel 959
Grosz, Wiktor 1415
Grot-Kwasnieski, Jerzy 1482
Groth, Alexander J. 1416
Grotowski, Jerzy 1565
Grove, William 822
Grudzinska-Gross, Irena 1477
Grudzinski, Tadeusz 765
Grzelonski, Bogdan 1248
Grzybowski, Każimierz 160
Gumkowski, Janusz 700
Gurney, Arthur E. 1381
Gutman, Ysrael 960
Gwiazdowska, Marie Ż. 961

Hadden, James C. 181
Hagen, William W. 1108
Haiman, Miecislaus 275, 276,
  277, 783, 1249, 1250, 1251,
  1252, 1253, 1254, 1255
Halecki, Oskar 24, 734, 735
Halicz, Emanuel 801
Hall, Adam, pseud. See
  Trevor, Elleston
Halpern, Ada 1154
Hamel, Joost van 416
Hamilton, F.E. 417
Hanley, Boniface 259
Hann, C.M. 1483
Hansen, Ernest R.B. 418
Hanson, Joanna K.M. 1580
Harjan, George 337
Harley, John H. 171, 736
Harrell, Jean G. 912
Harriman, Karl E. 1339
Harrow, Benjamin 225
Hart, Kitty 1131
Hayden, Joel B. 1256
Hartwig, Edward 475
Hayes, Florence 1340
Hebblethwaite, Peter 242
Hedley, Arthur 182
Heine, Marc E. 530, 1504

Heller, Celia S. 962
Hellman, Peter 1125
Hełm-Pirgo, Marian 1341, 1461
Henderson, N.W. 640
Hensel, Witold 75, 76
Herbert, Flight Lieutenant, pseud. See Meissner, Janusz
Herling, Gustaw 1155
Hersey, John R. 1016
Heymann, Frederick G. 823
Hilberg, Raul 963
Hill, Ninian 1382
Hill, Robert F. 1257
Hindus, Maurice G. 1342
Hine, Daryl 531
Hiscocks, Richard 1417
Hofmanowa 284
Holewinski, Jan 129, 1086
Holzer, Jerzy Z. 25
Horak, Stephan 641, 1109
Hordynski, Józef 802
Horn, David B. 160, 784
Hoskins, Janina W. 148, 149, 278, 329, 356
Hotchkiss, Christine 1418
Hoyle, Fred 209
Hubicz, Edward M. 1208
Hughes, Rupert 1343
Humphrey, Grace 343, 476, 491, 532
Huneker, James G. 183
Hutchinson, Alexander H. 534
Hutchison, Graham S. 419
Hutter, Catherine 888
Hyams, Joseph 964

Iranek-Osmecki, Kaźimierz 965
Irving, David J.C. 371
Iskra, Wiesław 905
Iwanicka, Halina 26
Iwańska, Alicja 27
Iwicki, John J. 1258
Izbicki, Roman 535

Jackowski, Aleksander 130
Jakimowicz, Irena 131
Jakubowski, August A. 51
Jamar, K. 101
Jankowski, Stanisław 490, 492
Janney, Russell 1344
Janowski, Robert W. 1375
Janta-Połczyński, Aleksander 1156, 1157
Jarecka, Louise L. 28
Jarociński, Stefan 1119
Jaron, Phillip 889
Jasienica, Paweł 766, 773
Jasienski, Alexander M. 1383
Jastrun, Mieczysław, pseud. See Agatstein, Mieczysław
Jaździewski, Konrad 77
Jędlicki, Marjan Z. 738
Jedruch, Jacek 739
Jędrychowski, Stefan 582
Jędrzejewicz, Wacław 344, 642
Johnpoll, Bernard K. 967
Johns, Joseph P. 279
Johnston, Russell R. 1158
Johnston, Ruth 1205, 1206
Jordan, Peter 841
Jordan, Zbigniew A. 420, 913
Juchniewicz, Mieczysław 1364

Kacewicz, George V. 842
Kaekenbeeck, Georges S.F.C. 421
Kajencki, Francis C. 253
Kąkol, Kaźimierz 1484, 1485
Kalkstein, Teresa 172
Kaltenbach, Frederick W. 422
Kane, William T. 379
Kanet, Roger E. 1402
Kantowicz, Edward R. 1259
Kaplan, Chaim A. 969
Kaplan, Herbert H. 785
Kapuścieńska, Marie 306
Karasowski, Moritz 184
Karol, K.S. 1419
Karolak, Tadeusz 243

Karolevitz, Robert F. 102
Karpiński, Andrzej 583, 584
Karpiński, Jakub 864
Karsavina, Jean 890
Karski, Jan 643, 1159
Karski, Stefan, pseud. See
 Filipowicz, Tytus
Karsov, Nina 970
Kasprzycki, Tadeusz 345
Katz, Alfred 971
Keefe, Eugene K. 29
Keller, Ulrich 1005
Kelley, Edgar S. 185
Kellogg, Charlotte 236, 237, 238, 330
Kelly, Eric P. 284, 891, 1034, 1035, 1036, 1037, 1038, 1039, 1040, 1555
Kennedy, Harriet E. 198
Kennedy, John F. 644
Kennedy, Robert M. 843
Kerns, Joseph E. 380
Kerstein, Edward S 865
Kesten, Hermann 210
Kielar, Wiesław 1133
Kieniewicz, Stefan 803
Kimmich, Christoph M. 423
Kirkien, Leszek 424
Kish, George 536
Klafkowski, Alfons 425
Klarkowski, Claude E. 163
Klarner, Czesław 585
Kmiecick, Jerzy 1160
Kmietowicz, Frank A. 78
Knapp, Stefan 1161
Knoll, Paul W. 767
Knox, Brian 86
Kobylańska, Krystyna 186
Koc, Leon W. 103
Kokot, Józef 645
Kolaja, Jiri T. 1486
Komarnicki, Tytus 629, 1420
Komorowski, Eugenjusz 1064
Komorowski, Tadeusz 104
Konopczyński, Władysław 357, 740
Konopko, Jóna 1505

Konovalov, Serge 646
Konwinski, Norbert 382
Kopczewski, Jan S. 280
Korbel, Josef 647
Korbonski, Andrzej 72
Korboński, Stefan 608, 701, 702, 703, 704, 1421
Korczak, Janusz, pseud. See
 Goldszmit, Henryk
Korczynski, Alexander 648
Korenblit, Michael 972
Korniłowicz, Maria 426
Korostovets, Vladimir K. 824
Korwin-Rhodes, Marta 844, 1162
Kos-Rabcewicz-Zubkowski, Ludwik 1209
Kościuszko, Tadeusz 281
Kościuszko Foundation 825
Kossak-Szczucka, Zofia 1163
Kostrowicki, Jerzy 537
Koszałki Opałki. English & Polish 622
Kot, Stanisław 649, 1077, 1462
Kotowska, Monika 705
Kowalak, Tadeusz 1517
Kowalczyk, Jan J. 1384
Kowalik, Jan 1260
Kozakiewicz, Stefan 132, 133
Kozakiewiczowa, Helena 133
Kozicki, Stanisław 1487
Kozłowski, Jerzy 1080
Kraitsir, Charles V. 741
Krakowski, Shmuel 973
Krasinska, Francoise. Countess 285
Krasinski, Walerjan 774
Krauze, Andrzej 134
Krawczyk, Monica 1345
Kridl, Manfred 307, 1087, 1422
Krok-Paszkowski, Jan 50
Krolikowski, Łucjan 1365
Kruszewski, Z.A. 427
Kryczynski, John W. 742
Krzesiński, Andrew J. 1423

Krzyżanowski, Jerzy R. 362
Krzyżanowski, Julian 1088, 1089
Krzyżanowski, Lech 538
Krzyzanowski, Włodzimierz 288
Kubiak, Wanda L. 1346
Kubrakiewicz, Michał 1385
Kucharski, Rajmund 1386
Kudlicki, Stanisław 428
Kukiel, Marjan 804, 826
Kukielko, Renya 974
Kula, Witold 586
Kulczycki, John L. 805
Kulka, Erich 1134
Kulski, Julian E. 1164
Kulski, Władysław W. 650
Kuncewiczowna, Maria 609, 914
Kuniczak, Wiesław S. 610, 892, 893, 1261
Kupiecki, Edmund 477
Kuron, Jacek 1436
Kurzman, Dan 1570
Kuśnierz, Bronisław 651
Kuszewski, Stanisław 1116
Kuzawa, Mary Grace, sister 1078
Kuzniewski, Anthony J. 1262
Kwiatkowski, Eugenjusz 587

Lachs, Manfred 429
Lanckorońska, Karolina 1463
Landau, Rom 331, 346
Landau, Zbigniew 588
Landowska, Wanda 290
Lane, Arthur B. 652
Lane, David S. 1488
Langer, Rulka 1165
Laserson, Max M. See Lazerson, Maksim Y.
Laskowski, Otton 374, 776
Lasok, Dominik 1072
Laudynowa, Stefania 975
Lavers, Norman 282
Lawton, Mary 333
Lazerson, Maksim Y. 446
Le Play Society 1506

Ledbetter, Eleanor 150, 151
Lédit, Joseph 203
Lednicki, Wacław 287, 291, 308, 370, 915, 916, 1090
Lemnis, Maria 501
Lengyel, Emil 332, 1110
Lengyel, Olga 1135
Lenski, Lois 1041
Lepszy, Leonard 478
Lerski, Jerzy J. 653, 1263
Leslie, Robert F. 806, 807, 808, 1387
Leszczycki, Stanisław 589
Levi, Primo 1136
Levine, Madeline G. 1091
Lewanski, Richard C. 152, 1081
Lewin, Isaac 976
Lewinski-Corwin, Edward T. 743
Lewis, Flora 866
Lewitt, Jan 539
Liberace, Władysław Valentino 296
Liberska, Barbara 604
Ligocki, Edward. See Elgoth-Ligocki
Lind, John 1388
Lineberry, William P. 30
Lippman, Theo, Jr. 323
Lipski, Jan J. 1424
Lipski, Józef 654
Lisowski, Bohdan 87
Listowel, Judith H. 845
Liszt, Franz 187, 188
Litman, Jacob 977
Little, Frances D. 540
Litwinski, Leon 917
Livinsky, Isidore 1389
London. Royal Academy of Arts 135
Lopata, Helena Z. 1264
Lord, Robert H. 786
Lorenc-Kot, Bogna 1507
Lorentz, Friedrich 1058
Lorentz, Leopold 105
Lorentz, Stanisław 136
Lorit, Sergius 260

Losk, I.M. 968
Lourie, Richard 611
Łozinski, Jerzy Z. 88
Łuczynska, Alfreda 1082
Lukas, Richard C. 655, 656, 706
Łukasiewicz, Juliusz 657
Lunde, Karl 1265
Lundgren-Nielsen, Kay 1390
Lutosławski, Wincenty 1391
Łychowski, Wincenty 590
Lyon, Norman T. 1226

McAlpine, Dale K. 1347
McBride, Robert 464
McCrea, Lilian 1556
Machray, Robert 430, 827, 828
Maciąg, Włodzimierz 224
Maciejewski, B.M. 385, 1120
Maciuszko, Jerzy J. 1092
Mackiewicz, Joseph 1065
Mackiewicz, Józef 612
Mackiewicz, Stanisław 658
Maclaren, Anna 106
McLaren, Moray 541, 1464
McLean, W.M. 164
MacShane, Denis 1526
Madej, Victor 119
Madison, Arnold 165
Majewski, Arthur J. 1267
Majkowski, Karol 906
Majkowski, Wladysław 1489
Makowski, William B. 1210
Maks, Leon 1166
Makucewicz, Peter 1167
Mała Encyklopedia Powszechna 31
Malak, Henryk M. 223
Malcher, George C. 107
Małcuzyński, Karol 1425
Malczewski, Antoni 1557
Malinski, Mieczysław 244
Manning, Clarence A. 358
Manteuffel, Tadeusz 768
Marcinkowski, Karol 787
Marcus, Joseph 978
Marczyński, Antoni 1204

Marek, George R. 189
Marek, Joseph 1155
Mark, Ber 1571
Markowska, Wanda 306
Marshall, Christabel 166
Martel, Rene 431
Mason, David S. 1426
Mason, John B. 468
Mason, Violet 542
Matejko, Alexander 1490
Matuszewski, Ignacy 432, 659
Matuszewski, Ryszard 234, 1093
Mayewski, Paweł 1079
Mazur, Stella M. 1268
McKown, Robin 1042
Meany, Thomas 320
Męclewski, Edmund 578
Meissner, Janusz 108, 1168, 1169
Mendelsohn, Ezra 979
Miąso, Józef 1269
Micewski, Andrzej 394
Michałek, Bolesław 1117
Michener, James A. 894
Mierzwa, Stefan P. See Mizwa
Mikołajczyk, Stanisław 867
Mikulski, John J. 1348
Mills, Lois 1043
Miłobedzki, Adam 88
Milostan, Harry 1270, 1271, 1272, 1273
Miłosz, Czesław 1094, 1104
Minc, Hilary 572
Miniter, Edith M. 1349
Mitchell, Harold 1366
Mizwa, Stephen P. 167, 190, 211, 1274
Młynarski, Bronisław
Młynarski, Feliks J. 591, 1170
Mocha, Frank 1290
Modjeska, Helena 317
Modrzejewska, Helena. See Modjeska, Helena
Monat, Paweł 1171
Montanus, B. 660
Montias, John M. 592, 597

Morawska, Ewa T. 1275, 1292
Morf, Gustaw 267, 268
Morfill, William R. 32, 33
Morgan, S.R. 613
Morison, George H. 469
Morkowicz-Olczakowa, Hanna 228
Morrison, James F. 1427
Morrow, Ian F.D. 433
Morton, John B. 788
Moses, Adolf 1017
Mostwin, Danuta 1276
Mowrer, Lilian T. 1172
Mur, Jan, pseud. 1173
Murdoch, William D. 191
Murdzek, Benjamin P. 1450
Murphy, Francis X. 245, 246
Murray, Kenneth M. 109
Murray, Michael 543
Musial, Nellie 1350
Musial, Stanley F. 321
Muskie, Donald C. 324
Muskie, Edmund S. 324
Myant, Martin 1428

Nadel, Norbert 846
Nadolski, Andrzej 123
Nagret, Paul 550
Naimark, Norman M. 1518
Nałkowska, Sofja R. 614
Nałkowski, Wacław 691
Napolska, Mary Remigia, sister 1277
Narkiewicz, Olga A. 1429
Natsolim. See Milostan, Harry
Nelson, Harold D. 41
Nemec, Ludwik 247
Nesterowicz, Stefan 1278
Nevin, David 325
New York City. Museum of Modern Art 137
Newman, Bernard 34, 35, 544, 545, 546, 1508
Newman, Simon 661
Niecks, Frederick 192
Niemcewicz, Julian U. 1279
Nieścior, Leon 1175

Niezabitowska, Małgorzata 980
Nirenstein, Albert 981
Noailles, Emmanuel H.V. de, marquis 1392
Nomberg-Przytyk, Sara 1137
Norris, Margaret 1351
Norwid-Neugebauer, Mieczysław 847
Nowak, Chester M. 153
Nowak, Jadwiga 158
Nowak, Jan 1176
Nowakowski, Tadeusz 359
Nowotarska, Róża 298
Nurowski, Roman 848

Obal, Thaddeus J. 154
Obidinski, Eugene E. 1280
Obojski, Robert 1044
Ochorowicz-Monatowa, Marja 502
Ocioszynski, Tadeusz 434
Oertzen, Friedrich W. von 1430
O'Konski, Alvin E. 662
Olszer, Krystyna M. 1414
Olszewicz, Bolesław 1281
Olszyk, Edmund 1282
Oram, James 248
Orga, Ates 193
Orłowicz, Miecysław 547
Oreme, Alexandra 1177, 1178
Ornano, Philippe Antoine, comte d' 389
Orpen, Neil 1581
Orska, Irena. See Bytniewska, Irena
Ortell, Gerald A. 688
Ortmayer, Louis L. 663
Orton, Lawrence D. 256
Orvis, Julia S. 744
Orzell, Laurence 1376
Osborne, Arthur 435
Osborne, Sidney 436
Ossowski, Stanisław 1491
Ostaszewski, Jan 868

Pack, Martin A. 1509

## Author Index

Paderewski, Ignacy J. 333
Palmer, Alicia T. 375
Paluszek, John L. 1283
Paneth, Philip 36
Parizeau, Alice 615
Parot, Joseph J. 1284
Pasek, Jan Chryzostom 338, 339
Patterson, Eric J. 347, 745
Pawełczyńska, Anna 1138
Pawełek, Anne J. 1179
Pawłowicz, Bohdan 110
Pawłowska, Harriet M. 623
Pawłowski, Jerome I. 38
Payne, Theodore 318
Peckwas, Edward A. 716
Pellowski, Anne 1352, 1353, 1354, 1355, 1356
Pember-Devereux, Margaret R. 548
Penzik, Irena 1180
Perkowski, Jan L. 1059, 1060
Pertek, Jerzy 694
Peszkowski, Zdzisław 1465
Peterson, Virgilia 1510
Pfeiffer, Christine 1045
Phillips, Charles J.M. 334, 549
Phillips, Janine 1181
Phillips, Walter A. 1393
Piasecki, Victor 1182
Piechotka, Każimierz 89
Piechotka, Maria 89
Piekałkiewicz, Jarosław 1431
Piekarski, Adam 1466
Pienkos, Angela 1286
Pienkos, Donald D. 1287
Pierce, Richard L. 1288
Pietrkiewicz, Jerzy 1217, 1467
Pietrucha, Jerzy 1451
Pilarski, Laura 168
Pilichowski, Czesław 707
Piłsudska, Aleksandra 348
Piłsudski, Józef 349, 350, 829
Piltz, Erasmus 39
Pinkowski, Edward 239
Pinkus, Oscar 982
Piótrkowski, Rufin 1183
Piótrowska, Irena 138
Piótrowski, Marian 1184
Piótrowski, Stanisław 708
Pirages, Dennis 1492
Pisar, Samuel 1139
Pitkiewicz, Józef 1394
Ploss, Sidney I. 664
Podolski, T.M. 593
Pogonowski, Iwo C. 746
Polak, W., pseud. See Giertych, Jędrzej
Poland. Central Statistical Office 1536
Poland. Głonna Komisja Badania Zbrodni Hitlerowskich w Polsce 1140
Poland. Komisariat Generalny. Nowjorska Wystawa Światowa, 1939-1940 40
Poland. Laws, Statutes, etc. 1073
Poland. Ministerstwo Informacji 849, 850, 851
Poland. Ministerstwo Przemysłu i Handlu 472
Poland. Ministerstwo Spraw Zagranicznych 710
Poland. Ministerstwo Spraw Zagranicznych. Department Prasi i Informacji 869
Poland. Rada Ochrony Pomników Walki i Męczenstwa 555, 983
Polanie Club. Mineapolis 503, 1121, 1511
Poliakoff, Vladimir 437, 438, 439
Polish American Congress 1293
Polish Day Association. Chicago 1296
Polish Institute of Arts and Sciences in America 1297

Polish Research Centre.
London 49, 440, 441, 470,
496, 709, 1469, 1470
Polish Roman Catholic Union
of America 156
Polish University College.
London. Library 157
Polland, Albert F. 1471
Polonius, Alexander, pseud.
1185
Polonsky, Antony 830, 1380
Polska Izba Handlu
Zagranicznego 497
Polskie Towarzystwo Naukowe
na Obczyźnie 158
Polzin, Theresita 1298
Pomian-Srzednicki, Maciej
919
Popescu, Julian 1046
Popiołek, Kaźimierz 443,
711
Poray, J.B. 895
Porazinska, Janina 1047
Porter, Bruce D. 860
Porter, Jane 896
Posner, Stanisław 1397
Potel, Jean-Yves 1528
Potichnyj, Peter J. 666
Potocka, Anna (Tyszkiewicz),
hrabina 352
Potocki, Alfred, hrabia 353
Pounds, Norman J.G. 444,
695, 719
Poznański, Czesław 667, 1218
Pruszynski, Ksawery 112,
309, 1186, 1219
Pruszynski, Xavier. See
Pruszynski, Ksawery
Przezdziecki, Rajnold,
hrabia 669
Przygoda, Jacek 1299, 1300
Przymanowski, Janusz 712
Przypkowski, Tadeusz 493
Pula, James S. 289

Rabinowicz, Harry M. 984
Rachwald, Arthur R. 670

Raczynski, Edward, hrabia
1220
Radecki, Henry 1211, 1212
Radio Free Europe. Audience
and Public Opinion Research
Dept. 1453
Radio Free Europe. Audience
Research Dept. 1493
Radio Free Europe. Research
and Analysis Dept. 1472
Radziwill, Michael, prince
360
Raina, Peter K. 920, 1435
Rajewski, Zdzisław 80
Rakowski, Mieczysław F. 671
Rashke, Richard L. 985
Rawicz, Slavomir 1187
Rayson, Ethel 1122
Read, Piers P. 897
Rchowicz, Henryk 445
Reddaway, William F. 351,
720
Renkiewicz, Frank 1301, 1302
Retinger, Joseph H. 52, 361
Revyuk, Emil 1111
Reynolds, Jaime 837
Rhode, Gotthold 672
Ricciardi, Antonio 367
Riekhoff, Harold von. See
von Riekhoff, Harold
Ringelblum, Emanuel 986, 987
Robinson, Paul 383
Rochman, Leyb 988
Rodzinska, Halina 363
Roemer, Ferdinand 81
Rogala, Tadeusz 1582
Roiter, Howard 989
Romanski, Andrzej K. 616
Roos, Hans 871
Rose, William J. 53, 265,
364, 748, 749, 750, 1095
Rosenthal, Harry K. 673
Ross, M. of Dunham 751
Rothenberg, Jerome 990
Rothschild, Joseph 831
Rottermund, Andrzej 83
Rousseau, Jean-Jacques 1437

Rozanow, Zofia 509
Rozek, Edward J. 674
Roxmaryn, Stefan 1438
Robinstein, Erna F. 991
Rudnicki, Adolf 898, 1141
Rudnicki, Józef 212, 481
Rudnicki, Klemens S. 113
Rusinek, Michał 213
Rutkowska, Neomisia, sister 326, 388
Rybczynski, Mieczysław 594
Rydel, W. 1188
Rysia, pseud. 504

Sadowski, Michał 556
Sagajllo, Witold 713
St. John, Christopher, pseud. See Marshall, Christabel
St. John-Stevas, Norman 249
Sandberg, Neil C. 1303
Sanders, Irwin T. 1292
Sanford, Albert H. 1304
Sanford, George 1439, 1440
Sapieha, Virgilia. See Peterson, Virgilia
Sarolea, Charles 1398
Sawicki, Jerzy 697
Saxton, Luther C. 789
Saysse-Tobiczyk, Każimierz 479, 557, 558
Scaevola, pseud. 1441
Schallenberg, Evert W. 194
Schaufele, William E. 872
Schedel, Hartmann 769
Scherer-Virski, Olga 1096
Schmitt, Bernadotte E. 54
Schneiderman, Samuel Loeb. See Shneiderman, Samuel L.
Schoor, Gene 322
Sebastian, Tim 1494
Secomski, Każimierz 595
Segal, Simon 714, 992
Segel, Harold B. 1105
Sehn, Jan 1140
Selz, Peter 137
Serafino, Frank 1305
Seroff, Victor 195

Serrailler, Ian 617, 1048
Shaifer, Norman 245
Sharp, Samuel L. 873
Shatyn, Bruno 993
Shneiderman, Samuel L. 874, 994, 995
Shneur, Zalman 1018
Shoskes, Henry 1572
Shotwell, James T. 446
Siekaniec, Ladislaus J. 1294, 1306
Sieniarski, Stefan 1535
Sienkiewicz, Henryk 319, 1357
Sigismund, brother 381
Simon, Brian 921
Simon, Maurice D. 1402, 1434
Singer, Daniel 675
Singer, Gusta 605
Singer, Isaac B. 1019, 1020, 1021
Singleton, Aileen M.W. 55, 56
Siuchiński, Mateusz 752
Skendzel, Edward A. 257
Skolimowski, Henryk 922
Skrzyński, Alexander J. 57
Skrzypek, Stanisław 447
Skubała-Tokarska, Zofia 923
Skurnowicz, Joan S. 293
Skurzynski, Gloria 899
Skwarczyński, Paweł 676
Skwarko, Krystyna 1223
Slocombe, Geroge E. 753, 754
Słomczynski, Każimierz 1495
Slomka, Jan 1512
Smogorzewski, Każimierz M. 448, 449
Smulikowska, Ewa 509
Sobański, Wacław 450
Smolen, Każimierz 1142
Sobieski, John 376
Sobolewski, Paweł 1097
Sokal, Franciszek 1496
Sołdaczuk, Józef 596
Solski, Wacław 900
Soltan, Christina 1189

Soltynski, Roman 90
Sopocko, Eryk K. 114
Spasowski, Romuald 377
Srokowski, Stanisław 692
Staar, Richard F. 1442
Stahl, Zdisław 1066
Stankiewicz, W. 597
Staniszkis, Jadwiga 1530
Starski, Stanisław 1531
Statkowski, Józef 58, 59
Stehle, Hansjakob 875
Steiner, Jean F. 996
Stern, Harold P. 876
Steven, Stewart 60
Stolica 465
Stone, Daniel 790
Stone, Rochelle H. 295
Strachey, Marjorie C. 196
Strakacz, Aniela 335
Strong, Anna L. 1443
Strybel, Robert 69
Strzelec, Karol W. 1473
Strzetelski, Stanisław 852, 1297
Styczyński, Jan 559
Stypułkowski, Zbigniew F. 1190
Styron, William 901
Sulikowski, Jerzy 1123
Sulimirski, Tadeusz 677
Super, Donald E. 451
Super, Margaret L. 678, 832
Super, Paul 62, 560, 755, 925
Surdykowski, Jerzy 561
Sutton, John L. 791
Swastek, Joseph 399, 1307
Swicz, V. 63
Świdziński, Natalia 64
Święcicki, Marek 115, 298, 1191
Swiętochowski, Tadeusz 648
Syrop, Konrad 877, 878, 879
Szafer, Władysław 403
Szajkowski, Bogdan 1474
Szalet, Leon 1192
Szambelan-Strevinsky, Christine 1049

Szaz, Zoltan M. 452
Szczepanski, Jan 1076, 1498
Szczypiorski, Andrzej 1445
Szechter, Szymon 970
Szmaglewska, Seweryna 1193, 1194
Szostak, John M. 250
Szturm de Sztrem, Edward 65
Szydłowski, Roman 1566
Szymański, Leszek 1532

Tabrah, Ruth M. 1358
Taplin, Michael R. 1568
Taras, Ray 926
Tarnowski, Michał 386
Tarnowski, Stanisław 197
Taylor, Jack 598
Tazbir, Janusz 1475
Tec, Nechama 997
Tenenbaum, Joseph 998, 999
Tennant, A.E. 756
Terlecki, Olgierd 116
Terlikowski, Maria 1050
Terry, Sarah M. 453
Teschner, Józef 1533
Thackeray, Frank W. 809
Thomas, Frederick W. 902
Thomas, William I. 1308
Thompson, Ewa M. 229
Tims, Richard W. 810
Todd, Mary I. 618
Tomiałajc, Ludwik 401
Tomkiewicz, Mina 1022
Topolińska, Zuzanna 1061
Toranska, Teresa 1446
Touraine, Alain 1529
Treece, Patricia 262
Trepczyński, Stanisław 1519
Treugutt, Stefan 373
Trevor, Elleston 619
Truscoe, Adam 98
Treciak, Przemysław 563
Turczynowicz, Lauara B. de G. 811
Turek, Wiktor 159, 161, 1213, 1214, 1215
Turkow Kaminska, Ruth 1000
Turska, Krystyna 1051

Tushnet, Leonard 1001, 1573
Tymieniecki, Kazimierz 757

Umiastowski, Roman 679, 680
Uminska, Zofia 198
Uminski, Sigmund H. 254, 1052, 1309, 1310, 1558
UNESCO 141
U.S. Library of Congress. Slavic and Central European Division 1071
Uszynska, Zofia 564

Vajiravudh, King of Siam 792
Van Norman, Louis E. 565
Vencenz, Stanisław de 1559
Vinecour, Earl 1002
Vinocur, Ana 1003
Viomenil, Antoine C. du Houx, Baron de 1195
Virski, Fred 1196
Vishniac, Roman 1004
Vitry, Henryk 501
Vogel, Joseph 1359
Vogler, Henryk 365
Volynska-Bogert, Rimma 311
von Riekhoff, Harold 681

Wagner, Wenceslas J. 1074
Wagner, Wolfgang 455, 672
Walux, Marguerite 1124
Waldo, Arthur 1311
Waldo, Harold 1360
Walicki, Andrzej 927
Walicki, Jerzy 1476
Waliszewski, Kazimierz 299, 812
Walker, Alan 199
Walska, Ganna 390
Wandycz, Piótr S. 682, 683, 684, 813
Warfield, Hania 1197
Wasilewska, Eugenia 1198
Wasilewski, Leon 1112
Wąsowicz, Józef 599
Wasserman, Charles 566
Watson, George Leo de St. M. 341
Watt, Richard M. 833
Wdowinski, David 1006
Wdowinski, Zdzisław 402
Wedda, Joseph 1361
Wedel, Janine 1513
Węgierski, Dominik 1199
Weinstein, J. 456
Weinryb, Bernard D. 1007
Weintraub, Wiktor 1098
Weit, Erwin 231, 1447
Wellisz, Leopold 600
Wellover, Maralyn 689
Wells, Leon W. 1008
Welsh, David J. 255, 283, 310
Wenkstern, Otto 1399
Wepsiec, Jan 928
Werstein, Irving 1053
Weschler, Lawrence, 880, 1534
Wesołowski, Zdzisław P. 511
West, Karen 505
Westerby, Robert 853
Weyers, J. 685
Wheeler, Opal 200
Wiatr, Jerzy J. 929, 1444
Whitton, Frederick E. 758
Wieczerzak, Joseph W. 814
Wieniewski, Ignacy 67
Wiepert, Friedrich von 457
Wierzbiańska, Alina 28
Wierzyński, Kazimierz 201, 1200
Wiewióra, Bolesław 458
Wilder, Jan A. 459
Willeby, Charles 202
Williams, George H. 251
Windeatt, Mary F. 233
Winiewicz, Józef M. 715
Winowska, Maria 263, 264
Winter, Nevin O. 567, 568
Wiślanski, Tadeusz 79
Wiśniewski, Joseph 170
Wiśniowski, Sygurd 1312
Wittlin, Tadeusz 1067, 1201
Włoszczewski, Stefan W. 1313
Włodarski, Szczepan 1377
Wnukowski, Joseph S. 903

Wojciechowska, Maia 1054, 1560
Wojciechowski, Aleksander 142
Wojciechowski, Zygmunt 759, 770
Wolanin, Alphonse S. 156
Wolfe, Rinna 252
Wołodkowicz, Andrzej 1216
Wolska, Helen 510
Wood, Arthur E. 1314
Woodall, Jean 601, 1527
Woods, William H. 881
World Power Conference. Polish National Committee 907
Woroniecki, Edouard 68
Woytak, Richard A. 1448
Wrobel, Paul 1315
Wrzos-Glinka, Stanisław 854
Wuorio, Eva-Lis 1055
Wylie, Ida A.R. 1362
Wynot, Edward D. 495, 1449
Wyszynski, Stefan, cardinal 395
Wytrwał, Joseph A. 1316, 1317, 1318, 1319, 1320

Yanow, Leonard 1009
Yarmolinsky, Avrahm 1321
Yastrzemski, Carl 396
Yeutter, Franklin W. 266
Yezierska, Anzia 397, 1368, 1369, 1370, 1371
Yurieff, Zoya 392

Zabelska, Janina 157
Zaborowski, Jan 411
Zachodnia Agencja Prasowa 460
Zachwatowicz, Jan 91, 92
Zagórski, Wacław 1583
Zajączkowski, Ananiasz 1056
Zajdlier, Zoë. See Girling, Zoë
Zakrzewska, Maria 398
Zaleski, August 760
Zalewski, Wojciech 311

Zaloga, Steven J. 118, 119
Zamoyski, Adam 336, 761, 834
Zand, Helen S. 1514
Zanoziński, Jerzy 143
Żarnowski, Janusz 835
Zatko, James J. 930
Zawisza, Olgierd 1202
Zawodny, Janusz K. 1068, 1584
Zbyszewski, Karol 120
Żeranski, Alina 506
Ziegfeld, Richard D. 294
Zieleniewicz, Andrzej 69
Zielinski, Adam K. 569
Zielinski, Anthony J. 815
Zielinski, Henryk 1452
Zielinski, Janusz G. 602
Ziemian, Joseph 1010
Ziffer, Bernard 931
Zimmer, Szczepan K. 393
Zins, Henryk 686
Znaniecki, Florian 1308, 1500
Żółkiewski, Stanisław 793
Zolobka, Vincent 161
Żółtowski, Adam, 461
Zubrzyski, Jerzy 1221
Zuckerman, Isaac 1011
Zuker-Bujanowska, Liliana 1012
Zurawski, Joseph W. 162, 882
Zweig, Ferdynand 603
Żychowski, Marian 717
Zylberberg, Michael 1013
Zyw, Aleksander 121
Żywulska, Krystyna 1203

# TITLE INDEX

Across Burning Frontiers 1202
Across Poland 563
Accident: The Death of General Sikorski 371
Adam Mickiewicz (Agatstein) 301
Adam Mickiewicz (Welsh) 310
Adam Mickiewicz: His Life and Work in Documents, Portraits and Illustrations 306
Adam Mickiewicz in English 303
Adam Mickiewicz in World Literature 308
Adam Mickiewicz, Poet of Poland 307
Adam Mickiewicz: the Life Story of the Greatest Polish Poet 309
Adam Mickiewicz, the National Poet of Poland 305
Adventures of a Polish Prisoner 1184
Aesthetics in Twentieth-Century Poland 912
After Bread 1357
After Pentecost 1326
After Thirty Years 519
Aims and Failures of the German New Order 715
Airlift to Warsaw 1581
All About Poland 52
Allied Wartime Diplomacy 674
Always Room at the Top 390
America and Poland, 1915-1925 817
America and the New Poland 821
America on Poland 662
American Beauty 1334
American Debut 319
An American in Poland 1179
An American Journey 1283
America's Polish Heritage 1316
Ameryka: A Globetrotter's View 1312
Amidst Forests and Lakes 402
Ancient Slavs 78
And My Children Did Not Know Me 1237
And The Sun Kept Shining ... 1151
And We Are Not Saved 1006
Anna Rose of Stairstep Farm 1352
The Anonymous Poet of Poland: Zygmunt Krasinski 286
Antecedents of Revolution 809
Anus Mundi 1133
The Apostle of Mercy from Chicago 223
An Appraisal of Thomas and Znaniecki's THE POLISH PEASANT IN EUROPE AND AMERICA 1229
Archaeological Research in Poland 75
Archbishop John Baptist Cieplak 203
The Architecture of Poland (Dmochowski) 84
The Architecture of Poland (Knox) 86
Area Handbook for Poland 29

An Army in Exile 93
Arrest and Exile 1172
Arrogant Beggar 1368
The Art of Poland 138
Art of Polish Cookery 506
Ascent to Heaven 898
Ashes to the Taste 1180
The Assimilation Myth 1205
Assistance to the Jews in Poland, 1939-1945 938
At the Red Summit 1447
Atlas of Warsaw's Architecture 83
Auschwitz 1137
The Auschwitz Album 1125
Auschwitz and the Allies 1130
Auschwitz 1940-1945, Guidebook Through the Museum 1142
Auschwitz: True Tales from a Grotesque Land 1137
Austrian Poland 20
The Authentic Biography of Colonel Beck 171
Authentic Memoirs of the Life of John Sobieski, Kind of Poland 375
Autocracy in Poland and Russia 1401

The Background of Polish-German Relations in Charts and Figures 451
Background to Crisis 1402
Baltic Tales 1057
Basic Concepts of Rural Sociology 1479
The Battle for the Marchlands 834
The Battle of Grunwald and the German DRANG NACH OSTEN 776
The Beginning of the Polish State 76
Behold: The Polish-Americans 1317

Belgium and Poland in International Relations, 1830-1831 794
Bells of Doom 846
Bernardo Bellotto 132
The Best of Polish Cooking 505
Betsy's Up-and-Down Years 1353
Between Fear and Hope 994
Between the Hammer and the Anvil 608
Between Tumbling Walls 941
Beyond Human Endurance 1143
A Bibliography for Genealogical Research Involving Polish Ancestry 154
Bibliography of Books in Polish or Relating to Poland Published Outside Poland Since September 1, 1939 157
Bibliography of Works by Polish Scholars and Scientists Published Outside Poland in Languages Other than Polish 158
Birds of Poland 401
Bishop Adam Naruszewicz and his HISTORY OF THE POLISH NATION: A CRITICAL STUDY 326
Biskupin Polish Excavations 80
Bitter Glory 833
Bitter Legacy 655
The Black Book of Poland 849
The Black Book of Polish Censorship 1403
The Black Book of Polish Jewry 932
The Blacksmith of Vilno 1034
The Blaze 1163
The Blood Shed Unites us 933
Bocheck in Poland 1024
Bolek 1032

Boleslaus the Bold Called Also the Bountiful and the Bishop Stanislaus 765
Bolesław Leśmian 295
Bolesław Limanowski, A Study in Socialism and Nationalism 297
The Bone Caves of Ojców in Poland 81
A Book Without a Title 1003
Border of Europe 461
Bound with Two Chains 1156
A Boy in the Gulag 1160
The Bravest Battle 1570
Bread Givers, a Novel 1369
The Bridge to the Other Side 705
The Bridgehead of East Prussia 440
A Brief History of Poland 744
A Brief Outline of Polish History 740
A Brigand, Two Queens and a Prankster 1547
British Public Opinion and the First Partition of Poland 784
The Broken Mirror 1079
Building and Architecture in Poland, 1945-1966 82
A Bulwark of Democracy 437
The Burning Bush 1473
By the Waters of the Danube 1177

Caen to Wilhelmshaven 105
Call Us to Witness 1197
The Cambridge History of Poland 720
Candle for Poland 1532
The Captain Leaves his Ship 219
Cardinal Wyszynski: A Biography 394
The Case for Poland 832
A Case History of Hope 866

Casimir Funk: Pioneer in Vitamins and Hormones 225
Casimir Pułaski 357
Casimir Pułaski, 1747-1779: A Selective List of Reading Materials in English 356
The Cassubian Civilization 1058
The Cauldron Boils 1110
Cavalry Hero: Casimir Pułaski 355
Central Planning in Poland 592
Child-Rearing and Reform 1507
Children of Loneliness 1370
Children of the Ghetto 954
Chopin (Bidou) 173
Chopin (Gronowicz) 180
Chopin (Hadden) 181
Chopin (Hedley) 182
Chopin (Marek & Gordon-Smith) 189
Chopin, A Pictorial Biography 174
Chopin: As Revealed by Extracts from His Diary 197
Chopin, His Life 191
Chopin: His Life and Times 193
Chopin in His Own Land 186
Chopin, The Child and the Lad 198
Chopin, The Composer 185
Chopin: The Man and His Music 183
Chopin The Unknown 179
Christian Poland's Millenary 18
The Christmas Nightingale 1555
The Chronicle of the Łodz Ghetto, 1941-1944 946
A Chronology of the Life, Activities and Works of Janusz Korczak 226
The Church in Poland 1466
The Cigarette Sellers of Three Crosses Square 1010

The Cinema of Adrzej Wajda 1117
The Cinema of Roman Polanski 1113
City and Regional Planning in Poland 463
A City Fights for Freedom 480
The Civilian Population and the Warsaw Uprising of 1944 1580
Class Structure and Social Mobility in Poland 1495
Class Structure in the Social Consciousness 1491
Class Struggle in Classless Poland 1531
Code: Polonaise 1055
Collections of Articles on Polish Heraldry 716
Colonel Beck and His Policy 658
Come With Me Through Kraków 476
Come With Me Through Warsaw 491
The Comedy of Poland 1150
Comes the Comrade 1178
Communist Local Government: A Study of Poland 1431
The Communist Party of Poland 1413
The Communists of Poland 1411
Communists on Communism 1409
Comparison of the Climate of the United States and Europe 690
Concentration Camp: Oświęcim-Brzezinka 1140
Concise Statistical Year-Book of Poland 1536
Conflict, Compromise and Conciliation 663
Conducted Tour 1154
Constitutions. Elections and Legislatures of Poland, 1493-1977 739

Contemporary Poland: Society, Politics, Economy 27
Contemporary Polish Cinematography 1114
Contemporary Polish Film 1116
Contemporary Polish Graphic Art 131
Contemporary Polish Painting (Wojciechowski) 142
Contemporary Polish Painting (Zanoziński) 143
Contemporary Polish Poetry, 1925-1975 1091
The Contemporary Polish Theatre (Csato) 1561
Contemporary Polish Theatre (Filler) 1563
Contemporary Polish Writers 1093
Conversations With the Kremlin 649
Co-operative Self-Government in People's Poland 576
Co-operatives in People's Poland 1517
Copernicus and His World 210
Copernicus, Scholar and Citizen 207
Copernicus, The Founder of Modern Astronomy 206
Costumes and Dances of Poland 1509
Count-Down, the Polish Upheavals of 1956, 1968, 1970, 1976, 1980 864
Courier From Warsaw 1176
Cracow (Hartwig) 475
Cracow (Saysse-Tobiczyk) 479
Cracow and Its University 474
Cracow: City of Museusm 125
Cracow: Landscape and Architecture 477
Cracow, The Royal Capital of Ancient Poland 478
The Crime of Katyn 1066
Crimes Against POWs 839

# Title Index

The Crisis of the Polish-Swedish War, 1655-1660 787
Crusades in the Secret War 845
The Crystal Spirit 1522
The Cultural Heritage of Jasna Gora 509
Cultural Policy in Poland 908
Culture in People's Poland 909
Culture in Poland 507
Cyprian Norwid 327
Czartoryski and European Unity, 1770-1861 804
Czechoslovak-Polish Confederation and the Great Powers, 1940-1943 682
Czechoslovak-Polish Relations, 1919-1939 153
Czesław Miłosz, An International Bibliography, 1930-1980 311

Dances of Poland 510
Dantzig and Poland 405
Danzig and the Corridor 467
Danzig and the Polish Problem 416
Danzig Dilemma 468
Danzig--What is it All About? 466
Danzig's Yesterday--And Tomorrow 469
Dark Hour of Noon 1049
The Dark Side of the Moon 838
A Day with Frederic Chopin 175
The Death Camp Proved Him Real 263
Death in the Forest 1068
Decorative Arts in Poland 124
The Deeds of Faith 395
Defeat in Victory 628
The Defense of Poland 847

Destiny Can Wait 98
Diplomat in Berlin, 1933-1939 654
Diplomat in Paris, 1936-1939 657
Diplomatic Ventures and Adventures 669
Divorce in Poland 480
The Dove and the Bear 862
Downfall 1018
Dust of Our Brothers' Blood 1505
Dying We Live 1164

Eagles Black and White 438
Early and Rare Polonica of the 15th-17th Centuries in American Libraries 148
The Early History of Panna Maria, Texas 1226
Early Polish Americana 1321
East Prussia (Machray) 430
East Prussia (Srokowski) 692
The Eastern Frontiers of Germany 431
Eastern Poland 49
The Eastern Pretender 340
The Economic Development of Poland, 1919-1950 598
The Economic Development of Poland's Western and Northern Regions 578
The Economic Independence of Poland 577
The Economic Progress of Poland 587
Economic Reforms in Polish Industry 602
The Economic Role of Jews in Medieval Poland 977
The Economic Theory of the Feudal System 586
The Economy of Modern Poland 573
Education and Youth Employment in Poland 604
Education in New Poland 921

The Eighteenth Decisive Battle of the World, Warsaw, 1920   819
Elements of Polish Culture as Seen by a Resident Foreigner   925
The Emancipation of the Polish Peasantry   803
Emigration in Polish Social Political Thought, 1870-1914   1450
Empirical Sociology in Poland   1076
Enduring Poles   1270
England and the Baltic in the Elizabethan Era   686
England's Baltic Trade in the Early Seventeenth Century   633
The English Atlas Containing a Description of Poland   524
The Errant Nun   1271
Escape From Auschwitz   1134
Escape From Sobibor   985
Escape From the Pit   974
Escape From Warsaw   617
Essays on Poland's Foreign Policy, 1918-1939   638
Ethnic Identity and Assimilation   1303
Ethnic Organizational Dynamics   1211
Ethnic Politics in Urban America   1286
Ethnic to Status Group   1280
Europe's Forgotten Territories   566
Events and Personalities in Polish History   755
Expedition to Moscow   793
Experiment "E"   1192
Exploring the Dimensions of Ethnicity   1257
Eyewitness: The Autobiography of Gomułka's Interpreter   231

Fair Rosalind   313
Faith and Fatherland   1262
Fall of Poland   789
The Fall of Poland in Contemporary American Opinion   783
The Fall of Poland in 1794   782
The Family Moskat   1019
A Fateful Meeting at Elsinore   676
A Field of Buttercups   964
15 Polish Painters   137
Fifteen Years of People's Poland   16
Fifty Years of Polish Independence   25
The Fight for Narvik   120
Fighting Auschwitz   1129
The Fighting Ghettos   1011
Fighting Warsaw   701
Filipowicz   224
Film and Television in Poland   1115
Final Report   624
Finger on the Trigger   895
First Farm in the Valley   1354
The First One Hundred Years   1258
The First Partition of Poland   785
The First Polish Americans   1227
The First Polish Colonies of America in Texas   1241
First to Fight   841
Five Centuries of Polish Learning   1077
Five Chimneys   1135
The Flaming Borders   667
Flashpoint Poland   856
Flight of Eagles   102
Folk Art in Poland (Czarnecka)   620
Folk Art in Poland (Jackowski)   130
Food for the Children   1575

## Title Index

Fool's White 1322
For God, Country and Polonia 1301
For Greater Things 379
For Liberty and Justice 289
For Your Freedom and Ours (Kridl) 1422
For Your Freedom and Ours (Olszer) 1414
Foreign Capital in Poland 600
The Foreign Policy of Poland, 1919-1939 632
The Foreign Policy of the Polish People's Republic 671
Foreigners on Poland 869
The Forester 609
The Forgotten Battlefield 1200
The Forgotten Holocaust 706
The Formation of the Polish State 768
The Formative Years of the Polish Seminary in the United States 1307
Four From the Old Town 1033
Frédéric Chopin (Gavoty) 177
Frédéric Chopin (Liszt) 188
Frédéric Chopin (Mizwa) 190
Frédéric Chopin (Schallenberg) 194
Frédéric Chopin (Seroff) 195
Frédéric Chopin, His Life and Letters 184
Frédéric Chopin: Profiles of the Man and Musician 199
Frédéric Chopin, Son of Poland 200
Frédéric Francois Chopin 202
Frederick Chopin, As a Man and Musician 192
The Free City: Danzig and German Foreign Policy, 1919-1934 423

Freedom Fighter: Casimir Pułaski 354
From a Ruined Garden 953
From Serfdom to Self-Government 1512
From Star to Star 1035
From Day to Day 956
From the History of KL-Auschwitz 1128
From Versailles to Locarno 629
The Frozen Revolution 863
The Fundamental Principles of Economic Policy in Industry 582

G-For Genevieve 1168
Galiant General 274
Gdańsk-Sopot-Gdynia 538
Gdynia, Poland's Gateway to the Sea 471
General Premises of Economic Policy 590
The Genesis of the Oder-Neisse Line 455
The Genesis of the Oder-Neisse Line in the Diplomatic Relations During World War II 672
Genocide, 1939-1945 840
The Gentleman from Michigan 298
Gerald Ford's Visit to Poland, 28-29 July 1975 636
German and Pole 673
The German Campaign in Poland (1939) 843
German Failures in Poland 709
The German Fifth Column in Poland 850
German Occupation of Poland 710
The German-Polish Frontier 412
German-Polish Relations, 1918 1918-1933 681

German Withdrawal in the East 441
Germanizing Prussian Poland 810
Germans, Poles and Jews 1108
Germany and Poland 650
Germany and Poland in their Historical Relations 626
Germany and Poland Through the Ages 738
Germany's Eastern Frontiers 452
Gierek's Poland 857
A Girl in the Karpathians 523
The Girl Who Ruled a Kingdom 236
A Girl Who Would be Queen 284
The Glass Rose 1327
Glimpses of Polish Architecture 90
The Glories of Częstochowa 508
Gnieżniks 1272
God's Playground 724
The Golden Bird 1545
The Golden Star of Halich 1036
Gomułka, His Poland and His Communism 230
The Gomułka Plan for a Nuclear Armaments Freeze in Central Europe 1425
Good Sense and Good Fortune 1541
The Goths in Ancient Poland 73
The Government of Poland 1437
The Great Battle on the Vistula 816
Great Britain, the Soviet Union, and the Polish Government-in-Exile, 1939-1945 1380

Great Britain's Obligations Towards Poland and Some Facts about the Curzon Line 659
A Great Lord 885
Great Men and Women of Poland 167
The Great Powers and Poland, 1919-1945 643
The Great Powers and the Polish Question, 1941-1945 1380
The Green Flag 1429
The Growth of a Church 1375
Guide to Architecture in Poland 88
A Guide to Polish Libraries and Archives 1081
The Gypsy and the Bear and Other Fairy Tales 1542
Gypsy Blood 1351

Hamtramck: A Sociological Study of a Polish-American Community 1314
The Hand in the Picture 1037
Handbook of the Sarmatian Heritage 1244
Hans Frank's Diary 708
Harvest in Poland 606
He Who Saves One Life 965
Hear Ye Sons 1335
Heart of Europe 725
Heirs 1328
Henryk Sienkiewicz 369
Henryk Sienkiewicz: A Retrospective Synthesis 370
Herbert Hoover and Poland 653
Heritage: The Foundation of Polish Culture 67
Hero's Oak 1329
His Will Alone 367
A Historical Phonology of the Kashubian Dialects of Polish 1061
Historical Sketch of the Rise, Progress, and Decline

of the Reformation in
 Poland 774
History and Integration of
 Poles in Canada 1210
A History of Modern Poland
 871
History of Poland (Gieysztor)
 737
A History of Poland (Halecki)
 734, 735
A History of Poland
 (Slocombe) 753
A History of Poland
 (Whitton) 758
A History of Poland from Its
 Foundation as a State to
 the Present Time 751
The History of Poland in
 One Volume 726
The History of Poland Since
 Eighteen Sixty-Three 806
History of Polish American
 Culture 1313
The History of Polish Cartography from the 15th to
 the 18th Century 693
A History of Polish Literature (Krzyżanowski) 1088
The History of Polish Literature (Miłosz) 1094
History of Polish Pomerania
 757
The History of the Education
 of Polish Immigrants in
 the United States 1269
History of the Jews in Russia and Poland, from the
 Earliest Times Until the
 Present Day 949
History of the Late Polish
 Revolution and the Events
 of the Campaign 802
History of the Polish Air
 Force, 1918-1968 70
History of the Polish
 People in Rochester 1266
A History of the "Proletariat" 1518

The Holocaust Kingdom 948
Home to Poland 1418
The Homebuilders 1339
Homecoming at Twilight 1014
Homeward Bound 1015
Hope Is the Last to Die 940
The Horse and His Shadow 1363
The House of Ashes 982
The Hundred Dresses 1027
Hungry Hearts 1371

I Came Back 1203
I Don't Want to Be Brave
 Anymore 1000
I Escaped From Germany 1167
I Lied to Live 1157
I Saw Poland Betrayed 652
I Saw the New Poland 1443
I Saw the Siege of Warsaw
 1185
I Survived Hell on Earth
 1175
Ideology in a Socialist State
 926
If the Branch Blossoms and
 Other Stories 1345
Ignace Paderewski, Musician
 and Statesman (Landau) 331
Ignace Paderewski, Musician
 and Statesman (Lengyel)
 332
Ignacy Jan Paderewski, 1860-
 1941 329
Ignacy Krasicki 283
An Illustrated History of
 Poland 752
Image Before My Eyes 947
Immigrant Assimilation 1206
Immigrant Destinations 1246
Immigrant Pastor 1400
In Allied London 1220
In Cracow 473
In Defence of My Country 19
In Search of a Lost People
 998
In Search of Chopin 176
In Sennamahoning Uplands
 1348

In Spite of Everything 1162
In the Bieszczady Mountains 535
In the Clutches of the Jews 961
In the Low Beskid Mountains 522
In the Footsteps of Pope John Paul II 250
In the Mirror of Literature 955
In the Name of Tomorrow 970
In Voytus' Little House 1047
In Western Pomerania 557
Incredible Warsaw 488
The Independent Satellite 875
Industrial Cooperation Between Poland and the West 635
The Industrial Development of Poland 905
Industrialization and Planning Under Polish Socialism 580
Information for Businessmen Trading with Poland 497
The Inhuman Land 1146
Institutional Changes in the Postwar Economy of Poland 597
Insurrection of Poland in 1830-31 800
Intellectual Poland 917
The International Experiment of Upper Silesia 421
The International Significance of the Depreciation of the Złoty in 1925 591
International Trade and Development, Theory and Policy 596
Introduction to Poland 5
An Introductory Polish-English Contrastive Grammar 1070
The Invaders 1324
Invitation to Moscow 1190

The Invited 1223
Is Poland Lost? 36
It Started in Poland 1148
Iwaszkiewicz 234

Jadwiga, Poland's Great Queen 237
Jadwiga, Queen of Poland 238
Jagiellonian Poland 773
Jamestown Pioneers from Poland 1293
Jan Kochanowski 255
Jan Parandowski 337
The Janowska Road 1008
Jasna Polana 1361
Jerzy Kosinski 282
The Jesuits in Poland 1471
The Jewish Community in Poland 976
Jewish Question in Poland 942
The Jews in Poland 1007
Jews in Poland, Yesterday and Today 966
The Jews of Warsaw, 1939-1943 960
Jim Konstanty 266
Joe-Pole, New American 1340
John F. Kennedy and Poland 644
John Paul II, A Pictorial Biography 242
John Paul II: A Son From Poland 245
John Paul II, the Pope from Poland 243
John Tyssowski 388
The Jolly Tailor and Other Fairy Tales 1543
Joseph Piłsudski: A European Federalist 342
Joseph Piłsudski, The Memories of a Polish Revolutionary and Soldier 350
Joseph Retinger: Memoirs of an Eminence Grise 361
Joseph Wittlin 392
The Journal of Countess Francoise Krasinska, Great

Grandmother of Victor
  Emmanuel  285
A Journey to Boston  1330
Journeys  324
Journeys to Glory  1455
Józef Piłsudski and His
  Ideas on International
  Peace  345
Juliusz Słowacki; a Romantic
  Poet  373

KL Auschwitz Seen by the
  SS/Hoss, Broad, Kremer
  1132
KZ Auschwitz  1127
The Kalish Book  968
Kane & Abel, A Novel  1325
Karaims in Poland  1056
Karol Szymanowski: His
  Life and Music  385
A Kashubian Ideolect in
  the United States  1059
Katyn  1062
The Katyn Wood Murders  1065
The King's Honor and the
  King's Cardinal  791
The Knotted Cord  1217
Kobiety (Women)  614
The Kolasinski Story  257
KOR: A History of the
  Workers' Defense Committee
  in Poland, 1976-1981  1424
Korczak Żiolkowski: Moun-
  tain Carner  399
Kościuszko: A Biographical
  Study with a Historical
  Background of the Times
  279
Kościuszko, a Biography
  272, 273
Kościuszko, a Short Biog-
  raphy of the Polish
  Patriot  270
Kościuszko and Pułaski  280
Kościuszko in the American
  Revolution  275, 276
Kościuszko, Leader and Exile
  277

The Kościuszko Letters  281

L-For Lucy  1169
The Lad Who Hiked to Heaven
  381
The Land and People of Poland
  1040
Land of Nicholas Copernicus
  213
The Land of the Polish People
  (1943)  1038
The Land of the Polish People
  (1952)  1039
The Land of the Rainbow  542
Landmarks of Polish History
  760
Landownership and Population
  in Pomerania  435
Landowska on Music  290
The Lands of Partitioned
  Poland  813
The Last Attempt to Germanize
  Opole Silesia  443
The Last Days of Maximilian
  Kolbe  260
The Last King of Poland and
  His Contemporaries  778
The Last of the War Horses
  113
Lazar, the Autobiography of
  My Father  1009
Lectures: Poland in Africa
  and Asia  1366
The Legacy of Polish Jewry
  984
Legends and History of Poland
  14
Lest We Forget  1141
Let Me Count the Ways  1332
Let's Visit Poland  1046
Letter from a Polish Patriot
  to the National Government
  of England  1394
Letters Concerning the Pre-
  sent State of Poland  1388
Letters on Polish Affairs
  1398
Lewis Littlepage  779

Liberace: An Autobiography 296
The Liberation of One 377
Libraries in Poland 1082
Life and Culture of Poland as Reflected in Polish Literature 1090
The Life and Death of Chopin 201
Life and Loves of Marie Walewska 389
Life in Both Hands 1153
Life of Chopin 187
The Life of Father Skarga 372
Life on the Modjeska Ranch in The Gay Nineties 318
The Life-Story and Personal Reminiscences of Colonel John Sobieski 376
The Lilacs are Blooming in Warsaw 615
Liliana's Journal 1012
Lincoln's Gadfly, Adam Gurowski 232
The "Lithuanian Metrica" in Moscow and Warsaw 733
A Little Book of Polish Saints 166
Little Man's Story 1188
The Little Worlds of Nellie Musial 1350
The Logic of the Oder-Neisse Frontier 645
Long-Term Planning and Spatial Structure of Poland's National Economy 589
The Long Walk 1187
Luser, the Watchmaker 1017

Madam Curie 215
Madame Curie, A Biography 216
Made in Poland 28
Magda 1342
The Magician of Lublin 1020
The Maintenance of Ethnicity 1275

A Man for Others 262
Man From a Far Country 241
Man in the Middle 713
The Man on the Moon 1548
The Manor 1021
Manwolf 899
Man's Courage 1359
The Maple Leaf and the White Eagle 1207
The March 892
March 1939: The British Guarantee to Poland 661
Marie Dąbrowska 221
Marie Curie 1042
Marie Curie, A Life 218
Marie Naimska; a Saga of Chicago 1347
Marshall Piłsudski 351
Martyrs and Fighters 952
Marya, A Tale of the Ukraine 1557
Marysieńka 299
The Mask of the Warriors 844
Master of Lancut 353
Matthew, The Young King 1553
Maximilian Kolbe: No Greater Love 259
"The Mayor" 382
The Melting Pot Revisited 1236
A Member of a Distinguished Family 1212
Memoir of Thaddeus Kośćiuszko 271
The Memoirs of a Polish Revolutionary and Soldier 349
A Memoir of the Warsaw Uprising 1574
Memoirs of Jan Chryzostom Pasek 338
Memoirs of Madame Piłsudska 354
Memoirs of Prince Adam Czartoryski 220
Memoirs of the Countess Potocka 352
Memoirs of the Polish Baroque 339

## Title Index

The Memoirs of Wladimir Krzyżanowski  288
Memories and Impressions of Helena Modjeska  317
The Mermaid and the Messerschmidt  1165
Merrily We Sing  623
Mickiewicz and the West  302
Mieszko I and the Rise of the Polish State  770
Military Rule in Poland  1439
Military Technique  1106
Millenium: A Thousand Years of the Polish State  730
The Mind of John Paul II  251
The Miracle of the Bells  1344
Mister Doctor; the Life of Janusz Korczak  228
Modern Architecture in Poland  87
Modern Mathematics: The Genesis of a School in Poland  1078
Modern Poland Between East and West  868
Modern Polish Literature  1083
The Modern Polish Mind  914
The Modern Polish Short Story  1096
Modernization and Political-Tension Management  1492
Modjeska, Her Life and Loves  315
More Tales by Polish Authors  1538
More Than a Knight  261
Moscow and the Polish Crisis  664
Music in Poland  1118
Muskie  323
Muskie of Maine  325
My Escape from Siberia  1183
My Felicia  1333
My Life in the Red Army  1196
My Name Is Million  1174

My Name is Million (Kuniczak)  1261
My Secret Diary  1181

The National Music of Poland  1124
Nationalism and Populism in Partitioned Poland  796
Nationalities in Pomerania  1112
The Nazi New Order in Poland  698
Nazi Rule in Poland  714
Nazi Rule in Poland, 1939-1945  697
The Neolithic in Poland  79
Never Came Morning  1323
A New England City and the November Uprising  797
New Life in Poland  3
The New Poland (Brant)  4
The New Poland (Cameron)  6
The New Poland (Newman)  544
The New Poland (Phillips)  549
The New Poland (Winter)  568
The New Poland and the Jews  992
The New Polish-German Border  404
Next to God  1474
Nice Promises  1494
Nicholas Copernicus (Mizwa)  211
Nicholas Copernicus (Rudnicki)  212
Nicholas Copernicus, the Country and Times  771
Nicolaus Copernicus, An Essay on His Life and Work  209
Nicolaus Copernicus and His Epoch  204
Night Never Ending  1064
The Nightingale  196
Nine Million Poles Abroad  1367
No Longer Poles Apart  514
No Time-Limit For These Crimes  707

Northern Lights 233
No Traveler Returns 1572
Notable Personages of Polish Ancestry 164
Notes from the Warsaw Ghetto 986
Notes on Chopin 178
Nothing But Honour 1584
November, 1918 835

O.R.P. Garland in Convoy to Russia 110
Oberländer: A Study in German East Policies 411
The Oder-Neisse Boundary and Poland's Modernization 427
Oder-Neisse Line 420
The Oder-Neisse Problem 457
Of Blood and Hope 1139
Of Bombs and Mice 1022
Official Catalog of the Polish Pavilion at the World's Fair, New York, 1939 40
Old Polish Legends 1537
Old Polish Traditions in Kitchen and at the Table 501
Old Swords 886
Old Warsaw Cook Book 504
On Cultural Freedom 911
On Some Fair Morning 888
On the Border of War and Peace 1448
On the Edge of Destruction 962
On the High Uplands 1559
One of the Radziwills 360
1000 Years of Art in Poland 135
An Orange Full of Dreams 316
The Origin and Growth of the Polish National Catholic Church 1377
The Origins of Poland 763
The Origins of Polish Socialism 1515

The Orthodox Eastern Church in Poland 1469
"Orzel's Patrol 114
Our Lady's Fool 264
Our Natupski Neighbors 1349
Our Two Lives 363
Our Way 1315
Outline History of Poland 717
Outline of Economic Geography 599
Outline of Polish History, Past and Present 732
Outline of Polish Morphology 1069
An Outline of Polish-Soviet Relations 640
An Outline of the History of Polish Literature 1086
Outlines of Polish History 727

PNA, A Centennial History of the Polish National Alliance 1287
Paderewski 330
Paderewski, a Biography of the Pianist and Statesman 336
Paderewski as I Knew Him 335
Paderewski, His Country and its Recent Progress 825
The Paderewski Memoirs 333
Paderewski: Pianist and Patriot 328
Paderewski, the Story of a Modern Immortal 334
A Page of Polish History: Lwów 481
Parisville Poles, First Polish Settlers in U.S.A. 1273
Partisan Warfare in 19th Century Poland 801
The Partitions of Poland 781
The Passion of Poland 880
Past and Present in Polish Sociology 929
Pastor of the Poles 1285

Patriot Novelist of Poland 368
Pattern for Peace 639
The Pattern of Life in Poland 37
The Pavement of Hell 1001
The Paving Stones of Hell 485
The Peace Settlement in the German Polish Borderlands 433
Pedalling Poland 545
The Penal Code of the Polish People's Republic 1073
The People of Poland 1508
People's Poland (Groth) 1416
People's Poland (Majkowski) 1489
The People's Pope 248
Periods of Polish Literary History 1084
The Persistance of Freedom 1564
Philosophy and Ideology 913
Philosophy and Romantic Nationalism 927
Piast Poland 766
The Piasts of Poland 23
The Pierced Heart 387
The Pilgrim Pope 246
Pills, Pens and Politics 239
Piłsudski, A Biography by His Wife 348
Piłsudski: A Life for Poland 344
Piłsudski and Poland 346
Piłsudski, Builder of Poland 343
Piłsudski, Marshal of Poland 347
Piłsudski, The Hero of Poland
Piłsudski's Coup d'Etat 831
Pit and the Trap 988
Playground of Satan 884

The Poetry of Adam Mickiewicz 1098
Poets and Poetry of Poland 1097
Pol-Am; A History of the Polish Americans in Pittsfield, Massachusetts, 1862-1945 1239
Poland (Alcuin) 1
Poland (Benes) 719
Poland (Brandys) 1023
Poland (Cazin) 521
Poland (Dyboski) 11
Poland (Elgoth-Ligocki) 15
Poland (Fournier) 527
Poland (Gardner) 528
Poland (Greene) 1031
Poland (Heine) 530
Poland (Jaździewski) 77
Poland (Kish) 536
Poland (Lewanski) 152
Poland (Lineberry) 30
Poland (Michener) 894
Poland (Morfill) 32
Poland (Nagret) 550
Poland (Patterson) 745
Poland (Phillips) 1393
Poland (Rose) 748
Poland (Schmitt) 54
Poland (Slocombe) 754
Poland (Zieleniewicz) 69
Poland (Zielinski) 569
Poland, A Country Study 41
Poland: A Crisis for Socialism 1438
Poland, A Guidebook for Tourists 515
Poland, A Handbook 42
Poland: A Historical Atlas 746
Poland, A Study in National Idealism 1085
Poland, A Study of the Land, People and Literature 518
Poland After One Year of War 851
Poland and Czechoslovakia 823

Poland and Danzig 470
Poland and Germany 415
Poland and Germany, Past and Future 677
Poland and Her Economic Development 581
Poland and Her National Minorities, 1919-1939 1109
Poland and Her People 38
Poland and Peace 57
Poland and Russia (Super) 678
Poland and Russia (Weyers) 685
Poland and Russia, 1919-1945 446
Poland and the Baltic 406
Poland and the Coming of the Second World War 625
Poland and the Discovery of America 1281
Poland and the Gregorian Reform 762
Poland and the Minority Races 958
Poland and the Poles 516
Poland and the Polish Nation 10
Poland and the Polish Question 1382
Poland and the Revolutionary War 1249
Poland and the Ukraine, Past and Present 666
Poland and the Western Powers 630
Poland and the World 915
Poland and the World Economy 583
Poland as a Geographical Entity 691
Poland as a Trading Partner 574
Poland as an Independent Economic Unit 1397
Poland at Arms 106

Poland Between East and West (Korbel) 647
Poland Between East and West (Pounds) 444
Poland Between Germany and Russia, 1926-1939 648
Poland, Between the Hammer and the Anvil 877
Poland Between the Superpowers 670
Poland Between Two Wars 603
Poland, Bridge for the Abyss? 1417
Poland: Communism Adrift 1412
Poland: Communism, Nationalism, Anti-Semitism 1407
Poland Discovers America 1309
Poland: Eagle in the East 881
Poland, Facts and Figures 551
Poland, Facts and Figures (Swidziński) 64
Poland Fights Back 112
Poland For Beginners 520
Poland: From the Baltic to the Carpathians 552
Poland From the Inside 8
Poland: General Sketch of History, 1569-1815 43
Poland: Genesis of a Revolution 858
Poland, Germany and the Corridor 448
Poland: Her People, History, Industries, etc. 39, 68
Poland: History and Historians 931
Poland in Christian Civilization 1454
Poland in Perspective 878
Poland in Pictures 1044
Poland in the British Parliament 642
Poland in the Collections of the Library of Congress 160
Poland in the Twentieth Century 861

Title Index

Poland in the World of Democracy 815
Poland in World Civilization 12
Poland Indomitable 55
Poland, Its People, Its Society, Its Culture 2
Poland: Key to Europe 1406
Poland: Land, History, Culture 31
Poland, Land of Freedom Fighters 1045
Poland, Land of the White Eagle (Arthurton) 718
Poland, Land of the White Eagle (Corsi) 722
Poland, Lights and Shadows in the Life of an Ancient Nation 9
Poland: Nature, Settlement, Architecture 537
Poland, 1914-1931 827
Poland, 1939-1947 837
Poland, 1931 990
Poland, 1944-1962 1442
Poland, 1945, A Red Cross Diary 1158
Poland 1980-81 1521
Poland 1981 1435
The Poland of Piłsudski 823
Poland of Today 44
Poland of To-Day and Yesterday 567
Poland, Old and New (Rose) 53
Poland, Old and New (Statkowski) 58
Poland, Old and New, Three Lectures 14
Poland on the Baltic 434
Poland: Painting of the Fifteenth Century 141
Poland, Past and Present (Filipowicz) 525
Pland, Past and Present (Harley) 736
Poland Reborn 548

Poland, Russia and Great Britain, 1941-1945 679
Poland, S.O.E. and the Allies 100
Poland Since 1956 1408
Poland: Sketch of Her History 723
Poland: Solidarity: Walsea 1523
Poland Still Unknown 63
Poland Struggles Forward 859
Poland: The Captive Satellite 882
Poland, The Country and Its People 553
Poland, The Country of Your Fathers 59
Poland, the Knight Among Nations 565
Poland, The Land of Copernicus 777
Poland, The Role of the Press in Political Change 1520
Poland: The Struggle for Power, 1772-1939 729
Poland the Unexplored 532
Poland, the Unknown 812
Poland Through the Ages 1030
Poland Today 1432
Poland Today (Humphrey) 533
Poland, Travel Guide 554
Poland, Travel Guide (Uszynska) 564
Poland Under Jaruzelski 1433
Poland Under Nazi Occupation 700
Poland Under the Communists 24
Poland, White Eagle on a Red Field 873
Poland, Yesterday, Today and Tomorrow 1459
Poland's Access to the Sea 449
Poland's Adventure in Grace 1465
Poland's Baltic Coast 561

Poland's Case for Independence 45
Poland's Economic Development 575
Poland's Freedom of the Sea 407
Poland's Ghettos at War 971
Poland's International Affairs, 1919-1960 641
Poland's Millenium of Catholicism 1468
Poland's New Generation 1493
Poland's Place in Europe (Rose) 749
Poland's Place in Europe (Terry) 453
Poland's Place in Europe (Wojciechowski) 759
Poland's Policy of Expansion as Revealed by Polish Testimonies 414
Poland's Politicized Army 107
Poland's Politics 1405
Poland's Progress, 1919-1939 543
Poland's Rights to Justice 1423
Poland's Self-Limiting Revolution 1530
Poland's Struggle for Independence 1386
Poland's Thousand Years 1464
Poland's Western and Northern Territories 417
Poland's Westward Trend 418
The Poles (Heine) 1504
The Poles (Steven) 60
Poles Against the "V" Weapons 94
The Poles in America (Fox) 1242
Poles in America (Mocha) 1290
Poles in America (Polish Day Association) 1296

The Poles in America (Renkiewicz) 1302
The Poles in America (Wytrwal) 1318
Poles in American History and Tradition 1319
The Poles in Canada 1209
Poles in History and Culture of the United States of America 1224
Poles in Manitoba 1213
Poles in Michigan 1289
Poles in New York in the 17th and the 18th Centuries 1250
The Poles in Oklahoma 1228
Poles in the Battle of Narvik 96
Poles in the Battle of Western Europe 97
The Poles in the Early History of Texas 1251
Poles in European Resistance Movement, 1939-1945 1364
Poles in the Italian Campaign, 1943-1945 116
Poles in the United States of America, 1776-1865 1248
The Poles in the United States of America, Preceded by the Earliest History, etc. 741
Poles in Uniform 121
The Poles in Wellington, New Zealand 1222
The Poles of Chicago, 1837-1937 1291
The Poles of Cleveland 1240
Poles on the High Seas 694
Policy and Politics in Contemporary Poland 1527
Polish Abbreviations, A Selective List 1071
Polish Aircraft, 1893-1939 71
Polish-American Community Life 1292
Polish American Encyclopedia 1294
Polish American History and Culture 162

# Title Index

Polish-American Politics in Chicago, 1880-1940   1259
The Polish American School System   1230
Polish Americans (Lopata)   1264
The Polish-Americans (Polzin)   1298
Polish Americans and their Communities of Cleveland   1247
Polish Americans, 1854-1939   1235
Polish Americans in California (Przygoda)   1299
Polish Americans in California (Haiman)   1253
Polish-Americans in the City of New York   1295
The Polish-Americans of Bridgeport   1234
Polish Analytical Philosophy   922
Polish and Proud   687
A Polish Anthology   1103
Polish Architecture up to the Mid-Nineteenth Century   91
Polish Armour, 1939-1945   122
Polish Arms, Side-Arms   123
The Polish Army and the Polish Navy   103
The Polish Army, 1939-45   118
Polish Artists in Great Britain   1218
Polish Atrocities in Ukraine   1111
The Polish August   855
Polish-Black Encounters   1320
Polish Blood   607
The Polish Blood in America's Veins   1243
Polish Books in English, 1945-1971   149

The Polish Campaign, 1939   119
Polish Catholics in Chicago, 1850-1920   1284
A Polish Chapter in Civil War America   814
A Polish Chapter in Jacksonian America   1263
The Polish Chiefs   902
Polish Churches in Manitoba   1208
Polish Circuit Rider   1225
Polish Cities in Photographs   465
Polish Civilization: Essays and Studies   17
Polish Communism in Crisis   1440
Polish Contribution to Arts and Sciences in Canada   1216
Polish Contribution to Early American Education   1306
Polish Cookbook (Culinary Arts Institute)   499
Polish Cookbook (Czerny)   500
Polish Cookery   502
Polish Cooking   498
The "Polish Corridor"   439
The Polish Corridor and the Consequences   410
Polish Countrysides   517
Polish Customs   1503
The Polish Defeat   1415
Polish Detroit and the Kolasinski Affair   256
Polish Dissident Publications   155
The Polish Drama, 1980-1982   860
The Polish Economy in the Twentieth Century   588
Polish Encyclopedia   46
A Polish Exile with Napoleon   341
A Polish Factory   1486
The Polish Fairy Book   1546

Polish Fairy Tales (Girling) 1551
Polish Fairy Tales (Glinski) 1552
Polish Family Law  1072
Polish Folk Tales  1544
Polish Folk Tales and Legends  1556
Polish-German Antagonism in History  413
The Polish-German Frontier  429
The Polish-German Frontier After World War II  425
Polish-German Frontiers from the Standpoint of International Law  459
The Polish Gold  853
Polish Greats  165
The Polish Handbook, 1925  7
Polish Health Resorts  558
The Polish Heritage of Joseph Conrad  267
The Polish Immigrant and His Reading  150
The Polish Immigrant in Detroit to 1914  1277
Polish Immigrants in Britain  1221
The Polish in America  1288
Polish Institute of Arts and Sciences in America  1297
Polish Institutions of Higher Learning  928
The Polish Insurrection of 1863 in the Light of New York Editorial Opinion  798
Polish Invasion  1219
Polish-Jewish Relations During the Second World War  987
Polish Jews: A Pictorial Record  1004
Polish Jews: The Final Chapter  1002

The Polish Land (Coleman)  1099
The Polish Land (Klub Polski)  1101
Polish Language and Heritage  47
The Polish-Language Press in Canada  1214
Polish Law Throughout the Ages  1074
Polish Literature  1095
Polish Literature in English Translation (Coleman)  1100
Polish Literature in English Translation (Ledbetter)  151
The Polish Memoirs of William Rose  364
Polish Music (Jarocinska)  1119
Polish Music (Sulikowski)  1123
Polish Music and Chopin  1122
The Polish Nation  1391
The Polish Nation in the Struggle for Peace and the 6-Year Plan  572
The Polish National Catholic Church  1374
The Polish National Catholic Church in America and Poland  1372
Polish National Income and Product in 1954, 1955 and 1956  570
The Polish Nobility in the Middle Ages  764
The Polish Ordeal  1445
Polish Orders, Medals, Badges and Insignia Military and Civilian 1750 to 1985  511
The Polish Orphan  613
Polish Painting  128
Polish Painting from the Enlightenment to Recent Times  127
Polish Paintings  126
Polish Panorama  539

Polish Paradox 872
Polish Parish Records of the Roman Catholic Church 688
Polish Past in America, 1608-1865 1252
The Polish Past in Canada 1215
The Polish Peasant in Europe and America 1308
The Polish People of Portage County 1304
Polish People's Republic 48
The Polish People's Republic (Morrison) 1427
The Polish Pioneers in Virginia 1310
Polish Pioneers of California 1253
Polish Pioneers of Pennsylvania 1254
Polish Pioneers of Virginia and Kentucky 1255
Polish Politics and National Reform, 1775-1788 790
Polish Politics and the Revolution of November 1830 807
Polish Politics: Edge of the Abyss 1434
Polish Politics in Transition 1449
Polish Portrait: An Autobiography 386
The Polish Poster 139
Polish Postwar Economy 571
The Polish Press in America (Kowalik) 1260
The Polish Press in America (Olszyk) 1282
The Polish Problem at the Paris Peace Conference 1390
Polish Profile 1510
Polish Profiles 529
Polish Proberbs 1514
The Polish Question 1387

The Polish Question and General Mouravieff 1395
The Polish Question as an International Problem 1396
The Polish Question in the Russian State Duma 1379
The Polish Regained Provinces 457
Polish Research Guide 1080
The Polish Revolution: Solidarity 1525
Polish Revolutionary Populism 1516
Polish Roads to Victory 712
Polish Romantic Drama 1105
Polish Romantic Literature 1089
Polish Scholars 1075
The Polish Self-Image 1453
The Polish Shades and Ghosts of Joseph Conrad 268
The Polish Short Story in English 1092
Polish Society 1498
Polish Society Under German Occupation 699
Polish Sociology 918
The Polish-Soviet Campaign of 1920 826
The Polish-Soviet Frontier 637
Polish-Soviet Relations in the Light of International Law 660
Polish-Soviet Relations, 1932-1939 627
The Polish State Budget 1950
Polish Studies 1506
Polish Subtitles 531
Polish Textiles 906
The Polish Theatre 1562
The Polish Tradition 62
Polish Troops in Norway 111
Polish-U.S. Industrial Cooperation in the 1980's 665
The Polish Underground 702
The Polish Underground State 1421

Polish Universities 923
The Polish Way 761
Polish Western Territories 442
Polish Wings in the West 95
Polish Wings over Europe 108
The Polish Worker 1481
The Political History of Poland 743
Political Opposition in Poland, 1954-1977 920
Politics in Independent Poland, 1921-1939 830
The Politics of Futility 967
Politics of Socialist Agriculture in Poland, 1945-1960 72
Polonaise (Girling) 1336
Polonaise (Read) 897
Polonaise Nevermore 1346
Polonica Buffalonensis 146
Polonica Canadiana (Turek) 159
Polonica Canadiana (Zolobka) 161
Polonica in English 156
The Pomeranian Vistula 594
The Pope and Poland in World War Two 1460
The Pope in Poland 1472
Pope John Paul II (Blazynski) 240
Pope John Paul II, A Festive Profile 247
Pope John Paul II: His Travels and Mission 249
Pope John Paul II, The Life of Karol Wojtyla 244
Population Changes in Poland, 1939-1950 1452
The Population of the Polish Commonwealth 1381
The Population of Western and Northern Poland 1451
The Port of Gdynia 472
Portrait of a Champion 380

Portrait of Poland (Krok-Paszkowski) 50
Portrait of Poland (Newman) 546
Postscript to Victory 634
Postwar Polish Poetry 1104
Power Sources in Poland and Their Utilization 907
Premises of the Five-Year Plan in Poland, 1956-1960 595
President Nixon's 24 Hours in Warsaw 668
Prince Godfrey, Knight of the Star of the Nativity 1554
A Prisoner of Martial Law 1173
Prisoners of the Night 616
The Private History of a Polish Insurrection 799
The Private Letters of Baron de Viomenil on Polish Affairs 1195
The Private Poland 1513
A Private War 993
The Problem of Eastern Galicia 447
Prominent Polish Pioneers of U.S.A., 1770-1790 1232
The Promise Hitler Kept 951
Protection of Historical Monuments in Poland 92
The Protestant Churches in Poland 1470
Protestantism in Poland 1457
Prussia and the Poles 1399
Prussian Poland 21
Prussian Poland, a Stronghold of German Militarism 1384
Prussian Poland in the German Empire (1871-2900) 795
Public Opinion and Political Change in Poland, 1980-1982 1426
Pulaski Place 1358

Queen Jadwiga of Poland 235
The Queen of Heaven 621

The Queen's Gems   163

The Radium Woman   217
The Radziwills   359
The Rape of Poland   867
The Ravishers   1204
The Real Poland   870
Realism in Polish Politics   1404
The Re-Birth of Poland   824
Rebirth of the Polish Republic   1420
Reborn Poland   1383
Reception of the Copernican Theory in Poland in the Seventeenth and Eighteenth Centuries   208
The Recovery of Poland   742
Red Cavalry   883
Red Ribbon on a White Horse   397
Red Star Over Poland   865
Reform and Insurrection in Russian Poland, 1856-1865   808
The Reformation in Poland   1458
Religious Changes in Contemporary Poland   919
Religious Life in Poland   1476
Religious Work Among Poles in America   1256
A Reluctant Traveler in Russia   1201
Remembrances of a Polish Exile   51
Reminiscences. The Adventure of a Modern Gil Blas During the Last War   271
Reminiscences of Poland   1389
Remnants: The Last Jews of Poland   980
The Renaissance in Poland (Kozakiewiczowa)   133
The Renaissance in Poland (Lorentz)   136

Rendezvous at Katyn   1063
A Republic of Nobles   747
Return to Auschwitz   1131
Revelations of Austria   1385
Revolution and Traditions in People's Poland   910
Revolutionary Marxist Students in Poland Speak Out   1436
Richard Anuszkiewicz   1265
The Riddle of Poland   56
Righteous Among Nations   934
The Rise of Polish Democracy   750
The Rise of the Polish Monarchy   767
The River Remembers   995
The Road to Gdańsk   675
Road to Nowhere   612
The Role of Opole Silesia in the Polish People's Republic   409
Roman Dmowski: Party, Tactics, Ideology, 1895-1907   222
Romantic Nationalism and Liberalism   293
Rome and the Validity of Orders in the Polish National Catholic Church   1376
Roots and Heritage of Polish People in Lowell, Massachusetts   1268
Royal Dragoons' Immortal Love   1341
The Royal Prince   254
Różewicz   365
Russia and the Polish Republic   680
Russia by the Back Door   1166
Russia, Poland and the Curzon Line   424
Russia, Poland and the West   916
The Russian Government in Poland   1410

Russian Poland, Lithuania
  and White Russia  22
Russian Year  1186
Russia's Neighbor  34
Russo-Polish Relations  646

The Sacral Art in Poland
  134
Sagittarius in Warsaw  611
Saint of Auschwitz  258
Saint Stanisław: Bishop of
  Kraków  378
The Samaritans  935
Sarmatia, the Early Polish
  Kingdom  769
Scenes of Fighting and
  Martyrdom  555
School Strikes in Prussian
  Poland, 1901-1907  805
Scroll of Agony  969
The Second Partition of
  Poland  786
The Secret Army  104
The Sejm and People's
  Councils in Poland  1438
Select Bibliography of Works
  in English on Polish History  145
Selected Polish Tales  1539
Selected Works in Polish
  Agrarian History and Agriculture  147
Self-determination, 1919
  422
September 1939  1199
The Servant of God, Mary
  Theresa Countess
  Ledochowska  292
Seven Rivers to Bologna
  1191
Seven Years in Russia and
  Siberia, 1914-1921  1149
Seventy Days  1583
The 79th Survivor  1170
Sewers of Warsaw  1582
Short History of the Life
  and Struggle of Bishop
  Francis Hodur  1373

Siege  486
Silent is the Vistula  1577
Silesia and Pomerania  585
Silesia in German Eyes,
  1939-1945  711
Silesia Revisited, 1929  419
The Silver Madonna  1198
The Silver Sword  1048
The Singing Pope  252
Six Centuries of Russo-Polish
  Relations  631
A Sketch of the History of
  Polish Art  129
Sketches in Poland  540
Smoke over Birkenau  1193
So This is Poland  1430
So Young a Queen  1043
Sobieski, King of Poland
  (Laskowski)  374
Sobieski, King of Poland
  (Martin)  788
Social and Political History
  of Jews in Poland, 1919-
  1939  978
Social and Political Transformation in Poland  1478
Social Change and Stratification in Eastern Europe
  1490
The Social Evolution of
  Poland in the Nineteenth
  Century  1487
Social Groups in Polish
  Society  1488
Social Insurance in Poland
  1496
Social Rights and Facilities
  in Poland  1484
The Social Security System in
  Poland  1485
Socialism and National Development  1519
Socialist Banking and Monetary Control  593
The Socialist Corporation and
  Technocratic Power  601
Society and Deviance in Communist Poland  1482

# Title Index

Socinianism in Poland 1462
The Sociology of the Struggle for Pomerania 1500
Soldier of Liberty, Casimir Pułaski 358
Solidarity, Poland in the Season of Its Passion 1534
Solidarity, Poland's Independent Trade Union 1526
Solidarity, the Analysis of a Social Movement, Poland, 1980-81 1529
Song, Dance and Customs of Peasant Poland 1502
Sophie's Choice 901
The Soul of a Queen 300
Southwestern Poland, Illustrated Guide 547
Soviet-Polish Relations, 1917-1921 683
The Sovietization of Culture in Poland 924
The Spirit of Polish History 721
The Spirit of Solidarity 1533
Sport in Poland 1535
Spring in October 879
Spy in the U.S. 1171
Squadron 303 99
A Square of Sky 944
The Square Sun 1161
Stalin and the Poles 651
The Stan Musial Story 322
Stan Musial: "The Man's Own Story" 321
Stanislaus Konarski 265
Stanisław Lem 294
Stanisław Wyśpiański 393
Stanley Frank Musial: The Man 320
Star On Many a Battlefield 253
The Stars Bear Witness 957
Stash of the Marsh Country 1360
A State Without Stakes 1475
Statistical Atlas of Poland 65
Stefanie Was the Good One 1029
Steffi, a Novel 1337
Stokowski 383
Stolen Childhood 1365
Stories from Polish History 1028
Story of a secret State 1159
The Story of Helena Modjeska 314
The Story of Poland (Morfill) 33
The Story of Poland (Newman) 35
The Story of the Kośćiuszko Foundation 1274
The Story of Wilno 496
The Strange Allies 656
Strangers are Coming 1362
Strike for Freedom 1524
The Strikes in Poland: August 1980 1497
Struggle, Death, Memory, 1939-1945 983
The Struggle for Poland 876
Studies in Polish Architecture 85
Studies in Polish Civilization 61
Studies in Polish Life and History 756
Studies in Polish Political System 1444
Studies on the Roman-Slavonic Rite in Poland 1463
Studies on the Theory of Reproduction and Prices 579
A Study in Forgery 1441
A Study of Acculturisation in the Polish Group in Buffalo, 1926-1928 1238
The Summer Before the Frost 1528
Sun, Stand Thou Still 205
Sun Without Warmth 903

A Survey of Polish Literature and Culture 1087
Survival in Auschwitz and the Reawakening 1136
The Survivor in us All 991
The Survivors 950
Symbolism in Poland 140
Szczecin 482
Szymanowski 384

Tadeusz Kościuszko, 1746-1817 278
Tales of Early Poland 1558
Tannenberg, 1410 and 1914 772
The Tatra Mountains 526
Teacher Education in a Communist State; Poland, 1956-1961 605
Ten Centuries of Poland's History 728
Teuton and Slav on the Polish Frontier 74
Texas Pioneers from Poland 1300
Thaddeus of Warsaw 896
The Theatre in Poland 1566
"Them:" Stalin's Polish Puppets 1446
They Came from Poland 168
They Fight for Poland 1147
The Third Adam 1467
This is Poland 562
This is Poland (Sadowski) 556
The Thousand Hour Day 893
1000 Years of Art in Poland 135
A Thousand Years of Polish Heritage 26
A Thousand Years of Polish History 731
Through a Woman's Eyes 696
Till the Break of Day 1054
Time Stopped at 6:30 1067
To Die With Honor 1573
To Live and Kill 1152

A Touch of Earth 945
Towards a Poor Theatre 1565
Towards Poland 2000 1499
A Tower from the Enemy 981
Towns and People of Modern Poland 464
The Towns of Copernicus 462
Tracing the Development of Polish Industry 904
Tracing Your Polish Roots 689
The Train Leaves at Midnight 900
Tramways of Czechoslovakia and Poland 1568
Transfer of the German Population from Poland 454
The Transplanted Family 1276
Travel Notes 1278
Travels into Poland, Russia, Sweden and Denmark 780
Treasured Polish Christmas Customs and Traditions 1511
Treasured Polish Folk Rhymes, Songs and Games 622
Treasured Polish Recipes for Americans 503
Treasured Polish Songs With English Translations 1121
Treblinka 996
A Tree Up to the Sky 1050
True Heroes of Jamestown 1311
The Trumpet Call from Poland 1540
The Trumpeter of Kraków 891
Try Cracow and the Carpathians 534
Twelve Polish Composers 1120
Twentieth-Century Polish Avant-garde Drama 1567
Twenty-five Years with the Poles 560
20: Twenty Years of Poland's Economic Development, 1944-1964 584
Twenty Years of the Polish People's Republic 66
Two Alone 889

# Title Index

Typhus and Doughboys 818

The Ukrainians in Poland 1107
Under Strange Skies 1189
Under the Vine and Fig Tree 1279
Underground, the Story of a People 999
United in Wrath 1194
The United States and Poland 684
The Unseen and the Silent 117
Until We Meet Again 972
Up the Hill 1025
Upper Silesia 428
Upper Silesia: A Country of Contrasts 456
The Upper Silesian Industrial Region 695
The Upper Silesian Question and Germany's Coal Problem 436
Uprising in the Warsaw Ghetto 1571
The Uprising of the Warsaw Ghetto, November 1940-May 1943 1053
Urban's Boys 1052

Valedictory 610
The Valley of Silence 930
Values and Violence in Auschwitz 1138
Vampires, Dwarves and Witches Among the Ontario Kashubs 1060
Vanished in Darkness 1126
The Vegetation of Poland 403
A Village Without Solidarity 1483
Vilna 943
Violina 618
Virgin Mary, Queen of Poland, Historical Essay 1461

Visa for Poland 1419
Vistula: The Story of a River 559
Vistual Voyage 1549
Voices From the Holocaust 989

The Wall 1016
Wanderers Twain 312
War Breaks Down Doors 1338
The War Hitler Won 836
War Losses in Poland, 1939-1945 848
The War of the Doomed 973
The War of Polish Succession 792
War Through Children's Eyes 1477
Warrior on Two Continents 269
War's Aftermath 822
Warsaw 494
Warsaw (Przypkowski) 493
Warsaw, A City Destroyed and Rebuilt 489
Warsaw Aflame 484
Warsaw Between the World Wars 495
Warsaw Death Ring, 1939-1944 483
A Warsaw Diary, 1939-1945 1013
A Warsaw Diary, 1978-1981 1145
The Warsaw Diary of Adam Czerniakow 963
The Warsaw Document 619
The Warsaw Ghetto: A Christian Testimony 936
Warsaw Ghetto, a Diary 939
The Warsaw Ghetto in Photographs 1005
The Warsaw Ghetto Memoirs of Janusz Korczak 227
The Warsaw Ghetto Revolt 1569
The Warsaw Heresy 874
Warsaw in Chains 703
Warsaw in Exile 704

Warsaw: 1939 Siege. 1959
  Warsaw Revisited  487
Warsaw 1945 and Today  492
Warsaw Rebuilt  490
Warsaw Rising  1579
The Warsaw Uprising,
  1 August-2 October 1944
  1576
The Warsaw Uprising of 1944
  1578
Way of the Lancer  1144
A Wayfarer in Poland  541
The Wayside Willow  1102
We Have Not Forgotten  854
We Live in the North  1041
We Stood Alone  1501
We, the Milwaukee Poles
  1233
Week in Agata's World:
  Poland  1026
West of Warsaw  1305
Western and Northern Poland
  (Kornilowicz)  426
Western and Northern Poland
  (Rechowicz)  445
Western and Northern Territories of Poland  460
Western and Northern Territories of Poland (Sobański)
  450
What I Saw in Poland-1946
  512
What is Poland?  1392
What Poland Wants  432
What to Read About Poland
  144
When Hamtramck and I Were
  Young  1267
When Light Pierced the
  Darkness  997
When the Prussians Came to
  Poland  811
Where the Storm Broke  852
Where There is Love  366
White Eagle, Dark Skies  890
The White Eagle of Poland
  1378
White Eagle, Red Star  820

White Eagles, a Story of 1812
  887
Who's Who in Poland  169
Who's Who in Poland
  (Wisniewski)  170
Who's Who in Polish America
  1231
Willow Wind Farm  1355
Winding Valley Farm  1356
Wings Over Poland  109
Winter in the Morning  937
With a Camera in the Ghetto
  959
With the Red Devils at Arnhem
  115
With the Tanks of the 1st
  Polish Armoured Division
  101
Within Two Years  408
Without Passport  1331
Winter Tales From Poland  1560
Witkacy  391
Witness to the Resurrection
  172
Witold Gombrowicz  229
Władysław Stanisław Reymont
  362
A Woman's Quest  398
The Woodcutter's Duck  1051
Wooden Synagogues  89
Woodrow Wilson and the Rebirth of Poland, 1914-1920
  1245
A World Apart  1155
The Word in the World  1456
A World Problem: Jews-Poland-Humanity  975
A World Remembered  1550
Wycinanki/Polish Cut-outs
  1585

Yaz  396
The Year 1920 and Its Climax,
  Battle of Warsaw  829
You'll Need a Guardian Angel
  1182
The Young Marie Curie  214
Young Mickiewicz  304

Your Guide to Poland 513

Zal, An International
 Romance 1343
Zionism in Poland 979
Żukrowski 400
Zygmunt Krasinski 287

NOV 1 5 1988